TEACHER'S EDITION

DESCUBRE 1A

Lengua y cultura del mundo hispánico

VISTA
HIGHER LEARNING

Boston, Massachusetts

On the cover: Mexican rattles (maracas), San Miguel de Allende, Guanajuato, Mexico

Publisher: José A. Blanco
Professional Development Director: Norah Lulich Jones
Editorial Development: Brian Contreras, Diego García, Sharla Zwirek
Project Management: Kayli Brownstein, Hillary Gospodarek, Sharon Inglis
Rights Management: Ashley Dos Santos, Jorgensen Fernandez, Caitlin O'Brien
Technology Production: Jamie Kostecki, Fabián Montoya, Paola Ríos Schaaf
Design: Gabriel Noreña, Andrés Vanegas
Production: Manuela Arango, Sergio Arias, Oscar Díez

© 2017 by Vista Higher Learning, Inc. All rights reserved.

No part of this work may be reproduced or distributed in any form or by any means, electronic or mechanical, including photocopying and recording, or by any information storage or retrieval system without prior written permission from Vista Higher Learning, 500 Boylston Street, Suite 620, Boston, MA 02116-3736.

Student Text ISBN: 978-1-68004-320-4
Teacher's Edition ISBN: 978-1-68004-325-9
Library of Congress Control Number: 2015948650

1 2 3 4 5 6 7 8 9 TC 21 20 19 18 17 16

Printed in Canada.

Contents

Teacher's Edition

Level 1A and Level 1B Scope and Sequence	T4
Level 1 Scope and Sequence	T5
Level 2 Scope and Sequence	T6
Level 3 Scope and Sequence	T7
Articulation	T8
Components	T12
Technology	T14
Walkthrough	T18
VHL Story	T30
ACTFL Standards	T31
Teaching with *Descubre*	T32
Assessment	T38
Pacing Guide	T42
Cultural Resources	T46

Student Edition Front Matter

Table of Contents of the Student Edition	iv
Map of the Spanish-Speaking World	viii
Map of Mexico	x
Map of Central America and the Caribbean	xi
Map of South America	xii
Map of Spain	xiii
Video Programs	xiv
Supersite	xvi
Icons	xvii
Studying Spanish	xviii
Getting Started	xxv
Acknowledgments	xxvii
Bios	xxix

Scope & Sequence: *Descubre 1A & 1B*

1A

contextos	cultura	estructura	adelante

Lección 1 Hola, ¿qué tal?

contextos	cultura	estructura	adelante
Greetings and leave-takings Identifying yourself and others Expressions of courtesy	**En detalle:** Saludos y besos en los países hispanos **Perfil:** La plaza principal	**1.1** Nouns and articles **1.2** Numbers 0–30 **1.3** Present tense of **ser** **1.4** Telling time	**Lectura:** *Teléfonos importantes* **Panorama:** Estados Unidos y Canadá

Lección 2 En la clase

contextos	cultura	estructura	adelante
The classroom and school life Fields of study and school subjects Days of the week Class schedules	**En detalle:** La escuela secundaria **Perfil:** El INFRAMEN	**2.1** Present tense of –**ar** verbs **2.2** Forming questions in Spanish **2.3** Present tense of **estar** **2.4** Numbers 31 and higher	**Lectura:** *¡Español en Madrid!* **Panorama:** España

Lección 3 La familia

contextos	cultura	estructura	adelante
The family Identifying people Professions and occupations	**En detalle:** ¿Cómo te llamas? **Perfil:** La familia real española	**3.1** Descriptive adjectives **3.2** Possessive adjectives **3.3** Present tense of –**er** and –**ir** verbs **3.4** Present tense of **tener** and **venir**	**Lectura:** *Gente... Las familias* **Panorama:** Ecuador

Lección 4 Los pasatiempos

contextos	cultura	estructura	adelante
Pastimes Sports Places in the city	**En detalle:** Real Madrid y Barça: rivalidad total **Perfil:** Miguel Cabrera and Paola Espinosa	**4.1** Present tense of **ir** **4.2** Stem-changing verbs: **e:ie, o:ue** **4.3** Stem-changing verbs: **e:i** **4.4** Verbs with irregular **yo** forms	**Lectura:** *No sólo el fútbol* **Panorama:** México

1B

contextos	cultura	estructura	adelante

Lección preliminar

A brief overview of the contexts and grammar from Level 1A

Lección 5 Las vacaciones

contextos	cultura	estructura	adelante
Travel and vacation Months of the year Seasons and weather Ordinal numbers	**En detalle:** Las cataratas del Iguazú **Perfil:** Punta del Este	**5.1** **Estar** with conditions and emotions **5.2** The present progressive **5.3** **Ser** and **estar** **5.4** Direct object nouns and pronouns	**Lectura:** *Turismo ecológico en Puerto Rico* **Panorama:** Puerto Rico

Lección 6 ¡De compras!

contextos	cultura	estructura	adelante
Clothing and shopping Negotiating a price and buying Colors More adjectives	**En detalle:** Los mercados al aire libre **Perfil:** Carolina Herrera	**6.1** **Saber** and **conocer** **6.2** Indirect object pronouns **6.3** Preterite tense of regular verbs **6.4** Demonstrative adjectives and pronouns	**Lectura:** *¡Real Liquidación en Corona!* **Panorama:** Cuba

Lección 7 La rutina diaria

contextos	cultura	estructura	adelante
Daily routine Personal hygiene Time expressions	**En detalle:** La siesta **Perfil:** El mate	**7.1** Reflexive verbs **7.2** Indefinite and negative words **7.3** Preterite of **ser** and **ir** **7.4** Verbs like **gustar**	**Lectura:** *¡Qué día!* **Panorama:** Perú

Lección 8 La comida

contextos	cultura	estructura	adelante
Food Food descriptions Meals	**En detalle:** Frutas y verduras de América **Perfil:** Ferran Adrià: arte en la cocina	**8.1** Preterite of stem-changing verbs **8.2** Double object pronouns **8.3** Comparisons **8.4** Superlatives	**Lectura:** *Gastronomía* **Panorama:** Guatemala

Lección 9 Las fiestas

contextos	cultura	estructura	adelante
Parties and celebrations Personal relationships Stages of life	**En detalle:** Semana Santa: vacaciones y tradición **Perfil:** Festival de Viña del Mar	**9.1** Irregular preterites **9.2** Verbs that change meaning in the preterite **9.3** ¿**Qué**? and ¿**cuál**? **9.4** Pronouns after prepositions	**Lectura:** *Vida social* **Panorama:** Chile

Scope & Sequence: *Descubre 1*

Lección 1 Hola, ¿qué tal?

contextos	cultura	estructura	adelante
Greetings and leave-takings Identifying yourself and others Expressions of courtesy	**En detalle:** Saludos y besos en los países hispanos **Perfil:** La plaza principal	1.1 Nouns and articles 1.2 Numbers 0–30 1.3 Present tense of **ser** 1.4 Telling time	**Lectura:** *Teléfonos importantes* **Panorama:** Estados Unidos y Canadá

Lección 2 En la clase

contextos	cultura	estructura	adelante
The classroom and school life Fields of study and school subjects Days of the week Class schedules	**En detalle:** La escuela secundaria **Perfil:** El INFRAMEN	2.1 Present tense of –ar verbs 2.2 Forming questions in Spanish 2.3 Present tense of **estar** 2.4 Numbers 31 and higher	**Lectura:** *¡Español en Madrid!* **Panorama:** España

Lección 3 La familia

contextos	cultura	estructura	adelante
The family Identifying people Professions and occupations	**En detalle:** ¿Cómo te llamas? **Perfil:** La familia real española	3.1 Descriptive adjectives 3.2 Possessive adjectives 3.3 Present tense of –**er** and –**ir** verbs 3.4 Present tense of **tener** and **venir**	**Lectura:** *Gente... Las familias* **Panorama:** Ecuador

Lección 4 Los pasatiempos

contextos	cultura	estructura	adelante
Pastimes Sports Places in the city	**En detalle:** Real Madrid y Barça: rivalidad total **Perfil:** Miguel Cabrera and Paola Espinosa	4.1 Present tense of **ir** 4.2 Stem-changing verbs: **e:ie, o:ue** 4.3 Stem-changing verbs: **e:i** 4.4 Verbs with irregular **yo** forms	**Lectura:** *No sólo el fútbol* **Panorama:** México

Lección 5 Las vacaciones

contextos	cultura	estructura	adelante
Travel and vacation Months of the year Seasons and weather Ordinal numbers	**En detalle:** Las cataratas del Iguazú **Perfil:** Punta del Este	5.1 **Estar** with conditions and emotions 5.2 The present progressive 5.3 **Ser** and **estar** 5.4 Direct object nouns and pronouns	**Lectura:** *Turismo ecológico en Puerto Rico* **Panorama:** Puerto Rico

Lección 6 ¡De compras!

contextos	cultura	estructura	adelante
Clothing and shopping Negotiating a price and buying Colors More adjectives	**En detalle:** Los mercados al aire libre **Perfil:** Carolina Herrera	6.1 **Saber** and **conocer** 6.2 Indirect object pronouns 6.3 Preterite tense of regular verbs 6.4 Demonstrative adjectives and pronouns	**Lectura:** *¡Real Liquidación en Corona!* **Panorama:** Cuba

Lección 7 La rutina diaria

contextos	cultura	estructura	adelante
Daily routine Personal hygiene Time expressions	**En detalle:** La siesta **Perfil:** El mate	7.1 Reflexive verbs 7.2 Indefinite and negative words 7.3 Preterite of **ser** and **ir** 7.4 Verbs like **gustar**	**Lectura:** *¡Qué día!* **Panorama:** Perú

Lección 8 La comida

contextos	cultura	estructura	adelante
Food Food descriptions Meals	**En detalle:** Frutas y verduras de América **Perfil:** Ferran Adrià: arte en la cocina	8.1 Preterite of stem-changing verbs 8.2 Double object pronouns 8.3 Comparisons 8.4 Superlatives	**Lectura:** *Gastronomía* **Panorama:** Guatemala

Lección 9 Las fiestas

contextos	cultura	estructura	adelante
Parties and celebrations Personal relationships Stages of life	**En detalle:** Semana Santa: vacaciones y tradición **Perfil:** Festival de Viña del Mar	9.1 Irregular preterites 9.2 Verbs that change meaning in the preterite 9.3 ¿**Qué**? and ¿**cuál**? 9.4 Pronouns after prepositions	**Lectura:** *Vida social* **Panorama:** Chile

Scope & Sequence: *Descubre 2*

contextos	cultura	estructura	adelante
Lección preliminar			
A brief overview of the contexts and grammar from Level 1			
Lección 1 En el consultorio			
Health and medical terms Parts of the body Symptoms and medical conditions Health professions	**En detalle:** Servicios de salud **Perfil:** Curanderos y chamanes	1.1 The imperfect tense 1.2 The preterite and the imperfect 1.3 Constructions with **se** 1.4 Adverbs	**Lectura:** *Libro de la semana* **Panorama:** Costa Rica
Lección 2 La tecnología			
Home electronics Computers and the Internet The car and its accessories	**En detalle:** Las redes sociales **Perfil:** Los mensajes de texto	2.1 Familiar commands 2.2 **Por** and **para** 2.3 Reciprocal reflexives 2.4 Stressed possessive adjectives and pronouns	**Lectura:** *A comic strip* **Panorama:** Argentina
Lección 3 La vivienda			
Parts of a house Household chores Table settings	**En detalle:** El patio central **Perfil:** Las islas flotantes del lago Titicaca	3.1 Relative pronouns 3.2 Formal commands 3.3 The present subjunctive 3.4 Subjunctive with verbs of will and influence	**Lectura:** *Bienvenidos al Palacio de las Garzas* **Panorama:** Panamá
Lección 4 La naturaleza			
Nature The environment Recycling and conservation	**En detalle:** ¡Los Andes se mueven! **Perfil:** La Sierra Nevada de Santa Marta	4.1 The subjunctive with verbs of emotion 4.2 The subjunctive with doubt, disbelief, and denial 4.3 The subjunctive with conjunctions	**Lectura:** *Dos fábulas de Félix María Samaniego y Tomás de Iriarte* **Panorama:** Colombia
Lección 5 En la ciudad			
City life Daily chores Money and banking At a post office	**En detalle:** Paseando en metro **Perfil:** Luis Barragán: arquitectura y emoción	5.1 The subjunctive in adjective clauses 5.2 **Nosotros/as** commands 5.3 Past participles used as adjectives	**Lectura:** *Esquina peligrosa de Marco Denevi* **Panorama:** Venezuela
Lección 6 El bienestar			
Health and well-being Exercise and physical activity Nutrition	**En detalle:** Spas naturales **Perfil:** La quinua	6.1 The present perfect 6.2 The past perfect 6.3 The present perfect subjunctive	**Lectura:** *Un día de éstos de Gabriel García Márquez* **Panorama:** Bolivia
Lección 7 El mundo del trabajo			
Professions and occupations The workplace Job interviews	**En detalle:** Beneficios en los empleos **Perfil:** César Chávez	7.1 The future 7.2 The future perfect 7.3 The past subjunctive	**Lectura:** *A Julia de Burgos de Julia de Burgos* **Panorama:** Nicaragua y La República Dominicana
Lección 8 Un festival de arte			
The arts Movies Television	**En detalle:** Museo de Arte Contemporáneo de Caracas **Perfil:** Fernando Botero: un estilo único	8.1 The conditional 8.2 The conditional perfect 8.3 The past perfect subjunctive	**Lectura:** *Tres poemas de Federico García Lorca* **Panorama:** El Salvador y Honduras
Lección 9 Las actualidades			
Current events and politics The media Natural disasters	**En detalle:** Protestas sociales **Perfil:** Dos líderes suramericanos	9.1 **Si** clauses 9.2 Summary of the uses of the subjunctive	**Lectura:** *Don Quijote de la Mancha de Miguel de Cervantes* **Panorama:** Paraguay y Uruguay

Scope & Sequence: *Descubre 3*

contextos	enfoques	estructura	lecturas y cine
Lección 1 Las relaciones personales			
La personalidad Los estados emocionales Los sentimientos Las relaciones personales	**En detalle:** Parejas sin fronteras **Perfil:** Isabel Allende y Willie Gordon	**1.1** The present tense **1.2 Ser** and **estar** **1.3** Progressive forms	**Cinemateca:** *Di algo* **Literatura:** *Poema 20* de Pablo Neruda **Cultura:** *Sonia Sotomayor: la niña que soñaba*
Lección 2 Las diversiones			
La música y el teatro Los lugares de recreo Los deportes Las diversiones	**En detalle:** El nuevo cine mexicano **Perfil:** Gael García Bernal	**2.1** Object pronouns **2.2 Gustar** and similar verbs **2.3** Reflexive verbs	**Cinemateca:** *Espíritu deportivo* **Literatura:** *Idilio* de Mario Benedetti **Cultura:** *El toreo: ¿Cultura o tortura?*
Lección 3 La vida diaria			
En casa De compras Expresiones La vida diaria	**En detalle:** La Familia Real **Perfil:** Letizia Ortiz	**3.1** The preterite **3.2** The imperfect **3.3** The preterite vs. the imperfect	**Cinemateca:** *Adiós mamá* **Literatura:** *Autorretrato* de Rosario Castellanos **Cultura:** *El arte de la vida diaria*
Lección 4 La salud y el bienestar			
Los síntomas y las enfermedades La salud y el bienestar Los médicos y el hospital Las medicinas y los tratamientos	**En detalle:** De abuelos y chamanes **Perfil:** La ciclovía de Bogotá	**4.1** The subjunctive in noun clauses **4.2** Commands **4.3 Por** and **para**	**Cinemateca:** *Éramos pocos* **Literatura:** *Mujeres de ojos grandes* de Ángeles Mastretta **Cultura:** *Colombia gana la guerra a una vieja enfermedad*
Lección 5 Los viajes			
De viaje El alojamiento La seguridad y los accidentes Las excursiones	**En detalle:** La ruta del café **Perfil:** El Canal de Panamá	**5.1** Comparatives and superlatives **5.2** Negative, affirmative, and indefinite expressions **5.3** The subjunctive in adjective clauses	**Cinemateca:** *El anillo* **Literatura:** *La luz es como el agua* de Gabriel García Márquez **Cultura:** *La ruta maya*
Lección 6 La naturaleza			
La naturaleza Los animales Los fenómenos naturales El medio ambiente	**En detalle:** Los bosques del mar **Perfil:** Parque Nacional Submarino La Caleta	**6.1** The future **6.2** The subjunctive in adverbial clauses **6.3** Prepositions: **a**, **hacia**, and **con**	**Cinemateca:** *El día menos pensado* **Literatura:** *El eclipse* de Augusto Monterroso **Cultura:** *La conservación de Vieques*
Lección 7 La tecnología y la ciencia			
La tecnología La astronomía y el universo Los científicos La ciencia y los inventos	**En detalle:** Argentina: tierra de animadores **Perfil:** Innovar	**7.1** The present perfect **7.2** The past perfect **7.3** Diminutives and augmentatives	**Cinemateca:** *Happy Cool* **Literatura:** *Ese bobo del móvil* de Arturo Pérez-Reverte **Cultura:** *Hernán Casciari: arte en la blogosfera*
Lección 8 La economía y el trabajo			
El trabajo Las finanzas La economía La gente en el trabajo	**En detalle:** Las telenovelas **Perfil:** Carolina Herrera	**8.1** The conditional **8.2** The past subjunctive **8.3 Si** clauses with simple tenses	**Cinemateca:** *Clown* **Literatura:** *La abeja haragana* de Horacio Quiroga **Cultura:** *Gustavo Dudamel: la estrella de "El Sistema"*
Lección 9 La cultura popular y los medios de comunicación			
La televisión, la radio y el cine La cultura popular Los medios de comunicación La prensa	**En detalle:** El mate **Perfil:** Las murgas y el candombe	**9.1** The present perfect subjunctive **9.2** Relative pronouns **9.3** The neuter **lo**	**Cinemateca:** *Sintonía* **Literatura:** *Dos palabras* de Isabel Allende **Cultura:** *Guaraní: la lengua vencedora*
Lección 10 La literatura y el arte			
La literatura Los géneros literarios Los artistas El arte Las corrientes artísticas	**En detalle:** Las casas de Neruda **Perfil:** Neruda en el cine	**10.1** The future perfect **10.2** The conditional perfect **10.3** The past perfect subjunctive	**Cinemateca:** *Las viandas* **Literatura:** *Continuidad de los parques* de Julio Cortázar **Cultura:** *De Macondo a McOndo*

Articulation: Traditional

Traditional
sequence of study

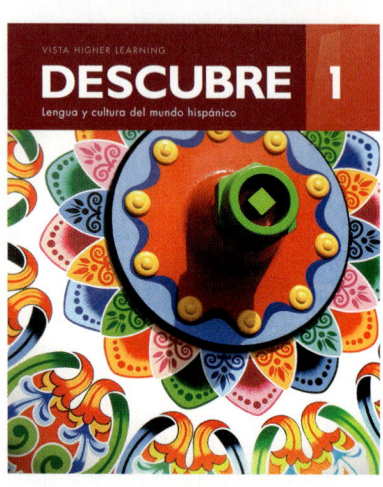

OR

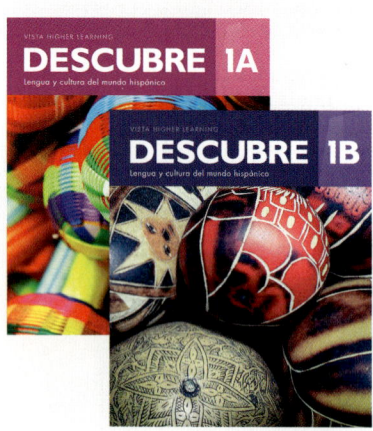

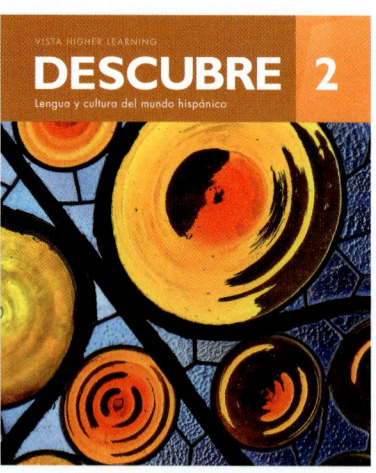

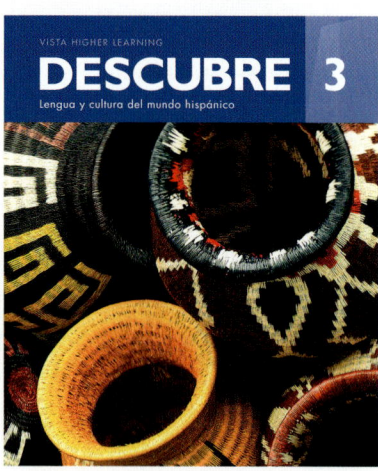

Year 1   Year 2   Year 3

- Sequenced instruction builds interpretive, interpersonal, and presentational communication skills
- Consistent pedagogy enables a seamless transition from year to year

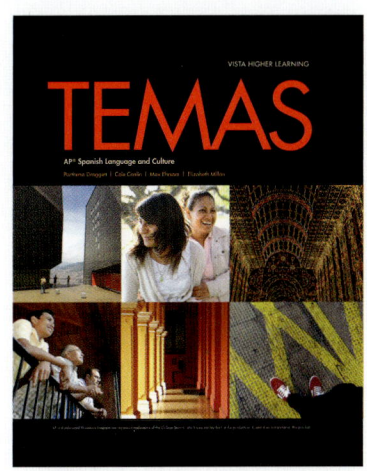
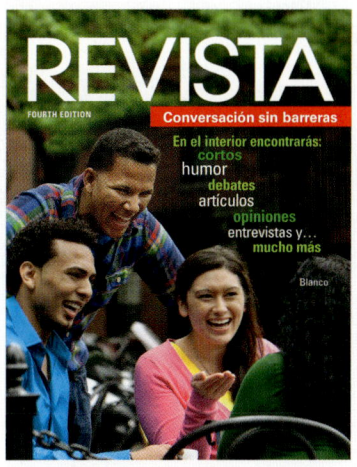

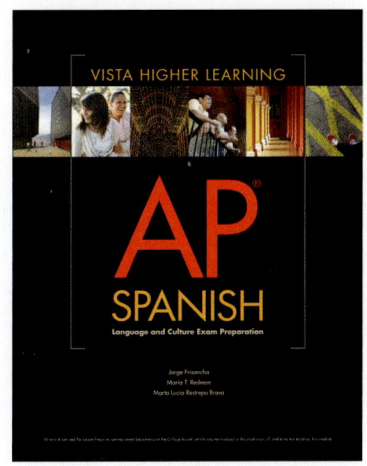

Year 4   **AP**   **Advanced**

- Focus on personalized language learning enhances the student experience
- A single technology portal—the Supersite—built specifically for world language education

Articulation: Alternate

Alternate sequence of study

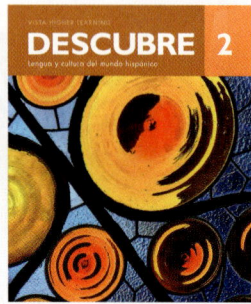

Descubre 1
Lecciones 1 – 6

- Hola, ¿qué tal? **1**
- En la clase **2**
- La familia **3**
- Los pasatiempos **4**
- Las vacaciones **5**
- ¡De compras! **6**

Descubre 1
Lecciones 7 – 9

- La rutina diaria **7**
- La comida **8**
- Las fiestas **9**

Descubre 2
Lecciones 1 – 3

- En el consultorio **1**
- La tecnología **2**
- La vivienda **3**

Descubre 2
Lecciones 4 – 9

- La naturaleza **4**
- En la ciudad **5**
- El bienestar **6**
- El mundo del trabajo **7**
- Un festival de arte **8**
- Las actualidades **9**

Year 1 — Year 2 — Year 3

Are you thinking of pacing **Descubre** more slowly? Then consider this alternative sequence of study successfully used in schools across the country.

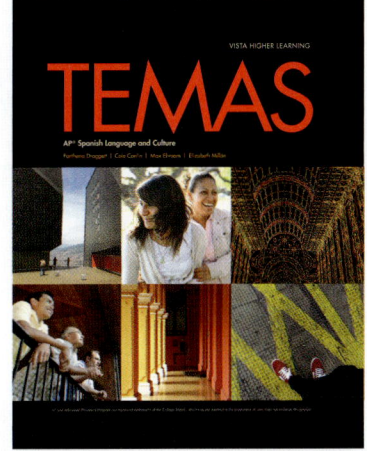

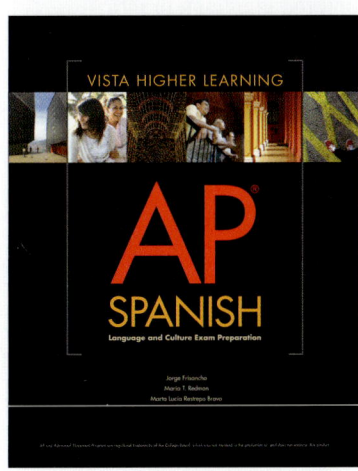

Year 4 **AP** **Advanced**

Pace **Descubre** 1 and 2 over three years to address the specific depth and breadth you need for your program. And no matter which sequence of study you choose, the Supersite is always there to support instruction and learning.

Components

For the Teacher: Plan

COMPONENT TITLE	WHAT IS IT?	📖	Ⓢ	💿
Teacher's Edition	Teacher support for core instruction	•	•	
Audio and Video Scripts	Scripts for all audio and video selections: • Textbook audio scripts • *Cuaderno de actividades comunicativas* scripts • Testing Program scripts • *Fotonovela, Flash cultura, En pantalla,* and *Panorama cultural* scripts • Supersite: Grammar Tutorial, Virtual Chat, and *Prueba escrita (Recapitulación)* scripts		•	•
Lesson Plans	Editable block and standard schedules		•	•
Pacing Guides	Guidelines for how to cover the level's instructional material for a variety of scenarios (standard, block, etc.)		•	•
Teacher's DVD Set	*Flash cultura/Fotonovela/Panorama cultural* DVD, Teacher Resources DVD			•
vText: Teacher's Edition	Complete Teacher's Edition in digital format		•	

For the Teacher: Teach

COMPONENT TITLE	WHAT IS IT?	📖	Ⓢ	💿
Activity Pack (includes AK)	Supplementary activities, including: • Additional structured language practice • Communication Activities worksheets for designated Student Edition activities • Additional activities using authentic sources • Communication activities for practicing interpersonal speaking • Chapter review activities • *¡Atrévete!* board game	•	•	•
Cuaderno de práctica y actividades comunicativas TE	Practice and communication WB with answers	•	•	•
Cuaderno para hispanohablantes AK	Heritage learners WB answers		•	•
Digital Image Bank	Images and maps from the text to use for presentation in class, plus a bank of illustrations to use with teacher-generated content		•	•
Grammar Presentation Slides	Textbook grammar presentation reformatted into PowerPoint format		•	•
Middle School Activity Pack (includes AK)	Hands-on vocabulary and grammar practice. Designed for younger learners, but effective for kinesthetic instruction for all level 1 students.		•	•

For the Teacher: Assess

COMPONENT TITLE	WHAT IS IT?	📖	Ⓢ	💿
I Can Worksheets	Lesson Objectives broken down by chapter section and written in student-friendly "I Can" statement format		•	•
Testing Program (includes AK)	Quizzes, Tests, and Exams; includes IPAs		•	•
Testing Program Audio	Audio to accompany all tests		•	•

For the Student

COMPONENT TITLE	WHAT IS IT?	Print	Supersite	DVD
Student Edition	Core instruction for students	•	•	
Audio Activities Audio	Audio to accompany all *Cuaderno de actividades comunicativas* activities		•	
Audio-synced Readings	Audio to accompany all *Lecturas*		•	
Cuaderno de práctica y actividades comunicativas	Written practice for vocabulary and grammar and Video, Audio, and Writing activities	•	•	
Cuaderno para hispanohablantes	Focused practice for heritage learners	•		
Dictionary	Easy digital access to a dictionary		•	
eBook	Downloadable Student Edition		•	
eCuaderno	Online versions of the *Cuaderno de práctica* and the *Cuaderno de actividades comunicativas*, embedded in the online gradebook, with many auto-graded options		•	
En pantalla Video	Authentic TV clips from across the Spanish-speaking world		•	
End-of-lesson Vocabulary Lists	Core vocabulary for each lesson, with linked audio online	•	•	
Flash cultura Video	Young broadcasters from across the Spanish-speaking world sharing cultural aspects of life		•	
Flashcards	Provide an easy way to study vocabulary		•	
Fotonovela Video	Engaging storyline video		•	
Grammar Tutorials	Animated grammar tutorial pairs lesson concepts with fun examples and interactive questions that check understanding		•	
Grammar Tutorials with Diagnostics*	Interactive grammar tutorial with embedded quick checks and multi-part diagnostic with active feedback and remediation		•	
My Vocabulary	A variety of tools to practice vocabulary		•	
News and Cultural Updates*	Monthly posting of authentic resource links with scaffolded activities		•	
Panorama cultural Video	Short video showcases the nations of the Spanish-speaking world		•	
Partner and Virtual Chats	Additional speaking activities online		•	
Practice Partner App*	Boost language skills on the go, with program video and tutorials		•	
Practice Tests with Diagnostics*	Students get feedback on what they need to study before an exam		•	
Vocab Hot Spots	Vocabulary presentations with embedded audio		•	
Textbook Audio	Audio to accompany all textbook listening activities		•	
Textbook Mouse Activities	Textbook activities that can also be completed digitally; many provide immediate feedback		•	
vText	Virtual interactive textbook for browser-based exploration • Links to all mouse-icon activities, audio, and video • Note-taking capabilities		•	
Vocabulary	Extensive practice with new vocabulary in digital portal		•	
Vocabulary Tutorials	Animated vocabulary tutorials allow students to practice lesson vocabulary and expressions at their own pace		•	
Vocabulary Tutorials with Diagnostics*	Lesson vocabulary and expressions taught in a three-mode process—listen and repeat, identification (Match), and production (Say It)—with diagnostics and personalized remediation		•	
Web-only Activities	Additional online practice for students		•	

 Print  Supersite DVD *Premium Supersite

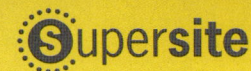

There's more to *Descubre* than meets the page

The **Descubre** Supersite provides a learning environment designed especially for world language instruction. Password-protected and program-specific, this website provides seamless textbook-technology integration that helps build students' love for language learning.

For students:
- engaging media
- motivating user experience
- superior performance
- helpful resources
- plenty of practice

For educators:
- proven instructional design
- powerful course management
- time-saving tools
- enhanced support

Integrated content means a more powerful student experience

- Streaming videos—episodic dramatic series, authentic TV clips, and cultural videos
- Interactive vocabulary tutorials
- Interactive grammar tutorials
- All program audio in downloadable MP3 format
- Textbook activities and additional online-only practice—most with automatic feedback
- Video Chat and Partner Chat activities for conversational skills practice
- My Vocabulary for personalized language study
- Audio-sync readings for all *Lecturas*
- Cultural readings in all levels and literary selections in volume 3
- Reference resources—online dictionary, audio flashcards, and grammar reference
- Online workbooks fully integrated with the Supersite gradebook

Specialized resources ensure a successful implementation

- Online assessments and Testing Program files in editable formats
- Audio and video scripts with English translations
- Grammar presentation slides
- Editable block and standard lesson plans
- Activity Pack
- Digital Image Bank
- Answer keys
- I Can worksheets

Educator tools facilitate instruction and save time

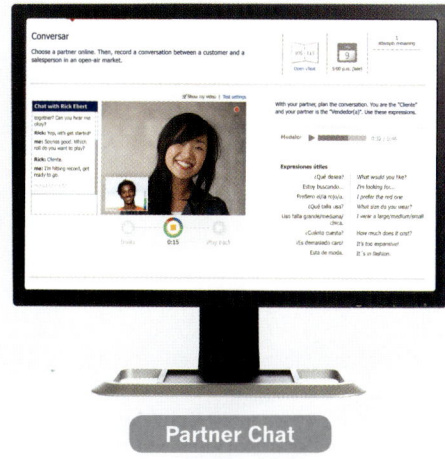
Partner Chat

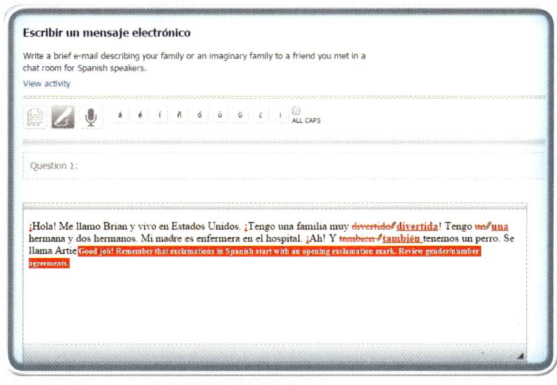
In-line editing

Easy course management

A powerful setup wizard lets you customize your course settings, copy previous courses to save time, and create your all-in-one gradebook. Grades for teacher-created assignments (e.g., pop quizzes, class participation) can be incorporated for a true, up-to-date cumulative grade.

Customized content

Tailor the Supersite to fit your needs. Create your own open-ended or video Partner Chat activities, add video or outside resources, and modify existing content with your own personalized notes.

Grading tools

Grade efficiently via spot-checking, student-by-student, and question-by-question options. Use in-line editing tools to give targeted feedback and voice comments—it's the perfect tool for busy language educators!

Assessment solutions

Administer online quizzes and tests from the Testing Program or develop your own—such as open-ended writing prompts or chat activities for an oral assessment portfolio. Plus, tools allow for time limits and password protection.

Plus!

- Single sign-on for easy integration with your school's Learning Management System*
- Live Chat for video chat, audio chat, and instant messaging with students
- A communication center for announcements, notifications, and student help requests
- Voiceboards for oral assignments, group discussions, homework, and more
- Reporting tools for summarizing student data

* available for select LMSs

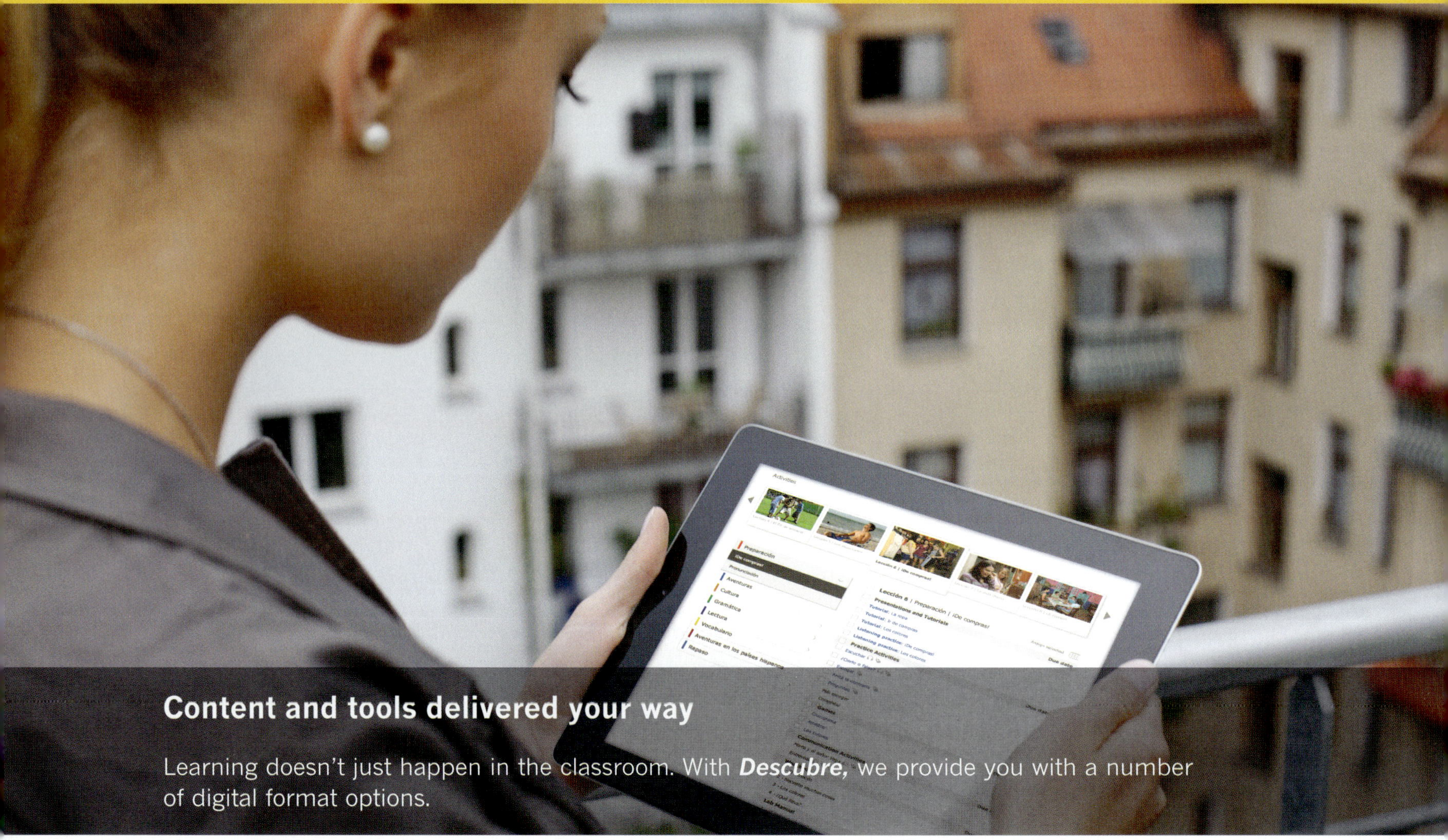

Content and tools delivered your way

Learning doesn't just happen in the classroom. With **Descubre,** we provide you with a number of digital format options.

vText (Online)

- Browser-based electronic text for online viewing
- Links to all mouse-icon textbook activities*, audio, and video
- Access to all Supersite resources
- Highlighting and note taking
- Easy navigation with searchable table of contents
- iPad®-friendly*
- Single- and double-page view and zooming
- Automatically adds auto-graded activities to the gradebook

Available on any PC or device that has Internet connectivity.

eBook (Downloadable for iPad®)

- Downloadable electronic text for offline viewing
- Embedded audio for anytime listening
- Easy navigation with searchable table of contents
- Highlighting and note taking
- Single-page view and zooming

When student is connected online:

- Links to all mouse-icon textbook activities*, audio, and video
- Access to all Supersite resources
- Automatically adds auto-graded activities in teacher gradebook

Available for iPad® via a Vista Higher Learning eBook app.

Visit **vistahigherlearning.com/interactive-texts** to learn more.

* Students must use a computer for audio recording.

Take learning to the next level with Premium Supersite

Monthly news and cultural updates

Receive monthly links to carefully curated authentic resources from across the Spanish-speaking world. From online newspaper articles to TV news segments, each source is chosen for its age-appropriate content, currency, and high interest to students. Each selection includes scaffolded pre-, during, and post-reading and viewing activities for a wide range of learning abilities.

A new way to master vocabulary

Using a variety of inputs including text, images, and audio, interactive tutorials guide students through three modes—listen and repeat, identification (Match), and production (Say It). Mastery is measured throughout, with targeted, individualized remediation recommendations based on individual student performance.

Grammar Tutorials with more diagnostics

The Grammar Tutorials on the Premium Supersite take learning to a new level with more diagnostics. In addition to the embedded tutorial self-check, these tutorials also offer concluding, multi-part diagnostic activities with active feedback.

Even more practice

The Premium Supersite includes even more practice for all levels of learning.

- Complete eCuaderno with added activities developed specifically to bolster student proficiency
- More Partner and Virtual Chat activities help build student confidence and oral proficiency
- All activities tied to the teacher gradebook for stress-free administration and reporting

Practice Tests with diagnostics

Multi-question practice tests provide students with a low-stakes tool for assessing their knowledge of vocabulary and grammar covered in each lesson. Only available at the Premium Supersite level, these tests are auto-graded and provide immediate feedback, as well as suggestions for additional practice based on performance.

* Available for use on iOS devices (iPhone®, iPad®, or iPod touch®) and Android devices.

Walkthrough

Beginning with the student in mind

Communicative Goals introduce the chapter's learning objectives.

Voiceboards for oral assignments, group discussions, homework, and projects.

Content summaries provide an at-a-glance view of the vocabulary, grammar, and cultural topics covered in the chapter.

All chapters open with images that provide visual context for the chapter theme.

Major sections are color-coded for easy use.

A primera vista questions jump-start the chapters, allowing students to use the Spanish they know to talk about the photos.

Look for the ⓢ located at the beginning of every section to see the corresponding resources available on the Supersite!

Setting the stage
for communication

Theme-related vocabulary is introduced through expansive, full-color illustrations and easy-to-reference lists.

Práctica starts the chapter's activity sequence with controlled practice.

Variación léxica highlights linguistic diversity.

Recursos boxes reference additional print and digital student resources.

Mouse icons indicate activities that teachers can assign on the Supersite. All close-ended practice activities are autograded with immediate feedback.

The **vText** online textbook is fully interactive. Students can click the links to access practice activities, audio, and video.

Teacher's Edition • Walkthrough T19

Walkthrough

Fotonovela bridges language and culture

Fotonovela storyline video brings chapter vocabulary and grammar to life. Students experience local life with a group of students living in Mexico City, Mexico.

Engaging storyline video follows characters through **Descubre** 1 and 2.

Products, perspectives, and practices are featured in every episode.

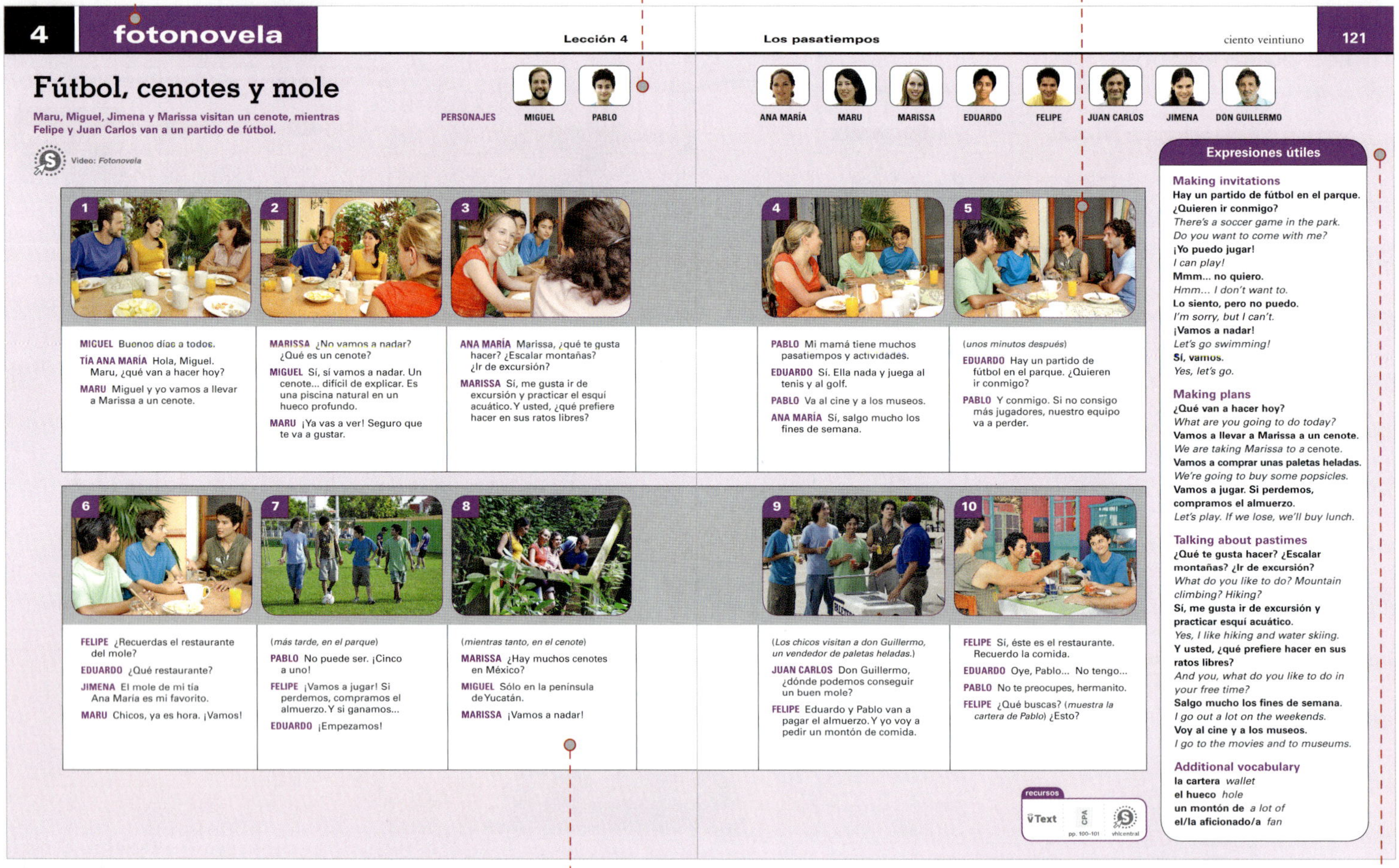

The easy-to-follow storyboard sets the context for the video and the dialogue boxes reinforce the lesson's vocabulary and preview the language structures that will be covered later in the lesson.

Expresiones útiles boxes organize the most important words and expressions from the episode by language function, showing how students can apply them in real, practical ways.

Assign pre- and post-viewing activities to test student comprehension of lesson vocabulary and key language functions.

Culture presented in context

En detalle explores the chapter's theme in-depth—in English in level 1A and in early chapters of level 1B and in Spanish thereafter for true cultural comprehension.

Así se dice presents familiar words and phrases related to the lesson's theme that are used in everyday spoken Spanish.

Perfil focuses on Spanish-speaking personalities and places in the Spanish-speaking world of high interest to students.

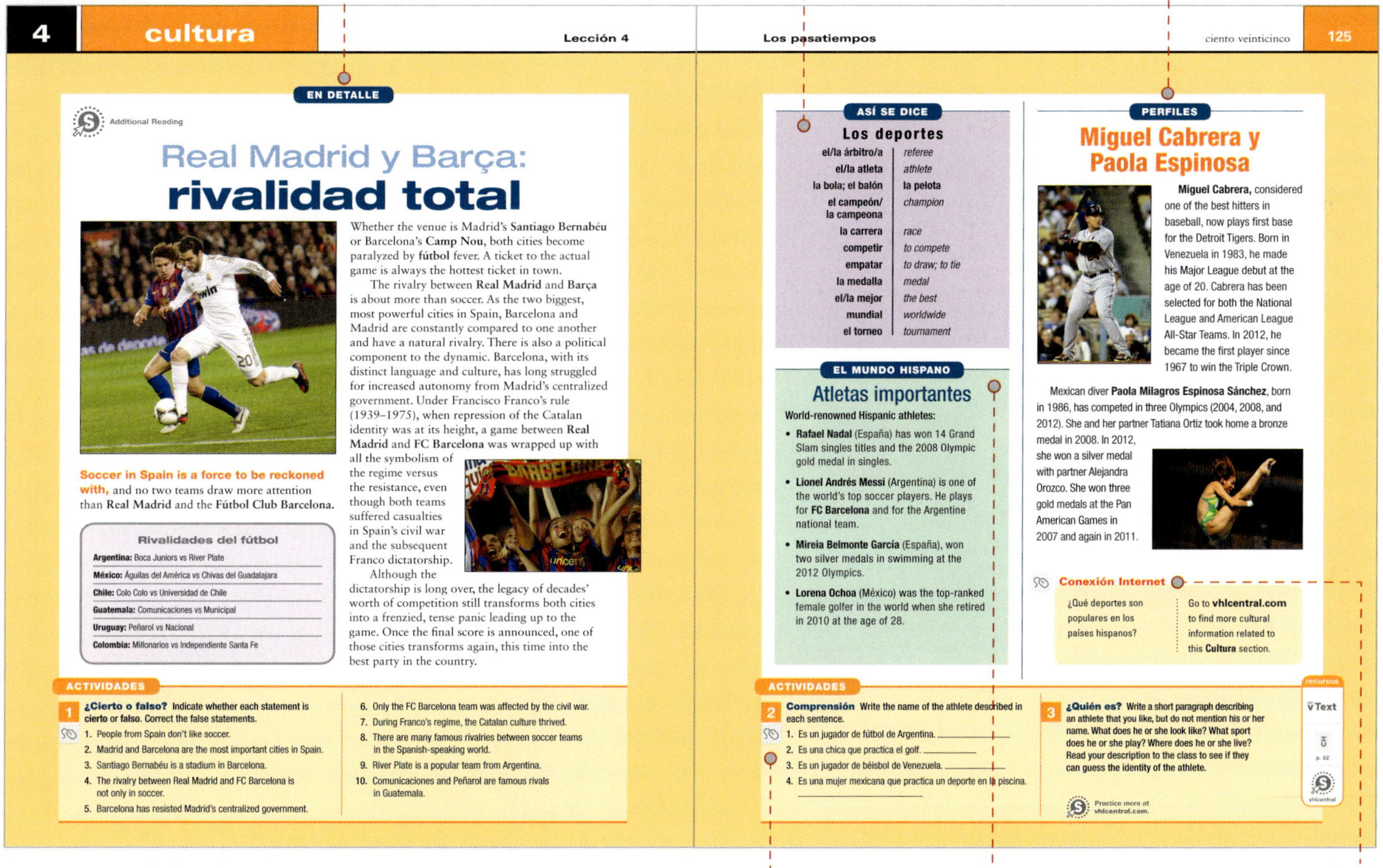

Comprehension activities solidify learning.

El mundo hispano continues the exploration of the lesson's cultural theme, but with a regional focus.

Conexión Internet features additional cultural explorations online.

Continue the communication-culture connection with additional readings and activities.

Walkthrough

Grammar
as a tool not a topic

Clear and concise explanations followed by visually appealing examples.

Sidebars connect previous and current learning.

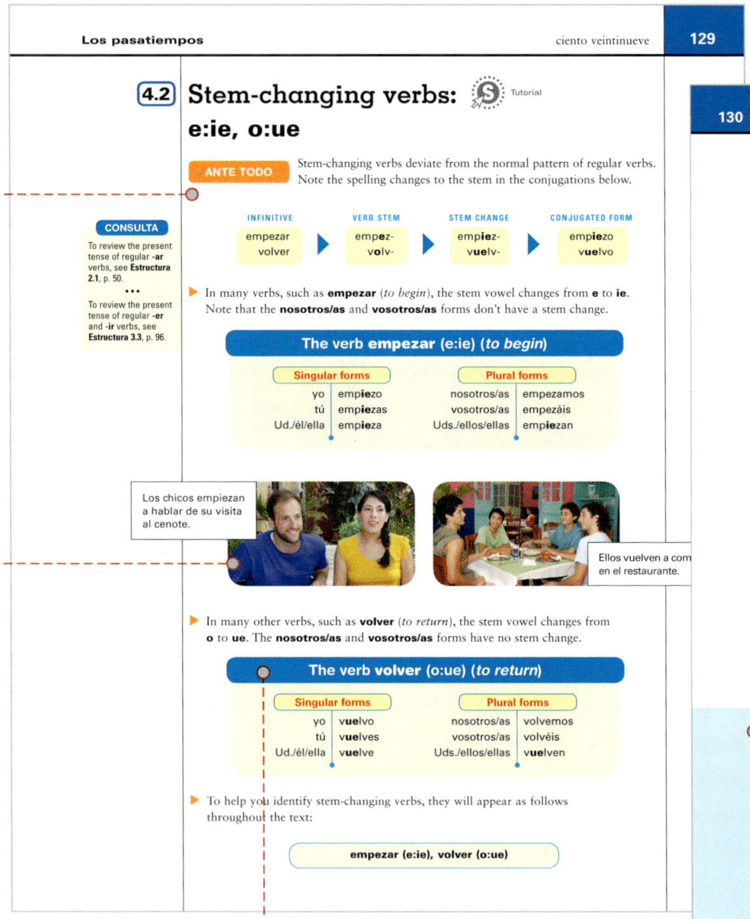

Photos from the **Fotonovela** show grammar in context.

Carefully designed charts and diagrams call out key grammatical structures and forms, as well as important related vocabulary.

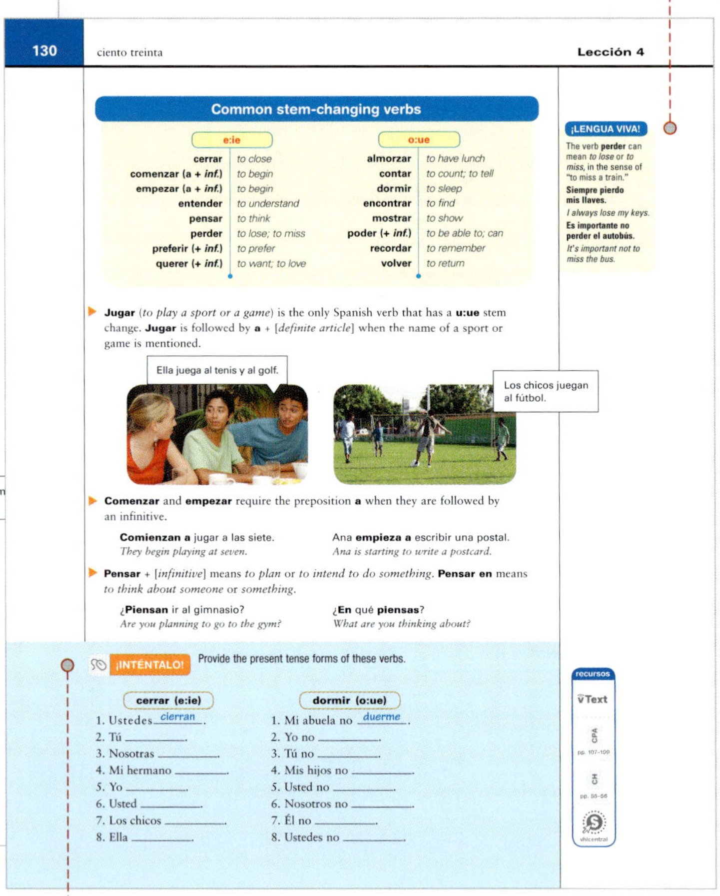

¡Inténtalo! offers students their first practice of each new grammar point.

Students can watch the grammar rules come alive with animated **Grammar Tutorials** featuring **el profesor**.

Visually engaging
and carefully scaffolded formats

Práctica sections include contextualized, personalized activities.

Comunicación sections feature pair and group activities for interpersonal and presentational practice.

Notas culturales sidebars expand coverage of the cultures of Spanish-speaking peoples and countries.

Síntesis activities integrate the current grammar point with previously learned material, providing built-in, consistent review and recycling.

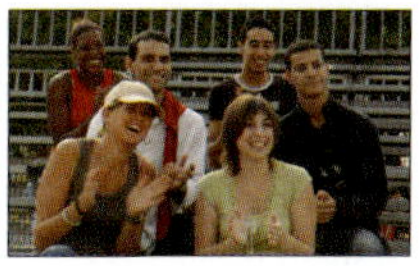

Incorporate additional in-class games and activities for beginning-level students from the **Middle School Activity Pack**.

Walkthrough

In-text and online diagnostic activities
provide targeted review

Scaffolded activities test students' comprehension of the chapter's key grammar points.

Resumen gramatical summarizes the grammatical points presented in the chapter.

Recapitulación on the Supersite
Assign **Recapitulación** online for a grade or as a self diagnostic. Additional activities are available for extra practice.

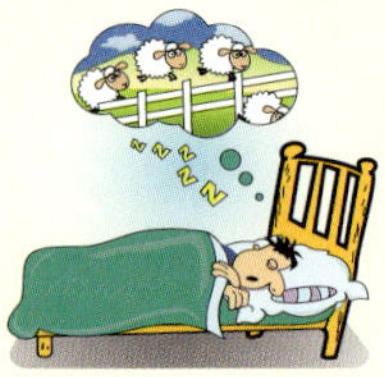

Reading skills
developed in context

Antes de leer includes reading strategies and pre-reading activities to develop confidence and skills.

Context-based readings pull all the chapter elements together.

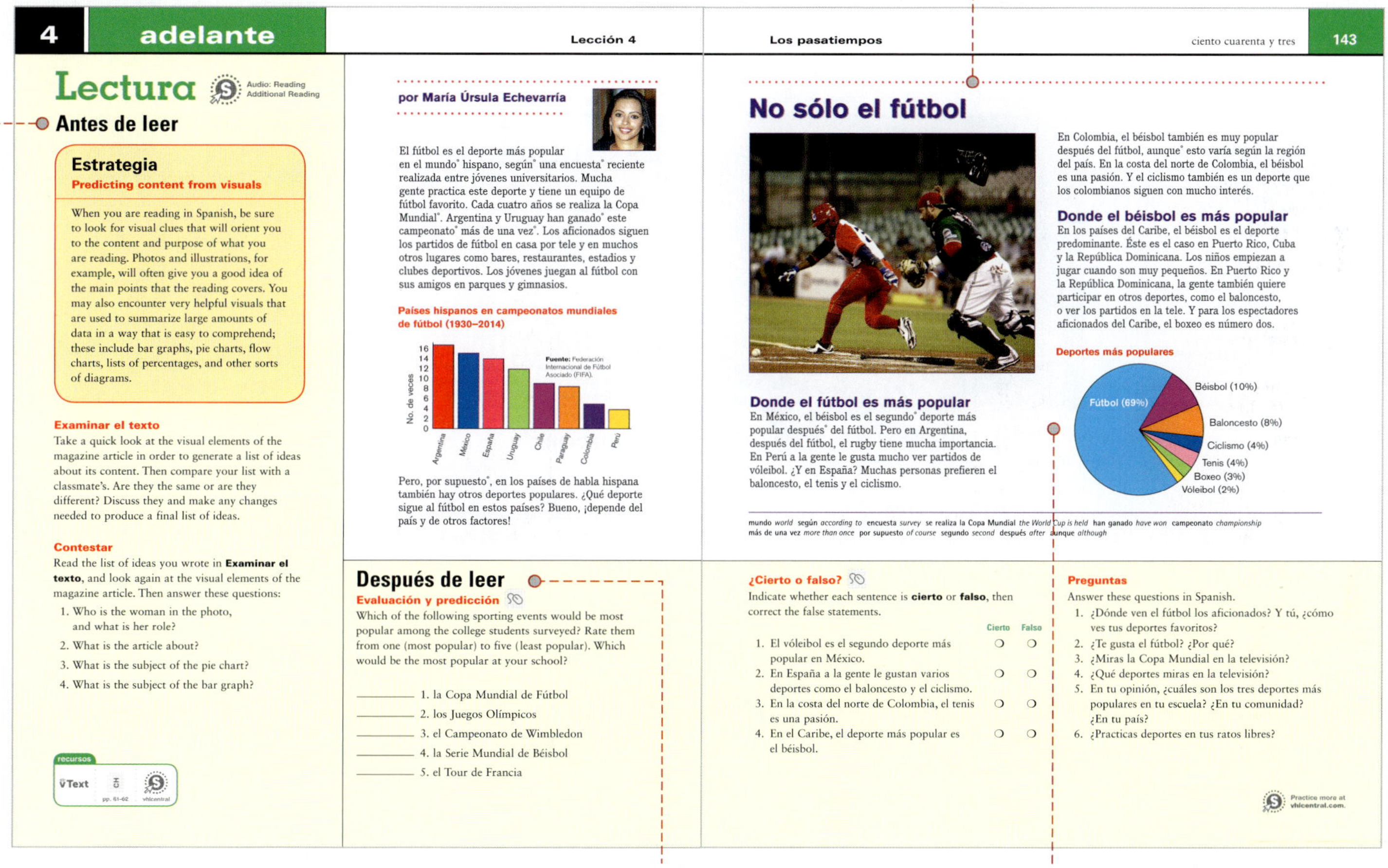

Después de leer activities include comprehension checks and post-reading expansion exercises.

Graphic organizers, photos, and other visual elements support reading comprehension.

Adelante on the Supersite
Students listen to native speakers as auto-sync highlighting of sentences guides students' eyes and comprehension.

Walkthrough

Writing and listening skills
developed in context

Estrategia provides strategies for preparation and execution of the writing task related to the chapter's theme.

Escuchar builds students' listening skills with a recorded conversation or narration.

Tema describes the writing topic and includes suggestions for approaching it.

Ahora escucha provides a variety of activities to support comprehension.

Assess writing and listening skills with auto-graded listening activities and teacher-graded composition activities on the Supersite.

Authentic cultural media
for interpretive communication

En pantalla presents TV clips from around the Spanish-speaking world connected to the language, vocabulary, and theme of the chapter.

Flash cultura videos feature young broadcasters from across the Spanish-speaking world sharing aspects of life related to the chapter's theme.

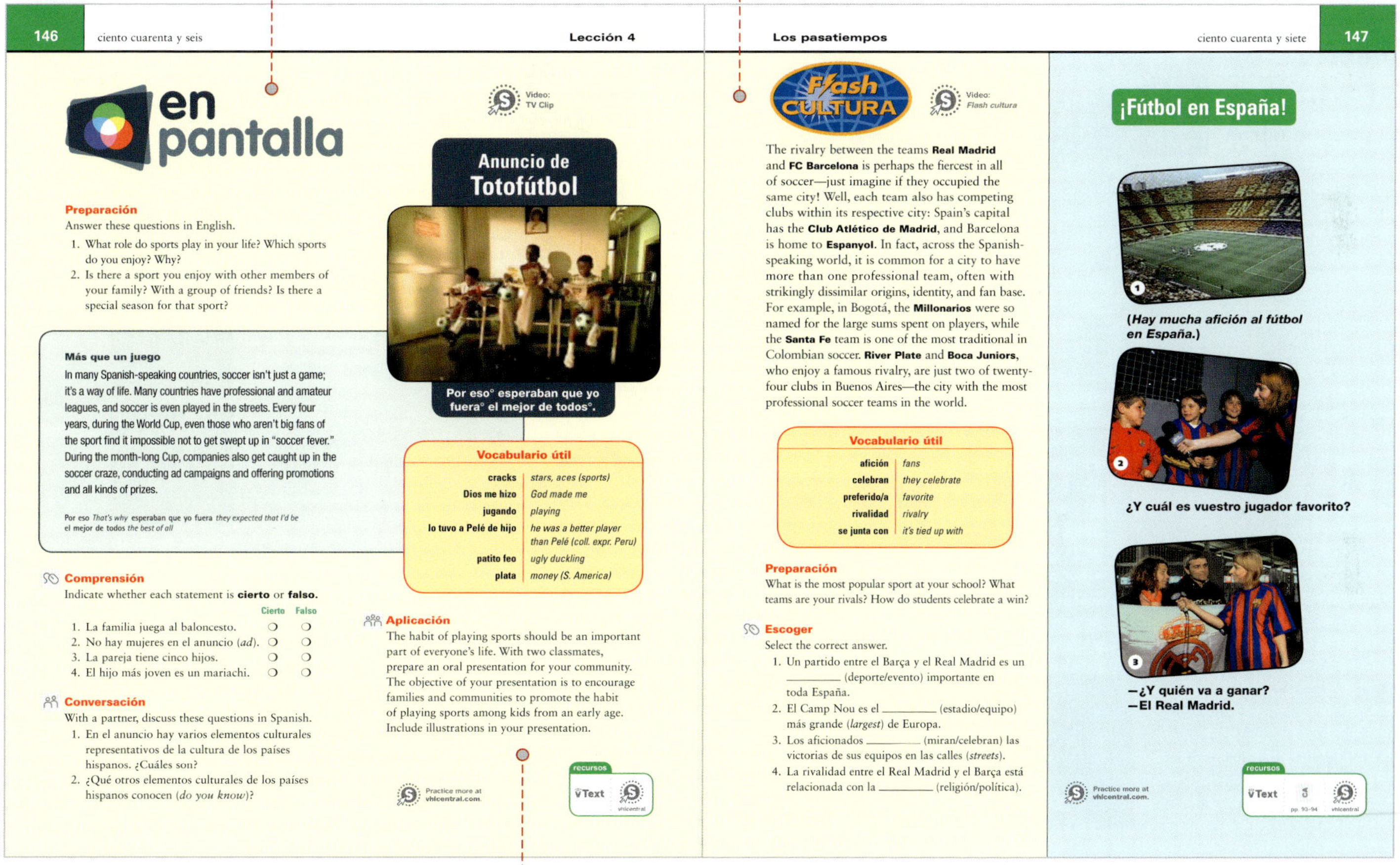

Scaffolded activity sequence really gets students engaged, understanding, and applying what they have seen.

Watch all the **En pantalla** and **Flash cultura** clips on the Supersite.

Walkthrough

Perspective through geography

El país en cifras presents interesting facts about the featured country.

Panorama showcases the nations of the Spanish-speaking world with short features about the country's culture—history, places, fine arts, literature, and aspects of everyday life.

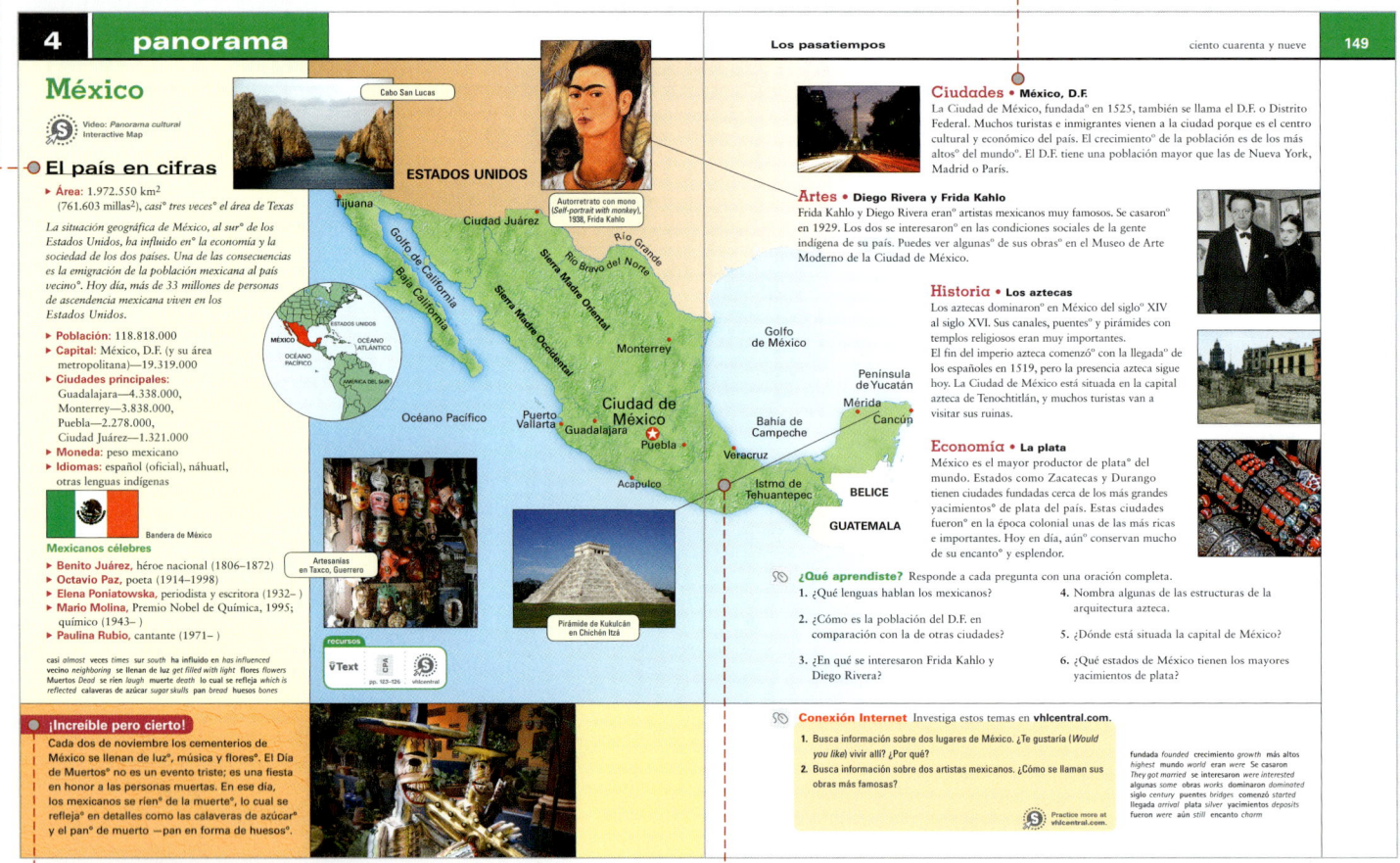

¡Increíble pero cierto! spotlights an intriguing, and often little-known fact about the featured country or its people.

Maps point out major cities, rivers, and geographical features and situate the country in the context of its immediate surroundings and the world.

Panorama cultural video on the Supersite
Authentic footage of the featured Spanish-speaking country exposes students to the sights and sounds of an aspect of its culture.

Vocabulary

Vocabulario summarizes all the active vocabulary in the chapter.

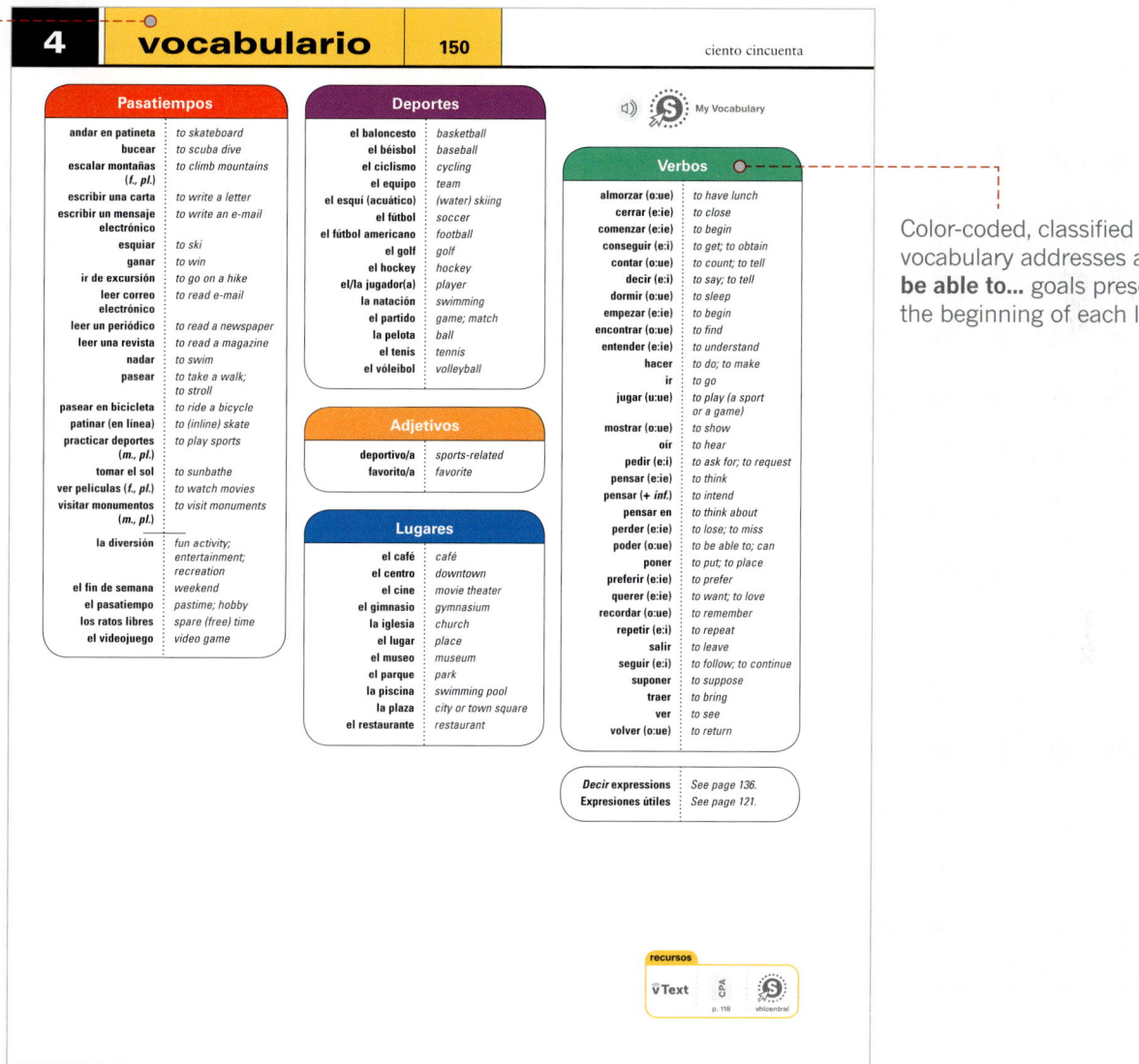

Color-coded, classified active vocabulary addresses all **I will be able to…** goals presented at the beginning of each lesson.

Active vocabulary is recorded for convenient study and practice. Flashcards for all terms are also available.

The Vista Higher Learning Story

Your Specialized Foreign Language Publisher

Independent, specialized, and privately owned, Vista Higher Learning was founded in 2000 with one mission: to raise the teaching and learning of world languages to a higher level. This mission is based on the following beliefs:

- It is essential to prepare students for a world in which learning another language is a necessity, not a luxury.
- Language learning should be fun and rewarding, and all students should have the tools they need to achieve success.
- Students who experience success learning a language will be more likely to continue their language studies both inside and outside the classroom.

With this in mind, we decided to take a fresh look at all aspects of language instructional materials. Because we are specialized, we dedicate 100 percent of our resources to this goal and base every decision on how well it supports language learning.

That is where you come in. Since our founding, we have relied on the invaluable feedback of language teachers and students nationwide. This partnership has proved to be the cornerstone of our success, allowing us to constantly improve our programs to meet your instructional needs.

The result? Programs that make language learning exciting, relevant, and effective through:

- unprecedented access to resources
- a wide variety of contemporary, authentic materials
- the integration of text, technology, and media
- a bold and engaging textbook design

By focusing on our singular passion, we let you focus on yours.

The Vista Higher Learning Team

www.vistahigherlearning.com

ACTFL Standards

World-Readiness Standards for Learning Languages

Descubre blends the underlying principles of the World-Readiness Standards with features and strategies tailored specifically to build students' language and cultural competencies.

THE FIVE C'S OF FOREIGN LANGUAGE LEARNING

Communication

Students:
1. Interact and negotiate meaning in spoken, signed, or written conversations to share information, reactions, feelings, and opinions. (Interpersonal mode)
2. Understand, interpret, and analyze what is heard, read, or viewed on a variety of topics. (Interpretive mode)
3. Present information, concepts, and ideas to inform, explain, persuade, and narrate on a variety of topics using appropriate media and adapting to various audiences of listeners, readers, or viewers. (Presentational mode)

Cultures

Students use Spanish to investigate, explain, and reflect on:
1. The relationship of the practices and perspectives of the culture studied.
2. The relationship of the products and perspectives of the culture studied.

Connections

Students:
1. Build, reinforce, and expand their knowledge of other disciplines while using Spanish to develop critical thinking and to solve problems creatively.
2. Access and evaluate information and diverse perspectives that are available through Spanish and its cultures.

Comparisons

Students use Spanish to investigate, explain, and reflect on:
1. The nature of language through comparisons of the Spanish language and their own.
2. The concept of culture through comparisons of the cultures studied and their own.

Communities

Students:
1. Use Spanish both within and beyond the school to interact and collaborate in their community and the globalized world.
2. Set goals and reflect on their progress in using languages for enjoyment, enrichment, and advancement.

Adapted from ACTFL's *Standards for Foreign Language Learning in the 21st Century*

Teaching with *Descubre*

Six-step instructional design

Take advantage of the unique, powerful six-step instructional design in *Descubre*. With a focus on personalization, authenticity, cultural immersion, and the seamless integration of text and technology, language learning comes to life in ways that are meaningful to each and every student.

STEP 1

Context

Begin each lesson by asking students to provide from their own experience words, concepts, categories, and opinions related to the theme. Spend quality time evoking words, images, ideas, phrases, and sentences; group and classify concepts. You are giving students the "hook" for their learning, focusing them on their most interesting topic—themselves—and encouraging them to invest personally in their learning.

STEP 2

Vocabulary

Now turn to the vocabulary section, inviting students to experience it as a new linguistic code to express what they already know and experience in the context of the lesson theme. Vocabulary concepts are presented in context, carefully organized, and frequently reviewed to reinforce student understanding. Involve students in brainstorming, classifying and grouping words and thoughts, and personalizing phrases and sentences. In this way, you will help students see Spanish as a new tool for self-expression.

STEP 3

Media

Once students see that Spanish is a tool for expressing their own ideas, bridge their experiences to those of Spanish speakers through the *Fotonovela* section. The *Fotonovela* Video Program storyline presents and reviews vocabulary and structure in accurate cultural contexts for effective training in both comprehension and personal communication.

STEP 4

Culture
Now bring students into the experience of culture as seen from the perspective of those living in it. Here we share Spanish-speaking cultures' unique geography, history, products, perspectives, and practices. Through *Flash cultura* and *Panorama cultural* (instructional videos) and *En pantalla* (authentic video) students experience and reflect on cultural experiences beyond their own.

STEP 5

Structure
Through context, media, and culture, students have incorporated both previously-learned and new grammatical structures into their personalized communication. Now a formal presentation of relevant grammar demonstrates that grammar is a tool for clearer and more effective communication. Clear presentations and invitations to compare Spanish to English build confidence, fluency, and accuracy.

STEP 6

Skill synthesis
Pulling all their learning together, students now integrate context, personal experience, communication tools, and cultural products, perspectives, and practices. Through extended reading, writing, listening, speaking, and cultural exploration in scaffolded progression, students apply all their skills for a rich, personalized experience of Spanish.

Teaching with *Descubre*

Differentiation

Knowing how to appeal to learners of different abilities and learning styles will allow you to foster a positive teaching environment and motivate all your students. Here are some strategies for creating inclusive learning environments. Consider also the ideas at the base of the Teacher's Edition (TE) pages. Extension and expansion activities are also suggested.

Learners with Special Needs

Learners with special needs include students with attention priority disorders or learning disabilities, slower-paced learners, at-risk learners, and English-language learners. Some inclusion strategies that work well with such students are:

Clear Structure By teaching concepts in a predictable order, you can help students organize their learning. Encourage students to keep outlines of materials they read, classify words into categories such as colors, or follow prewriting steps.

Frequent Review and Repetition Preview material to be taught and review material covered at the end of each lesson. Pair proficient learners with less proficient ones to practice and reinforce concepts. Help students retain concepts through continuous practice and review.

Multi-sensory Input and Output Use visual, auditory, and kinesthetic tasks to add interest and motivation, and to achieve long-term retention. For example, vary input with the use of audio recordings, video, guided visualization, rhymes, and mnemonics.

Additional Time Consider how physical limitations may affect participation in special projects or daily routines. Provide additional time and recommended accommodations.

Different Learning Styles

Visual Learners learn best by seeing, so engage them in activities and projects that are visually creative. Encourage them to write down information and think in pictures as a long-term retention strategy; reinforce their learning through visual displays such as diagrams, videos, and handouts.

Auditory Learners best retain information by listening. Engage them in discussions, debates, and role-playing. Reinforce their learning by playing audio versions of texts or reading aloud passages and stories. Encourage them to pay attention to voice, tone, and pitch to infer meaning.

Kinesthetic Learners learn best through moving, touching, and doing hands-on activities. Involve such students in skits and dramatizations; to infer or convey meaning, have them observe or model gestures such as those used for greeting someone or getting someone's attention.

Advanced Learners

Advanced learners have the potential to learn language concepts and complete assignments at an accelerated pace. They may benefit from assignments that are more challenging than the ones given to their peers. The key to differentiating for advanced learners is adding a degree of rigor to a given task. Examples include sharing perspectives on texts they have read with the class, retelling detailed stories, preparing analyses of texts, or adding to discussions. Here are some other strategies for engaging advanced learners:

Timed Answers Have students answer questions within a specified time limit.

Persuading Adapt activities so students have to write or present their points of view in order to persuade an audience. Pair or group advanced learners to form debating teams.

Pre-AP®

While Pre-AP® strategies are associated with advanced students, all students can benefit from the activities and strategies that are categorized as Pre-AP® in *Descubre.* Long-term success in language learning starts in the first year of instruction, so these strategies should be incorporated throughout students' language-learning career.

Descubre is particularly strong in fostering interpretive communication skills. Students are offered a variety of opportunities to read and listen to spoken language. The *Lectura* sections provide various types of authentic written texts, and the *En pantalla* and *Flash cultura* videos feature Spanish spoken at a natural pace. Encourage students to interact with as much authentic language as possible, as this will lead to long-term success.

Advanced Placement, Advanced Placement Program, and AP are registered trademarks of the College Board, which was not involved in the production of, and does not endorse, this product.

Heritage Language Learners

Heritage language learners are students who come from homes where a language other than English is spoken. Spanish heritage learners are likely to have adequate comprehension and conversation skills, but they could require as much explicit instruction of reading and writing skills as their non-heritage peers. Because of their background, heritage language learners can attain, with instruction adapted to their needs, a high level of proficiency and literacy in Spanish. Use these strategies to support them:

Support and Validate Experiences Acknowledge students' experiences with their heritage culture and encourage them to share what they know.

Focus on Accuracy Alert students to common spelling and grammatical errors made by native speakers, such as distinguishing between **c, s,** and **z** or **b** and **v** and appropriate use of irregular verb forms such as **hubo** instead of **hubieron.**

Develop Literacy and Writing Skills Help students focus on reading as well as grammar, punctuation, and syntax skills, but be careful not to assign a workload significantly greater than what is assigned to non-heritage learners.

For each level of the **Descubre** program, the *Cuaderno para hispanohablantes* provides materials developed specifically for heritage learners.

Best Practices

The creators of **Descubre** understand that there are many different approaches to successful language teaching and that no one method works perfectly for all teachers or all learners. These strategies and tips may be applied to any language-teaching method.

Maintain the Target Language
As much as possible, create an immersion environment by using Spanish to *teach* Spanish. Encourage the exclusive use of the target language in your classroom, employing visual aids, mnemonics, circumlocution, or gestures to complement what you say. Encourage students to perceive meaning directly through careful listening and observation, and by using cognates and familiar structures and patterns to deduce meaning.

Cultivate Critical Thinking
Prompt students to reflect, observe, reason, and form judgments in Spanish. Engaging students in activities that require them to compare, contrast, predict, criticize, and estimate will help them to internalize the language structures they have learned.

Encourage Use of Circumlocution
Prompt students to discover various ways of expressing ideas and of overcoming potential blocks to communication through the use of circumlocution and paraphrasing.

Teaching with *Descubre*

TELL: Teacher Effectiveness for Language Learning

The TELL Project's goal is to define and focus on the skills, behaviors, and professional growth of world language educators. Find specific TELL suggestions in this Teacher's Edition wrap. Each suggestion asks "why" are we doing this activity and "what" do we do to address the TELL Project goals. Please visit the TELL Project website for more information.

- **Environment:** How do you create a safe and supportive learning environment to prepare for student learning?
- **Planning:** How does your planning of learning experiences prepare for student learning?
- **The Learning Experience:** How do you provide meaningful learning experiences that advance student learning?
- **Performance and Feedback:** How do you and your students use performance and feedback to advance student learning?
- **Learning Tools:** How do you and your students capitalize on a variety of learning tools to maximize student learning?
- **Collaboration:** How does your collaboration with stakeholders support student learning?
- **Professionalism:** How does your continued growth as a professional support student learning?

21st Century Skills

The Partnership for 21st Century Skills ("P21") has developed a framework to identify and classify skills that high school students need to meet today's workplace requirements. In collaboration with ACTFL, P21 has created a map to illustrate the integration of these skills with the World Language Curriculum. Categories include:

- **Interdisciplinary Themes:** Global Awareness; Financial, Economic, Business, and Entrepreneurial Literacy; Civic Literacy; and Health Literacy
- **Information, Media, and Technology Skills:** Communication, Collaboration, Critical Thinking and Problem Solving, Creativity and Innovation, Information and Media Literacy, and Technology Literacy
- **Life and Career Skills:** Flexibility and Adaptability, Initiative and Self-Direction, Social and Cross-Cultural Skills, Productivity and Accountability, Leadership and Responsibility

"I Can" Statements

Students can assess their own progress by using "I Can" (or "Can-Do") Statements. The template below may be customized with the Student Objectives found in **Descubre** to guide student learning, and to train students to assess their progress.

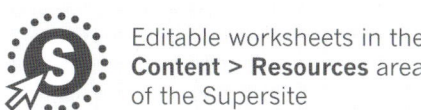

Editable worksheets in the **Content > Resources** area of the Supersite

---

"I Can" Statements

STUDENT OBJECTIVES
Lección 4 Descubre 1

Nombre _____   Fecha _____

Objetivos: Contextos	Fecha	¿Cómo voy?
1. I can name some sports and other pastimes.		
2. I can identify places in a city.		

¿Cómo voy?

4 ¡Excelente!: I know this well enough to teach it to someone.

3 Muy bien: I can do this with almost no mistakes.

2 Más o menos: I can do much of this but I have questions.

1 Es difícil: I can do this only with help.

0 ¡Ayúdame!: I can't do this, even with help.

Notas: _____

_____

_____

_____

Assessment

Assessment

As you use the **Descubre** program, you can employ a variety of assessments to evaluate progress. The program provides comprehensive, discrete answer assessments, as well as more communicative assessments that elicit open-ended, personalized responses.

Diagnostic Testing

The *Recapitulación* section in each lesson of Levels 1 and 2 provides you with an informal opportunity to assess students' readiness for the listening, reading, and writing activities in the *Adelante* section. If some students need additional practice or instruction in a particular area, you can identify this before students move on.

If students have moderate or high access to computers, they could complete the *Recapitulación* auto-graded quiz, also available for Level 3, on the **Descubre** Supersite. After finishing the quiz, each student receives an evaluation of his or her progress, indicating areas where he or she needs to focus. The student is then presented with several options—viewing a summary chart, accessing an online tutorial, or completing some practice items—to reach an appropriate level before beginning the activities in the Adelante section. You will be able to monitor how well students have done through the online gradebook and be able to recommend appropriate study paths until they develop as reflective learners and can decide on their own what works best for them.

Writing Assessment

In each lesson of Levels 1 and 2, the *Adelante* section includes an *Escritura* page that introduces a writing strategy, which students apply as they complete the writing activity. The Teacher's Edition contains suggested rubrics for evaluating students' written work.

You can also apply these rubrics to the process writing activities in the *Cuaderno de práctica y actividades comunicativas* and the *Cuaderno para hispanohablantes* for all three levels of **Descubre.** These activities include suggestions for peer- and self-editing that will focus students' attention on what is important for attaining clarity in written communication.

Testing Program

The **Descubre** Testing Program now offers two Quizzes for each *Contextos* section and every grammar point in *Estructura*. Each Quiz A uses discrete answer formats, such as multiple-choice, fill-in-the-blanks, matching and completing charts, while Quiz B uses more open-ended formats, such as asking students to write sentences using prompts or respond to a topic in paragraph format. There is no listening comprehension section for the Quizzes.

Six Tests are available for Levels 1 and 2. Versions A and B are interchangeable, for purposes of administering make-up tests. Tests C and D are shorter versions of Tests A and B. New to this edition, Tests E and F provide a third interchangeable pair that check students' mastery of lesson vocabulary and grammar. All of the Tests contain a listening comprehension section. Level 3 has four Tests for each lesson. Tests A and B contain a greater proportion of controlled activities, while Tests C and D have more open-ended activities. Cumulative Exams are available for all levels.

The tests are also available on the Teacher Resources DVD and the Supersite so that you can customize them by adding, eliminating, or moving items according to your classroom and student needs.

Portfolio Assessment

Portfolios can provide further valuable evidence of your students' learning. They are useful tools for evaluating students' progress in Spanish and also suggest to students how they are likely to be assessed in the real world. Since portfolio activities often comprise classroom tasks that you would assign as part of a lesson or as homework, you should think of the planning, selecting, recording, and interpreting of information about individual performance as a way of blending assessment with instruction.

You may find it helpful to refer to portfolio contents, such as drafts, essays, and samples of presentations when writing student reports and conveying the status of a student's progress to his or her parents.

Ask students regularly to consider which pieces of their own work they would like to share with family and friends, and help them develop criteria for selecting representative samples of essays, stories, poems, recordings of plays or interviews, mock documentaries, and so on. Prompt students to choose a variety of media in their activities wherever possible to demonstrate development in all four language skills. Encourage them to seek peer and parental input as they generate and refine criteria to help them organize and reflect on their own work.

Strategies for Differentiating Assessment

Here are some strategies for modifying tests and other forms of assessment according to your students' needs and your own purposes for administering the assessment.

Adjust Questions Direct complex or higher-level questions to students who are equipped to answer them adequately and modify questions for students with greater needs. Always ask questions that elicit thinking, but keep in mind the students' abilities.

Provide Tiered Assignments Assign tasks of varying complexity depending on individual student needs. Appealing to learners of different abilities and learning styles will allow you to foster a positive teaching environment.

Promote Flexible Grouping Encourage movement among groups of students so that all learners are appropriately challenged. Group students according to interest, oral proficiency levels, or learning styles.

Adjust Pacing Pace the sequence and speed of assessments to suit your students' learning needs. Time advanced learners to challenge them and allow slower-paced learners more time to complete tasks or answer questions.

Assessment

Integrated Performance Assessment

Integrated performance assessments (IPA) begin with a real-life task that engages students' interest. To complete the task, students progress through the three modes of communication: they read, view, and listen for information (interpretive mode); they talk and write with classmates about what they have experienced (interpersonal mode); and they share formally what they have learned (presentational mode).

Editable worksheets in the **Content > Resources** area of the Supersite

ASSESSMENT   Lección 4

Integrated Performance Assessment Rubric

	5 points	3 points	1 point
Interpretive	The student can identify characteristics of each speaker.	The student can identify characteristics of each speaker with some difficulty.	The student can barely identify characteristics of each speaker.
Interpersonal	The student can complete an interview demonstrating mutual understanding. The result of the interview is a clear description for the class.	The student can complete an interview with only some difficulty in mutual understanding. The result of the interview is a clear description for the class.	The student can complete an interview but does not reach mutual understanding. The student is not able to prepare a clear description for the class.
Presentational	The student can provide relevant information about his or her recommendation and the reasoning for his or her choice.	Details are missing about the student's recommendation.	The presentation lacks detail, and the reasoning for the decision is unclear.

Nombre _____   Fecha _____

PERFORMANCE TASK   Lección 4

All responses and communication must be in Spanish.

Context
Your school is having an election for student council, and you need to decide what attributes are important in the person you elect. You are going to listen to two people describe themselves. Then, you and a partner will talk about the characteristics that would make each of them a better candidate. Finally, you will describe the characteristics of your ideal candidate to the class.

Interpretive task
Listen to the audio for the **Escuchar** activity on page 145 of your textbook. As you listen to the two people describe themselves, make a list of three characteristics that would make each of them good members of your school's student council. Then, make a list of three additional characteristics you would like to see in your student council members.

Interpersonal task
Compare your lists with your partner's lists. Take turns asking each other what characteristics you wrote down, and why you feel those characteristics are important. Work together to write a description of your ideal candidate, including at least five characteristics you think are important.

Presentational task
Prepare a presentation describing your ideal candidate to the class. Mention at least five characteristics of your ideal student council member, and describe why those characteristics are important for you and your school.

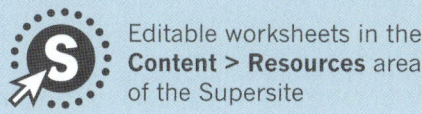
Editable worksheets in the **Content > Resources** area of the Supersite

A critical step in administering the IPA is to define and share rubrics with students before beginning the task. They need to be aware of what successful performance should look like.

Descubre 1A Pacing Guide

DAYS		WARM-UP / ACTIVATE	PRESENT / PRACTICE / COMMUNICATE	REFLECT / CONCLUDE / CONNECT
1, 2	Context for Communication	Evoke student experiences & vocabulary for context [5] Present **A primera vista** [5] 10 minutes	Present vocabulary using illustrations, phrases, categories, association [15] Students demonstrate, role-play, illustrate, classify, associate, & define [10] 25 minutes	Students restate context [5] Introduce homework: Complete selected **Práctica** activities (text and/or **Supersite**) [5] 10 minutes
3, 4	Vocabulary as a Tool	Students restate context and connect to vocabulary [5] **Assessment: Contextos** [5] 10 minutes	Students complete **Práctica** [5] Students do **Comunicación** activities [20] 25 minutes	Students review and personalize key vocabulary in context [5] Introduce homework: **Supersite** flashcards, context illustrations & audio; end-of-chapter list and audio; remaining auto-graded activities [5] 10 minutes
5, 6	Media as a Bridge	Student pairs/small groups review vocabulary [5] **Assessment: Contextos** [5] 10 minutes	Present **Pronunciación** using **Supersite** or DVD [10] Orient students to **Fotonovela** and **Expresiones útiles** through video stills with observation, role-play, and prediction [5] First viewing of **Fotonovela** [10] 25 minutes	Student pairs reflect on **Fotonovela** content and connection to vocabulary and context [5] Introduce homework: Complete (selected) text or **Supersite ¿Qué pasó?** activities [5] 10 minutes
7, 8	Media as a Bridge	Choral (whole-class) pronunciation review [5] Role-play or review of homework activities [5] 10 minutes	Second viewing of **Fotonovela** [10] **¿Qué pasó?** activities [10] Student pairs/small groups write/illustrate sentences on context-vocabulary-**Fotonovela** connections [5] 25 minutes	Students share sentences/illustrations with whole class [5] Introduce homework: Watch **Fotonovela** again on **Supersite**; complete remaining auto-graded activities [5] 10 minutes
9, 10	Culture for Communication	**Assessment: Fotonovela** 10 minutes	Present (select) **Cultura** features in whole class or in small groups using jigsaw, numbered heads together, etc. [20] Student pairs/small groups do selected item(s) from **Actividades** [10] 30 minutes	Introduce homework: Use **Supersite** to do **Conexión Internet** and/or **Actividades** [5] 5 minutes
11, 12	Grammar as a Tool	**Assessment: Cultura** 5 minutes	Present **Flash cultura** using DVD or **Supersite** [15] Present grammatical concept using text, **Supersite** (tutorials, slides), and **Fotonovela** segments [15] Students complete **Inténtalo**, sharing results with partners [5] 35 minutes	Introduce homework: Complete (selected) **Práctica** activities using text and/or **Supersite**; watch tutorials as desired [5] 5 minutes
13, 14	Grammar in Context	Student pairs re-present grammatical structures to each other and share results of completed **Práctica** activities 10 minutes	Student pairs/small groups complete **Práctica** activities [5] Students do **Comunicación** activities [20] 25 minutes	Student pairs/small groups preview **Síntesis** [5] Introduce homework: Complete (selected) **Práctica** and/or **Comunicación** activities in text and/or **Supersite** [5] 10 minutes
15, 16	Grammar as a Tool	Student groups present **Síntesis** and/or review homework activities [5] **Assessment: Estructura** [10] 15 minutes	Present grammatical concept using text, **Supersite** (tutorials, slides), and **Fotonovela** segments [15] Students complete **Inténtalo**, sharing results with partners [5] 20 minutes	Student pairs explain grammatical structure to partner; begin **Práctica** activities [5] Introduce homework: Complete (selected) **Práctica** activities using text and/or **Supersite**; watch tutorials as desired [5] 10 minutes
17, 18	Grammar in Context	Student pairs re-present grammatical structures to each other and share results of completed **Práctica** activities 10 minutes	Student pairs/small groups complete **Práctica** activities [5] Students do **Comunicación** activities [20] 25 minutes	Student pairs/small groups preview **Síntesis** [5] Introduce homework: Complete (selected) **Práctica** and/or **Comunicación** activities in text and/or **Supersite** [5] 10 minutes
19, 20	Grammar as a Tool	Student groups present **Síntesis** and/or review homework activities [5] **Assessment: Estructura** [10] 15 minutes	Present grammatical concept using text, **Supersite** (tutorials, slides), and **Fotonovela** segments [15] Students complete **Inténtalo**, sharing results with partners [5] 20 minutes	Student pairs explain grammatical structure to partner; begin **Práctica** activities [5] Introduce homework: Complete (selected) **Práctica** activities using text and/or **Supersite**; watch tutorials as desired [5] 10 minutes

Traditional Schedule

DAYS		WARM-UP / ACTIVATE	PRESENT / PRACTICE / COMMUNICATE	REFLECT / CONCLUDE
21, 22	Grammar in Context	Student pairs re-present grammatical structures to each other and share results of completed Práctica activities 10 minutes	Student pairs/small groups complete Práctica activities [5] Students do Comunicación activities [20] 25 minutes	Student pairs/small groups preview Síntesis [5] Introduce homework: Complete (selected) Práctica and/or Comunicación activities in text and/or Supersite [5] 10 minutes
23, 24	Grammar as a Tool	Student groups present Síntesis and/or review homework activities [5] Assessment: Estructura [10] 15 minutes	Present grammatical concept using text, Supersite (tutorials, slides), and Fotonovela segments [15] Students complete Inténtalo, sharing results with partners [5] 20 minutes	Student pairs explain grammatical structure to partner; begin Práctica activities [5] Introduce homework: Complete (selected) Práctica activities using text and/or Supersite; watch tutorials as desired [5] 10 minutes
25, 26	Grammar in Context	Student pairs re-present grammatical structures to each other and share results of completed Práctica activities 10 minutes	Student pairs/small groups complete Práctica activities [5] Students do Comunicación activities [20] 25 minutes	Student pairs/small groups preview Síntesis [5] Introduce homework: Complete (selected) Práctica and/or Comunicación activities in text and/or Supersite [5] 10 minutes
27, 28	Skill Synthesis: Interpretive (Reading)	Assessment: Estructura 10 minutes	Guide students through Antes de leer, including Estrategia [10] Students read Lectura (whole class or small groups) [15] 25 minutes	Student pairs/small groups begin Después de leer [5] Introduce homework: Reread Lectura and complete Después de leer activities (text or Supersite) [5] 10 minutes
29, 30	Skill Synthesis: Presentational (Writing)	Assessment: Lectura 15 minutes	Guide students through Escritura, including Estrategia and Tema [15] Students prepare writing plan, sharing with partner [10] 25 minutes	Introduce homework: First draft of Tema writing assignment 5 minutes
31, 32	Skill Synthesis: Interpretive (Listening)	Student pairs read partner's first draft of Tema of Escritura and share comments 10 minutes	Guide students through Estrategia and Preparación in Escuchar and present selection [15] Students (individuals, pairs, or small groups) do Comprensión activities [15] 30 minutes	Introduce homework: Complete second draft of Escritura assignment 5 minutes
33, 34	Skill Synthesis: Interpretive (Viewing)	Student group peer review of second draft of Tema of Escritura 10 minutes	Guide students through the introduction and Vocabulario útil of En pantalla and show clip using Supersite [20] Student pairs do post-viewing activities; show clip again as necessary [10] 30 minutes	Introduce homework: Final version of Escritura assignment 5 minutes
35, 36	Geographical Context	Assessment: Escuchar or En pantalla 5 minutes	Present Panorama to whole class or to small groups using jigsaw, numbered heads together, etc. [20] Present Panorama cultural using DVD or Supersite [15] 35 minutes	Introduce homework: Panorama: selected activities (text or Supersite) 5 minutes
37, 38	Communication-based Synthesis and Review	Assessment: Panorama 5 minutes	Student pairs/small groups/whole class prepare and check Recapitulación [20] Guide review of lesson context, vocabulary, structures, skills [10] 30 minutes	Confirm understanding of assessment content and grading rubric [5] Introduce homework: Prepare for lesson test using text and Supersite [5] 10 minutes
39, 40	Assessment	Orientation Students look over lesson content in preparation 5 minutes	Assessment Lesson Test: 40 minutes	

Descubre 1A Pacing Guide

DAYS	WARM-UP / ACTIVATE	PRESENT / PRACTICE / COMMUNICATE
1, 2 — Context for Communication	Evoke student experiences & vocabulary for context [5] Present **A primera vista** [5] 10 minutes	Present vocabulary using illustrations, phrases, categories, association [15] Students demonstrate, role-play, illustrate, classify, associate, & define [15] 30 minutes
3, 4 — Media as a Bridge	Student pairs/small groups review vocabulary [5] Assessment: **Contextos** [5] 10 minutes	Present **Pronunciación** using **Supersite** or DVD [15] Orient students to **Fotonovela** and **Expresiones útiles** through video stills with observation, role-play, and prediction [10] First viewing of **Fotonovela** [10] 35 minutes
5, 6 — Culture for Communication	Assessment: **Fotonovela** 10 minutes	Present (select) **Cultura** features in whole class or in small groups using jigsaw, numbered heads together, etc. [20] Student pairs/small groups do selected item(s) from **Actividades** [15] 35 minutes
7, 8 — Grammar as a Tool	Assessment: **Cultura** 10 minutes	Present grammatical concept using text, **Supersite** (tutorials, slides), and **Fotonovela** segments [25] Students complete **Inténtalo**, sharing results with partners [5] 30 minutes
9, 10 — Grammar as a Tool	Assessment: **Estructura** 10 minutes	Present grammatical concept using text, **Supersite** (tutorials, slides), and **Fotonovela** segments [25] Students complete **Inténtalo**, sharing results with partners [5] 30 minutes
11, 12 — Grammar as a Tool	Assessment: **Estructura** 10 minutes	Present grammatical concept using text, **Supersite** (tutorials, slides), and **Fotonovela** segments [25] Students complete **Inténtalo**, sharing results with partners [5] 30 minutes
13, 14 — Grammar as a Tool	Assessment: **Estructura** 10 minutes	Present grammatical concept using text, **Supersite** (tutorials, slides), and **Fotonovela** segments [25] Students complete **Inténtalo**, sharing results with partners [5] 30 minutes
15, 16 — Skill Synthesis	Assessment: **Estructura** 10 minutes	Interpretive (Reading) Guide students through **Antes de leer**, including **Estrategia** [10] Students read **Lectura** (whole class or small groups) and do **Después de leer** [25] 35 minutes
17, 18 — Skill Synthesis and Review	Student group peer review of drafts of **Tema** of **Escritura** [5] Assessment: **Lectura** [10] 15 minutes	Interpretive (Listening) Guide students through **Estrategia** and **Preparación** in **Escuchar** and present selection [10] Students (individuals, pairs, or small groups) do **Comprensión** activities [15] 25 minutes
19, 20 — Assessment and Geography	Guide review of lesson context, vocabulary, structures, skills 5 minutes	Present **Panorama** features to whole class or to small groups using jigsaw, numbered heads together, etc. [25] Present **Panorama cultural** video using DVD or **Supersite** [10] 35 minutes

Block Schedule

REFLECT	PRESENT / PRACTICE / COMMUNICATE	REFLECT / CONCLUDE	DAYS
Students restate context (individually or in pairs) and create personalized sentences 5 minutes	Students do select **Práctica** activities [15] Students do **Comunicación** activities [15] 30 minutes	Students review key vocabulary through personalized phrases and sentences [5] Introduce homework: **Supersite** flashcards, context illustrations & audio; end-of-lesson list and audio; auto-graded activities [5] 10 minutes	1 2
Student pairs reflect on **Fotonovela** and begin ¿Qué pasó? comprehension activities 10 minutes	Second viewing of **Fotonovela** [10] Students complete ¿Qué pasó? activities [5] Student pairs/small groups write/illustrate vocabulary-**Fotonovela** connections [5] 20 minutes	Students reflect on connection of vocabulary and video to lesson context [5] Introduce homework: Watch **Fotonovela** again on **Supersite**; complete remaining auto-graded activities [5] 10 minutes	3 4
Individual students reflect on information presented and identify concept or topic of initial personal interest 5 minutes	Orient students to **Flash cultura** vocabulary, content, and learning outcomes on **Supersite** [10] Present **Flash cultura** using DVD or **Supersite** and discuss [15] 25 minutes	Student pairs/small groups do selected item(s) from **Actividades** [5] Introduce homework: Use **Supersite** to do **Flash cultura** activities, **Conexión Internet**, and/or **Actividades** [5] 10 minutes	5 6
Student pairs explain grammatical structure to partner 5 minutes	Student pairs do select **Práctica** activities [15] Students do **Comunicación** activities [15] 30 minutes	Student pairs/small groups preview **Síntesis** [5] Introduce homework: Complete (selected) **Práctica** and/or **Comunicación** activities in text and/or **Supersite** [5] 10 minutes	7 8
Student pairs explain grammatical structure to partner 5 minutes	Student pairs/small groups do select **Práctica** activities [15] Students do **Comunicación** activities [15] 30 minutes	Student pairs/small groups preview **Síntesis** [5] Introduce homework: Complete (selected) **Práctica** and/or **Comunicación** activities in text and/or **Supersite** [5] 10 minutes	9 10
Student pairs explain grammatical structure to partner 5 minutes	Student pairs/small groups do select **Práctica** activities [15] Students do **Comunicación** activities [15] 30 minutes	Student pairs/small groups preview **Síntesis** [5] Introduce homework: Complete (selected) **Práctica** and/or **Comunicación** activities in text and/or **Supersite** [5] 10 minutes	11 12
Student pairs explain grammatical structure to partner 5 minutes	Student pairs/small groups do select **Práctica** activities [15] Students do **Comunicación** activities [15] 30 minutes	Student pairs/small groups preview **Síntesis** [5] Introduce homework: Complete (selected) **Práctica** and/or **Comunicación** activities in text and/or **Supersite** [5] 10 minutes	13 14
	Presentational (Writing) Guide students through **Escritura**, including **Estrategia** and **Tema** [10] Place students in pairs/small groups and orient to process writing through **Supersite** or **CPA** [5] Students begin writing [15] 30 minutes	Student pairs share writing plan with partner [5] Introduce homework: First draft of **Tema** writing assignment [5] 10 minutes	15 16
	Interpretive (Viewing) Guide students through the introduction and **Vocabulario útil** of **En pantalla** and show clip via **Supersite** [10] Student pairs do post-viewing activities; show clip again as necessary [10] 20 minutes	Students do **Recapitulación** [15] Confirm understanding of assessment content and grading rubric [5] Introduce homework: Complete **Escritura** writing assignment and review **Recapitulación** and lesson vocabulary (text or **Supersite**) [5] 25 minutes	17 18
Introduce homework: **Panorama**: selected activities (text or **Supersite**) 5 minutes	**Assessment** Lesson Test: 40 minutes		19 20

Index of Cultural References

Animals
colibrí abeja (*bee hummingbird, world's smallest bird,* Cuba), 222
llamas *and* alpacas, 259
quetzal (Guatemala), 297

Artists
Guayasamín, Oswaldo (Ecuador), 113
Kahlo, Frida (Mexico), 149
Rivera, Diego (Mexico), 149
Velázquez, Diego (Spain), 75

Celebrations
bautismo (*baptism, christening*), 322
Carnaval de Oruro (Bolivia), 309
comer doce uvas, 306
Desfile de las palmas (El Salvador), 309
Desfile puertorriqueño (United States), 37
Día de los Reyes Magos, 327
Día de Muertos (*Day of the Dead*),148
Feria Juniana (Honduras), 309
Festival de Viña del Mar (Chile), 309
Festival Internacional de la Canción (*International Song Festival* (Chile), 309
Fiesta de quince años, 323
Fiestas Patrias (Chile), 326
matrimonio (*wedding*), 322
Mes de las Artes (*Arts Month*), 309
Semana Santa (*Holy Week*), 297, 308
Tomatina, la (Valencia, Spain), 74

Countries and Regions
Argentina, 162
Canada (**Canadá**), 36–37
Chile, 328–329
Cuba, 222–223
Ecuador, 112–113
Guatemala, 296–297
 Antigua Guatemala, 297
Mexico (**México**), 48, 148–149
 México, D.F., 149
Peru (**el Perú**), 258–259
 Lima, 259
Puerto Rico, 176, 186–187
Spain (**España**), 74–75
 Rastro (*market*), 198
 royal family, 87
United States (**Estados Unidos**), 36–37

Economics
 silver (la plata, Mexico), 149
 sugar and tobacco (Cuba), 223
Maya, 297
Hispanos en Canadá, 37
Historical figures
 Alfonso X (Spain), 257
 Franco, Francisco (Spain), 220
piratas (*pirates*), 245
population (Cuba), 223
status of Puerto Rico, 187

Education
INFRAMEN (El Salvador), 49
secondary, 48
Spain, 68–69, 220
universities, 62
 Universidad Nacional Autónoma de México, 48, 73
 Universidad Autónoma Española, 68–69

Fashion Design
Domínguez, Adolfo (Spain), 199
Herrera, Carolina (Venezuela), 199
Renta, Óscar de la (Dominican Republic), 199
Rodríguez, Narciso (USA), 199
Tcherassi, Silvia (Colombia), 199

Food
Adrià, Ferran (chef, Spain), 273
aguacate (*avocado*), see frutas y verduras
Andrés, José (chef, Spain), 75
arroz (*rice*), 266, 273
breakfast foods (*desayunos típicos*), 264
cacao, 272
café con leche, 238
ceviche (Peru), 273
enchiladas (Mexico, Honduras), 272
flan, 312
frutas y verduras (*fruits and vegetables*), 272, 295
machas a la parmesana (*Chilean clam dish*), 319
mate, 235
menú, 290
Mexican
 in the U.S., 37
mole, 272
sancocho (Colombia), 273
Spanish
 gazpacho andaluz, 273
 paella, 75
 tamales, 290
 tapas, 257
vino (*wine,* Chile), 329
yuca (*cassava*), 273

History
Aztecs, 149
diversity (Spain), 75
Mayans, 297

Indigenous Peoples
Amazonas, 112
Aztecs (**los aztecas**), 149, 272
Incas (**los incas**), 112, 185, 259, 272
Maya (**los mayas**), 272, 296–297
Nazca (**los nazca**), 258

Languages
English (*inglés*), 186
spoken in Latin America
 aimará, 258
 cakhiquel (maya), 296
 kekhícomo (maya), 296
 mapuche, 328
 náhuatl, 148
 quechua, 112, 258
 quiché (maya), 296
 quichua, 112
spoken in Spain
 castellano (*Castilian*), 74
 catalán, 74
 eusquera/euskera (*Basque*), 74
 gallego (*Galician*), 74
 valenciano, 74

Literature
Writers
 Fuentes, Carlos (Mexico), 91
 García Márquez, Gabriel (Colombia), 86
 Martí, José (Cuba), 204
 Paz, Octavio (Mexico), 73

Media in Spanish
Advertisements
    Asepxia, 256
    Chilevisión, 326
    Jumbo, 72
    MasterCard, 34
    Pentel, 110
    Santander LANPASS, 184
    Sopas Roa, 294
    tiendas Galerías, 220
    Totofútbol, 146
Television, 132

Monuments and Buildings
Casa Rosada (Argentina), 35
Catedral Metropolitana (Argentina), 35
Equatorial Line Monument (**Mitad del Mundo, la**), 113
Gran Teatro de La Habana (Cuba), 222
Iglesia de la Merced (Guatemala), 296
Iglesia de Ponce (Puerto Rico), 186
Morro, El (Puerto Rico), 187
Palacio Nacional de la Cultura (Guatemala), 296
Sagrada Familia Church (Spain), 74

Museums
El Prado (Madrid, Spain), 75
Museo de Arte Moderno de la Ciudad de México (*Museum of Modern Art*), 149
Museo del Oro del Perú (*Gold Museum*), 259
Museo Nacional de Antropología y Arqueología, Perú (*National Museum of Anthropology and Archeology*), 259

Music and Dance
Dance
    Alonso, Alicia (Cuba), dancer, 223
    Ballet Nacional de Cuba, 223
    flamenco (Spain), 74
Genres
    música andina, 259
    salsa, 187
    son (Cuba), 223
Instruments, musical
    quena (type of flute), 259
    zampoña (type of flute), 259

Musicians
    Buena Vista Social Club (Cuba), 223

Points of Interest
Álamo, El (USA), 36
Andes Mountains (**Cordillera de los Andes**), 112
    observatories in, 329
Arecibo Observatory (**Observatorio de Arecibo**), 187
Atacama Desert (Chile), 328
Aztec ruins (Mexico), 149
Bariloche (Argentina), 193
Bosque de Chapultepec (Mexico), 134
Camino Inca, el (*Inca Trail*), 185
Chichén Itzá (Mexico), 148
Cueva de los Tres Pueblos (Puerto Rico), 186
Galápagos, Las islas, 113
Iguazú, Las cataratas del, 162
Latitud 0 (Ecuador), 113
Machu Picchu (Peru), 259
Moai, see **La isla de Pascua**
Nazca Lines (**Líneas de Nazca**, Peru), 258
Old Havana (**La Habana Vieja**), 204, 222
Otavalo Market, 198
Pasaje Santa Rosa de Lima (Peru), 258
Pascua, La isla de (*Easter Island,* Chile), 315, 329
Patagonia (Chile, Argentina), 184
Pequeña Habana, La (USA), 37
Plaza del Capitolio (Cuba), 222
Plaza de Mayo (Argentina), 35
Plaza Mayor (Madrid, Spain), 74
Punta del Este (Uruguay), 163
Strait of Magellan (**Estrecho de Magallanes,** Chile), 328
Torres del Paine (Chile), 328
Viña del Mar (Chile), 302, 309, 328
volcanoes (**volcanes**), 112–113
    Cotopaxi (Ecuador), 112

Social Customs and Daily Life
bargaining (at open-air markets), 198
dating, 110
family size, 87
godparents, 87
huipil (traditional clothing, Guatemala), 297
mercados al aire libre (*open-air markets*), 198
naming customs, 86
plaza principal, la, 11
reuniones familiares, 111
siesta, 234
specialty shops, 221
styles of greeting, 10
textiles (**telas,** Guatemala), 296

Spanish Speakers in the U.S.
Cubans, 37
numbers of, xx–xxi
Puerto Ricans, 37

Sports and Pastimes
Athletes (**atletas**), 125
    Belmonte García, Mireia (Spain), swimmer, 125
    Cabrera, Miguel (Venezuela/U.S.), baseball player, 125
    Casillas, Iker (Spain), soccer player, 132
    Espinosa Sanchez, Paola Milagros (Mexico), diver, 125
    Messi, Lionel (Argentina), soccer player, 125
    Nadal, Rafael (Spain), tennis player, 125
    Ochoa, Lorena (Mexico), golfer, 125
Baseball (**el béisbol**), 143
Dominoes (**el dominó**), 131
Soccer (**el fútbol**), 124, 142–143, 146–147
Trekking, 113
Winter sports (**deportes de invierno,** Chile), 329

DESCUBRE 1A

Lengua y cultura del mundo hispánico

VISTA
HIGHER LEARNING

Boston, Massachusetts

On the cover: Mexican rattles (maracas), San Miguel de Allende, Guanajuato, Mexico

Publisher: José A. Blanco
Professional Development Director: Norah Lulich Jones
Editorial Development: Brian Contreras, Diego García, Sharla Zwirek
Project Management: Kayli Brownstein, Hillary Gospodarek, Sharon Inglis
Rights Management: Ashley Dos Santos, Jorgensen Fernandez, Caitlin O'Brien
Technology Production: Jamie Kostecki, Fabián Montoya, Paola Ríos Schaaf
Design: Gabriel Noreña, Andrés Vanegas
Production: Manuela Arango, Sergio Arias, Oscar Díez

© 2017 by Vista Higher Learning, Inc. All rights reserved.
No part of this work may be reproduced or distributed in any form or by any means, electronic or mechanical, including photocopying and recording, or by any information storage or retrieval system without prior written permission from Vista Higher Learning, 500 Boylston Street, Suite 620, Boston, MA 02116-3736.

Student Text ISBN: 978-1-68004-320-4
Library of Congress Control Number: 2015948650

1 2 3 4 5 6 7 8 9   TC   20 19 18 17 16 15

Printed in Canada.

DESCUBRE 1A

Lengua y cultura del mundo hispánico

Table of Contents

contextos	fotonovela

Map of the
  Spanish-Speaking World viii
Map of Mexico............... x
Map of Central America
  and the Caribbean xi
Map of South America xii

Lección 1
Hola, ¿qué tal?

Greetings and goodbyes 2
Identifying yourself
  and others................. 2
Courtesy expressions 2

Bienvenida, Marissa 6
Pronunciación
  The Spanish alphabet 9

Lección 2
En la clase

The classroom and
  school life 40
Fields of study and
  school subjects 40
Days of the week 42
Class schedules 43

¿Qué estudias? 44
Pronunciación
  Spanish vowels............ 47

Lección 3
La familia

The family 78
Identifying people 78
Professions and occupations .. 78

Un domingo en familia 82
Pronunciación
  Diphthongs and linking 85

iv Student Edition • Table of Contents

cultura	estructura	adelante
Map of Spain . . . . xiii Video Programs. . . . . xiv Supersite . . . . xvi Icons xvii	Studying Spanish . . . . xviii Getting Started. . . . . xxv Acknowledgments. . . . . xxvii Bios xxix	
En detalle: Saludos y besos en los países hispanos . . . . 10 **Perfil:** La plaza principal 11	**1.1** Nouns and articles . . . . . . 12 **1.2** Numbers 0–30 . . . . 16 **1.3** Present tense of **ser** . . . . . 19 **1.4** Telling time . . . . 24 **Recapitulación** 28	**Lectura:** *Teléfonos importantes* . . . . 30 **Escritura** . . . . 32 **Escuchar** . . . . 33 **En pantalla** . . . . 34 **Flash cultura** . . . . 35 **Panorama:** Estados Unidos y Canadá 36
En detalle: La escuela secundaria . . . . 48 **Perfil:** El INFRAMEN 49	**2.1** Present tense of **-ar** verbs . . . . 50 **2.2** Forming questions in Spanish . . . . 55 **2.3** Present tense of **estar** . . . . 59 **2.4** Numbers 31 and higher . . 63 **Recapitulación** 66	**Lectura:** *¡Español en Madrid!* . . 68 **Escritura** . . . . 70 **Escuchar** . . . . 71 **En pantalla** . . . . 72 **Flash cultura** . . . . 73 **Panorama:** España 74
En detalle: ¿Cómo te llamas? . . 86 **Perfil:** La familia real española 87	**3.1** Descriptive adjectives . . . 88 **3.2** Possessive adjectives . . . . 93 **3.3** Present tense of **-er** and **-ir** verbs . . . . 96 **3.4** Present tense of **tener** and **venir** . . . . 100 **Recapitulación** 104	**Lectura:** *Gente... Las familias* . . . . 106 **Escritura** . . . . 108 **Escuchar** . . . . 109 **En pantalla** . . . . 110 **Flash cultura** . . . . 111 **Panorama:** Ecuador 112

Table of Contents

Lección 4
Los pasatiempos

contextos

Pastimes 116
Sports 116
Places in the city 118

fotonovela

Fútbol, cenotes y mole 120
Pronunciación
  Word stress
  and accent marks 123

Consulta

Apéndice A
Glossary of Grammatical Terms 152
Apéndice B
Verb Conjugation Tables 156
Vocabulario
Spanish-English Vocabulary 166
English-Spanish Vocabulary 177

cultura

En detalle: Real Madrid y Barça: rivalidad total 124
Perfiles: Miguel Cabrera and Paola Espinosa 125

estructura

4.1 Present tense of **ir** 126
4.2 Stem-changing verbs: **e:ie, o:ue** 129
4.3 Stem-changing verbs: **e:i** 133
4.4 Verbs with irregular **yo** forms 136
Recapitulación 140

adelante

Lectura: *No sólo el fútbol* 142
Escritura 144
Escuchar 145
En pantalla 146
Flash cultura 147
Panorama: México 148

References 188
Índice 200
Credits 202

The Spanish-Speaking World

Mexico

Central America and the Caribbean

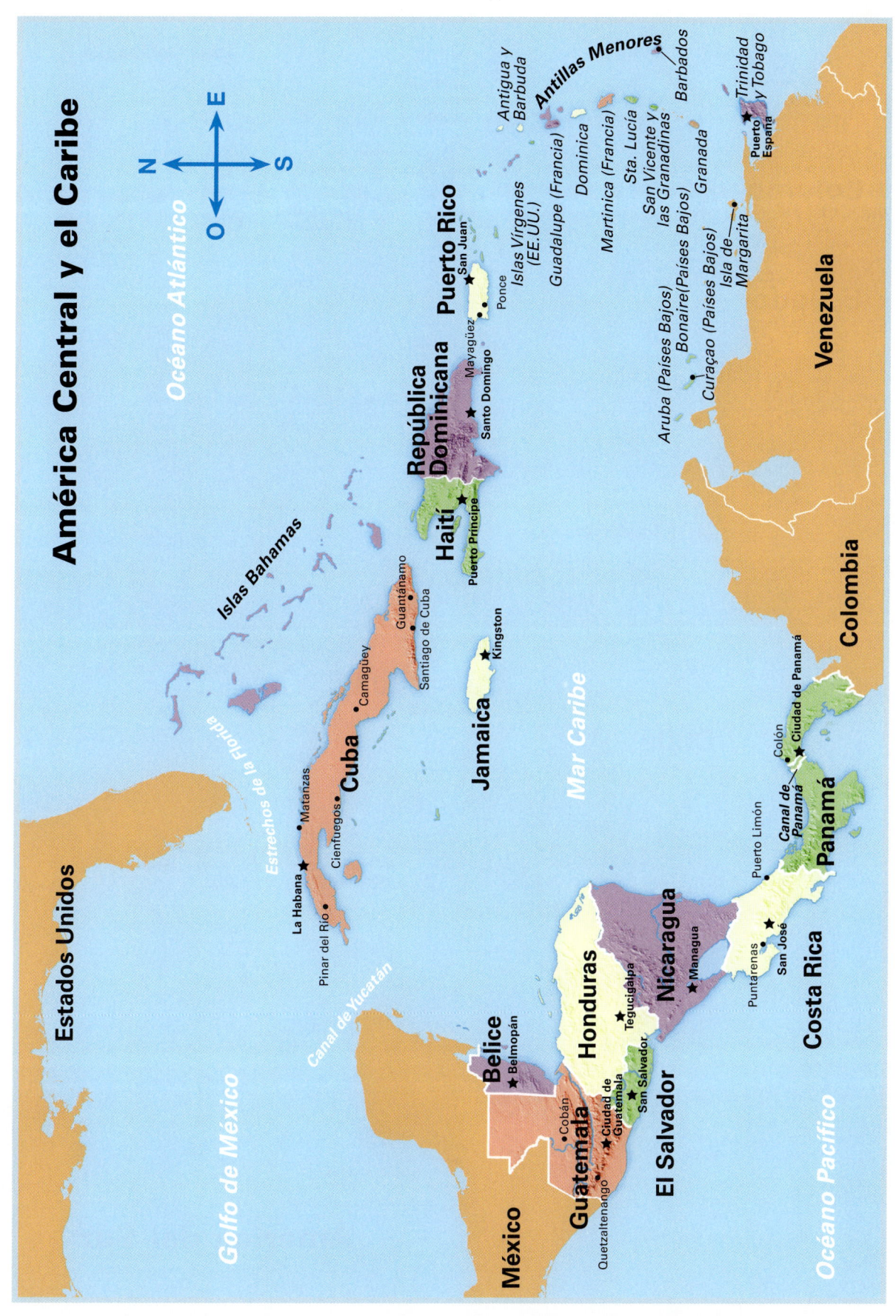

South America

Spain

Video Programs

Fotonovela video program

The Cast

Here are the main characters you will meet in the **Fotonovela** Video:

From Mexico, Jimena Díaz Velázquez

From Argentina, Juan Carlos Rossi

From the U.S., Marissa Wagner

From Mexico, Felipe Díaz Velázquez

From Mexico, María Eugenia (Maru) Castaño Ricaurte

From Spain, Miguel Ángel Lagasca Martínez

Fully integrated with your text, the **Descubre Fotonovela** Video is a dynamic and contemporary window into the Spanish language. The video centers around the Díaz family, whose household includes two college-aged children and a visiting student from the U.S. Over the course of an academic year, Jimena, Felipe, Marissa, and their friends explore **el D.F.** and other parts of Mexico as they make plans for their futures. Their adventures take them through some of the greatest natural and cultural treasures of the Spanish-speaking world, as well as the highs and lows of everyday life.

The **Fotonovela** section in each textbook lesson is actually an abbreviated version of the dramatic episode featured in the video. Therefore, each **Fotonovela** section can be done before you see the corresponding video episode, after it, or as a section that stands alone.

In each dramatic segment, the characters interact using the vocabulary and grammar you are studying. As the storyline unfolds, the episodes combine new vocabulary and grammar with previously taught language, exposing you to a variety of authentic accents along the way. At the end of each episode, the **Resumen** section highlights the grammar and vocabulary you are studying.

We hope you find the **Fotonovela** Video to be an engaging and useful tool for learning Spanish!

En pantalla video program

The **Descubre** Supersite features an authentic video clip for each lesson. Clip formats include commercials and newscasts. These clips have been carefully chosen to be comprehensible for students learning Spanish, and are accompanied by activities and vocabulary lists to facilitate understanding. More importantly, though, these clips are a fun and motivating way to improve your Spanish!

Here are the countries represented in each lesson in **En pantalla**:

Lesson 1 **U.S.A.**
Lesson 2 **Chile**
Lesson 3 **Spain**
Lesson 4 **Peru**

Flash cultura video program

In the dynamic **Flash cultura** Video, young people from all over the Spanish-speaking world share aspects of life in their countries with you. The similarities and differences among Spanish-speaking countries that come up through their adventures will challenge you to think about your own cultural practices and values. The segments provide valuable cultural insights as well as linguistic input; the episodes will introduce you to a variety of accents and vocabulary as they gradually move into Spanish.

Panorama cultural video program

The **Panorama cultural** Video is integrated with the **Panorama** section in each lesson. Each segment is 2–3 minutes long and consists of documentary footage from each of the countries featured. The images were specially chosen for interest level and visual appeal, while the all-Spanish narrations were carefully written to reflect the vocabulary and grammar covered in the textbook.

Supersite

Supersite

Each section of your textbook comes with resources and activities on the **Descubre** Supersite. You can access them from any computer with an Internet connection. Visit **vhlcentral.com** to get started.

My Vocabulary Tutorials	**CONTEXTOS** Listen to audio of the **Vocabulary**, watch dynamic **Tutorials**, and practice using Flashcards.
Video: *Fotonovela*	**FOTONOVELA** Travel with Marissa to Mexico and meet her host family. Watch the **Video** again at home to see the characters use the vocabulary in a real context.
Audio	**PRONUNCIACIÓN** Improve your accent by listening to native speakers, then recording your voice and comparing it to the samples provided.
Additional Reading	**CULTURA** Explore cultural topics through the **Conexión Internet** activity or reading the *Más cultura* selection.
Tutorial	**ESTRUCTURA** Watch an animated **Tutorial**, and then answer *el profesor*'s questions to make sure you got it.
Audio: Reading Additional Reading Audio Video: TV Clip Video: *Flash cultura* Video: *Panorama cultural* Interactive Map	**ADELANTE** Listen along as the **reading** is read aloud. Read another selection related to the chapter's theme. Listen again to the audio from *Escuchar*. Watch the **En pantalla**, **Flash cultura**, and **Panorama cultural Videos** again outside of class so that you can pause and repeat to really understand what you hear. Use the **Interactive Map** to explore the places you might want to visit.
My Vocabulary Diagnostics	**VOCABULARIO - RECAPITULACIÓN** Just what you need to get ready for the test! Review the **vocabulary** with **audio**. Practice vocabulary with Flashcards in **My Vocabulary**. Complete the Diagnostic *Recapitulación* to see what you might still need to study. Get additional **Remediation Activities**.

Icons

Familiarize yourself with these icons that appear throughout *Descubre*.

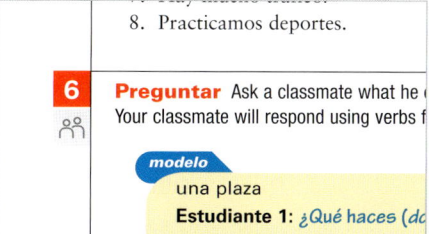
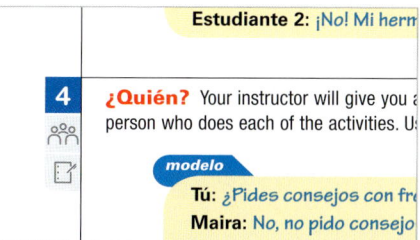

Listening
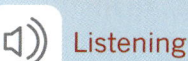
The listening icon indicates that audio is available. You will see it in the lesson's **Contextos**, **Pronunciación**, **Escuchar**, and **Vocabulario** sections.

Pair Activities

Two heads indicate a pair activity.

Handout
The activities marked with this icon require handouts that your teacher will give you to help you complete the activity.

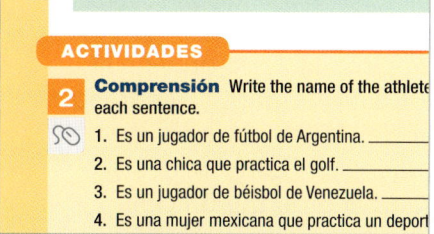
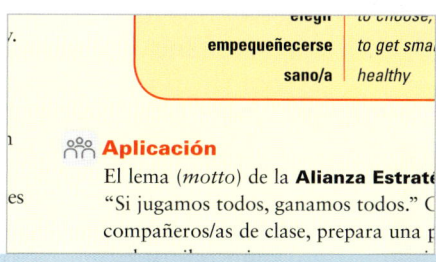
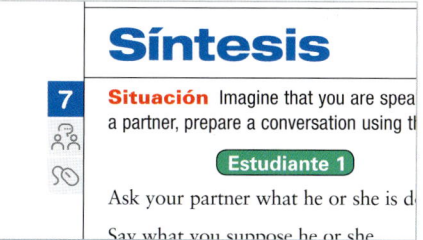

Activity Online
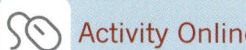
The mouse icon indicates when an activity is also available on the Supersite.

Group Activities
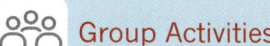
Three heads indicate a group activity.

Partner Chat/Virtual Chat Activities
Two heads with a speech bubble indicate that the activity may be assigned as a Partner Chat or a Virtual Chat activity on the Supersite.

Recursos

Recursos boxes let you know exactly which print and technology ancillaries you can use to reinforce and expand on every section of the lessons in your textbook. They even include page numbers when applicable.

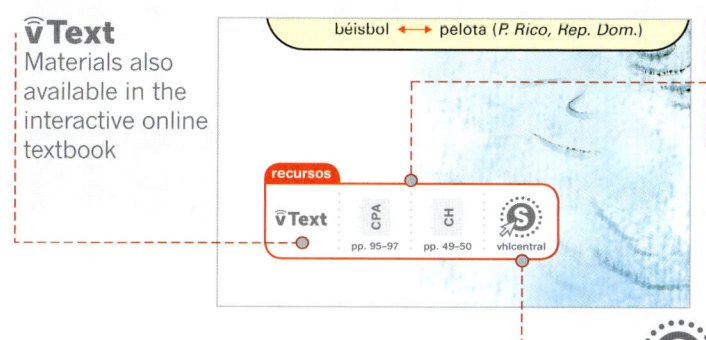

vText Materials also available in the interactive online textbook

CPA Cuaderno de práctica y actividades comunicativas

CH Cuaderno para hispanohablantes

Two workbooks with additional vocabulary and grammar practice; audio activities; and pre-, during, and post-viewing activities for the video programs.

Supersite Additional practice on the Supersite, not included in the textbook.

Studying Spanish

The Spanish-Speaking World

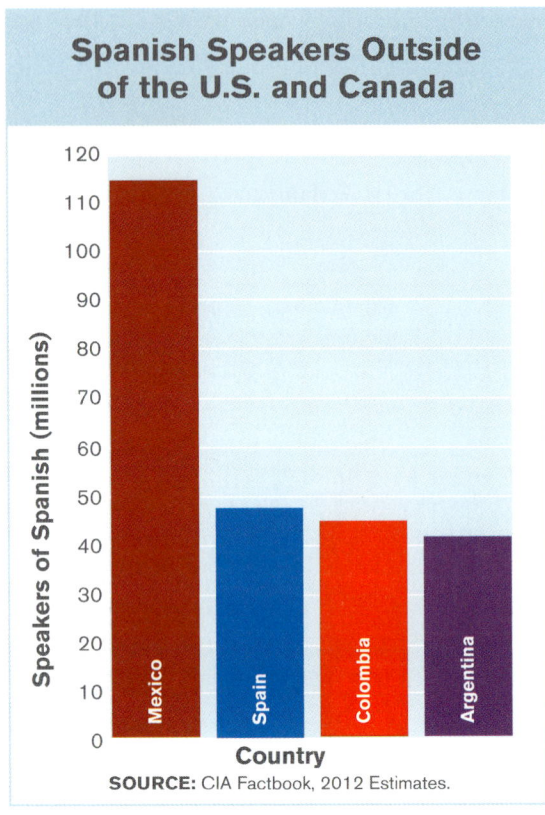

Do you know someone whose first language is Spanish? Chances are you do! More than approximately forty million people living in the U.S. speak Spanish; after English, it is the second most commonly spoken language in this country. It is the official language of twenty-two countries and an official language of the European Union and United Nations.

The Growth of Spanish

Have you ever heard of a language called Castilian? It's Spanish! The Spanish language as we know it today has its origins in a dialect called Castilian (**castellano** in Spanish). Castilian developed in the 9th century in north-central Spain, in a historic provincial region known as Old Castile. Castilian gradually spread towards the central region of New Castile, where it was adopted as the main language of commerce. By the 16th century, Spanish had become the official language of Spain and eventually, the country's role in exploration, colonization, and overseas trade led to its spread across Central and South America, North America, the Caribbean, parts of North Africa, the Canary Islands, and the Philippines.

Spanish in the United States

1500

16th Century
Spanish is the official language of Spain.

1565
The Spanish arrive in Florida and found St. Augustine.

1600

1610
The Spanish found Santa Fe, today's capital of New Mexico, the state with the most Spanish speakers in the U.S.

1700

Spanish in the United States

Spanish came to North America in the 16th century with the Spanish who settled in St. Augustine, Florida. Spanish-speaking communities flourished in several parts of the continent over the next few centuries. Then, in 1848, in the aftermath of the Mexican-American War, Mexico lost almost half its land to the United States, including portions of modern-day Texas, New Mexico, Arizona, Colorado, California, Wyoming, Nevada, and Utah. Overnight, hundreds of thousands of Mexicans became citizens of the United States, bringing with them their rich history, language, and traditions.

This heritage, combined with that of the other Hispanic populations that have immigrated to the United States over the years, has led to the remarkable growth of Spanish around the country. After English, it is the most commonly spoken language in 43 states. More than 12 million people in California alone claim Spanish as their first or "home" language.

You've made a popular choice by choosing to take Spanish in school. Not only is Spanish found and heard almost everywhere in the United States, but it is the most commonly taught foreign language in classrooms throughout the country! Have you heard people speaking Spanish in your community? Chances are that you've come across an advertisement, menu, or magazine that is in Spanish. If you look around, you'll find that Spanish can be found in some pretty common places. For example, most ATMs respond to users in both English and Spanish. News agencies and television stations such as **CNN** and **Telemundo** provide Spanish-language broadcasts. When you listen to the radio or download music from the Internet, some of the most popular choices are Latino artists who perform in Spanish. Federal government agencies such as the Internal Revenue Service and the Department of State provide services in both languages. Even the White House has an official Spanish-language webpage! Learning Spanish can create opportunities within your everyday life.

1800

1848 Mexicans who choose to stay in the U.S. after the Mexican-American War become U.S. citizens.

1900

1959 After the Cuban Revolution, thousands of Cubans emigrate to the U.S.

2010

2010 Spanish is the 2nd most commonly spoken language in the U.S., with more than approximately 40 million speakers.

Studying Spanish

Why Study Spanish?

Learn an International Language

There are many reasons to learn Spanish, a language that has spread to many parts of the world and has along the way embraced words and sounds of languages as diverse as Latin, Arabic, and Nahuatl. Spanish has evolved from a medieval dialect of north-central Spain into the fourth most commonly spoken language in the world. It is the second language of choice among the majority of people in North America.

Understand the World Around You

Knowing Spanish can also open doors to communities within the United States, and it can broaden your understanding of the nation's history and geography. The very names Colorado, Montana, Nevada, and Florida are Spanish in origin. Just knowing their meanings can give you some insight into, of all things, the landscapes for which the states are renowned. Colorado means "colored red;" Montana means "mountain;" Nevada is derived from "snow-capped mountain;" and Florida means "flowered." You've already been speaking Spanish whenever you talk about some of these states!

Connect with the World

Learning Spanish can change how you view the world. While you learn Spanish, you will also explore and learn about the origins, customs, art, music, and literature of people in close to two dozen countries. When you travel to a Spanish-speaking country, you'll be able to converse freely with the people you meet. And whether in the U.S., Canada, or abroad, you'll find that speaking to people in their native language is the best way to bridge any culture gap.

State Name	Meaning in Spanish
Colorado	"colored red"
Florida	"flowered"
Montana	"mountain"
Nevada	"snow-capped mountain"

Why Study Spanish?

Expand Your Skills

Studying a foreign language can improve your ability to analyze and interpret information and help you succeed in many other subject areas. When you first begin learning Spanish, your studies will focus mainly on reading, writing, grammar, listening, and speaking skills. You'll be amazed at how the skills involved with learning how a language works can help you succeed in other areas of study. Many people who study a foreign language claim that they gained a better understanding of English. Spanish can even help you understand the origins of many English words and expand your own vocabulary in English. Knowing Spanish can also help you pick up other related languages, such as Italian, Portuguese, and French. Spanish can really open doors for learning many other skills in your school career.

Explore Your Future

How many of you are already planning your future careers? Employers in today's global economy look for workers who know different languages and understand other cultures. Your knowledge of Spanish will make you a valuable candidate for careers abroad as well as in the United States or Canada. Doctors, nurses, social workers, hotel managers, journalists, businessmen, pilots, flight attendants, and many other professionals need to know Spanish or another foreign language to do their jobs well.

Studying Spanish

How to Learn Spanish

Start with the Basics!

As with anything you want to learn, start with the basics and remember that learning takes time! The basics are vocabulary, grammar, and culture.

Vocabulary | Every new word you learn in Spanish will expand your vocabulary and ability to communicate. The more words you know, the better you can express yourself. Focus on sounds and think about ways to remember words. Use your knowledge of English and other languages to figure out the meaning of and memorize words like **conversación, teléfono, oficina, clase,** and **música**.

Grammar | Grammar helps you put your new vocabulary together. By learning the rules of grammar, you can use new words correctly and speak in complete sentences. As you learn verbs and tenses, you will be able to speak about the past, present, or future, express yourself with clarity, and be able to persuade others with your opinions. Pay attention to structures and use your knowledge of English grammar to make connections with Spanish grammar.

Culture | Culture provides you with a framework for what you may say or do. As you learn about the culture of Spanish-speaking communities, you'll improve your knowledge of Spanish. Think about a word like **salsa**, and how it connects to both food and music. Think about and explore customs observed on **Nochevieja** (New Year's Eve) or at a **fiesta de quince años** (a girl's fifteenth birthday party). Watch people greet each other or say good-bye. Listen for idioms and sayings that capture the spirit of what you want to communicate!

Teenagers celebrating at a **fiesta de quince años**.

Listen, Speak, Read, and Write

Listening | Listen for sounds and for words you can recognize. Listen for inflections and watch for key words that signal a question such as **cómo** (*how*), **dónde** (*where*), or **qué** (*what*). Get used to the sound of Spanish. Play Spanish pop songs or watch Spanish movies. Borrow books on CD from your local library, or try to visit places in your community where Spanish is spoken. Don't worry if you don't understand every single word. If you focus on key words and phrases, you'll get the main idea. The more you listen, the more you'll understand!

Speaking | Practice speaking Spanish as often as you can. As you talk, work on your pronunciation, and read aloud texts so that words and sentences flow more easily. Don't worry if you don't sound like a native speaker, or if you make some mistakes. Time and practice will help you get there. Participate actively in Spanish class. Try to speak Spanish with classmates, especially native speakers (if you know any), as often as you can.

Reading | Pick up a Spanish-language newspaper or a pamphlet on your way to school, read the lyrics of a song as you listen to it, or read books you've already read in English translated into Spanish. Use reading strategies that you know to understand the meaning of a text that looks unfamiliar. Look for cognates, or words that are related in English and Spanish, to guess the meaning of some words. Read as often as you can, and remember to read for fun!

Writing | It's easy to write in Spanish if you put your mind to it. And remember that Spanish spelling is phonetic, which means that once you learn the basic rules of how letters and sounds are related, you can probably become an expert speller in Spanish! Write for fun—make up poems or songs, write e-mails or instant messages to friends, or start a journal or blog in Spanish.

Studying Spanish

Tips for Learning Spanish

Practice, practice, practice!
Seize every opportunity you find to listen, speak, read, or write Spanish. Think of it like a sport or learning a musical instrument—the more you practice, the more you will become comfortable with the language and how it works. You'll marvel at how quickly you can begin speaking Spanish and how the world that it transports you to can change your life forever!

- **Listen** to Spanish radio shows. Write down words that you can't recognize or don't know and look up the meaning.
- **Watch** Spanish TV shows or movies. Read subtitles to help you grasp the content.
- **Read** Spanish-language newspapers, magazines, or blogs.
- **Listen** to Spanish songs that you like—anything from Shakira to a traditional mariachi melody. Sing along and concentrate on your pronunciation.

- **Seek** out Spanish speakers. Look for neighborhoods, markets, or cultural centers where Spanish might be spoken in your community. Greet people, ask for directions, or order from a menu at a Mexican restaurant in Spanish.
- **Pursue** language exchange opportunities (**intercambio cultural**) in your school or community. Try to join language clubs or cultural societies, and explore opportunities for studying abroad or hosting a student from a Spanish-speaking country in your home or school.
- **Connect** your learning to everyday experiences. Think about naming the ingredients of your favorite dish in Spanish. Think about the origins of Spanish place names in the U.S., like Cape Canaveral and Sacramento, or of common English words like *adobe, chocolate, mustang, tornado,* and *patio.*
- **Use** mnemonics, or a memorizing device, to help you remember words. Make up a saying in English to remember the order of the days of the week in Spanish (L, M, M, J, V, S, D).
- **Visualize** words. Try to associate words with images to help you remember meanings. For example, think of a **paella** as you learn the names of different types of seafood or meat. Imagine a national park and create mental pictures of the landscape as you learn names of animals, plants, and habitats.
- **Enjoy** yourself! Try to have as much fun as you can learning Spanish. Take your knowledge beyond the classroom and find ways to make the learning experience your very own.

Getting Started

Useful Spanish Expressions

The following expressions will be very useful in getting you started learning Spanish. You can use them in class to check your understanding or to ask and answer questions about the lessons. Read **En las instrucciones** ahead of time to help you understand direction lines in Spanish, as well as your teacher's instructions. Remember to practice your Spanish as often as you can!

Expresiones útiles *Useful expressions*

¿Cómo se dice _____ en español?	How do you say _____ in Spanish?
¿Cómo se escribe _____?	How do you spell _____?
¿Comprende(n)?	Do you understand?
Con permiso.	Excuse me.
De acuerdo.	Okay.
De nada.	You're welcome.
¿De veras?	Really?
¿En qué página estamos?	What page are we on?
Enseguida.	Right away.
Más despacio, por favor.	Slower, please.
Muchas gracias.	Thanks a lot.
No entiendo.	I don't understand.
No sé.	I don't know.
Perdone.	Excuse me.
Pista	Clue
Por favor.	Please.
Por supuesto.	Of course.
¿Qué significa _____?	What does _____ mean?
Repite, por favor.	Please repeat.
Tengo una pregunta.	I have a question.
¿Tiene(n) alguna pregunta?	Do you have questions?
Vaya(n) a la página dos.	Go to page 2.

En las instrucciones *In direction lines*

Cierto o falso	True or false
Completa las oraciones de una manera lógica.	Complete the sentences logically.
Con un(a) compañero/a...	With a classmate...
Contesta las preguntas.	Answer the questions.
Corrige la información falsa.	Correct the false information.
Di/Digan...	Say...
En grupos...	In groups...
En parejas...	In pairs...
Entrevista...	Interview...
Forma oraciones completas.	Create/Make complete sentences.
Háganse preguntas.	Ask each other questions.
Haz el papel de...	Play the role of...
Haz los cambios necesarios.	Make the necessary changes.
Indica/Indiquen si las oraciones...	Indicate if the sentences...
Lee/Lean en voz alta.	Read aloud.
...que mejor completa...	...that best completes...
Toma nota...	Take note...
Tomen apuntes.	Take notes.
Túrnense...	Take turns...

Getting Started

Common Names

Get started learning Spanish by using a Spanish name in class. You can choose from the lists on these pages, or you can find one yourself. How about learning the Spanish equivalent of your name? The most popular Spanish female names are Lucía, María, Paula, Sofía, and Valentina. The most popular male names in Spanish are Alejandro, Daniel, David, Mateo, and Santiago. Is your name, or that of someone you know, in the Spanish top five?

Más nombres masculinos	Más nombres femeninos
Alfonso	Alicia
Antonio (Toni)	Beatriz (Bea, Beti, Biata)
Carlos	Blanca
César	Carolina (Carol)
Diego	Claudia
Ernesto	Diana
Felipe	Emilia
Francisco (Paco)	Irene
Guillermo	Julia
Ignacio (Nacho)	Laura
Javier (Javi)	Leonor
Leonardo	Liliana
Luis	Lourdes
Manolo	Margarita (Marga)
Marcos	Marta
Oscar (Óscar)	Noelia
Rafael (Rafa)	Patricia
Sergio	Rocío
Vicente	Verónica

Los 5 nombres masculinos más populares	Los 5 nombres femeninos más populares
Alejandro	Lucía
Daniel	María
David	Paula
Mateo	Sofía
Santiago	Valentina

Acknowledgments

On behalf of its authors and editors, Vista Higher Learning expresses its sincere appreciation to the many instructors and teachers across the U.S. and Canada who contributed their ideas and suggestions. Their insights and detailed comments were invaluable to us as we created **Descubre.**

In-depth reviewers

Patrick Brady
Tidewater Community College, VA

Christine DeGrado
Chestnut Hill College, PA

Martha L. Hughes
Georgia Southern University, GA

Aida Ramos-Sellman
Goucher College, MD

Reviewers

Kathleen Aguilar
Fort Lewis College, CO

Aleta Anderson
Grand Rapids Community College, MI

Gunnar Anderson
SUNY Potsdam, NY

Nona Anderson
Ouachita Baptist University, AR

Ken Arant
Darton College, GA

Vicki Baggia
Phillips Exeter Academy, NH

Jorge V. Bajo
Oracle Charter School, NY

Ana Basoa-McMillan
Columbia State Community College, TN

Timothy Benson
Lake Superior College, MN

Georgia Betcher
Fayetteville Technical Community College, NC

Teresa Borden
Columbia College, CA

Courtney Bradley
The Principia, MO

Vonna Breeze-Marti
Columbia College, CA

Christa Bucklin
University of Hartford, CT

Mary Cantu
South Texas College, TX

Christa Chatrnuch
University of Hartford, CT

Tina Christodouleas
SUNY Cortland, NY

Edwin Clark
SUNY Potsdam, NY

Donald Clymer
Eastern Mennonite University, VA

Ann Costanzi
Chestnut Hill College, PA

Patricia Crespo-Martin
Foothill College, CA

Miryam Criado
Hanover College, KY

Thomas Curtis
Madison Area Technical College, WI

Patricia S. Davis
Darton College, GA

Danion Doman
Truman State University, MO

Deborah Dubiner
Carnegie Mellon University, PA

Benjamin Earwicker
Northwest Nazarene University, ID

Deborah Edson
Tidewater Community College, VA

Matthew T. Fleming
Grand Rapids Community College, MI

Ruston Ford
Indian Hills Community College, IA

Marianne Franco
Modesto Junior College, CA

Elena García
Muskegon Community College, MI

María D. García
Fayetteville Technical Community College, NC

Lauren Gates
East Mississippi Community College, MS

Marta M. Gómez
Gateway Academy, MO

Danielle Gosselin
Bishop Brady High School, NH

Charlene Grant
Skidmore College, NY

Betsy Hance
Kennesaw State University, GA

Marti Hardy
Laurel School, OH

Dennis Harrod
Syracuse University, NY

Fanning Hearon
Brunswick School, CT

Richard Heath
Kirkwood Community College, IA

Óscar Hernández
South Texas College, TX

Yolanda Hernández
Community College of Southern Nevada, North Las Vegas, NV

Martha L. Hughes
Georgia Southern University, GA

Martha Ince
Cushing Academy, MA

Acknowledgments

Reviewers

Stacy Jazan
Glendale Community College, CA

María Jiménez Smith
Tarrant County College, TX

Emory Kinder
Columbia Prep School, NY

Marina Kozanova
Crafton Hills College, CA

Tamara Kunkel
Alice Lloyd College, KY

Anna Major
The Westminster Schools, GA

Armando Maldonado
Morgan Community College, CO

Molly Marostica Smith
Canterbury School of Florida, FL

Jesús G. Martínez
Fresno City College, CA

Laura Martínez
Centralia College, WA

Daniel Millis
Verde Valley School, AZ

Deborah Mistron
Middle Tennessee State University, TN

Mechteld Mitchin
Village Academy, OH

Anna Montoya
Florida Institute of Technology, FL

Robert P. Moore
Loyola Blakefield Jesuit School, MD

S. Moshir
St. Bernard High School, CA

Javier Muñoz-Basols
Trinity School, NY

William Nichols
Grand Rapids Community College, MI

Bernice Nuhfer-Halten
Southern Polytechnic State University, GA

Amanda Papanikolas
Drew School, CA

Elizabeth M. Parr
Darton College, GA

Julia E. Patiño
Dillard University, LA

Martha Pérez
Kirkwood Community College, IA

Teresa Pérez-Gamboa
University of Georgia, GA

Marion Perry
The Thacher School, CA

Molly Perry
The Thacher School, CA

Melissa Pytlak
The Canterbury School, CT

Ana F. Sache
Emporia State University, KS

Celia S. Samaniego
Cosumnes River College, CA

Virginia Sánchez-Bernardy
San Diego Mesa College, CA

Frank P. Sanfilippo
Columbia College, CA

Piedad Schor
South Kent School, CT

David Schuettler
The College of St. Scholastica, MN

Romina Self
Ankeny Christian Academy, IA

David A. Short
Indian Hills Community College, IA

Carol Snell-Feikema
South Dakota State University, SD

Matias Stebbings
Columbia Grammar & Prep School, NY

Mary Studer Shea
Napa Valley College, CA

Cathy Swain
University of Maine, Machias, ME

Cristina Szterensus
Rock Valley College, IL

John Tavernakis
College of San Mateo, CA

David E. Tipton
Circleville Bible College, OH

Larry Thornton
Trinity College School, ON

Linda Tracy
Santa Rosa Junior College, CA

Beverly Turner
Truckee Meadows Community College, OK

Christine Tyma DeGrado
Chestnut Hill College, PA

Fanny Vera de Viacava
Canterbury School, CT

Luis Viacava
Canterbury School, CT

María Villalobos-Buehner
Grand Valley State University, MI

Hector Villarreal
South Texas College, TX

Juanita Villena-Álvarez
University of South Carolina, Beaufort, SC

Marcella Anne Wendzikowski
Villa Maria College of Buffalo, NY

Doug West
Sage Hill School, CA

Paula Whittaker
Bishop Brady High School, NH

Mary Zold-Herrera
Glenbrook North High School, IL

Bios

About the Authors

José A. Blanco founded Vista Higher Learning in 1998. A native of Barranquilla, Colombia, Mr. Blanco holds degrees in Literature and Hispanic Studies from Brown University and the University of California, Santa Cruz. He has worked as a writer, editor, and translator for Houghton Mifflin and D.C. Heath and Company, and has taught Spanish at the secondary and university levels. Mr. Blanco is also the co-author of several other Vista Higher Learning programs: **Vistas, Panorama, Aventuras,** and **¡Viva!** at the introductory level; **Ventanas, Facetas, Enfoques, Imagina,** and **Sueña** at the intermediate level; and **Revista** at the advanced conversation level.

Philip Redwine Donley received his M.A. in Hispanic Literature from the University of Texas at Austin in 1986 and his Ph.D. in Foreign Language Education from the University of Texas at Austin in 1997. Dr. Donley taught Spanish at Austin Community College, Southwestern University, and the University of Texas at Austin. He published articles and conducted workshops about language anxiety management and the development of critical thinking skills, and was involved in research about teaching languages to the visually impaired. Dr. Donley was also the co-author of **Vistas, Aventuras,** and **Panorama,** three introductory college Spanish textbook programs published by Vista Higher Learning. Dr. Donley passed away in 2003.

About the Illustrators

Yayo, an internationally acclaimed illustrator, was born in Colombia. He has illustrated children's books, newspapers, and magazines, and has been exhibited around the world. He currently lives in Montreal, Canada.

Pere Virgili lives and works in Barcelona, Spain. His illustrations have appeared in textbooks, newspapers, and magazines throughout Spain and Europe.

Born in Caracas, Venezuela, **Hermann Mejía** studied illustration at the Instituto de Diseño de Caracas. Hermann currently lives and works in the United States.

Hola, ¿qué tal?

1

Communicative Goals
I will be able to:
- Greet people in Spanish
- Say goodbye
- Identify myself and others
- Talk about the time of day

Lesson Goals
In **Lección 1**, students will be introduced to the following:
- identifying where one is from
- courtesy expressions
- greetings in the Spanish-speaking world
- the **plaza principal**
- nouns and articles (definite and indefinite)
- numbers 0–30
- present tense of **ser**
- telling time
- recognizing cognates
- reading a telephone list
- writing a telephone/address list in Spanish
- listening for known vocabulary
- a television commercial for MasterCard
- a video about **plazas** and greetings
- demographic and cultural information about Hispanics in the U.S. and Canada

A primera vista Have students look at the photo. Ask: *What do you think the people are doing?* Say: *It is common in Hispanic cultures for friends to greet each other with a kiss (or two) on the cheek. Young men typically shake hands.* Ask: *How do you greet your friends?*

21st Century Skills

Initiative and Self-Direction
Students can monitor their progress online using the Supersite activities and assessments.

---

contextos
pages 2–5
- Greetings and goodbyes
- Identifying yourself and others
- Courtesy expressions

fotonovela
pages 6–9
Marissa arrives from the U.S. for a year abroad in Mexico City. She meets her Mexican hosts, the Díaz family, survives a practical joke, and settles in to unpack.

cultura
pages 10–11
- Greetings in the Spanish-speaking world
- The **plaza principal**

estructura
pages 12–29
- Nouns and articles
- Numbers 0–30
- Present tense of **ser**
- Telling time
- **Recapitulación**

adelante
pages 30–37
Lectura: Telephone list
Escritura: Address list in Spanish
Escuchar: Conversation in a bus station
En pantalla
Flash cultura
Panorama: Estados Unidos y Canadá

A PRIMERA VISTA
- Guess what the people in the photo are saying:
  a. Adiós   b. Hola   c. Salsa
- Most likely they would also say:
  a. Gracias   b. Fiesta   c. Buenos días
- The girls are:
  a. amigas   b. chicos   c. señores

SUPPORT FOR BACKWARD DESIGN

Lección 1 Essential Questions
1. How do people greet one another?
2. How do people make introductions?
3. What influence do Spanish speakers have in the U.S. and Canada?

Lección 1 Integrated Performance Assessment
Before teaching this chapter, review the Integrated Performance Assessment (IPA) and its accompanying scoring rubric provided in the Testing Program. Use the IPA to assess students' progress toward proficiency targets at the end of the chapter.
IPA Context: You are meeting many students in Spanish class for the first time. You will prepare a brief presentation to introduce yourself to the class.

Voice boards on the Supersite allow you and your students to record and share up to five minutes of audio. Use voice boards for presentations, oral assessments, discussions, directions, etc.

Teacher's Edition • Lesson One   **1**

Section Goals

In **Contextos**, students will learn and practice:
- basic greetings
- introductions
- courtesy expressions

Communication 1.2
Comparisons 4.1

Student Resources
Cuaderno de práctica y actividades comunicativas, pp. 1–3
Cuaderno para hispanohablantes, pp. 1–2
Supersite: Activities, *eCuaderno*

Teacher Resources
Workbook TE; Digital Image Bank; Textbook and Audio Activities MP3s; Audio Scripts; Testing Program Quizzes; Activity Pack; Middle School Activity Pack

Teaching Tips
- For sample lesson plans, go to **vhlcentral.com** to access the instructor's part of the **DESCUBRE** Supersite.
- Use the **Lección 1 Contextos** Digital Image Bank to support this presentation.
- Write a few greetings, farewells, and courtesy expressions on the board, explain their meaning, and model their pronunciation. Circulate around the class, greeting students, making introductions, and encouraging responses. Then have students open their books to pages 2–3 and ask them to identify which conversations seem to be exchanges between friends and which seem more formal. Draw attention to the use of **usted** vs. **tú** in these conversations. Explain situations in which each form is appropriate.

1 contextos

Lección 1

Hola, ¿qué tal?

 My Vocabulary Tutorials

Más vocabulario

Buenos días.	Good morning.
Buenas noches.	Good evening; Good night.
Hasta la vista.	See you later.
Hasta pronto.	See you soon.
¿Cómo se llama usted?	What's your name? (form.)
Le presento a…	I would like to introduce you to (name). (form.)
Te presento a…	I would like to introduce you to (name). (fam.)
el nombre	name
¿Cómo estás?	How are you? (fam.)
No muy bien.	Not very well.
¿Qué pasa?	What's happening?; What's going on?
por favor	please
De nada.	You're welcome.
No hay de qué.	You're welcome.
Lo siento.	I'm sorry.
Gracias.	Thank you; Thanks.
Muchas gracias.	Thank you very much; Thanks a lot.

Variación léxica

Items are presented for recognition purposes only.

Buenos días.	⟷	Buenas.
De nada.	⟷	A la orden.
Lo siento.	⟷	Perdón.
¿Qué tal?	⟷	¿Qué hubo? (*Col.*)
chau	⟷	ciao, chao

1
ELENA Patricia, éste es el señor Perales.
PATRICIA Encantada.
SEÑOR PERALES Igualmente. ¿De dónde es usted, señorita?
PATRICIA Soy de México. ¿Y usted?
SEÑOR PERALES De Puerto Rico.

2
TOMÁS ¿Qué tal, Alberto?
ALBERTO Regular. ¿Y tú?
TOMÁS Bien. ¿Qué hay de nuevo?
ALBERTO Nada.

3
SEÑOR VARGAS Buenas tardes, señora Wong. ¿Cómo está usted?
SEÑORA WONG Muy bien, gracias. ¿Y usted, señor Vargas?
SEÑOR VARGAS Bien, gracias.
SEÑORA WONG Hasta mañana, señor Vargas. Saludos a la señora Vargas.
SEÑOR VARGAS Adiós.

recursos
vText | CPA pp. 1–3 | CH pp. 1–2 | vhlcentral

EXPANSION

Extra Practice Bring in photos or magazine images of people greeting each other or saying goodbye. Ask pairs to write dialogue captions for each photo. Remind students to use formal and informal expressions as appropriate.
Groups Write questions and possible answers from the new set of expressions in **Contextos** on separate note cards. Give each student one note card and have them find the student with the

EXPANSION

matching card that completes their question/answer. Then have students work with other pairs to see if they can create a longer dialogue with their expressions.
Extra Practice Prepare name tags with a variety of names, titles, and ages. Ex: **señora López, 63; Carlos de la Vega, 22,** etc. Each student should wear a name tag and greet their classmates according to the information on their tags.

Práctica

1 Escuchar Listen to each question or statement, then choose the correct response.

1. a. Muy bien, gracias. b. Me llamo Graciela. **b**
2. a. Lo siento. b. Mucho gusto. **b**
3. a. Soy de Puerto Rico. b. No muy bien. **a**
4. a. No hay de qué. b. Regular. **a**
5. a. Mucho gusto. b. Hasta pronto. **b**
6. a. Nada. b. Igualmente. **a**
7. a. Me llamo Guillermo Montero. b. Muy bien, gracias. **b**
8. a. Buenas tardes. ¿Cómo estás? b. El gusto es mío. **a**
9. a. Saludos a la Sra. Ramírez. b. Encantada. **b**
10. a. Adiós. b. Regular. **b**

2 Identificar You will hear a series of expressions. Identify the expression (**a**, **b**, **c**, or **d**) that does not belong in each series.

1. **c**   3. **b**
2. **a**   4. **c**

3 Escoger For each expression, write another word or phrase that expresses a similar idea.

modelo
¿Cómo estás? ¿Qué tal?

1. De nada. *No hay de qué.*
2. Encantado. *Mucho gusto.*
3. Adiós. *Chau. / Hasta luego/mañana/pronto.*
4. Te presento a Antonio. *Éste es Antonio.*
5. Hasta la vista. *Hasta luego.*
6. Mucho gusto. *El gusto es mío.*

4 Ordenar Work with a partner to put this scrambled conversation in order. Then act it out.

—Muy bien, gracias. Soy Rosabel.
—Soy de México. ¿Y tú?
—Mucho gusto, Rosabel.
—Hola. Me llamo Carlos. ¿Cómo estás?
—Soy de Argentina.
—Igualmente. ¿De dónde eres, Carlos?

CARLOS *Hola. Me llamo Carlos. ¿Cómo estás?*
ROSABEL *Muy bien, gracias. Soy Rosabel.*
CARLOS *Mucho gusto, Rosabel.*
ROSABEL *Igualmente. ¿De dónde eres, Carlos?*
CARLOS *Soy de México. ¿Y tú?*
ROSABEL *Soy de Argentina.*

AYUDA
In Spanish, people can be addressed either formally or informally. Dialogues 1 and 3 are formal exchanges and use **usted** (formal *you*) forms. Dialogues 2, 4, and 5 are informal and use the **tú** (informal *you*) form or other informal expressions. You will learn more about this in **Estructura 1.3**.

BERTA Hasta luego, Tere.
TERESA Chau, Berta. Nos vemos mañana.

CARMEN Buenas tardes. Me llamo Carmen. ¿Cómo te llamas tú?
ANTONIO Buenas tardes. Me llamo Antonio. Mucho gusto.
CARMEN El gusto es mío. ¿De dónde eres?
ANTONIO Soy de los Estados Unidos, de California.

5 Completar
Work with a partner to complete these dialogues. Use expressions from the word bank.

> Buenos días.   De nada.   Muy bien, gracias.
> ¿Cómo te llamas?   Encantado/a.   ¿Qué pasa?
> ¿De dónde eres?   Hasta luego.   ¿Qué tal?

1. **Estudiante 1:** Buenos días.
   Estudiante 2: Buenos días. ¿Qué tal?
2. **Estudiante 1:** ¿Cómo te llamas?
   Estudiante 2: Me llamo Carmen Sánchez.
3. **Estudiante 1:** ¿De dónde eres?
   Estudiante 2: De Canadá.
4. **Estudiante 1:** Te presento a Marisol.
   Estudiante 2: Encantado/a.
5. **Estudiante 1:** Gracias.
   Estudiante 2: De nada.
6. **Estudiante 1:** ¿Qué tal?
   Estudiante 2: Regular.
7. **Estudiante 1:** ¿Qué pasa?
   Estudiante 2: Nada.
8. **Estudiante 1:** ¡Hasta la vista!
   Estudiante 2: Hasta luego.

6 Responder
Work with a partner to complete these dialogues. *Answers will vary.*

modelo
Estudiante 1: ¿Qué tal?
Estudiante 2: Bien. ¿Y tú?

1. **Estudiante 1:** Hasta mañana, señora Ramírez. Saludos al señor Ramírez.
   Estudiante 2: _____
2. **Estudiante 1:** ¿Qué hay de nuevo, Alberto?
   Estudiante 2: _____
3. **Estudiante 1:** Gracias, Tomás.
   Estudiante 2: _____
4. **Estudiante 1:** Miguel, ésta es la señorita Perales.
   Estudiante 2: _____
5. **Estudiante 1:** ¿De dónde eres, Antonio?
   Estudiante 2: _____
6. **Estudiante 1:** ¿Cómo se llama usted?
   Estudiante 2: _____
7. **Estudiante 1:** ¿Qué pasa?
   Estudiante 2: _____
8. **Estudiante 1:** Buenas tardes, señor. ¿Cómo está usted?
   Estudiante 2: _____

Teaching notes (margin)

5 Teaching Tip Have pairs share their responses with the class.

5 Expansion Have pairs or small groups create conversations that include the expressions used in **Actividad 5**. Ask volunteers to present their conversations to the class.

6 Teaching Tips
- Discuss the **modelo** before assigning the activity to pairs.
- Have volunteers write each mini-conversation on the board. Work as a class to identify and explain any errors.
- After students have completed the activity, have pairs role-play the corrected mini-conversations. Ask them to substitute their own names and personal information where possible.

¡Lengua viva! Have students locate examples of the titles in **Actividad 6**. Then ask them to create short sentences in which they use the titles with people they know.

¡LENGUA VIVA!
The titles **señor, señora,** and **señorita** are abbreviated **Sr., Sra.,** and **Srta**. Note that these abbreviations are capitalized, while the titles themselves are not.
...
There is no Spanish equivalent for the English title *Ms.;* women are addressed as **señora** or **señorita**.

Practice more at vhlcentral.com.

EXPANSION

Extra Practice Add an auditory activity to this vocabulary practice. Read some phrases aloud and ask if students would use them with a person of the same age or someone older. Ex: **1. Te presento a Luis.** (same age) **2. ¿Cómo estás?** (same age) **3. Buenos días, doctor Soto.** (older) **4. ¿De dónde es usted, señora?** (older) **5. Chau, Teresa.** (same age) **6. No hay de qué, señor Perales.** (older)

TEACHING OPTIONS

Game Prepare a series of response statements using language in **Contextos**. Divide the class into two teams and invite students to guess the question or statement that would have elicited each of your responses. Read one statement at a time. The first team to correctly guess the question or statement earns a point. Ex: **Me llamo Lupe Torres Garza.** (¿Cómo se llama usted? / ¿Cómo te llamas?) The team with the most points at the end wins.

Hola, ¿qué tal? cinco **5**

Comunicación

7 **Diálogos** With a partner, complete and act out these conversations. Answers will vary.

Conversación 1
—Hola. Me llamo Teresa. ¿Cómo te llamas tú?
—_____
—Soy de Puerto Rico. ¿Y tú?
—_____

Conversación 2
—_____
—Muy bien, gracias. ¿Y usted, señora López?
—_____
—Hasta luego, señora. Saludos al señor López.
—_____

Conversación 3
—_____
—Regular. ¿Y tú?
—_____
—Nada.

8 **Conversaciones** This is the first day of class. Write four short conversations based on what the people in this scene would say. Answers will vary.

9 **Situaciones** In groups of three, write and act out these situations. Answers will vary.

1. On your way out of class on the first day of school, you strike up a conversation with the two students who were sitting next to you. You find out each student's name and where he or she is from before you say goodbye and go to your next class.
2. At the next class you meet up with a friend and find out how he or she is doing. As you are talking, your friend Elena enters. Introduce her to your friend.
3. As you're leaving school, you meet your parents' friends Mrs. Sánchez and Mr. Rodríguez. You greet them and ask how each person is. As you say goodbye, you send greetings to Mrs. Rodríguez.
4. Make up and act out a real-life situation that you and your classmates can role-play with the language you have learned.

EXPANSION

Extra Practice Have students circulate around the classroom and conduct unrehearsed mini-conversations in Spanish with other students, using the words and expressions that they learned on pages 2–3. Monitor students' work and offer assistance if requested.

DIFFERENTIATION

Heritage Speakers Ask heritage speakers to role-play some of the conversations and situations in these **Comunicación** activities, modeling correct pronunciation and intonation for the class. Remind students that, just as in English, there are regional differences in the way Spanish is pronounced. Help clarify unfamiliar vocabulary as necessary.

Communication 1.1, 1.2

7 Expansion
- Have students work in small groups to write a few mini-conversations modeled on this activity. Then ask them to copy the dialogues, omitting a few exchanges. Have groups exchange papers and fill in the blanks.
- Have students rewrite **Conversaciones 1** and **3** in the formal register and **Conversación 2** in the informal register.

8 Teaching Tip To simplify, have students brainstorm who the people in the illustration are and what they are talking about. Ask students which groups would be speaking to each other in the **usted** form, and which would be using the **tú** form.

8 Expansion In pairs, have students take turns selecting a person from the drawing and providing 2–3 statements that he or she might be saying. The partner will try to guess who it is.

21st Century Skills

9 Collaboration
If you have access to students in a Spanish-speaking country, ask them to write a dialogue as described in item 4 for your students to act out.

9 Teaching Tip To challenge students, have each group pick a situation to prepare and perform. Tell groups not to memorize every word of the conversation, but rather to re-create it.

The Affective Dimension
Have students rehearse the situations a few times, so that they will feel more comfortable with the material and less anxious when presenting before the class.

Contextos **5**

Section Goals

In **Fotonovela**, students will:
- receive comprehensible input from free-flowing discourse
- learn functional phrases that preview lesson grammatical structures

Communication 1.2
Cultures 2.1, 2.2

Student Resources
Cuaderno de práctica y actividades comunicativas, pp. 4–5
Supersite: *Fotonovela* video, Activities, *eCuaderno*

Teacher Resources
Workbook TE; Video Script & Translation

Video Synopsis **Marissa**, an American college student, arrives in Mexico City for a year abroad. She meets her Mexican hosts, **Carolina** and **Roberto Díaz**, and their doorman, **Don Diego**. As **Marissa** unpacks, the **Díaz** children, **Felipe** and **Jimena**, take away her English-Spanish dictionary as a joke. **Marissa** accepts the challenge and leaves the dictionary with **Carolina**.

Teaching Tips
- Hand out the **Antes de ver el video** and the **Mientras ves el video** activities from the *Cuaderno de práctica y actividades comunicativas* and go over the **Antes de ver** questions before starting the **Fotonovela**.
- In small groups, have students cover the captions and guess the plot based on the video stills. Write their predictions on the board. After students have watched the video, compare their predictions to what actually happened in the episode.
- Point out that **don** is a title of respect and neither equivalent nor related to the English name *Don*. Ask if students think **Diego** is the doorman's first or last name. (It is his first name.) Students will learn more about the titles **don** and **doña** on page 8.

---

 fotonovela   Lección 1

Bienvenida, Marissa

Marissa llega a México para pasar un año con la familia Díaz.

PERSONAJES  MARISSA    SRA. DÍAZ

Video: *Fotonovela*

MARISSA ¿Usted es de Cuba?
SRA. DÍAZ Sí, de La Habana. Y Roberto es de Mérida. Tú eres de Wisconsin, ¿verdad?
MARISSA Sí, de Appleton, Wisconsin.

MARISSA ¿Quiénes son los dos chicos de las fotos? ¿Jimena y Felipe?
SRA. DÍAZ Sí. Ellos son estudiantes.

DON DIEGO Buenas tardes, señora. Señorita, bienvenida a la Ciudad de México.
MARISSA ¡Muchas gracias!

SRA. DÍAZ Ahí hay dos maletas. Son de Marissa.
DON DIEGO Con permiso.

SR. DÍAZ ¿Qué hora es?
FELIPE Son las cuatro y veinticinco.

SRA. DÍAZ Marissa, te presento a Roberto, mi esposo.
SR. DÍAZ Bienvenida, Marissa.
MARISSA Gracias, señor Díaz.

TEACHING OPTIONS

Bienvenida, Marissa Have students make a three-column chart with the headings *Greetings, Self-Identification,* and *Courtesy Expressions*. Have students suggest two or three possible phrases for each category. Then play the **Bienvenida, Marissa** episode once and ask students to fill in the first column with the basic greetings that they hear. Repeat this process for the second column, where they should list the expressions the characters use to identify themselves. Play the video a third time for students to jot down courtesy expressions, such as ways to say "pleased to meet you" and "pardon me."

Hola, ¿qué tal?

DON DIEGO SR. DÍAZ FELIPE JIMENA

4

MARISSA ¿Cómo se llama usted?
DON DIEGO Yo soy Diego. Mucho gusto.
MARISSA El gusto es mío, don Diego.

5

DON DIEGO ¿Cómo está usted hoy, señora Carolina?
SRA. DÍAZ Muy bien, gracias. ¿Y usted?
DON DIEGO Bien, gracias.

9

JIMENA ¿Qué hay en esta cosa?
MARISSA Bueno, a ver, hay tres cuadernos, un mapa... ¡Y un diccionario!
JIMENA ¿Cómo se dice mediodía en inglés?
FELIPE "Noon".

10

FELIPE Estás en México, ¿verdad?
MARISSA ¿Sí?
FELIPE Nosotros somos tu diccionario.

Expresiones útiles

Identifying yourself and others
¿Cómo se llama usted?
What's your name?
Yo soy Diego, el portero. Mucho gusto.
I'm Diego, the doorman. Nice to meet you.
¿Cómo te llamas?
What's your name?
Me llamo Marissa.
My name is Marissa.
¿Quién es...? / ¿Quiénes son...?
Who is...? / Who are...?
Es mi esposo.
He's my husband.
Tú eres..., ¿verdad?/¿cierto?/¿no?
You are..., right?

Identifying objects
¿Qué hay en esta cosa?
What's in this thing?
Bueno, a ver, aquí hay tres cuadernos...
Well, let's see, here are three notebooks...
Oye/Oiga, ¿cómo se dice suitcase en español?
Hey, how do you say suitcase in Spanish?
Se dice maleta.
You say maleta.

Saying what time it is
¿Qué hora es?
What time is it?
Es la una. / Son las dos.
It's one o'clock. / It's two o'clock.
Son las cuatro y veinticinco.
It's four twenty-five.

Polite expressions
Con permiso.
Pardon me; Excuse me. (to request permission)
Perdón.
Pardon me; Excuse me. (to get someone's attention or excuse yourself)
¡Bienvenido/a! *Welcome!*

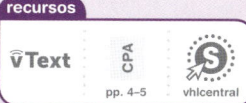

Communication 1.1, 1.2

1 Expansion Give students these true/false statements as items 8–10: **8. En la mochila de Marissa hay una foto de Jimena y Felipe. (Cierto.) 9. No hay cuadernos en la mochila de Marissa. (Falso. Hay tres cuadernos.) 10. Hay cuatro personas en la familia Díaz. (Cierto.)**

2 Expansion Ask volunteers to call out more statements from the **Fotonovela**. The class guesses which character made each.

¡Lengua viva! Ask students how they might address **Sr. Díaz** (**don Roberto**).

Nota cultural **Señor(a)** and **señorita** may also be used with a person's first name as a sign of respect. Using these titles with a first name also shows a greater level of intimacy or warmth; **señor Díaz** sounds more formal than **señor Roberto**.

3 Teaching Tip Have volunteers take the roles of **don Diego** and **Marissa**.

Pre-AP*

4 Interpersonal Speaking Have students prepare by reading through the cues and jotting down possible phrases for each one.

4 Possible Conversation
E1: Buenas tardes. ¿Cómo te llamas?
E2: Hola. Me llamo Felipe. ¿Y tú?
E1: Me llamo Luisa. Mucho gusto.
E2: El gusto es mío.
E1: ¿Cómo estás?
E2: Bien, gracias.
E1: ¿De dónde eres?
E2: Soy de Venezuela.
E1: ¡Uf! Es la una. ¡Adiós!
E2: Chau.

4 Partner Chat You can also assign activity 4 on the Supersite. Students work in pairs to record the activity online. The pair's recorded conversation will appear in your gradebook.

8 | Teacher's Edition • Lesson One

---

8 ocho **Lección 1**

¿Qué pasó?

1 **¿Cierto o falso?** Indicate if each statement is **cierto** or **falso**. Then correct the false statements.

	Cierto	Falso
1. La Sra. Díaz es de Caracas.	○	✓ La Sra. Díaz es de La Habana.
2. El Sr. Díaz es de Mérida.	✓	○
3. Marissa es de Los Ángeles, California.	○	✓ Marissa es de Appleton, Wisconsin.
4. Jimena y Felipe son profesores.	○	✓ Jimena y Felipe son estudiantes.
5. Las dos maletas son de Jimena.	○	✓ Las dos maletas son de Marissa.
6. El Sr. Díaz pregunta "¿qué hora es?".	✓	○
7. Hay un diccionario en la mochila (*backpack*) de Marissa.	✓	○

2 **Identificar** Indicate which person would make each statement. One name will be used twice.

1. Son las cuatro y veinticinco, papá. **Felipe**
2. Roberto es mi esposo. **Sra. Díaz**
3. Yo soy de Wisconsin, ¿de dónde es usted? **Marissa**
4. ¿Qué hay de nuevo, doña Carolina? **don Diego**
5. Yo soy de Cuba. **Sra. Díaz**
6. ¿Qué hay en la mochila, Marissa? **Jimena**

MARISSA   FELIPE   SRA. DÍAZ

DON DIEGO   JIMENA

¡LENGUA VIVA!
In Spanish-speaking countries, **don** and **doña** are used with first names to show respect: **don Diego, doña Carolina**. Note that these titles, like **señor** and **señora**, are not capitalized.

3 **Completar** Complete the conversation between Don Diego and Marissa.

DON DIEGO Hola, (1) _señorita_ .
MARISSA Hola, señor. ¿Cómo se (2) _llama_ usted?
DON DIEGO Yo me llamo Diego, ¿y (3) _usted_ ?
MARISSA Yo me llamo Marissa. (4) _Encantada_ .
DON DIEGO (5) _Igualmente_ , señorita Marissa.
MARISSA Nos (6) _vemos_ , don Diego.
DON DIEGO Hasta (7) _luego/pronto/la vista_ , señorita Marissa.

4 **Conversar** Imagine that you are chatting with a traveler you just met at the airport. With a partner, prepare a conversation using these cues. *Some answers will vary.*

Estudiante 1	**Estudiante 2**
Say "good afternoon" to your partner and ask for his or her name. →	Say hello and what your name is. Then ask what your partner's name is.
Say what your name is and that you are glad to meet your partner. →	Say that the pleasure is yours.
Ask how your partner is. →	Say that you're doing well, thank you.
Ask where your partner is from. →	Say where you're from.
Say it's one o'clock and say goodbye. →	Say goodbye.

Practice more at vhlcentral.com.

TEACHING OPTIONS

Small Groups Ask students to work in small groups to ad-lib the exchanges between **Marissa** and **Sra. Díaz**, **Marissa** and **don Diego**, and **Marissa**, **Felipe**, and **Jimena**. Tell them to convey the general meaning using vocabulary and expressions they know, and assure them that they do not have to stick to the original dialogues word for word. Then, ask volunteers to present their exchanges to the class.

EXPANSION

Extra Practice Choose four or five lines of the **Fotonovela** to use as a dictation. Read the lines twice slowly to give students sufficient time to write. Then read them again at normal speed to allow students to correct any errors or fill in any gaps. You may have students correct their own work by checking it against the **Fotonovela** text and ask follow-up questions to check comprehension.

Hola, ¿qué tal?

Pronunciación  Audio

The Spanish alphabet

The Spanish and English alphabets are almost identical, with a few exceptions. For example, the Spanish letter **ñ (eñe)** doesn't appear in the English alphabet. Furthermore, the letters **k (ka)** and **w (doble ve)** are used only in words of foreign origin. Examine the chart below to find other differences.

Letra	Nombre(s)	Ejemplos	Letra	Nombre(s)	Ejemplos
a	a	adiós	o	o	once
b	be	bien, problema	p	pe	profesor
c	ce	cosa, cero	q	cu	qué
d	de	diario, nada	r	ere	regular, señora
e	e	estudiante	s	ese	señor
f	efe	foto	t	te	tú
g	ge	gracias, Gerardo, regular	u	u	usted
h	hache	hola	v	ve	vista, nuevo
i	i	igualmente	w	doble ve	walkman
j	jota	Javier	x	equis	existir, México
k	ka, ca	kilómetro	y	i griega, ye	yo
l	ele	lápiz	z	zeta, ceta	zona
m	eme	mapa			
n	ene	nacionalidad	**Dígrafo**		**Ejemplos**
ñ	eñe	mañana	ch		chico
			ll		llave

AYUDA

The letter combination **rr** produces a strong trilled sound which does not have an English equivalent. English speakers commonly make this sound when imitating the sound of a motor. This trilled sound occurs between vowels or at the beginning of a word: **puertorriqueño, terrible, Roberto,** etc.

¡LENGUA VIVA!

Note that **ch** and **ll** are not letters but *digraphs*, or two letters that together produce one sound. Traditionally they were considered part of the alphabet and they were called **che** and **elle**, but nowadays **ch** and **ll** do not have their own entries when placing words in alphabetical order, as in a glossary.

El alfabeto Repeat the Spanish alphabet and example words after your instructor.

Práctica Spell these words aloud in Spanish.

1. nada
2. maleta
3. quince
4. muy
5. hombre
6. por favor
7. San Fernando
8. Estados Unidos
9. Puerto Rico
10. España
11. Javier
12. Ecuador
13. Maite
14. gracias
15. Nueva York

Refranes Read these sayings aloud.

Ver es creer.[1]

En boca cerrada no entran moscas.[2]

[1] Seeing is believing. [2] Silence is golden.

recursos: vText, CPA p. 6, CH p. 3, vhlcentral

1 cultura

Lección 1

Section Goals

In **Cultura**, students will:
- read about greetings in Spanish-speaking countries
- learn informal greetings and goodbyes
- read about famous friends and couples
- read about the **plaza principal**

Communication 1.1, 1.2
Cultures 2.1, 2.2
Connections 3.1, 3.2
Comparisons 4.2

Student Resources
Cuaderno para hispanohablantes, p. 4
Supersite: Activities

 21st Century Skills

Global Awareness
Students will gain perspectives on the Spanish-speaking world.

En detalle

Antes de leer Ask students to share how they normally greet friends and family.

Lectura
- In the U.S., friends generally remain at least 18 inches apart while chatting. Hispanic friends would probably deem 18 inches to be excessive.
- Show students the locations mentioned here on the maps on pp. x–xv of their books.
- Explain that an "air kiss" is limited to a grazing of cheeks.

Después de leer Call on two volunteers to stand in front of the class. Point out the natural distance between them; then have the volunteers face each other with their toes touching and start a conversation. Tell the rest of the class to do the same. Ask students to share their feelings on this change in personal space.

1 Expansion Ask students to write three true/false statements for a classmate to do.

EN DETALLE

Additional Reading

Saludos y besos en los países hispanos

In Spanish-speaking countries, kissing on the cheek is a customary way to greet friends and family members. Even when people are introduced for the first time, it is common for them to kiss, particularly in non-business settings. Whereas North Americans maintain considerable personal space when greeting, Spaniards and Latin Americans tend to decrease their personal space and give one or two kisses (**besos**) on the cheek, sometimes accompanied by a handshake or a hug. In formal business settings, where associates do not know one another on a personal level, a simple handshake is appropriate.

Greeting someone with a **beso** varies according to gender and region. Men generally greet each other with a hug or warm handshake, except in Argentina, where male friends and relatives lightly kiss on the cheek. Greetings between men and women, and between women, can differ depending on the country and context. In Spain, it is customary to give **dos besos**, starting with the right cheek first. In Latin American countries, including Mexico, Costa Rica, Colombia, and Chile, a greeting consists of a single "air kiss" on the right cheek. Peruvians also "air kiss," but strangers will simply

shake hands. In Colombia, female acquaintances tend to simply pat each other on the right forearm or shoulder.

Tendencias

País	Beso	País	Beso
Argentina	💋	España	💋💋
Bolivia	💋	México	💋
Chile	💋	Paraguay	💋💋
Colombia	💋	Puerto Rico	💋
El Salvador	💋	Venezuela	💋 / 💋💋

ACTIVIDADES

1 **¿Cierto o falso?** Indicate whether these statements are true (**cierto**) or false (**falso**). Correct the false statements.

1. Hispanic people use less personal space when greeting than non-Hispanics in the U.S. **Cierto**
2. Men never greet with a kiss in Spanish-speaking countries. **Falso.** Argentine men can greet with a light kiss.
3. Shaking hands is not appropriate for a business setting in Latin America. **Falso.** In most business settings, people greet one another by shaking hands.
4. Spaniards greet with one kiss on the right cheek. **Falso.** They greet with one kiss on each cheek.
5. In Mexico, people greet with an "air kiss." **Cierto**
6. Gender can play a role in the type of greeting given. **Cierto**
7. If two women acquaintances meet in Colombia, they should exchange two kisses on the cheek. **Falso.** They pat one another on the right forearm or shoulder.
8. In Peru, a man and a woman meeting for the first time would probably greet each other with an "air kiss." **Falso.** They would probably shake hands.

TEACHING OPTIONS

Game Divide the class into two teams. Give situations in which people greet one another and have one member from each team identify the appropriate way to greet. Ex: Two male friends in Argentina. (light kiss on the cheek) Give one point for each correct answer. The team with the most points at the end wins.

EXPANSION

Culture Note Kisses are not only a form of greeting in Hispanic cultures. It is also common to end phone conversations and close letters or e-mails with the words **un beso** or **besos**. Additionally, friends may use **un abrazo** to end a written message. In a more formal e-mail, one can write **un saludo (cordial)** or **saludos**.

Hola, ¿qué tal?

ASÍ SE DICE
Saludos y despedidas

¿Cómo te/le va?	How are things going (for you)?
¡Cuánto tiempo!	It's been a long time!
Hasta ahora.	See you soon.
¿Qué hay?	What's new?
¿Qué onda? (Méx., Arg., Chi.); ¿Qué más? (Ven., Col.)	What's going on?

EL MUNDO HISPANO
Parejas y amigos famosos

Here are some famous couples and friends from the Spanish-speaking world.

- **Penélope Cruz** (España) y **Javier Bardem** (España) Cruz and Bardem first appeared on film together in the 1992 film *Jamón jamón*, but didn't start dating until 2007. They were married in 2010 and had a son, Leonardo, in 2011.

- **Gael García Bernal** (México) y **Diego Luna** (México) These lifelong friends were made famous by their roles in the 2001 Mexican film *Y tu mamá también*. They continue to work together in other projects, such as the films *Rudo y Cursi* (2008) and *Casa de mi padre* (2012).

- **Selena Gomez** (Estados Unidos) y **Demi Lovato** (Estados Unidos) These close friends are both from Texas and have parents of Mexican descent. They've know each other since working together on *Barney* when they were 6 years old.

PERFIL
La plaza principal

In the Spanish-speaking world, public space is treasured. Small city and town life revolves around the **plaza principal**. Often surrounded by cathedrals or municipal buildings like the **ayuntamiento** (city hall), the pedestrian **plaza** is designated as a central meeting place for family and friends. During warmer months, when outdoor cafés usually line the **plaza**, it is a popular spot to have a leisurely cup of coffee, chat, and people watch. Many town festivals, or **ferias**, also take place in this space. One of the most famous town squares

La Plaza Mayor de Salamanca

is the **Plaza Mayor** in the university town of Salamanca, Spain. Students gather underneath its famous clock tower to meet up with friends or simply take a coffee break.

La Plaza de Armas, Lima, Perú

Conexión Internet

What are the **plazas principales** in large cities such as Mexico City and Caracas?

Go to **vhlcentral.com** to find more cultural information related to this **Cultura** section.

ACTIVIDADES

2 Comprensión Answer these questions.
Some answers may vary. Suggested answers:
1. What are two types of buildings found on the **plaza principal**? *municipal buildings and cathedrals*
2. What two types of events or activities are common at a **plaza principal**? *meeting with friends and festivals*
3. Would Penélope Cruz greet her friends with one kiss or two? *two*
4. What would Diego Luna say when greeting a friend? *¿Qué onda?*

3 Saludos Role-play these greetings with a partner. Include a verbal greeting as well as a handshake, as appropriate. *Role-plays will vary according to student gender.*
1. friends in Mexico
2. business associates at a conference in Chile
3. friends in Madrid's Plaza Mayor
4. Peruvians meeting for the first time
5. Relatives in Argentina

Section Goals

In **Estructura 1.1**, students will be introduced to:
- gender of nouns
- definite and indefinite articles

Communication 1.1
Comparisons 4.1

Student Resources
Cuaderno de práctica y actividades comunicativas, pp. 7–8
Cuaderno para hispanohablantes, pp. 5–6
Supersite: Activities, *eCuaderno*

Teacher Resources
Workbook TE; Grammar Slides; Audio Activities MP3s; Audio Script; Testing Program Quizzes; Activity Pack; Middle School Activity Pack

Teaching Tips
- Write these nouns from the **Fotonovela** on the board: **chicos, diccionario, estudiantes, maleta.** Ask volunteers what each means. Point out the different endings and introduce grammatical gender in Spanish. Explain what a noun is and give examples of people (**chicos**), places (**universidad**), things (**documentos**), and ideas (**nacionalidad**). Ask volunteers to point out which of these nouns are singular or plural and why.
- Point out that while nouns for male beings are generally masculine and those for female beings are generally feminine, grammatical gender does not necessarily correspond to the actual gender of the being.
- Point out patterns of noun endings **–o, –a; –or, –ora.** Stress that **–ista** can refer to males or females, and give additional examples: **el/la artista, el/la dentista.**

1 estructura

Lección 1

1.1 Nouns and articles

Spanish nouns

ANTE TODO A noun is a word used to identify people, animals, places, things, or ideas. Unlike English, all Spanish nouns, even those that refer to non-living things, have gender; that is, they are considered either masculine or feminine. As in English, nouns in Spanish also have number, meaning that they are either singular or plural.

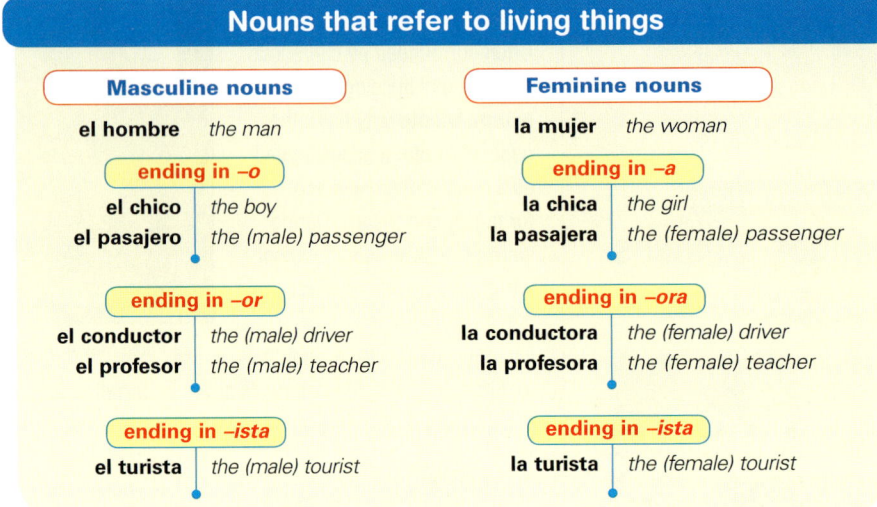

▶ Generally, nouns that refer to males, like **el hombre**, are masculine, while nouns that refer to females, like **la mujer**, are feminine.

▶ Many nouns that refer to male beings end in **–o** or **–or**. Their corresponding feminine forms end in **–a** and **–ora**, respectively.

el conductor

la profesora

▶ The masculine and feminine forms of nouns that end in **–ista**, like **turista**, are the same, so gender is indicated by the article **el** (masculine) or **la** (feminine). Some other nouns have identical masculine and feminine forms.

el joven
the youth; the young man

la joven
the youth; the young woman

el estudiante
the (male) student

la estudiante
the (female) student

¡LENGUA VIVA!
Profesor(a) and **turista** are *cognates*—words that share similar spellings and meanings in Spanish and English. Recognizing cognates will help you determine the meaning of many Spanish words. Here are some other cognates:
**la administración,
el animal,
el apartamento,
el cálculo, el color,
la decisión, la historia,
la música,
el restaurante,
el/la secretario/a**

AYUDA
Cognates can certainly be very helpful in your study of Spanish. However, beware of "false" cognates, those that have similar spellings in Spanish and English, but different meanings:
la carpeta *file folder*
el/la conductor(a) *driver*
el éxito *success*
la fábrica *factory*

EXPANSION
Extra Practice Write ten singular nouns on the board. Make sure the nouns represent a mix of the different types of noun endings. In a rapid-response drill, call on students to give the appropriate gender. For **–ista** words, accept either masculine or feminine, but clarify that both are used. You may also do this as a completely oral drill by not writing the words on the board.

TEACHING OPTIONS
Game Divide the class into teams of three or four. Bring in photos or magazine pictures showing objects or people. Hold up each photo and say the Spanish noun without the article. Call on teams to indicate the object or person's gender. Give one point for each correct answer. Deduct one point for each incorrect answer. The team with the most points at the end wins.

12 Teacher's Edition • Lesson One

Hola, ¿qué tal? trece **13**

Nouns that refer to non-living things

Masculine nouns

ending in –o
el cuaderno	the notebook
el diario	the diary
el diccionario	the dictionary
el número	the number
el video	the video

ending in –ma
| el problema | the problem |
| el programa | the program |

ending in –s
| el autobús | the bus |
| el país | the country |

Feminine nouns

ending in –a
la cosa	the thing
la escuela	the school
la computadora	the computer
la maleta	the suitcase
la palabra	the word

ending in –ción
| la lección | the lesson |
| la conversación | the conversation |

ending in –dad
| la nacionalidad | the nationality |
| la comunidad | the community |

¡LENGUA VIVA!
The Spanish word for *video* can be pronounced with the stress on the **i** or the **e**. For that reason, you might see the word written with or without an accent: **video** or **vídeo**.

▶ As shown above, certain noun endings are strongly associated with a specific gender, so you can use them to determine if a noun is masculine or feminine.

▶ Because the gender of nouns that refer to non-living things cannot be determined by foolproof rules, you should memorize the gender of each noun you learn. It is helpful to memorize each noun with its corresponding article, **el** for masculine and **la** for feminine.

▶ Another reason to memorize the gender of every noun is that there are common exceptions to the rules of gender. For example, **el mapa** (*map*) and **el día** (*day*) end in **–a**, but are masculine. **La mano** (*hand*) ends in **–o**, but is feminine.

Plural of nouns

▶ To form the plural, add **–s** to nouns that end in a vowel. Nouns that end in a consonant add **–es**. Nouns that end in **–z** change the **z** to **c**, then add **–es**.

el chic**o** → los chic**os**   la nacionalida**d** → las nacionalida**des**

el diari**o** → los diari**os**   el paí**s** → los paí**ses**

el problem**a** → los problem**as**   el lápi**z** (*pencil*) → los lápi**ces**

CONSULTA
You will learn more about accent marks in **Lección 4, Pronunciación**, p. 123.

▶ In general, when a singular noun has an accent mark on the last syllable, the accent is dropped from the plural form.

la lecc**ión** → las lecc**iones**   el autob**ús** → los autob**uses**

▶ Use the masculine plural form to refer to a group that includes both males and females.

1 pasajer**o** + 2 pasajer**as** = 3 pasajer**os**   2 chic**os** + 2 chic**as** = 4 chic**os**

14 catorce Lección 1

Spanish articles

ANTE TODO As you know, English often uses definite articles (*the*) and indefinite articles (*a, an*) before nouns. Spanish also has definite and indefinite articles. Unlike English, Spanish articles vary in form because they agree in gender and number with the nouns they modify.

Definite articles

▶ Spanish has four forms that are equivalent to the English definite article *the*. Use definite articles to refer to specific nouns.

| **el** diccionario | **los** diccionarios | **la** computadora | **las** computadoras |
| *the dictionary* | *the dictionaries* | *the computer* | *the computers* |

Indefinite articles

▶ Spanish has four forms that are equivalent to the English indefinite article, which according to context may mean *a, an,* or *some*. Use indefinite articles to refer to unspecified persons or things.

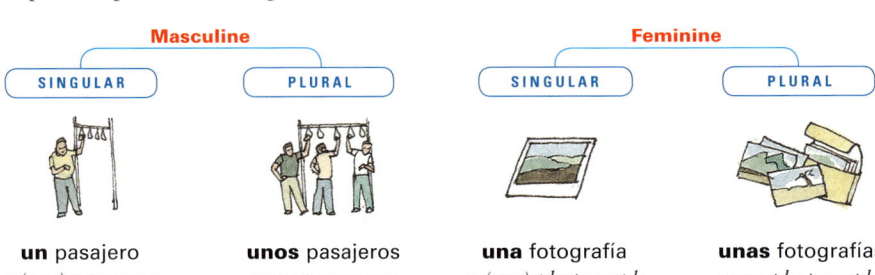

| **un** pasajero | **unos** pasajeros | **una** fotografía | **unas** fotografías |
| *a (one) passenger* | *some passengers* | *a (one) photograph* | *some photographs* |

¡LENGUA VIVA!
Feminine singular nouns that begin with stressed **a-** or **ha-** require the masculine articles **el** and **un**. The plural forms still use the feminine articles.
el agua *water*
las aguas *waters*
un hacha *ax*
unas hachas *axes*

¡LENGUA VIVA!
Since **la fotografía** is feminine, so is its shortened form, **la foto,** even though it ends in –**o**.

¡INTÉNTALO! Provide a definite article for each noun in the first column and an indefinite article for each noun in the second column.

¿el, la, los o las?
1. _la_ chica
2. _el_ chico
3. _la_ maleta
4. _los_ cuadernos
5. _el_ lápiz
6. _las_ mujeres

¿un, una, unos o unas?
1. _un_ autobús
2. _unas_ escuelas
3. _una_ computadora
4. _unos_ hombres
5. _una_ señora
6. _unos_ lápices

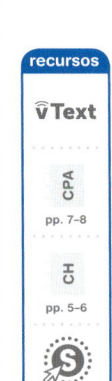

Teaching Tips (margin)

- Write **¿El, la, los o las?** on the board and ask students to identify the correct definite article for these words. **1. hombre (el) 2. computadora (la) 3. profesor (el) 4. universidades (las) 5. turistas (los/las) 6. diccionario (el) 7. problema (el) 8. mujeres (las)**
- Write **¿Un, una, unos o unas?** on the board and ask students to identify the correct indefinite article for these words. **1. pasajeros (unos) 2. chico (un) 3. escuela (una) 4. lecciones (unas) 5. autobuses (unos) 6. maleta (una) 7. programas (unos) 8. cosa (una)**
- Do a pair of conversion activities. Students respond with the article and the noun:
Definido → Indefinido
1. los turistas (unos turistas) 2. la computadora (una computadora) 3. el hombre (un hombre) 4. las mujeres (unas mujeres) 5. el programa (un programa) 6. el hacha (un hacha)
Indefinido → Definido
1. unas lecciones (las lecciones) 2. una maleta (la maleta) 3. unos lápices (los lápices) 4. unas pasajeras (las pasajeras) 5. un diario (el diario) 6. una foto (la foto)

TELL Connection

Performance and Feedback 2
Why: We can't fix a problem unless we know it exists. *What:* Throughout **DESCUBRE**, use **¡Inténtalo!** activities to provide immediate and specific feedback to students. You will quickly be able to gauge what additional explanation or practice they need.

EXPANSION

Extra Practice Add a visual aspect to this grammar practice. Hold up or point to objects whose names students are familiar with (Ex: **diccionario, lápiz, computadora, foto[grafía]**). Ask students to indicate the appropriate definite article and the noun. Include a mix of singular and plural nouns. Repeat the exercise with indefinite articles.

TEACHING OPTIONS

Pairs Have pairs jot down a mix of ten singular and plural nouns, without their articles. Have them exchange their lists with another pair. Each pair then has to write down the appropriate definite and indefinite articles for each item. After pairs have finished, have them exchange lists and correct them.

Hola, ¿qué tal? quince **15**

Práctica

1 **¿Singular o plural?** If the word is singular, make it plural. If it is plural, make it singular.

1. el número los números
2. un diario unos diarios
3. la estudiante las estudiantes
4. el conductor los conductores
5. el país los países
6. las cosas la cosa
7. unos turistas un turista
8. las nacionalidades la nacionalidad
9. unas computadoras una computadora
10. los problemas el problema
11. una fotografía unas fotografías
12. los profesores el profesor
13. unas señoritas una señorita
14. el hombre los hombres
15. la maleta las maletas
16. la señora las señoras

2 **Identificar** For each drawing, provide the noun with its corresponding definite and indefinite articles.

modelo
las maletas, unas maletas

1. la computadora, una computadora

2. los cuadernos, unos cuadernos

3. las mujeres, unas mujeres

4. el chico, un chico

5. la escuela, una escuela

6. las fotos, unas fotos

7. los autobuses, unos autobuses

8. el diario, un diario

Practice more at vhlcentral.com.

Comunicación

3 **Charadas** In groups, play a game of charades. Individually, think of two nouns for each charade, for example, a boy using a computer (**un chico; una computadora**). The first person to guess correctly acts out the next charade. Answers will vary.

Communication 1.1
Comparisons 4.1

1 Expansion Reverse the activity by reading the on-page answers and having students convert the singular to plural and vice versa. Make sure they close their books. Give the nouns in random order.

2 Expansion As an additional visual exercise, bring in photos or magazine pictures that illustrate items whose names students know. Ask students to indicate the definite article and the noun. Include a mix of singular and plural nouns. Repeat the exercise with indefinite articles.

3 Teaching Tip Model the game of charades by writing some new cognates on the board (Ex: **la guitarra, el teléfono, la televisión**). Act out sitting on a couch and flipping channels on a remote and invite students to guess. Emphasize that the student acting out the charade must not speak and that he or she may show the number of syllables by using fingers.

3 Expansion Split the class into two teams, with volunteers from each team acting out the charades. Give a point to each team for correctly guessing the charade. The team with the most points wins.

EXPANSION

Video Show the **Fotonovela** episode again to offer more input on singular and plural nouns and articles. With their books closed, have students write down every noun and article that they hear. After viewing the video, ask volunteers to list the nouns and articles they heard. Explain that the **las** used when telling time refers to **las horas** (Ex: **Son las cinco = Son las cinco horas**).

EXPANSION

Extra Practice To challenge students, slowly read aloud a short passage from a novel, story, poem, or newspaper article written in Spanish, preferably one with a great number of nouns and articles. As a listening exercise, have students write down every noun and article they hear, even unfamiliar ones (the articles may cue when nouns appear).

Estructura **15**

Section Goals

In **Estructura 1.2**, students will be introduced to:
- numbers 0–30
- the verb form **hay**

Communication 1.1
Comparisons 4.1

Student Resources
Cuaderno de práctica y actividades comunicativas, pp. 9–12
Cuaderno para hispanohablantes, pp. 7–8
Supersite: Activities, *eCuaderno*

Teacher Resources
Workbook TE; Grammar Slides; Audio Activities MP3s; Audio Script; Testing Program Quizzes; Activity Pack; Middle School Activity Pack

Teaching Tips
- Introduce numbers by asking students if they can count to ten in Spanish. Model the pronunciation of each number. Write individual numbers on the board and call on students at random to say the number.
- Say numbers aloud at random and have students hold up the appropriate number of fingers. Then reverse the drill; hold up varying numbers of fingers at random and ask students to shout out the corresponding number in Spanish.
- Emphasize the variable forms of **uno** and **veintiuno**, giving examples of each. Ex: **veintiún profesores, veintiuna profesoras.**
- Ask questions like these: **¿Cuántos estudiantes hay en la clase? (Hay _____ estudiantes en la clase.)**

1.2 Numbers 0–30

 Tutorial

Los números 0 a 30

0	cero				
1	uno	11	once	21	veintiuno
2	dos	12	doce	22	veintidós
3	tres	13	trece	23	veintitrés
4	cuatro	14	catorce	24	veinticuatro
5	cinco	15	quince	25	veinticinco
6	seis	16	dieciséis	26	veintiséis
7	siete	17	diecisiete	27	veintisiete
8	ocho	18	dieciocho	28	veintiocho
9	nueve	19	diecinueve	29	veintinueve
10	diez	20	veinte	30	treinta

▶ The number **uno** (*one*) and numbers ending in **–uno**, such as **veintiuno**, have more than one form. Before masculine nouns, **uno** shortens to **un**. Before feminine nouns, **uno** changes to **una**.

un hombre ⟶ veint**iún** hombres   **una** mujer ⟶ veint**iuna** mujeres

▶ **¡Atención!** The forms **uno** and **veintiuno** are used when counting (**uno, dos, tres… veinte, veintiuno, veintidós…**). They are also used when the number *follows* a noun, even if the noun is feminine: **la lección uno**.

▶ To ask *how many people* or *things* there are, use **cuántos** before masculine nouns and **cuántas** before feminine nouns.

▶ The Spanish equivalent of both *there is* and *there are* is **hay**. Use **¿Hay…?** to ask *Is there…?* or *Are there…?* Use **no hay** to express *there is not* or *there are not*.

—**¿Cuántos** estudiantes **hay**?
How many students are there?

—**Hay** seis estudiantes en la foto.
There are six students in the photo.

—**¿Hay** chicos en la fotografía?
Are there guys in the picture?

—**Hay** tres chicas y **no hay** chicos.
There are three girls, and there are no guys.

 **¡INTÉNTALO!** Provide the Spanish words for these numbers.

1. 7 siete
2. 16 dieciséis
3. 29 veintinueve
4. 1 uno
5. 0 cero
6. 15 quince
7. 21 veintiuno
8. 9 nueve
9. 23 veintitrés
10. 11 once
11. 30 treinta
12. 4 cuatro
13. 12 doce
14. 28 veintiocho
15. 14 catorce
16. 10 diez

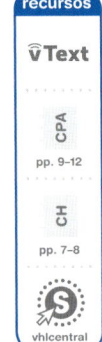
recursos
vText
CPA pp. 9–12
CH pp. 7–8
vhlcentral

TEACHING OPTIONS

TPR Assign ten students a number from 0–30 and line them up in front of the class. Call out one of the numbers at random, and have the student assigned that number step forward. When two students have stepped forward, ask them to repeat their numbers. Then ask individuals to add (Say: **Suma**) or subtract (Say: **Resta**) the two numbers, giving the result in Spanish.

TEACHING OPTIONS

Game Ask students to write B-I-N-G-O across the top of a blank piece of paper. Have them draw five squares vertically under each letter and randomly fill in the squares with numbers from 0–30, without repeating any numbers. Draw numbers from a hat and call them out in Spanish. The first student to mark five in a row (horizontally, vertically, or diagonally) yells **¡Bingo!** and wins. Have the winner confirm the numbers for you in Spanish.

Práctica

1 Contar Following the pattern, write out the missing numbers in Spanish.

1. 1, 3, 5, ..., 29 7, 9, 11, 13, 15, 17, 19, 21, 23, 25, 27
2. 2, 4, 6, ..., 30 8, 10, 12, 14, 16, 18, 20, 22, 24, 26, 28
3. 3, 6, 9, ..., 30 12, 15, 18, 21, 24, 27
4. 30, 28, 26, ..., 0 24, 22, 20, 18, 16, 14, 12, 10, 8, 6, 4, 2
5. 30, 25, 20, ..., 0 15, 10, 5
6. 28, 24, 20, ..., 0 16, 12, 8, 4

2 Resolver Solve these math problems with a partner.

modelo
5 + 3 = **Estudiante 1:** *cinco más tres son...*
Estudiante 2: *ocho*

AYUDA
+ → más
− → menos
= → son

1. **2 + 15 =** Dos más quince son diecisiete.
2. **20 − 1 =** Veinte menos uno son diecinueve.
3. **5 + 7 =** Cinco más siete son doce.
4. **18 + 12 =** Dieciocho más doce son treinta.
5. **3 + 22 =** Tres más veintidós son veinticinco.
6. **6 − 3 =** Seis menos tres son tres.
7. **11 + 12 =** Once más doce son veintitrés.
8. **7 − 2 =** Siete menos dos son cinco.
9. **8 + 5 =** Ocho más cinco son trece.
10. **23 − 14 =** Veintitrés menos catorce son nueve.

3 ¿Cuántos hay? How many persons or things are there in these drawings?

modelo
Hay tres maletas.

1. Hay veinte lápices.

2. Hay un hombre.

3. Hay veinticinco chicos.

4. Hay una conductora.

5. Hay cuatro fotos.

6. Hay treinta cuadernos.

7. Hay seis turistas.

8. Hay diecisiete chicas.

Practice more at vhlcentral.com.

Teaching Tips
- Before beginning the activity, make sure students know each pattern: odds (**los números impares**), evens (**los números pares**), count by threes (**contar de tres en tres**), etc.
- To simplify, write complete patterns out on the board.

1 Expansion Explain that a prime number (**un número primo**) is any number that can only be evenly divided by itself and 1. To challenge students, ask the class to list the prime numbers up to 30. (They are: 1, 2, 3, 5, 7, 11, 13, 17, 19, 23, 29.)

2 Expansion Do simple multiplication and division problems. Introduce the phrases **multiplicado por** and **dividido por**. Ex: **Cinco multiplicado por cinco son...** (**veinticinco**). **Veinte dividido por cuatro son...** (**cinco**).

3 Teaching Tip Have students read the directions and the model. Cue student responses by asking questions related to the drawings. Ex: **¿Cuántos lápices hay?** (**Hay veinte lápices.**)

3 Expansion Add an additional visual aspect to this activity. Hold up or point to classroom objects and ask how many there are. Since students will not know the names of many items, a simple number or **hay** + [*the number*] will suffice to signal comprehension. Ex: —**¿Cuántos diccionarios hay aquí?** —(**Hay**) **Dos**.

TEACHING OPTIONS

TPR Give ten students each a card that contains a different number from 0–30. The cards should be visible to the other students. Then call out simple math problems (addition or subtraction) involving the assigned numbers. When the first two numbers are called, each student steps forward. The student whose assigned number completes the math problem then has five seconds to join them.

EXPANSION

Extra Practice Ask questions about your school and the town or city in which it is located. Ex: **¿Cuántos profesores de español hay? ¿Cuántas escuelas secundarias hay en _____? ¿Cuántas pizzerías hay en _____?** Encourage students to guess the number. If a number exceeds 30, write that number on the board and model its pronunciation.

**Communication 1.1
Comparisons 4.1**

4 Teaching Tip If there are no examples of the item listed, students should say: **No hay _____**.

4 Expansion After completing the activity, call on individuals to give rapid responses for the same items. To challenge students, mix up the order of items.

4 Virtual Chat You can also assign activity 4 on the Supersite. Students record individual responses that appear in your gradebook.

5 Teaching Tip Remind students that they will be forming sentences with **hay** and a number. Give them four minutes to do the activity. You might also have students write out their answers.

5 Expansion After pairs have finished analyzing the drawing, call on individuals to respond. Convert the statements into questions in Spanish. Ask: **¿Cuántos chicos hay? ¿Cuántas mujeres hay?**

5 Expansion In pairs, have students role-play conversations between one of the family members in the drawing and an exchange student that has come to live with them. Encourage students to use phrases they learned in **Contextos**, as well as simple questions about the host family, such as **¿Cuántas personas hay en la casa?**

5 Partner Chat (Premium) You can also assign activity 5 on the Supersite. Students work in pairs to record the activity online. The pair's recorded conversation will appear in your gradebook.

Teaching Tip See the Communication Activities in the *Activity Pack* for an additional activity to practice the material presented in this section.

---

18   dieciocho   Lección 1

Comunicación

4   En la clase With a classmate, take turns asking and answering these questions about your classroom. *Answers will vary.*

1. ¿Cuántos estudiantes hay?
2. ¿Cuántos profesores hay?
3. ¿Hay una computadora?
4. ¿Hay una maleta?
5. ¿Cuántos mapas hay?
6. ¿Cuántos lápices hay?
7. ¿Hay cuadernos?
8. ¿Cuántos diccionarios hay?
9. ¿Hay hombres?
10. ¿Cuántas mujeres hay?

5   Preguntas With a classmate, take turns asking and answering questions about the drawing. Talk about: *Answers will vary.*

1. how many children there are
2. how many women there are
3. if there are some photographs
4. if there is a boy
5. how many notebooks there are
6. if there is a bus
7. if there are tourists
8. how many pencils there are
9. if there is a man
10. how many computers there are

TEACHING OPTIONS

Pairs Have each student draw a scene similar to the one on this page. Stick figures are perfectly acceptable! Give them three minutes to draw the scene. Encourage students to include multiple numbers of particular items (**cuadernos, maletas, lápices,** etc.). Then have pairs take turns describing what is in their partner's picture. The student that created the drawing should verify the accuracy of the description.

TEACHING OPTIONS

Pairs Divide the class into pairs. Give half of the pairs magazine pictures that contain images of familiar words or cognates. Give the other half written descriptions of the pictures, using **hay**. Ex: **En la foto hay dos mujeres, un chico y una chica**. Have pairs circulate around the room to match the descriptions with the corresponding pictures.

Hola, ¿qué tal? diecinueve 19

1.3 Present tense of ser Tutorial

Subject pronouns

ANTE TODO In order to use verbs, you will need to learn about subject pronouns. A subject pronoun replaces the name or title of a person or thing and acts as the subject of a verb. In both Spanish and English, subject pronouns are divided into three groups: first person, second person, and third person.

Subject pronouns

	SINGULAR		PLURAL	
FIRST PERSON	yo	I	nosotros	we (masculine)
			nosotras	we (feminine)
SECOND PERSON	tú	you (familiar)	vosotros	you (masc., fam.)
	usted (Ud.)	you (formal)	vosotras	you (fem., fam.)
			ustedes (Uds.)	you (form.)
THIRD PERSON	él	he	ellos	they (masc.)
	ella	she	ellas	they (fem.)

▶ Spanish has two subject pronouns that mean *you* (singular). Use **tú** when addressing a friend, a family member, or a child. Use **usted** to address a person with whom you have a formal or more distant relationship, such as a superior at work, a professor, or a person older than you.

Tú eres de Canadá, ¿verdad, David?
You are from Canada, right, David?

¿Usted es la profesora de español?
Are you the Spanish professor?

▶ The masculine plural forms **nosotros, vosotros,** and **ellos** refer to a group of males or to a group of males and females. The feminine plural forms **nosotras, vosotras,** and **ellas** can refer only to groups made up exclusively of females.

nosotros, vosotros, ellos

nosotros, vosotros, ellos

nosotras, vosotras, ellas

▶ There is no Spanish equivalent of the English subject pronoun *it*. Generally *it* is not expressed in Spanish.

Es un problema.
It's a problem.

Es una computadora.
It's a computer.

¡LENGUA VIVA!

In Latin America, **ustedes** is used as the plural for both **tú** and **usted**. In Spain, however, **vosotros** and **vosotras** are used as the plural of **tú**, and **ustedes** is used only as the plural of **usted**.

...

Usted and **ustedes** are abbreviated as **Ud.** and **Uds.**, or occasionally as **Vd.** and **Vds.**

EXPANSION

Extra Practice Explain that students are to give subject pronouns based on their point of view. Ex: Point to yourself (**usted**), a female student (**ella**), everyone in the class (**nosotros**).

Extra Practice Ask students to indicate whether certain people would be addressed as **tú** or **usted**. Ex: A classmate, a friend's grandfather, a doctor, a neighbor's child.

DIFFERENTIATION

Heritage Speakers Ask heritage speakers how they address elder members of their family, such as parents, grandparents, aunts, and uncles—whether they use **tú** or **usted**. Also ask them if they use **vosotros/as** (they typically will not unless they or their family are from Spain) or **voseo**. Explain that **voseo** is the use of the second-person subject pronoun **vos** instead of **tú**. It is used extensively in much of Latin America.

Section Goals

In **Estructura 1.3**, students will be introduced to:
- subject pronouns
- present tense of the verb **ser**
- the use of **ser** to identify, to indicate possession, to describe origin, and to talk about professions or occupations

Communication 1.1
Comparisons 4.1

Student Resources

Cuaderno de práctica y actividades comunicativas, pp. 13–15
Cuaderno para hispanohablantes, pp. 9–10
Supersite: Activities, eCuaderno

Teacher Resources

Workbook TE; Grammar Slides; Audio Activities MP3s; Audio Script; Testing Program Quizzes; Activity Pack; Middle School Activity Pack

Teaching Tips

- Point to yourself and say: **Yo soy profesor(a)**. Then point to a student and ask: **¿Tú eres profesor(a) o estudiante?** (estudiante) Say: **Sí, tú eres estudiante.** Indicate the whole class and tell them: **Ustedes son estudiantes.** Once the pattern has been established, include other subject pronouns and forms of **ser** while indicating other students. Ex: **Él es..., Ella es..., Ellos son...**
- Remind students of the familiar and formal forms of address they learned in **Contextos**.
- You may want to point out that while **usted** and **ustedes** are second-person forms of address equivalent to the English *you*, they take third-person verb forms.

Note: While the **vosotros/as** forms are listed in verb paradigms in **DESCUBRE**, they will not be actively practiced.

Estructura 19

The present tense of ser

ANTE TODO In **Contextos** and **Fotonovela**, you have already used several present-tense forms of **ser** (*to be*) to identify yourself and others, and to talk about where you and others are from. **Ser** is an irregular verb; its forms do not follow the regular patterns that most verbs follow. You need to memorize the forms, which appear in this chart.

The verb ser (to be)

SINGULAR FORMS	yo	soy	*I am*
	tú	eres	*you are* (fam.)
	Ud./él/ella	es	*you are* (form.); *he/she is*
PLURAL FORMS	nosotros/as	somos	*we are*
	vosotros/as	sois	*you are* (fam.)
	Uds./ellos/ellas	son	*you are* (form.); *they are*

Uses of ser

▶ Use **ser** to identify people and things.

—¿Quién **es** él?
Who is he?

—**Es** Felipe Díaz Velázquez.
He's Felipe Díaz Velázquez.

—¿Qué **es**?
What is it?

—**Es** un mapa de España.
It's a map of Spain.

Es Marissa.

Es una maleta.

▶ **Ser** also expresses possession, with the preposition **de**. There is no Spanish equivalent of the English construction [*noun*] + *'s* (*Maru's*). In its place, Spanish uses [*noun*] + **de** + [*owner*].

—¿De quién **es**?
Whose is it?

—**Es** el diario **de** Maru.
It's Maru's diary.

—¿De quién **son**?
Whose are they?

—**Son** los lápices **de** la chica.
They are the girl's pencils.

▶ When **de** is followed by the article **el**, the two combine to form the contraction **del**. **De** does *not* contract with **la**, **las**, or **los**.

—**Es** la computadora **del** conductor.
It's the driver's computer.

—**Son** las maletas **del** chico.
They are the boy's suitcases.

Hola, ¿qué tal?

¡LENGUA VIVA!

Some geographic locations can be referred to either with or without a definite article:

Soy de Estados Unidos./Soy de los Estados Unidos.

• • •

Sometimes a definite article is a part of a proper name, as in **El Salvador**, **El Paso**, and **Los Ángeles**. In these cases, **de** and **el** do not contract:

Soy de El Salvador.

CONSULTA

You will learn more about adjectives in **Estructura 3.1**, pp. 88–90.

NOTA CULTURAL

Created in 1998, LAN Perú is an affiliate of the Chilean-based LAN Airlines, one of the largest carriers in South America. LAN Perú operates out of Lima, offering domestic flights and international service to select major cities in the Americas and Spain.

▶ **Ser** also uses the preposition **de** to express origin.

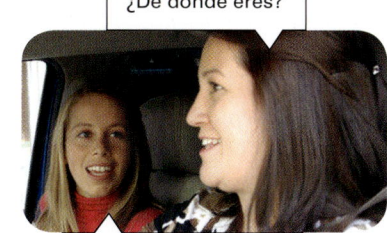

¿De dónde eres?
Yo soy de Wisconsin.

¿De dónde es usted?
Yo soy de Cuba.

—¿**De** dónde **es** Juan Carlos?
Where is Juan Carlos from?

—**Es de** Argentina.
He's from Argentina.

—¿**De** dónde **es** Maru?
Where is Maru from?

—**Es de** Costa Rica.
She's from Costa Rica.

▶ Use **ser** to express profession or occupation.

Don Francisco **es conductor**.
Don Francisco is a driver.

Yo **soy estudiante**.
I am a student.

▶ Unlike English, Spanish does not use the indefinite article (**un**, **una**) after **ser** when referring to professions, unless accompanied by an adjective or other description.

Marta **es** profesora.
Marta is a teacher.

Marta **es una** profesora excelente.
Marta is an excellent teacher.

Somos Perú
LanPerú

¡INTÉNTALO! Provide the correct subject pronouns and the present forms of **ser**. The first item has been done for you.

1. Gabriel — él — es
2. Juan y yo — nosotros — somos
3. Óscar y Flora — ellos — son
4. Adriana — ella — es
5. las turistas — ellas — son
6. el chico — él — es
7. los conductores — ellos — son
8. los señores Ruiz — ellos — son

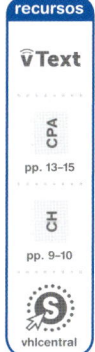

recursos
vText
CPA pp. 13–15
CH pp. 9–10
vhlcentral

EXPANSION

Extra Practice Write cognates on the board and ask students to identify the professions of famous people. Ex: **actor/actriz, presidente, artista, pianista.** Ask: ¿Qué es Brad Pitt? (Es actor.) ¿Quién es presidente? (_____ es presidente.)

TEACHING OPTIONS

Pairs Have pairs interview each other. Write sample questions on the board. Have students report about their partners. Students should begin by saying **Él/Ella es…**

Teaching Tips

• Explain **ser** + **de** to express origin. Start practicing this construction by indicating where you are from. Ex: **Soy de _____.** You may also want to further practice and contrast the contraction **del**. Ex: **Soy del estado de _____ /de la región (de) _____.** Introduce ¿**de dónde**? and ask students where they are from. Ex: _____, ¿**de dónde eres**? After a student answers, ask another student: ¿**De dónde es _____**? (Es de _____.)

• Explain the use of **ser** to describe professions or occupations. Say: **Yo soy profesor(a) de español. ¿Qué eres tú?** Response: **Soy estudiante.** Say: **Sí, eres estudiante.**

• Emphasize that the indefinite articles **un** and **una** are not used with **ser** and professions: **Él es arquitecto. Somos estudiantes.** However, stress that **un** and **una** are required if there is a descriptor present. Ex: **Él es un arquitecto importante. Somos unos estudiantes inteligentes.**

Communication 1.1
Comparisons 4.1

1 Teaching Tip Review **tú** and **usted**, asking students which pronoun they would use in a formal situation and which they would use in an informal situation.

2 Expansion Once students have identified the correct subject pronouns, ask them to give the form of **ser** they would use when *addressing* each person and when *talking about* each person.

2 Expansion Give additional names of well-known Spanish speakers and ask students to tell where they are from. Have students give the country names in English if they do not know the Spanish equivalent. Ex: **¿De dónde es Gael García Bernal? (Es de México.)**

3 Teaching Tips
- To simplify, before beginning the activity, guide students in identifying the objects.
- You might tell students to answer the second part of the question (**¿De quién es?**) with any answer they wish. Have students take turns asking and answering questions.

Práctica

1 Pronombres What subject pronouns would you use to (a) talk *to* these people directly and (b) talk *about* them to others?

modelo
un joven tú, él

1. una chica tú, ella
2. el presidente de México Ud., él
3. tres chicas y un chico Uds., ellos
4. un estudiante tú, él
5. la señora Ochoa Ud., ella
6. dos profesoras Uds., ellas

2 Identidad y origen With a partner, take turns asking and answering these questions about the people indicated: **¿Quién es?/¿Quiénes son?** and **¿De dónde es?/¿De dónde son?**

modelo
Selena Gomez (Estados Unidos)
Estudiante 1: ¿Quién es?   **Estudiante 1:** ¿De dónde es?
Estudiante 2: Es Selena Gomez.   **Estudiante 2:** Es de los Estados Unidos.

1. Enrique Iglesias (España) E1: ¿Quién es? E2: Es Enrique Iglesias. E1: ¿De dónde es? E2: Es de España.
2. Robinson Canó (República Dominicana) E2: ¿Quién es? E1: Es Robinson Canó. E2: ¿De dónde es? E1: Es de la República Dominicana.
3. Eva Mendes y Prince Royce (Estados Unidos) E1: ¿Quiénes son? E2: Son Eva Mendes y Prince Royce. E1: ¿De dónde son? E2: Son de los Estados Unidos.
4. Carlos Santana y Salma Hayek (México) E2: ¿Quiénes son? E1: Son Carlos Santana y Salma Hayek. E2: ¿De dónde son? E1: Son de México.
5. Shakira (Colombia) E1: ¿Quién es? E2: Es Shakira. E1: ¿De dónde es? E2: Es de Colombia.
6. Antonio Banderas y Penélope Cruz (España) E2: ¿Quiénes son? E1: Son Antonio Banderas y Penélope Cruz. E2: ¿De dónde son? E1: Son de España.
7. Taylor Swift y Demi Lovato (Estados Unidos) E1: ¿Quiénes son? E2: Son Taylor Swift y Demi Lovato. E1: ¿De dónde son? E2: Son de los Estados Unidos.
8. Daisy Fuentes (Cuba) E2: ¿Quién es? E1: Es Daisy Fuentes. E2: ¿De dónde es? E1: Es de Cuba.

3 ¿Qué es? Ask your partner what each object is and to whom it belongs.

modelo
Estudiante 1: ¿Qué es?   **Estudiante 1:** ¿De quién es?
Estudiante 2: Es un diccionario.   **Estudiante 2:** Es del profesor Núñez.

 1.    2.   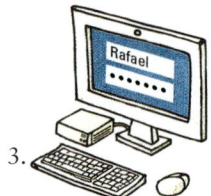 3.    4.

1. E1: ¿Qué es? E2: Es una maleta. E1: ¿De quién es? E2: Es de la Sra. Valdés.
2. E1: ¿Qué es? E2: Es un cuaderno. E1: ¿De quién es? E2: Es de Gregorio.
3. E1: ¿Qué es? E2: Es una computadora. E1: ¿De quién es? E2: Es de Rafael.
4. E1: ¿Qué es? E2: Es un diario. E1: ¿De quién es? E2: Es de Marisa.

 Practice more at vhlcentral.com.

EXPANSION

Video Replay the **Fotonovela**, having students focus on subject pronouns and the verb **ser**. Ask them to copy down as many examples of sentences that use forms of **ser** as they can. Stop the video where appropriate to ask comprehension questions on what the characters said.

DIFFERENTIATION

Heritage Speakers Encourage heritage speakers to describe themselves and their family briefly. Make sure they use the cognates **familia**, **mamá**, and **papá**. Call on students to report the information given. Ex: **Francisco es de la Florida. La mamá de Francisco es de España. Ella es profesora. El papá de Francisco es de Cuba. Él es dentista.**

Hola, ¿qué tal? veintitrés 23

Comunicación

4 Preguntas Using the items in the word bank, ask your partner questions about the ad. Be imaginative in your responses. Answers will vary.

¿Cuántas?   ¿De dónde?   ¿Qué?
¿Cuántos?   ¿De quién?   ¿Quién?

SOMOS ECOTURISTA, S.A.
Los autobuses oficiales de la Ruta Maya

- 25 autobuses en total
- 30 conductores del área
- pasajeros internacionales
- mapas de la región

¡Todos a bordo!

5 ¿Quién es? In small groups, take turns pretending to be a famous person from a Spanish-speaking country (such as Spain, Mexico, Puerto Rico, Cuba, or the United States). Use the list of professions to think of people from a variety of backgrounds. Your partners will ask you questions and try to guess who you are. Answers will vary.

actor	*actor*	cantante	*singer*	escritor(a)	*writer*
actriz	*actress*	deportista	*athlete*	músico/a	*musician*

modelo

Estudiante 3: ¿Eres de Puerto Rico?
Estudiante 1: No. Soy de Colombia.
Estudiante 2: ¿Eres hombre?
Estudiante 1: Sí. Soy hombre.
Estudiante 3: ¿Eres escritor?
Estudiante 1: No. Soy actor.
Estudiante 2: ¿Eres John Leguizamo?
Estudiante 1: ¡Sí! ¡Sí!

NOTA CULTURAL

John Leguizamo was born in Bogotá, Colombia. John is best known for his work as an actor and comedian. He has appeared in movies such as *Moulin Rouge*, *The Happening*, and *The Lincoln Lawyer*. Other Hispanic celebrities: Laura Esquivel (writer from Mexico), Andy García (actor from Cuba), and Don Omar (singer from Puerto Rico).

TEACHING OPTIONS

Small Groups Bring in personal photos or magazine pictures that show people. In small groups, have students invent stories about the people: who they are, where they are from, and what they do. Circulate around the room and assist with unfamiliar vocabulary as necessary, but encourage students to use terms they already know.

TEACHING OPTIONS

Game Hand out individual strips of paper with names of famous people on them. There should be several duplicates of each name. Then describe one of the famous people (**Es de ____. Es** [*profession*].), including cognate adjectives if you wish (**inteligente, pesimista**). The first person to stand and indicate that the name they have is the one you are describing (**¡Yo lo tengo!**) wins that round.

Communication 1.1
Comparisons 4.1

TELL Connection

Learning Experience 5
Why: Extend activities to real-world contexts to expand learning opportunities. *What:* Using the context in activity 4, ask: What would they be planning if they encountered this ad outside of class? Ask them to brainstorm questions they would want to ask. Have them use these ideas to prepare their questions and answers.

4 Teaching Tip If students ask, explain that the abbreviation **S.A.** in the ad stands for **Sociedad Anónima** and is equivalent to the English abbreviation *Inc.* (*Incorporated*).

4 Expansion Ask pairs to write four true/false statements about the ad. Call on volunteers to read their sentences aloud. The class will indicate whether the statements are true (**cierto**) or false (**falso**) and correct the false statements.

4 Partner Chat (Premium) You can also assign activity 4 on the Supersite.

5 Teaching Tips
- To simplify, have students brainstorm a list of names in the categories suggested.
- Have three students read the **modelo** aloud.

5 Expansion Have each group select a famous person and write a description of him or her. Brainstorm some useful cognate adjectives that students can use and tell them to be sure not to give the person's name in their descriptions. Then have groups take turns reading their descriptions aloud for the class to guess the person's identity. If guessing proves too difficult, allow the class to ask for a hint (**una pista**), such as a song or movie title.

Estructura 23

Section Goals

In **Estructura 1.4**, students will be introduced to:
- asking and telling time
- times of day

 Communication 1.1
Comparisons 4.1

Student Resources
Cuaderno de práctica y actividades comunicativas, pp. 16–20
Cuaderno para hispanohablantes, pp. 11–12
Supersite: Activities, *eCuaderno*

Teacher Resources
Workbook TE; Grammar Slides; Digital Image Bank; Audio Activities MP3s; Audio Script; Testing Program Quizzes; Activity Pack; Middle School Activity Pack

Teaching Tips
- To prepare students for telling time, review **es** and **son** and numbers 0–30.
- Use the **Lección 1** Grammar Presentation Slides to support this presentation.
- Introduce **es la una** and **son las dos (tres, cuatro…)**. Remind students that **las** in time constructions refers to **las horas**. Introduce **y cinco (diez, veinte…)**, **y quince/cuarto**, and **y treinta/media**.
- Draw three clocks on the board, each displaying a different time. Ask the class: **¿Qué hora es?** and have students identify the time for each one. Concentrate on this until students are relatively comfortable with expressing the time in Spanish.
- Introduce **menos diez (cuarto, veinte…)** and explain this method of telling time in Spanish. It typically takes students longer to master this aspect of telling time. Spend about five minutes with your moveable-hands clock and ask students to state the times shown.

1.4 Telling time  Tutorial

ANTE TODO In both English and Spanish, the verb *to be* (**ser**) and numbers are used to tell time.

▶ To ask what time it is, use **¿Qué hora es?** When telling time, use **es + la** with **una** and **son + las** with all other hours.

Es la una. **Son las** dos. **Son las** seis.

▶ As in English, you express time from the hour to the half hour in Spanish by adding minutes.

Son las cuatro **y cinco**. Son las once **y veinte**.

▶ You may use either **y cuarto** or **y quince** to express fifteen minutes or quarter past the hour. For thirty minutes or half past the hour, you may use either **y media** or **y treinta**.

Es la una **y cuarto**. Son las nueve **y quince**. Son las doce **y media**. Son las siete **y treinta**.

▶ You express time from the half hour to the hour in Spanish by subtracting minutes or a portion of an hour from the next hour.

Es la una **menos cuarto**. Son las tres **menos quince**. Son las ocho **menos veinte**. Son las tres **menos diez**.

EXPANSION

Extra Practice Draw a large clock face on the board with numbers but without hands. Say a time and ask a volunteer to come up to the board and draw the hands to indicate that time. The rest of the class verifies that their classmate has written the correct time. Continue until several volunteers have participated.

TEACHING OPTIONS

Pairs Tell the class **tengo** means *I have*. Have pairs take turns telling each other what time their classes are this semester/quarter. (Ex: **Tengo una clase a las…**) For each time given, the other student draws a clock face with the corresponding time. The first student verifies the time. To challenge students, give a list of course names (**las matemáticas, la biología,** etc.)

24 Teacher's Edition • Lesson One

Hola, ¿qué tal?

▶ To ask at what time a particular event takes place, use the phrase **¿A qué hora (...)?** To state at what time something takes place, use the construction **a la(s)** + *time*.

¿**A qué hora** es la clase de biología?
(At) what time is biology class?

La clase es **a las dos**.
The class is at two o'clock.

¿**A qué hora** es la fiesta?
(At) what time is the party?

A las ocho.
At eight.

▶ Here are some useful words and phrases associated with telling time.

Son las ocho **en punto**.
It's 8 o'clock on the dot/sharp.

Son las nueve **de la mañana**.
It's 9 a.m./in the morning.

Es **el mediodía**.
It's noon.

Son las cuatro y cuarto **de la tarde**.
It's 4:15 p.m./in the afternoon.

Es **la medianoche**.
It's midnight.

Son las diez y media **de la noche**.
It's 10:30 p.m./at night.

¡LENGUA VIVA!
Other useful expressions for telling time:
Son las doce (del día).
It is twelve o'clock (p.m.).
Son las doce (de la noche).
It is twelve o'clock (a.m.).

¿Qué hora es? — Son las cuatro menos diez.

¿Qué hora es? — Son las cuatro y veinticinco.

¡INTÉNTALO!

Practice telling time by completing these sentences. The first item has been done for you.

1. (1:00 a.m.) Es la ___una___ de la mañana.
2. (2:50 a.m.) Son las tres ___menos___ diez de la mañana.
3. (4:15 p.m.) Son las cuatro y ___cuarto/quince___ de la tarde.
4. (8:30 p.m.) Son las ocho y ___media/treinta___ de la noche.
5. (9:15 a.m.) Son las nueve y quince de la ___mañana___.
6. (12:00 p.m.) Es el ___mediodía___.
7. (6:00 a.m.) Son las seis de la ___mañana___.
8. (4:05 p.m.) Son las cuatro y cinco de la ___tarde___.
9. (12:00 a.m.) Es la ___medianoche___.
10. (3:45 a.m.) Son las cuatro menos ___cuarto/quince___ de la mañana.
11. (2:15 a.m.) Son las ___dos___ y cuarto de la mañana.
12. (1:25 p.m.) Es la una y ___veinticinco___ de la tarde.
13. (6:50 a.m.) Son las ___siete___ menos diez de la mañana.
14. (10:40 p.m.) Son las once menos veinte de la ___noche___.

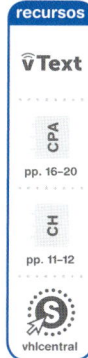

recursos
vText
CPA pp. 16–20
CH pp. 11–12
vhlcentral

Teaching Tips

- Review **¿Qué hora es?** and introduce **¿A qué hora?** and make sure students know the difference between them. Ask a few questions to contrast the constructions. Ex: **¿Qué hora es? ¿A qué hora es la clase de español?** Emphasize the difference between the questions by looking at your watch as you ask **¿Qué hora es?** and shrugging your shoulders with a quizzical look when asking **¿A qué hora es?**
- Go over **en punto, mediodía,** and **medianoche**. Explain that **medio/a** means *half*.
- Go over **de la mañana/tarde/noche**. Ask students what time it is now.
- You may wish to explain that Spanish speakers tend to view times of day differently than English speakers do. In many countries, only after someone has eaten lunch does one say **Buenas tardes**. Similarly, with the evening, Spanish speakers tend to view 6:00 and even 7:00 as **de la tarde**, not **de la noche**.

¡Lengua viva! Introduce the Spanish equivalents for noon (**las doce del día**) and midnight (**las doce de la noche**).

EXPANSION

Extra Practice Give half of the class slips of paper with clock faces depicting certain times. Give the corresponding times written out in Spanish to the other half of the class. Have students circulate around the room to match their times. To increase difficulty, include duplicates of each time with **de la mañana** or **de la tarde/noche** on the written-out times and a sun or a moon on the clock faces.

DIFFERENTIATION

Heritage Speakers Ask heritage speakers if they generally tell time as presented in the text or if they use different constructions. Some ways Hispanics use time constructions include (1) forgoing **menos** and using a number from 31–59 and (2) asking the question **¿Qué horas son?** Stress, however, that the constructions presented in the text are the ones students should focus on.

Práctica

1 Ordenar Put these times in order, from the earliest to the latest.

a. Son las dos de la tarde. 4
b. Son las once de la mañana. 2
c. Son las siete y media de la noche. 6
d. Son las seis menos cuarto de la tarde. 5
e. Son las dos menos diez de la tarde. 3
f. Son las ocho y veintidós de la mañana. 1

2 ¿Qué hora es? Give the times shown on each clock or watch.

modelo
Son las cuatro y cuarto/quince de la tarde.

p.m.   p.m.

1. Son las doce y media/treinta de la tarde.
2. Es la una de la mañana.
3. Son las cinco y cuarto/quince de la tarde.
4. Son las ocho y diez de la noche.
5. Son las siete y media/treinta de la mañana.

a.m.   a.m.   p.m.

6. Son las once menos cuarto/quince de la mañana.
7. Son las dos y doce de la tarde.
8. Son las siete y cinco de la mañana.
9. Son las cuatro menos cinco de la tarde.
10. Son las doce menos veinticinco de la noche.

3 ¿A qué hora? Ask your partner at what time these events take place. Your partner will answer according to the cues provided.

modelo
la clase de matemáticas (2:30 p.m.)
Estudiante 1: ¿A qué hora es la clase de matemáticas?
Estudiante 2: Es a las dos y media de la tarde.

1. el programa *Las cuatro amigas* (11:30 a.m.)
2. el drama *La casa de Bernarda Alba* (7:00 p.m.)
3. el programa *Las computadoras* (8:30 a.m.)
4. la clase de español (10:30 a.m.)
5. la clase de biología (9:40 a.m.)
6. la clase de historia (10:50 a.m.)
7. el partido (*game*) de béisbol (5:15 p.m.)
8. el partido de tenis (12:45 p.m.)
9. el partido de baloncesto (*basketball*) (7:45 p.m.)

1. E1: ¿A qué hora es el programa *Las cuatro amigas*?
   E2: Es a las once y media/treinta de la mañana.
2. E1: ¿A qué hora es el drama *La casa de Bernarda Alba*?
   E2: Es a las siete de la noche.
3. E1: ¿A qué hora es el programa *Las computadoras*?
   E2: Es a las ocho y media/treinta de la mañana.
4. E1: ¿A qué hora es la clase de español?
   E2: Es a las diez y media/treinta de la mañana.
5. E1: ¿A qué hora es la clase de biología?
   E2: Es a las diez menos veinte de la mañana.
6. E1: ¿A qué hora es la clase de historia?
   E2: Es a las once menos diez de la mañana.
7. E1: ¿A qué hora es el partido de béisbol?
   E2: Es a las cinco y cuarto/quince de la tarde.
8. E1: ¿A qué hora es el partido de tenis?
   E2: Es a la una menos cuarto/quince de la tarde.
9. E1: ¿A qué hora es el partido de baloncesto?
   E2: Es a las ocho menos cuarto/quince de la noche.

NOTA CULTURAL

Many Spanish-speaking countries use both the 12-hour clock and the 24-hour clock (that is, military time). The 24-hour clock is commonly used in written form on signs and schedules. For example, 1 p.m. is **13 h** or **13:00**, 2 p.m. is **14 h** or **14:00**, and so on. See the photo on p. 33 for a sample schedule.

NOTA CULTURAL

La casa de Bernarda Alba is a famous play by Spanish poet and playwright **Federico García Lorca** (1898–1936). Lorca was one of the most famous writers of the 20th century and a close friend of Spain's most talented artists, including the painter Salvador Dalí and the filmmaker Luis Buñuel.

Practice more at vhlcentral.com.

Comunicación

4 En la televisión With a partner, take turns asking questions about these television listings.

Answers will vary.

modelo
Estudiante 1: ¿A qué hora es el documental *Las computadoras*?
Estudiante 2: Es a las nueve en punto de la noche.

NOTA CULTURAL

Telenovelas are the Latin American version of soap operas, but they differ from North American soaps in many ways. Many **telenovelas** are prime-time shows enjoyed by a large segment of the population. They seldom run for more than one season and they are sometimes based on famous novels.

TV Hoy – Programación

11:00 am	Telenovela: *La casa de la familia Díaz*		5:00 pm	Telenovela: *Tres mujeres*
12:00 pm	Película: *El cóndor* (drama)		6:00 pm	Noticias
2:00 pm	Telenovela: *Dos mujeres y dos hombres*		7:00 pm	Especial musical: *Música folclórica de México*
3:00 pm	Programa juvenil: *Fiesta*		7:30 pm	La naturaleza: *Jardín secreto*
3:30 pm	Telenovela: *¡Sí, sí, sí!*		8:00 pm	Noticiero: *Veinticuatro horas*
4:00 pm	Telenovela: *El diario de la Sra. González*		9:00 pm	Documental: *Las computadoras*

5 Preguntas With a partner, answer these questions based on your own knowledge.

Some answers will vary.

1. Son las tres de la tarde en Nueva York. ¿Qué hora es en Los Ángeles?
   Es el mediodía./Son las doce.
2. Son las ocho y media en Chicago. ¿Qué hora es en Miami?
   Son las nueve y media.
3. Son las dos menos cinco en San Francisco. ¿Qué hora es en San Antonio?
   Son las cuatro menos cinco.
4. ¿A qué hora es el programa *Saturday Night Live*? ¿A qué hora es el programa *American Idol*?
   Es a las once y media/treinta. Es a las ocho de la noche.

6 Más preguntas Using the questions in the previous activity as a model, make up four questions of your own. Then get together with a classmate and take turns asking and answering each other's questions.

Answers will vary.

Síntesis

7 Situación With a partner, play the roles of a student on the school newspaper interviewing the new Spanish teacher (**profesor(a) de español**) from Venezuela. Be prepared to act out the conversation for your classmates. Answers will vary.

Estudiante	Profesor(a) de español
Ask the teacher his/her name.	→ Ask the student his/her name.
Ask the teacher what time his/her Spanish classes are.	→ Ask the student where he/she is from.
Ask how many students are in his/her classes.	→ Ask to whom the notebook belongs.
Say thank you and goodbye.	→ Say thank you and you are pleased to meet him/her.

TEACHING OPTIONS

Small Groups Have small groups prepare skits. Students can choose any situation they wish, provided that they use material presented in the **Contextos** and **Estructura** sections. Possible situations include: meeting to go on an excursion, meeting between classes, and introducing friends to teachers.

DIFFERENTIATION

Heritage Speakers Ask heritage speakers to describe popular shows that are currently featured on Spanish-language television, noting the type of show (**telenovela, reality**, etc.), the channel (**canal**), and time when they are shown. As a class, try to think of English-language versions or similar programs. Examples may include *American Idol, Big Brother, Dancing with the Stars*, and their respective Latin American counterparts.

Communication 1.1
Comparisons 4.1

4 Teaching Tip Before beginning the activity, have students scan the schedule for cognates and predict their meanings. Guide them in understanding the meanings of other programming categories: **película, programa juvenil, noticias/noticiero**.

4 Expansion Ask students what time popular TV programs are shown in the U.S. Ex: —¿A qué hora es el programa *Dancing with the Stars?* —Es a las ocho.

4 Virtual Chat (Premium) You can also assign activity 4 on the Supersite.

5 Teaching Tip Remind students that there are four time zones in the continental United States, and that when it is noon in the Eastern Time zone, it is 9 a.m. in the Pacific Time zone.

6 Expansion Have pairs give their two most challenging questions to another pair to see if they can stump them.

Communication 1.1

7 Partner Chat You can also assign activity 7 on the Supersite. Students work in pairs to record the activity online.

21st Century Skills

Productivity and Accountability Provide students with the oral testing rubric found in the Teacher Resources on the Supersite. Ask them to keep these strategies in mind as they prepare their oral exchanges.

Teaching Tip See the Communication Activities in the *Activity Pack* for an additional activity to practice the material presented in this section.

Recapitulación

Diagnostics

Review the grammar concepts you have learned in this lesson by completing these activities.

1 Completar Complete the charts according to the models. **28 pts.**

Masculino	Femenino
el chico	la chica
el profesor	la profesora
el amigo	la amiga
el señor	la señora
el pasajero	la pasajera
el estudiante	la estudiante
el turista	la turista
el joven	la joven

Singular	Plural
una cosa	unas cosas
un libro	unos libros
una clase	unas clases
una lección	unas lecciones
un conductor	unos conductores
un país	unos países
un lápiz	unos lápices
un problema	unos problemas

2 En la clase Complete each conversation with the correct word. **22 pts.**

 César  Beatriz

CÉSAR ¿(1) _Cuántas_ (Cuántos/Cuántas) chicas hay en la (2) _clase_ (maleta/clase)?
BEATRIZ Hay (3) _catorce_ (catorce/cuatro) [14] chicas.
CÉSAR Y, ¿(4) _cuántos_ (cuántos/cuántas) chicos hay?
BEATRIZ Hay (5) _trece_ (tres/trece) [13] chicos.
CÉSAR Entonces (*Then*), en total hay (6) _veintisiete_ (veintiséis/veintisiete) (7) _estudiantes_ (estudiantes/chicas) en la clase.

 Ariana  Daniel

ARIANA ¿Tienes (*Do you have*) (8) _un_ (un/una) diccionario?
DANIEL No, pero (*but*) aquí (9) _hay_ (es/hay) uno.
ARIANA ¿De quién (10) _es_ (son/es)?
DANIEL (11) _Es_ (Son/Es) de Carlos.

RESUMEN GRAMATICAL

1.1 Nouns and articles *pp. 12–14*

Gender of nouns

Nouns that refer to living things

	Masculine		Feminine
-o	el chico	-a	la chica
-or	el profesor	-ora	la profesora
-ista	el turista	-ista	la turista

Nouns that refer to non-living things

	Masculine		Feminine
-o	el libro	-a	la cosa
-ma	el programa	-ción	la lección
-s	el autobús	-dad	la nacionalidad

Plural of nouns

▶ ending in vowels + *-s*   la chica → las chicas
▶ ending in consonant + *-es*
   el señor → los señores
   (-z → -ces un lápiz → unos lápices)

Spanish articles

▶ Definite articles: **el, la, los, las**
▶ Indefinite articles: **un, una, unos, unas**

1.2 Numbers 0–30 *p. 16*

0	cero	8	ocho	16	dieciséis
1	uno	9	nueve	17	diecisiete
2	dos	10	diez	18	dieciocho
3	tres	11	once	19	diecinueve
4	cuatro	12	doce	20	veinte
5	cinco	13	trece	21	veintiuno
6	seis	14	catorce	22	veintidós
7	siete	15	quince	30	treinta

1.3 Present tense of *ser* *pp. 19–21*

yo	soy	nosotros/as	somos
tú	eres	vosotros/as	sois
Ud./él/ella	es	Uds./ellos/ellas	son

Hola, ¿qué tal? veintinueve 29

3 Presentaciones
Complete this conversation with the correct form of the verb **ser**. *12 pts.*

JUAN ¡Hola! Me llamo Juan. (1) __Soy__ estudiante en la clase de español.

DANIELA ¡Hola! Mucho gusto. Yo (2) __soy__ Daniela y ella (3) __es__ Mónica. ¿De dónde (4) __eres__ (tú), Juan?

JUAN De California. Y ustedes, ¿de dónde (5) __son__?

MÓNICA Nosotras (6) __somos__ de Florida.

1.4 Telling time pp. 24–25

Es la **una**.	It's 1:00.
Son las **dos**.	It's 2:00.
Son las tres **y diez**.	It's 3:10.
Es la una **y cuarto/ quince**.	It's 1:15.
Son las siete **y media/ treinta**.	It's 7:30.
Es la una **menos cuarto/quince**.	It's 12:45.
Son las once **menos veinte**.	It's 10:40.
Es **el mediodía**.	It's noon.
Es **la medianoche**.	It's midnight.

4 ¿Qué hora es?
Write out in words the following times, indicating whether it's morning, noon, afternoon, or night. *10 pts.*

1. It's 12:00 p.m.
   Es el mediodía./Son las doce del día.
2. It's 7:05 a.m.
   Son las siete y cinco de la mañana.
3. It's 9:35 p.m.
   Son las diez menos veinticinco de la noche.
4. It's 5:15 p.m.
   Son las cinco y cuarto/quince de la tarde.
5. It's 1:30 p.m.
   Es la una y media/treinta de la tarde.

5 ¡Hola!
Write five sentences introducing yourself and talking about your classes. You may want to include: your name, where you are from, who your Spanish teacher is, the time of your Spanish class, how many students are in the class, etc. *28 pts.* Answers will vary.

_____
_____
_____
_____

6 Canción
Write the missing words to complete this children's song. *4 EXTRA points!*

cinco   media
cuántas   quiénes
cuatro

" ¿ __Cuántas__ patas°
tiene un gato°?
Una, dos, tres y
__cuatro__ . "

patas *legs*   tiene un gato *does a cat have*

TEACHING OPTIONS

Game Have students make a five-column, five-row chart with B-I-N-G-O written across the top of the columns. Tell them to fill in the squares at random with different times of day. (Remind them to use only full, quarter, or half hours.) Draw times from a hat and call them out in Spanish. The first student to mark five in a row (horizontally, vertically, or diagonally) yells ¡Bingo! and wins.

PRE-AP*

Interpersonal Writing Have students imagine they have a new penpal in a Spanish-speaking country. Ask them to write a short e-mail in which they introduce themselves, state where they are from, and give information about their class schedule. (You may want to give students the verb form **tengo** and class subjects vocabulary.) Encourage them to finish the message with questions about their penpal.

---

3 Teaching Tip Before beginning the activity, orally review the conjugation of **ser**.

3 Expansion Ask questions about the characters in the dialogue. Ex: ¿Quién es Juan? (Juan es un estudiante en la clase de español.) ¿De dónde es? (Es de California.)

4 Teaching Tip Go over the answers with the class and point out that items 1, 4, and 5 may be written two ways.

4 Expansion To challenge students, give them these times as items 6–10:
6. It's 3:13 p.m.
7. It's 4:29 a.m.
8. It's 1:04 a.m.
9. It's 10:09 a.m.
10. It's 12:16 a.m.

4 Expansion Have students write down five additional times in Spanish. Then have them get together with a partner and take turns reading the times aloud. The partner will draw a clock showing the appropriate time, plus a sun or moon to indicate a.m. or p.m. Students should check each other's drawings to verify accuracy.

5 Expansion For further practice with **ser** and **hay**, ask students to share the time and size of their other classes. Be certain to list necessary vocabulary on the board, such as **matemáticas**, **ciencias**, **inglés**, and **historia**.

6 Teaching Tip Point out the word **Una** in line 3 of the song. To challenge students, have them work in pairs to come up with an explanation for why **Una** is used. (It refers to **pata** [una pata, dos patas...]).

Estructura 29

Section Goals

In **Lectura**, students will:
- learn to recognize cognates
- use prefixes and suffixes to recognize cognates
- read a telephone list rich in cognates

 Communication 1.1, 1.2, 1.3
Cultures 2.1, 2.2
Connections 3.1, 3.2
Comparisons 4.2

Student Resources
Cuaderno para hispanohablantes, pp. 13–14
Supersite: Activities

 **Pre-AP***

Interpretive Reading: Estrategia
Have students look at the cognates in the **Estrategia** box. Write some of the common suffix correspondences between Spanish and English on the board: **–ción/–sión** = *–tion/–sion* (**nación, decisión**); **–ante/–ente** = *–ant/–ent* (**importante, inteligente**); **–ia/–ía** = *–y* (**farmacia, sociología**); **–dad** = *–ty* (**oportunidad**).

The Affective Dimension
Tell students that reading in Spanish will be less anxiety-provoking if they follow the advice in the **Estrategia** sections, which are designed to reinforce and improve reading comprehension skills.

Examinar el texto Ask students to tell you what type of text **Teléfonos importantes** is and how they can tell. (It is a list and it contains names and telephone numbers.)

Cognados Ask students to mention any cognates they see in the phone list. Discuss them and explain any discrepancies with the list of suffixes given above. Ex: **policía** = *police*, not *policy*.

---

1 adelante

Lección 1

Lectura  Audio: Reading
Additional Reading

Antes de leer

Estrategia
Recognizing cognates

As you learned earlier in this lesson, cognates are words that share similar meanings and spellings in two or more languages. When reading in Spanish, it's helpful to look for cognates and use them to guess the meaning of what you're reading. But watch out for false cognates. For example, **librería** means *bookstore*, not *library*, and **embarazada** means *pregnant*, not *embarrassed*. Look at this list of Spanish words, paying special attention to prefixes and suffixes. Can you guess the meaning of each word?

importante	oportunidad
farmacia	cultura
inteligente	activo
dentista	sociología
decisión	espectacular
televisión	restaurante
médico	policía

Examinar el texto
Glance quickly at the reading selection and guess what type of document it is. Explain your answer.

Cognados
Read the document and make a list of the cognates you find. Guess their English equivalents, then compare your answers with those of a classmate.

Teléfonos importantes

Policía

Médico

Dentista

Pediatra

Farmacia

Banco Central

Aerolíneas Nacionales

Cine Metro

Hora/Temperatura

Profesora Salgado (escuela)

Papá (oficina)

Gimnasio Gente Activa

Restaurante Roma

Supermercado Famoso

Librería El Inteligente

DIFFERENTIATION

Heritage Speakers Ask heritage speakers to model reading and writing the numbers in **Teléfonos importantes**, and to discuss how digits are grouped and punctuated (periods instead of hyphens). For example, 732.5722 may be pronounced by a combination of tens (**siete, treinta y dos, cincuenta y siete, veintidós**) or hundreds and tens (**setecientos treinta y dos, cincuenta y siete, veintidós**).

EXPANSION

Extra Practice Write some Spanish words on the board and have students name the English cognate: **democracia, actor, eficiente, nacionalidad, diferencia, guitarrista, artista, doctora, dificultad, exploración**. Then write some words with less obvious cognates: **ciencias, población, número, signo, remedio**.

54.11.11	
54.36.92	
54.87.11	
53.14.57	
54.03.06	
54.90.83	
54.87.40	
53.45.96	
53.24.81	
54.15.33	
54.84.99	
54.36.04	
53.75.44	
54.77.23	
54.66.04	

Después de leer

¿Cierto o falso?

Indicate whether each statement is **cierto** or **falso**. Then correct the false statements.

1. There is a child in this household.
   Cierto.

2. To renew a prescription, you would dial 54.90.83.
   Falso. To renew a prescription you would dial 54.03.06.

3. If you wanted the exact time and information about the weather you'd dial 53.24.81.
   Cierto.

4. Papá probably works outdoors.
   Falso. Papá works in an office.

5. This household probably orders a lot of Chinese food.
   Falso. They probably order a lot of Italian food.

6. If you had a toothache, you would dial 54.87.11.
   Cierto.

7. You would dial 54.87.40 to make a flight reservation.
   Cierto.

8. To find out if a best-selling book were in stock, you would dial 54.66.04.
   Cierto.

9. If you needed information about aerobics classes, you would dial 54.15.33.
   Falso. If you needed information about aerobics classes, you would call Gimnasio Gente Activa at 54.36.04.

10. You would call **Cine Metro** to find out what time a movie starts.
    Cierto.

Números de teléfono

Make your own list of phone numbers like the one shown in this reading. Include emergency phone numbers as well as frequently called numbers. Use as many cognates from the reading as you can. **Answers will vary.**

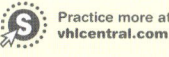
Practice more at vhlcentral.com.

¿Cierto o falso?
- Go over the activity orally as a class. If students have trouble inferring the answer to any question, help them identify the cognate or provide additional corresponding context clues.
- Ask students to work with a partner to use cognates and context clues to determine whether each statement is **cierto** or **falso**. Go over the answers as a class.

Números de teléfono
- As a class, brainstorm possible categories of phone numbers students may wish to include in their lists. Begin an idea map on the board or overhead transparency, jotting down the students' responses in Spanish. Explain unfamiliar vocabulary as necessary.
- You may wish to have students include e-mail addresses (**direcciones electrónicas**) in their lists.
- To add an auditory aspect to this exercise, have groups of three read aloud entries from their lists. The listeners should copy down the items that they hear. Have group members switch roles so each has a chance to read. Have groups compare and contrast their lists.

21st Century Skills

Creativity and Innovation
Ask students to prepare a presentation on the vital telephone numbers in your area, inspired by the information on these two pages.

EXPANSION

Variación léxica How a Spanish speaker answers the telephone may reveal their origin. A telephone call in Mexico is likely answered **¿Bueno?** In other parts of the Spanish-speaking world you may hear the greetings **Diga, Dígame, Oigo, ¿Sí?,** and **Aló**.

DIFFERENTIATION

Heritage Speakers Ask heritage speakers to share phone etiquette they may know, such as answering the phone or the equivalents of "Is ___ there?" (¿**Está** ___?), "Speaking" (**Soy yo.** or **Al habla.**), and identifying oneself, "This is ___." (**Te/Le habla** ___. or **Soy** ___.).

Section Goals

In **Escritura**, students will:
- learn to write a telephone/address list in Spanish
- integrate lesson vocabulary, including cognates and structures

 Communication 1.3

Student Resources
Cuaderno de práctica y actividades comunicativas, pp. 21–22
Cuaderno para hispanohablantes, pp. 15–16
Supersite: Activities, eCuaderno

Teacher Resources
Workbook TE

Pre-AP*

Interpersonal Writing: Estrategia
Go over the strategy as a class. Encourage students to give examples of how they will use the suggestions for this activity.

Tema Introduce students to standard headings used in a telephone/address list. They may wish to add notes pertaining to home (**número de casa**), cellular (**número de celular/móvil**), or office (**número de oficina**) phone numbers.

Spanish Characters in Word Processing

Macintosh
á Á, etc.	opt + e then a or A, etc.
ñ Ñ	opt + n then n or N
ü Ü	opt + u then u or U
¿	opt + shift + ?
¡	opt + !

PC (Windows)
á Á, etc.	ctrl + ' then a or A, etc.
ñ Ñ	ctrl + shift + ~ then n or N
ü Ü	ctrl + shift + : then u or U
¿	ctrl + alt + shift + ?
¡	ctrl + alt + shift + !

Escritura

Estrategia
Writing in Spanish

Why do we write? All writing has a purpose. For example, we may write an e-mail to share important information or compose an essay to persuade others to accept a point of view. Proficient writers are not born, however. Writing requires time, thought, effort, and a lot of practice. Here are some tips to help you write more effectively in Spanish.

DO
- Try to write your ideas in Spanish
- Use the grammar and vocabulary that you know
- Use your textbook for examples of style, format, and expression in Spanish
- Use your imagination and creativity
- Put yourself in your reader's place to determine if your writing is interesting

AVOID
- Translating your ideas from English to Spanish
- Simply repeating what is in the textbook or on a web page
- Using a dictionary until you have learned how to use foreign language dictionaries

recursos
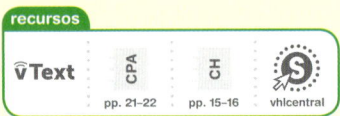

Tema

Hacer una lista

Create a telephone/address list that includes important names, numbers, and websites that will be helpful to you in your study of Spanish. Make whatever entries you can in Spanish without using a dictionary. You might want to include this information:

- The names, phone numbers, and e-mail addresses of at least four classmates
- Your teacher's name, e-mail address, and phone number
- Three phone numbers and e-mail addresses of locations related to your study of Spanish
- Five electronic resources for students of Spanish, such as sites dedicated to the study of Spanish as a second language

Nombre Sally
Teléfono 655-8888
Dirección electrónica sally@uru.edu

Nombre Profesor José Ramón Casas
Teléfono 655-8090
Dirección electrónica jrcasas@uru.edu

Nombre Biblioteca 655-7000
Dirección electrónica library@uru.edu

EVALUATION: Lista

Criteria	Scale
Content	1 2 3 4 5
Organization	1 2 3 4 5
Accuracy	1 2 3 4 5
Creativity	1 2 3 4 5

Scoring	
Excellent	18–20 points
Good	14–17 points
Satisfactory	10–13 points
Unsatisfactory	< 10 points

Hola, ¿qué tal?   treinta y tres   **33**

Escuchar  Audio

Estrategia
Listening for words you know

You can get the gist of a conversation by listening for words and phrases you already know.

🔊 To help you practice this strategy, listen to the following sentence and make a list of the words you have already learned.

Preparación

Based on the photograph, what do you think Dr. Cavazos and Srta. Martínez are talking about? How would you get the gist of their conversation, based on what you know about Spanish? *Answers will vary.*

Ahora escucha 🔊

Now you are going to hear Dr. Cavazos's conversation with Srta. Martínez. List the familiar words and phrases each person says. *Answers will vary.*

Dr. Cavazos	Srta. Martínez
1. _____	9. _____
2. _____	10. _____
3. _____	11. _____
4. _____	12. _____
5. _____	13. _____
6. _____	14. _____
7. _____	15. _____
8. _____	16. _____

With a classmate, use your lists of familiar words as a guide to come up with a summary of what happened in the conversation. *Answers will vary.*

recursos
vText vhlcentral

Comprensión

Identificar
Who would say the following things, Dr. Cavazos or Srta. Martínez?

1. Me llamo… *Dr. Cavazos*
2. De nada. *Srta. Martínez*
3. Gracias. Muchas gracias. *Dr. Cavazos*
4. Aquí tiene usted los documentos de viaje, señor. *Srta. Martínez*
5. Usted tiene tres maletas, ¿no? *Srta. Martínez*
6. Tengo dos maletas. *Dr. Cavazos*
7. Hola, señor. *Srta. Martínez*
8. ¿Viaja usted a Buenos Aires? *Srta. Martínez*

Contestar
1. Does this scene take place in the morning, afternoon, or evening? How do you know? *The scene takes place in the morning, as indicated by **Buenos días**.*
2. How many suitcases does Dr. Cavazos have? *two*
3. Using the words you already know to determine the context, what might the following words and expressions mean? *Answers will vary.*
   - boleto
   - pasaporte
   - un viaje de ida y vuelta
   - ¡Buen viaje!

Practice more at **vhlcentral.com**.

Script DR. CAVAZOS: Buenos días, señorita.
SRTA. MARTÍNEZ: Buenos días, señor. ¿En qué le puedo servir?
C: Yo soy el doctor Alejandro Cavazos. Voy a Quito. Aquí tiene mi boleto. Deseo facturar mis maletas.
M: ¿Alejandro Cavazos? ¿C-A-V-A-Z-O-S?
C: Sí, señorita.
M: ¿Un viaje de ida y vuelta a Quito?

C: Sí.
M: ¿Cuántas maletas tiene usted? ¿Tres?
C: Dos.
M: Bueno, aquí tiene usted su boleto.
C: Muchas gracias, señorita.
M: No hay de qué, doctor Cavazos. ¡Buen viaje!
C: Gracias. ¡Adiós!

Section Goals

In **En pantalla**, students will:
- read about advertising geared toward Hispanics in the United States
- watch a television commercial for MasterCard

 Communication 1.1, 1.2
Cultures 2.1, 2.2
Connections 3.2
Comparisons 4.2

Student Resources
Supersite: *En pantalla* video, Activities

Teacher Resources
Transcript & Translation

Anuncios para los latinos
To check comprehension, ask these questions: 1. By which year will Hispanic population double? (2050) 2. What are the two major Spanish-language TV stations? (**Univisión** and **Telemundo**) 3. Why are marketing campaigns targeting Spanish-speaking audiences? (Spending power of $1.7 trillion in 2017)

Antes de ver
Read through the **Vocabulario útil** with students. Assure students that they do not have to understand every word they hear in the video. Tell them to rely on visual clues, cognates, and the **Vocabulario útil**.

 **Pre-AP***

Audiovisual Interpretive Communication
Antes de ver strategy
Invite students to identify the key words in each entry in the **Vocabulario útil**. Then have them infer Spanish word order compared to that of English.

 **21st Century Skills**

Social and Cross-Cultural Skills
Have students write down two aspects of the ad that they identify as different from what they would expect in their daily life.

 Video: TV Clip

Preparación
Answer these questions in English. *Answers will vary.*
1. Name some foods your family buys at the supermarket.
2. What is something you consider precious that cannot be bought?

Anuncios para los latinos
Latinos form the fastest-growing minority group in the United States; Census Bureau projections show Hispanic populations doubling from 2015–2050, to 106 million. Viewership of the two major Spanish language TV stations, **Univisión** and **Telemundo**, has skyrocketed, sometimes surpassing that of the four major English-language networks. With Latino purchasing power estimated at $1.7 trillion for 2017, many companies have responded by adapting successful marketing campaigns to target a Spanish-speaking audience. Along with the change in language, there often come cultural adaptations important to Latino viewers.

Anuncio de **MasterCard**

Un domingo en familia…

Vocabulario útil

aperitivo	appetizer
carne en salsa	beef with sauce
copa de helado	cup of ice cream
no tiene precio	priceless
plato principal	main dish
postre	dessert
un domingo en familia	Sunday with the family

Comprensión
Complete the chart below based on what you see in the video.

aperitivo	salami	$8
plato principal	carne en salsa	$15
postre	copa de helado	$6

Conversación
Based on the video, discuss in English the following questions with a partner. *Answers will vary.*
1. In what ways do the food purchasing choices of this family differ from your own? In what ways are they alike?
2. How does the role of the pet in this video reflect that of your family or culture? How is it different?

Aplicación
With a partner, use a dictionary to prepare an ad in Spanish like that in the video. Present your ad to the class. How did your food choices vary from the ad? What was your "priceless" item? *Answers will vary.*

 Practice more at vhlcentral.com.

 recursos
vText
vhlcentral

DIFFERENTIATION

Heritage Speakers Ask heritage speakers to identify some products of their cultures that are seldom seen in the U.S., and explain their value and purpose. How do products vary from culture to culture? In which ways are they similar? Why are there such differences? For this activity, students may also access print and video ads from various Spanish-speaking cultures through the Internet.

EXPANSION

Culture Note The perception of pets (**animales domésticos** or **mascotas**) in Latin America has shifted in the last 20 years, particularly in upper-income households. Dogs and cats once held the status of guardians or were peripheral to the household; today they are increasingly considered members of the family.

Hola, ¿qué tal? treinta y cinco 35

Video: Flash cultura

Encuentros en la plaza

The **Plaza de Mayo** in Buenos Aires, Argentina, is perhaps best known as a place of political protest due to its weekly demonstrations. Despite this reputation, for many it is also a traditional **plaza**, a spot to escape from the hustle of city life. In warmer months, office workers from neighboring buildings flock to the plaza during lunch hour. **Plaza de Mayo** is also a favorite spot for families, couples, and friends to gather, stroll, or simply sit and chat. Tourists come year-round to take in the iconic surroundings: **Plaza de Mayo** is flanked by the rose-colored presidential palace (**Casa Rosada**), city hall (**municipalidad**), a colonial-era museum (**Cabildo**), and a spectacular cathedral (**Catedral Metropolitana**).

Vocabulario útil

abrazo	hug
¡Cuánto tiempo!	It's been a long time!
encuentro	encounter
plaza	city or town square
¡Qué bueno verte!	It's great to see you!
¡Qué suerte verlos!	How lucky to see you!

Preparación

Where do you and your friends usually meet? Are there public places where you get together? What activities do you take part in there? *Answers will vary.*

Identificar

Identify the person or people who make(s) each of these statements.

1. ¿Cómo están ustedes? d
2. ¡Qué bueno verte! b
3. Bien, ¿y vos? a
4. Hola. a, b, c, d
5. ¡Qué suerte verlos! d

a. Gonzalo
b. Mariana
c. Mark
d. Silvina

Today we are at the Plaza de Mayo.

People come to walk and get some fresh air...

And children come to play...

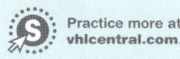

Practice more at vhlcentral.com.

Section Goal
In **Panorama**, students will read demographic and cultural information about Hispanics in the United States and Canada.

Communication 1.3
Cultures 2.1, 2.2
Connections 3.1, 3.2
Comparisons 4.2

Student Resources
Cuaderno de práctica y actividades comunicativas, pp. 25–28
Supersite: *Panorama cultural* video, Activities, *eCuaderno*

Teacher Resources
Workbook TE; Digital Image Bank; Video Script & Translation

Global Awareness
Students will gain perspectives on the Spanish-speaking world.

Teaching Tips
- Use **Lección 1 Panorama** Digital Image Bank to support this presentation.
- Have volunteers read aloud the labeled cities and geographic features.

El país en cifras Point out cognates and clarify unfamiliar words. Explain that numerals in Spanish have a comma where English would use a decimal point (**3,5%**) and a period where English would use a comma (**14.013.719**). Explain that **EE.UU.** is the abbreviation of **Estados Unidos**, and the doubling of the initials indicates plural. For perspective, give the populations for the five states: California, 37,253,956; Texas, 25,145,561; Florida, 18,801,310; New York, 19,378,102; Illinois, 12,830,632.

¡Increíble pero cierto! Tell students that they are not expected to produce numbers over 30 at this point.

---

1 panorama

Lección 1

Video: *Panorama cultural*
Interactive Map

Estados Unidos
El país en cifras°
- **Población° de los EE.UU.:** 317 millones
- **Población de origen hispano:** 51 millones
- **Lugar de origen de hispanos en los EE.UU.:**

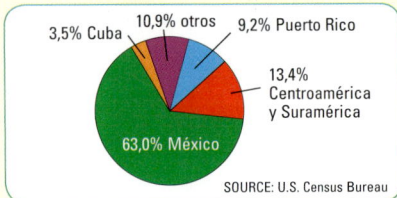

3,5% Cuba 10,9% otros 9,2% Puerto Rico
13,4% Centroamérica y Suramérica
63,0% México
SOURCE: U.S. Census Bureau

- **Estados con la mayor° población hispana:**

California 14.013.719
Texas 9.460.921
Florida 4.223.806
Nueva York 3.416.922
Illinois 2.027.578
SOURCE: U.S. Census Bureau

Canadá
El país en cifras
- **Población de Canadá:** 35 millones
- **Población de origen hispano:** 700.000
- **País de origen de hispanos en Canadá:**

12,4% México
11,6% Chile
67% otros
9% El Salvador

- **Ciudades° con la mayor población hispana:**
Montreal, Toronto, Vancouver

en cifras *by the numbers* Población *Population* mayor *largest*
Ciudades *Cities* creció *grew* más *more* cada *every* niños *children*
Se estima *It is estimated* va a ser *it is going to be*

¡Increíble pero cierto!
La población hispana en los EE.UU. creció° un 48% entre los años 2000 (dos mil) y 2011 (dos mil once) (16,7 millones de personas más°). Hoy, uno de cada° cinco niños° en los EE.UU. es de origen hispano. Se estima° que en el año 2034 va a ser° uno de cada tres.

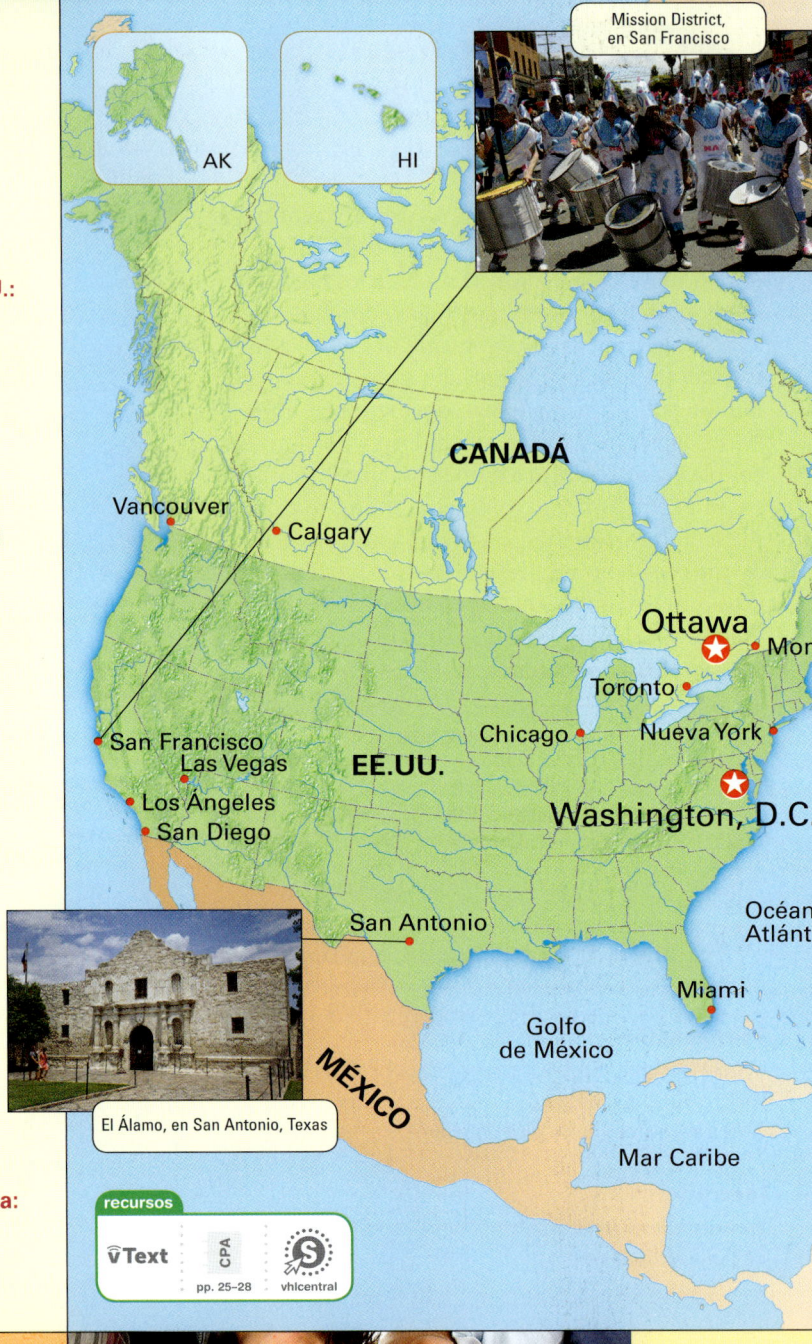

Mission District, en San Francisco

AK HI

CANADÁ
Vancouver Calgary
Ottawa Mont
Toronto
San Francisco Chicago Nueva York
Las Vegas
Los Ángeles EE.UU. Washington, D.C.
San Diego
San Antonio
Océano Atlántic
Miami
Golfo de México
MÉXICO
Mar Caribe

El Álamo, en San Antonio, Texas

recursos
vText CPA pp. 25–28 vhlcentral

DIFFERENTIATION
Heritage Speakers Ask heritage speakers to describe the celebrations that are held in their families' countries of origin. Ask them to tell the date when the celebration takes place, the event it commemorates, and some of the particulars of the celebration. Possible celebrations: **Cinco de Mayo, Día de la Raza, Día de los Muertos, Fiesta de San Juan, Carnaval.**

TEACHING OPTIONS
Game Divide the class into teams of five. Give teams five minutes to brainstorm place names (cities, states, lakes, rivers, mountain ranges) in the United States that have Spanish origins. One team member should jot down the names in a numbered list. After five minutes, go over the names with the class, confirming the accuracy of each name. The team with the greatest number wins.

Hola, ¿qué tal?

Comida • La comida mexicana
La comida° mexicana es muy popular en los Estados Unidos. Los tacos, las enchiladas, las quesadillas y los frijoles frecuentemente forman parte de las comidas de muchos norteamericanos. También° son populares las variaciones de la comida mexicana en los Estados Unidos: el tex-mex y el cali-mex.

Lugares • La Pequeña Habana
La Pequeña Habana° es un barrio° de Miami, Florida, donde viven° muchos cubanoamericanos. Es un lugar° donde se encuentran° las costumbres° de la cultura cubana, los aromas y sabores° de su comida y la música salsa. La Pequeña Habana es una parte de Cuba en los Estados Unidos.

Costumbres • Desfile puertorriqueño
Cada junio, desde° 1958 (mil novecientos cincuenta y ocho), los puertorriqueños celebran su cultura con un desfile° en Nueva York. Es un gran espectáculo con carrozas° y música salsa, merengue y hip-hop. Muchos espectadores llevan° la bandera° de Puerto Rico en su ropa° o pintada en la cara°.

Comunidad • Hispanos en Canadá
En Canadá viven° muchos hispanos. Toronto y Montreal son las ciudades° con mayor° población hispana. La mayoría de ellos tienen estudios universitarios° y hablan° una de las lenguas° oficiales: inglés o francés°. Los hispanos participan activamente en la vida cotidiana° y profesional de Canadá.

 ¿Qué aprendiste? Completa las oraciones con la información adecuada (*appropriate*).

1. Hay __51 millones__ de personas de origen hispano en los Estados Unidos.
2. Los cuatro estados con las poblaciones hispanas más grandes son (en orden) __California__, Texas, Florida y __Nueva York__.
3. Toronto, Montreal y __Vancouver__ son las ciudades con más población hispana de Canadá.
4. Las quesadillas y las enchiladas son platos (*dishes*) __mexicanos__.
5. La Pequeña __Habana__ es un barrio de Miami.
6. En Miami hay muchas personas de origen __cubano__.
7. Cada junio se celebra en Nueva York un gran desfile para personas de origen __puertorriqueño__.
8. Muchos hispanos en Canadá hablan __inglés__ o francés.

 Conexión Internet Investiga estos temas en **vhlcentral.com**.

1. Haz (*Make*) una lista de seis hispanos célebres de los EE.UU. o Canadá. Explica (*Explain*) por qué (*why*) son célebres.
2. Escoge (*Choose*) seis lugares en los Estados Unidos con nombres hispanos e investiga sobre el origen y el significado (*meaning*) de cada nombre.

 Practice more at **vhlcentral.com**.

comida *food* También *Also* La Pequeña Habana *Little Havana* barrio *neighborhood* viven *live* lugar *place* se encuentran *are found* costumbres *customs* sabores *flavors* Cada junio desde *Each June since* desfile *parade* con carrozas *with floats* llevan *wear* bandera *flag* ropa *clothing* cara *face* viven *live* ciudades *cities* mayor *most* tienen estudios universitarios *have a degree* hablan *speak* lenguas *languages* inglés o francés *English or French* vida cotidiana *daily life*

EXPANSION

Variación léxica Hispanic groups in the United States refer to themselves with various names. The most common of these terms, **hispano** and **latino**, refer to all people who come from Hispanic backgrounds, regardless of the country of origin of their ancestors. **Puertorriqueño**, **cubanoamericano**, and **mexicoamericano** refer to Hispanics whose ancestors came from Puerto Rico, Cuba, and Mexico, respectively. Many Mexican Americans also refer to themselves as **chicanos**. This word has stronger sociopolitical connotations than **mexicoamericano**. Use of the word **chicano** implies identification with Mexican Americans' struggle for civil rights and equal opportunity in the United States. It also suggests an appreciation of the indigenous aspects of Mexican and Mexican-American culture.

1 vocabulario 38

Student Resources
Cuaderno de práctica y actividades comunicativas, p. 18
Supersite: Activities, eCuaderno

Teacher Resources
Workbook TE; Textbook and Testing Audio MP3s; Testing Audio Script; Testing Program Tests

Teaching Tip Tell students that this is active vocabulary for which they are responsible and that it will appear on tests and exams.

21st Century Skills

Creativity and Innovation
Ask students to prepare a list of the three products or perspectives they learned about in this lesson to share with the class. You may ask them to focus specifically on the **Cultura** and **Panorama** sections.

21st Century Skills

Leadership and Responsibility Extension Project
Establish a partner classroom in a Spanish-speaking country. As a class, have students decide on three questions they want to ask the partner class related to the topic of the lesson they have just completed. Based on the responses they receive, work as a class to explain to the Spanish-speaking partners one aspect of their responses that surprised the class and why.

 My Vocabulary

Saludos
Hola.	Hello; Hi.
Buenos días.	Good morning.
Buenas tardes.	Good afternoon.
Buenas noches.	Good evening; Good night.

Despedidas
Adiós.	Goodbye.
Nos vemos.	See you.
Hasta luego.	See you later.
Hasta la vista.	See you later.
Hasta pronto.	See you soon.
Hasta mañana.	See you tomorrow.
Saludos a...	Greetings to...
Chau.	Bye.

¿Cómo está?
¿Cómo está usted?	How are you? (form.)
¿Cómo estás?	How are you? (fam.)
¿Qué hay de nuevo?	What's new?
¿Qué pasa?	What's happening?; What's going on?
¿Qué tal?	How are you?; How is it going?
(Muy) bien, gracias.	(Very) well, thanks.
Nada.	Nothing.
No muy bien.	Not very well.
Regular.	So-so; OK.

Expresiones de cortesía
Con permiso.	Pardon me; Excuse me.
De nada.	You're welcome.
Lo siento.	I'm sorry.
(Muchas) gracias.	Thank you (very much); Thanks (a lot).
No hay de qué.	You're welcome.
Perdón.	Pardon me; Excuse me.
por favor	please

Títulos
señor (Sr.); don	Mr.; sir
señora (Sra.); doña	Mrs.; ma'am
señorita (Srta.)	Miss

Presentaciones
¿Cómo se llama usted?	What's your name? (form.)
¿Cómo te llamas?	What's your name? (fam.)
Me llamo...	My name is...
¿Y usted?	And you? (form.)
¿Y tú?	And you? (fam.)
Mucho gusto.	Pleased to meet you.
El gusto es mío.	The pleasure is mine.
Encantado/a.	Delighted; Pleased to meet you.
Igualmente.	Likewise.
Éste/Ésta es...	This is...
Le presento a...	I would like to introduce you to (name). (form.)
Te presento a...	I would like to introduce you to (name). (fam.)
el nombre	name

¿De dónde es?
¿De dónde es usted?	Where are you from? (form.)
¿De dónde eres?	Where are you from? (fam.)
Soy de...	I'm from...

Palabras adicionales
¿cuánto(s)/a(s)?	how much/many?
¿de quién...?	whose...? (sing.)
¿de quiénes...?	whose...? (plural)
(no) hay	there is (not); there are (not)

Países
Argentina	Argentina
Canadá	Canada
Costa Rica	Costa Rica
Cuba	Cuba
Ecuador	Ecuador
España	Spain
Estados Unidos (EE.UU.)	United States
México	Mexico
Puerto Rico	Puerto Rico

Verbo
ser	to be

Sustantivos
el autobús	bus
la capital	capital city
el chico	boy
la chica	girl
la computadora	computer
la comunidad	community
el/la conductor(a)	driver
la conversación	conversation
la cosa	thing
el cuaderno	notebook
el día	day
el diario	diary
el diccionario	dictionary
la escuela	school
el/la estudiante	student
la foto(grafía)	photograph
el hombre	man
el/la joven	youth; young person
el lápiz	pencil
la lección	lesson
la maleta	suitcase
la mano	hand
el mapa	map
la mujer	woman
la nacionalidad	nationality
el número	number
el país	country
la palabra	word
el/la pasajero/a	passenger
el problema	problem
el/la profesor(a)	teacher
el programa	program
el/la turista	tourist
el video	video

Numbers 0–30	See page 16.
Telling time	See pages 24–25.
Expresiones útiles	See page 7.

recursos

vText | CPA p. 18 | vhlcentral

En la clase

2

Communicative Goals

I will be able to:
- Talk about my classes and school life
- Discuss everyday activities
- Ask questions in Spanish
- Describe the location of people and things

A PRIMERA VISTA
- ¿Hay dos chicas en la foto?
- ¿Hay una computadora o dos?
- ¿Son turistas o estudiantes?
- ¿Qué hora es, la una de la mañana o de la tarde?

contextos
pages 40–43
- The classroom and school life
- Days of the week
- Fields of study and school subjects
- Class schedules

fotonovela
pages 44–47
Felipe takes Marissa around Mexico City. Along the way, they meet some friends and discuss the upcoming semester.

cultura
pages 48–49
- Secondary school in the Spanish-speaking world
- The INFRAMEN

estructura
pages 50–67
- Present tense of -ar verbs
- Forming questions in Spanish
- Present tense of estar
- Numbers 31 and higher
- Recapitulación

adelante
pages 68–75
Lectura: A brochure for a summer course in Madrid
Escritura: A description of yourself
Escuchar: A conversation about courses
En pantalla
Flash cultura
Panorama: España

Lesson Goals

In **Lección 2**, students will be introduced to the following:
- classroom- and school-related words
- names of school courses and fields of study
- class schedules
- days of the week
- secondary school in Mexico
- the **INFRAMEN** (El Salvador)
- present tense of regular -ar verbs
- forming negative sentences
- the verb **gustar**
- forming questions
- the present tense of **estar**
- prepositions of location
- numbers 31 and higher
- using text formats to predict content
- brainstorming and organizing ideas for writing
- writing descriptions of themselves
- listening for cognates
- a television commercial for **Jumbo**, a Chilean superstore chain
- a video about the **Universidad Nacional Autónoma de México (UNAM)**
- cultural and geographic information about Spain

21st Century Skills

Initiative and Self-Direction
Students can monitor their progress online using the Supersite activities and assessments.

A primera vista Have students look at the photo. Say: **Es una foto de unos jóvenes.** Then ask: **¿Qué son los jóvenes? (Son estudiantes/amigos.) ¿Cuántas computadoras hay? (Hay una.)**

SUPPORT FOR BACKWARD DESIGN

Lección 2 Essential Questions
1. How do students talk about their classes and school life?
2. How do people ask and answer questions about their daily activities?
3. How is school in Latin America the same as and different from school in the U.S.?

Lección 2 Integrated Performance Assessment
Before teaching this chapter, review the Integrated Performance Assessment (IPA) and its accompanying scoring rubric provided in the Testing Program. Use the IPA to assess students' progress toward proficiency targets at the end of the chapter.
IPA Context: You and your classmates want to know about each others' class schedules and your opinions about the classes you take. First, you will interview one of your classmates to find out about his/her classes. Then you will present your own schedule to the class.

 Voice boards on the Supersite allow you and your students to record and share up to five minutes of audio. Use voice boards for presentations, oral assessments, discussions, directions, etc.

Section Goals

In **Contextos**, students will learn and practice:
- names for people, places, and things at school
- names of academic courses

 Communication 1.2
Comparisons 4.1

Student Resources
Cuaderno de práctica y actividades comunicativas, pp. 29–31
Cuaderno para hispanohablantes, pp. 17–18
Supersite: Activities, *eCuaderno*

Teacher Resources
Workbook TE; Digital Image Bank; Textbook and Audio Activities MP3s; Audio Scripts; Testing Program Quizzes; Activity Pack; Middle School Activity Pack

Teaching Tips
- Introduce vocabulary for classroom objects such as **mesa, libro, pluma, lápiz, papel**. Hold up or point to an object and say: **Es un lápiz.** Ask questions that include **¿Hay/No hay…?** and **¿Cuántos/as…?**
- Use the **Lección 2 Contextos** Digital Image Bank to support this presentation.
- Point to objects in the classroom and ask questions such as: **¿Qué es? ¿Es una mesa? ¿Es un reloj?** Vary by asking: **¿Qué hay en el escritorio? ¿Qué hay en la mesa? ¿Cuántas tizas hay en la pizarra? ¿Hay una pluma en el escritorio de ____?**

Successful Language Learning
Encourage students to make flash cards to help them memorize new vocabulary words.

---

2 contextos

Lección 2

En la clase

 My Vocabulary Tutorials

Más vocabulario

la biblioteca	library
la cafetería	cafeteria
la casa	house; home
el estadio	stadium
el laboratorio	laboratory
la librería	bookstore
la residencia estudiantil	dormitory
la universidad	university; college
el/la compañero/a de clase	classmate
el/la compañero/a de cuarto	roommate
la clase	class
el curso	course
la especialización	major
el examen	test; exam
el horario	schedule
la prueba	test; quiz
el semestre	semester
la tarea	homework
el trimestre	trimester; quarter
la administración de empresas	business administration
el arte	art
la biología	biology
las ciencias	sciences
la computación	computer science
la contabilidad	accounting
la economía	economics
el español	Spanish
la física	physics
la geografía	geography
la música	music

Variación léxica

pluma ↔ bolígrafo
pizarra ↔ tablero (*Col.*)

recursos
vText pp. 29–31
CPA pp. 17–18
CH
vhlcentral

Labels in illustration: el reloj, la ventana, la puerta, la profesora, el estudiante, la mesa, la calculadora, el libro, la pluma

---

DIFFERENTIATION

Heritage Speakers Ask heritage speakers to tell the class any other terms they or their families use to talk about people, places, or things at school. Ask them to tell where these terms are used. Possible responses: **el boli, el profe, el profesorado, la asignatura, el gimnasio, el pizarrón, el salón de clases, el aula, el pupitre, el gis, el alumno.**

TEACHING OPTIONS

Game Divide the class into two teams. Then, in English, name an academic course and ask one of the teams to provide the Spanish equivalent. If the team provides the correct term, it gets a point. If not, the second team gets a chance at the same item. Alternate between teams until you have read all the course names. The team with the most points at the end wins.

En la clase

cuarenta y uno 41

- el mapa
- la pizarra
- LAS MATERIAS / COURSES
  - la historia / history
  - las humanidades / humanities
  - el inglés / English
  - las lenguas extranjeras / foreign languages
  - la literatura / literature
  - las matemáticas / mathematics
  - el periodismo / journalism
  - la psicología / psychology
  - la química / chemistry
  - la sociología / sociology
- el papel
- el borrador
- la tiza
- la papelera
- el escritorio
- la mochila
- la estudiante
- la silla

Práctica

1 Escuchar Listen to Professor Morales talk about her Spanish classroom, then check the items she mentions.

puerta ✓	tiza ✓	plumas ✓
ventanas ✓	escritorios ✓	mochilas ○
pizarra ✓	sillas ○	papel ✓
borrador ○	libros ✓	reloj ✓

2 Identificar You will hear a series of words. Write each one in the appropriate category.

Personas	Lugares	Materias
el estudiante	el estadio	la química
la profesora	la biblioteca	las lenguas extranjeras
el compañero de clase	la residencia estudiantil	el inglés

3 Emparejar Match each question with its most logical response. ¡Ojo! (Careful!) One response will not be used.

1. ¿Qué clase es? d
2. ¿Quiénes son? g
3. ¿Quién es? e
4. ¿De dónde es? c
5. ¿A qué hora es la clase de inglés? f
6. ¿Cuántos estudiantes hay? a

a. Hay veinticinco.
b. Es un reloj.
c. Es de Perú.
d. Es la clase de química.
e. Es el señor Bastos.
f. Es a las nueve en punto.
g. Son los profesores.

4 Identificar Identify the word that does not belong in each group.

1. examen • casa • tarea • prueba casa
2. economía • matemáticas • biblioteca • contabilidad biblioteca
3. pizarra • tiza • borrador • librería librería
4. lápiz • cafetería • papel • calculadora cafetería
5. veinte • diez • pluma • treinta pluma
6. conductor • laboratorio • autobús • pasajero laboratorio

5 ¿Qué clase es? Name the class associated with the subject matter.

modelo
los elementos, los átomos   Es la clase de química.

1. Abraham Lincoln, Winston Churchill Es la clase de historia.
2. Picasso, Leonardo da Vinci Es la clase de arte.
3. Freud, Jung Es la clase de psicología.
4. África, el océano Pacífico Es la clase de geografía.
5. la cultura de España, verbos Es la clase de español.
6. Hemingway, Shakespeare Es la clase de literatura.
7. geometría, trigonometría Es la clase de matemáticas.

EXPANSION

Extra Practice Ask students what phrases or vocabulary words they associate with these items: **1. la pizarra** (Ex: **la tiza, el borrador**) **2. las ciencias** (Ex: **la biología, la física, la química, el laboratorio**) **3. el reloj** (Ex: **¿Qué hora es?, Son las…, Es la…**) **4. la biblioteca** (Ex: **los libros, los exámenes, las materias**)

EXPANSION

Extra Practice On the board, write **¿Qué clases tomas?** and **Tomo…** Explain the meaning of these phrases and ask students to circulate around the classroom and imagine that they are meeting their classmates for the first time. Tell them to introduce themselves, find out where each person is from, and ask what classes they are taking. Follow up by asking individual students what their classmates are taking.

 Communication 1.1

1 Expansion Have students circle the items that they see in their own classroom.

1 Script ¿Qué hay en mi clase de español? ¡Muchas cosas! Hay una puerta y cinco ventanas. Hay una pizarra con tiza. Hay muchos escritorios para los estudiantes. En los escritorios de los estudiantes hay libros y plumas. En la mesa de la profesora hay papel. Hay un mapa y un reloj en la clase también.
Teacher Resources DVD

2 Teaching Tip To simplify, have students prepare for listening by predicting a few words for each category.

2 Script el estudiante, la química, el estadio, las lenguas extranjeras, la profesora, la biblioteca, el inglés, el compañero de clase, la residencia estudiantil
Teacher Resources DVD

3 Expansion Have student pairs ask each other the questions and answer based on your class. Ex: **1. ¿Qué clase es? (Es la clase de español.)** For items 2–4, the questioner should indicate specific people in the classroom.

4 Expansion Have students write four additional items for a classmate to complete.

5 Expansion Have the class associate famous people with these fields: **periodismo, computación, humanidades.** Then have them guess the field associated with these people: Albert Einstein (**física**), Charles Darwin (**biología**).

TELL Connection

Environment 4
Why: A culture-rich environment encourages use of the target language. *What:* Use materials in your classroom to teach the vocabulary in **Contextos**.

Contextos 41

Teaching Tip Review the captions, explaining their meaning as you do so.

42   cuarenta y dos   Lección 2

Los días de la semana

¿Qué día es hoy (today)?
Hoy es martes.
¿Cuándo (When) es el examen?
Es el viernes.

septiembre

lunes	martes	miércoles	jueves	viernes	sábado	domingo
		1	2	3	4	5	6
7	8	9	10			

¡LENGUA VIVA!
The days of the week are never capitalized in Spanish.

Monday is usually considered the first day of the week in Spanish-speaking countries.

AYUDA
Note that September in Spanish is **septiembre**.

---

6 Expansion To challenge students, ask them questions such as: **Mañana es viernes… ¿qué día fue ayer? (miércoles); Ayer fue domingo… ¿qué día es mañana? (martes)**

6 **¿Qué día es hoy?** Complete each statement with the correct day of the week.

1. Hoy es martes. Mañana es __miércoles__. Ayer fue (*Yesterday was*) __lunes__.
2. Ayer fue sábado. Mañana es __lunes__. Hoy es __domingo__.
3. Mañana es viernes. Hoy es __jueves__. Ayer fue __miércoles__.
4. Ayer fue domingo. Hoy es __lunes__. Mañana es __martes__.
5. Hoy es jueves. Ayer fue __miércoles__. Mañana es __viernes__.
6. Mañana es lunes. Hoy es __domingo__. Ayer fue __sábado__.

7 Teaching Tip To simplify, before doing this activity, have students review the list of **sustantivos** on page 38 and numbers 0–30 on page 16.

7 **Analogías** Use these words to complete the analogies. Some words will not be used.

arte	día	martes	pizarra
biblioteca	domingo	matemáticas	profesor
catorce	estudiante	mujer	reloj

1. maleta ↔ pasajero ⊜ mochila ↔ __estudiante__
2. chico ↔ chica ⊜ hombre ↔ __mujer__
3. pluma ↔ papel ⊜ tiza ↔ __pizarra__
4. inglés ↔ lengua ⊜ miércoles ↔ __día__
5. papel ↔ cuaderno ⊜ libro ↔ __biblioteca__
6. quince ↔ dieciséis ⊜ lunes ↔ __martes__
7. Cervantes ↔ literatura ⊜ Dalí ↔ __arte__
8. autobús ↔ conductor ⊜ clase ↔ __profesor__
9. los EE.UU. ↔ mapa ⊜ hora ↔ __reloj__
10. veinte ↔ veintitrés ⊜ jueves ↔ __domingo__

 Practice more at vhlcentral.com.

EXPANSION

Extra Practice Have students prepare a day-planner for the upcoming week. Tell them to list each day of the week and the things they expect to do each day, including classes, homework, tests, appointments, and social events. Provide unfamiliar vocabulary as needed. Tell them to include the time each activity takes place. Have them exchange their day-planners with a partner and check each other's work for accuracy.

TEACHING OPTIONS

Game Have groups of five or six play a "word-chain" game in which the first group member says a word in Spanish (e.g., **estudiante**). The next student has to say a word that begins with the last letter of the first person's word (e.g., **español**). If a student cannot think of a word, he or she is eliminated and it is the next student's turn. The last student left in the game is the winner.

Comunicación

8 Horario Choose three classes from the chart to create your own class schedule, then discuss it with a classmate. *Answers will vary.*

materia	horas	días	profesor(a)
inglés	9:50	lunes, miércoles, viernes	Prof. Ordóñez
historia	9:00–10:30	martes, jueves	Profa. Dávila
biología	1:30–3:00	martes, jueves	Profa. Quiñones
matemáticas	2:10–3:00	lunes, miércoles, viernes	Prof. Jiménez
arte	10:40–12:10	jueves	Prof. Molina

modelo

Estudiante 1: Tomo (*I take*) historia los martes y jueves, de 9 a 10:30, con (*with*) la profesora Dávila.
Estudiante 2: ¿Sí? Yo no tomo historia. Yo tomo arte los jueves, de 10:40 a 12:10, con el profesor Molina.

¡ATENCIÓN!

Use **el** + [*day of the week*] when an activity occurs on a specific day and **los** + [*day of the week*] when an activity occurs regularly.
El lunes tengo un examen.
On Monday I have an exam.
Los lunes y miércoles tomo biología.
On Mondays and Wednesdays I take biology.
•••
Except for **sábados** and **domingos**, the singular and plural forms for days of the week are the same.

9 Memoria How well do you know your Spanish classroom? Take a good look around and then close your eyes. Your partner will ask you questions about the classroom, using these words and other vocabulary. Each person should answer six questions and switch roles every three questions. *Answers will vary.*

escritorio	mapa	pizarra	reloj
estudiante	mesa	profesor(a)	silla
libro	mochila	puerta	ventana

modelo

Estudiante 1: ¿Cuántas ventanas hay?
Estudiante 2: Hay cuatro ventanas.

10 Nuevos amigos During the first week of class, you meet a new student in the cafeteria. With a partner, prepare a conversation using these cues. Then act it out for the class. *Answers will vary.*

Estudiante 1	Estudiante 2
Greet your new acquaintance. →	Introduce yourself.
Find out about him or her. →	Tell him or her about yourself.
Ask about your partner's class schedule. →	Compare your schedule to your partner's.
Say nice to meet you and goodbye. →	Say nice to meet you and goodbye.

Section Goals

In **Fotonovela**, students will:
- receive comprehensible input from free-flowing discourse
- learn functional phrases that preview lesson grammatical structures

Communication 1.2
Cultures 2.1, 2.2

Student Resources
Cuaderno de práctica y actividades comunicativas, pp. 32–33
Supersite: *Fotonovela* video, Activities, *eCuaderno*

Teacher Resources
Workbook TE; Video Script & Translation

Video Recap: Lección 1
Before doing this **Fotonovela** section, review the previous episode with these questions:
1. En la familia Díaz, ¿quiénes son estudiantes? (Felipe y Jimena son estudiantes.)
2. ¿Quién es Roberto? (Es el esposo de Carolina.) 3. ¿De dónde es Marissa? (Es de Wisconsin.) 4. ¿De dónde es la señora Díaz? (Es de Cuba.)
5. ¿Es de Felipe el diccionario? (No, es de Marissa.)

Video Synopsis Felipe takes **Marissa** around Mexico City. Along the way, they meet some friends, **Juan Carlos** and **Miguel**. Felipe, Marissa, and **Juan Carlos** compare schedules for the upcoming semester, while **Miguel** rushes off to meet **Maru**.

Teaching Tip Hand out the **Antes de ver el video** and the **Mientras ves el video** activities from the *Cuaderno de práctica y actividades comunicativas* and go over the **Antes de ver** questions before starting the **Fotonovela**.

2 fotonovela
Lección 2

¿Qué estudias?

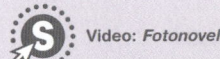

Felipe, Marissa, Juan Carlos y Miguel visitan Chapultepec y hablan de las clases.

Video: *Fotonovela*

PERSONAJES  MARISSA FELIPE

FELIPE Dos boletos, por favor.

EMPLEADO Dos boletos son 64 pesos.
FELIPE Aquí están 100 pesos.
EMPLEADO 100 menos 64 son 36 pesos de cambio.

FELIPE Ésta es la Ciudad de México.

FELIPE Juan Carlos, ¿quién enseña la clase de química este semestre?
JUAN CARLOS El profesor Morales. Ah, ¿por qué tomo química y computación?
FELIPE Porque te gusta la tarea.

FELIPE Los lunes y los miércoles, economía a las 2:30. Tú tomas computación los martes en la tarde, y química, a ver... Los lunes, los miércoles y los viernes ¿a las 10? ¡Uf!

FELIPE Y Miguel, ¿cuándo regresa?
JUAN CARLOS Hoy estudia con Maru.
MARISSA ¿Quién es Maru?

TEACHING OPTIONS

¿Qué estudias? Play the **¿Qué estudias?** episode of the **Fotonovela** and have students give you a "play-by-play" description of the action. Write their descriptions on the board. Give the class a moment to read the descriptions you have written and then play the episode a second time so that students can add more details to the descriptions or consolidate information. Finally, discuss the material on the board with the class and call attention to any incorrect information. Help students prepare a brief plot summary.

En la clase

JUAN CARLOS

MIGUEL

EMPLEADO

MARU

FELIPE Oye, Marissa, ¿cuántas clases tomas?

MARISSA Tomo cuatro clases: español, historia, literatura y también geografía. Me gusta mucho la cultura mexicana.

MIGUEL Marissa, hablas muy bien el español... ¿Y dónde está tu diccionario?

MARISSA En casa de los Díaz. Felipe necesita practicar inglés.

MIGUEL ¡Ay, Maru! Chicos, nos vemos más tarde.

MIGUEL ¿Hablas con tu mamá?

MARU Mamá habla. Yo escucho. Es la 1:30.

MIGUEL Ay, lo siento. Juan Carlos y Felipe...

MARU Ay, Felipe.

MARU Y ahora, ¿adónde? ¿A la biblioteca?

MIGUEL Sí, pero primero a la librería. Necesito comprar unos libros.

Expresiones útiles

Talking about classes
¿Cuántas clases tomas?
How many classes are you taking?
Tomo cuatro clases.
I'm taking four classes.
Mi especialización es en arqueología.
My major is archeology.
Este año, espero sacar buenas notas y, por supuesto, viajar por el país.
This year, I hope / I'm hoping to get good grades. And, of course, travel through the country.

Talking about likes/dislikes
Me gusta mucho la cultura mexicana.
I like Mexican culture a lot.
Me gustan las ciencias ambientales.
I like environmental science.
Me gusta dibujar.
I like to draw.
¿Te gusta este lugar?
Do you like this place?

Paying for tickets
Dos boletos, por favor.
Two tickets, please.
Dos boletos son sesenta y cuatro pesos.
Two tickets are sixty-four pesos.
Aquí están cien pesos.
Here's a hundred pesos.
Son treinta y seis pesos de cambio.
That's thirty-six pesos change.

Talking about location and direction
¿Dónde está tu diccionario?
Where is your dictionary?
Está en casa de los Díaz.
It's at the Díaz's house.
Y ahora, ¿adónde? ¿A la biblioteca?
And now, where to? To the library?
Sí, pero primero a la librería.
Está al lado.
Yes, but first to the bookstore. It's next door.

recursos
vText CPA
pp. 32–33 vhlcentral

Communication 1.1, 1.2

1 Teaching Tips
- Before doing this activity, review the names of courses, pages 40–41, and the days of the week, page 42.
- Alternatively, reformat this activity as a matching exercise, in which students match the name of the character with the corresponding information.

2 Expansion Give these statements to the class as items 7–10: **7. La cultura mexicana es interesante. (Marissa) 8. Mi diccionario está en la casa de Felipe. (Marissa) 9. Yo compro los boletos. (Felipe) 10. Necesito comprar unas cosas en la librería. (Miguel)**

3 Expansion Point out that one of the answers in the word bank will not be used. After students complete this activity, have them write a sentence that includes the unused item (**clase**).

Nota cultural The name **Chapultepec** derives from *Chapoltepēc*, which means "at the grasshopper hill" in Nahuatl. Covering 1,800 acres, **El Bosque de Chapultepec** consists of forest, lakes, and landscaped areas. It also houses a zoo, an amusement park, and **Los Pinos**, the official residence of the President of Mexico.

4 Expansion Ask volunteers to reenact their conversation for the class.

4 Virtual Chat You can also assign activity 4 on the Supersite. Students record individual responses that appear in your gradebook.

The Affective Dimension
If students appear anxious about speaking, reassure them that perfect pronunciation is not necessary for communication and that their pronunciation will improve with practice.

46 Teacher's Edition • Lesson Two

---

46 cuarenta y seis Lección 2

¿Qué pasó?

1 Escoger Choose the answer that best completes each sentence.

1. Marissa toma (*is taking*) ___c___ en la universidad.
   a. español, psicología, economía y música   b. historia, inglés, sociología y periodismo
   c. español, historia, literatura y geografía

2. El profesor Morales enseña (*teaches*) ___a___.
   a. química   b. matemáticas   c. historia

3. Juan Carlos toma química ___b___.
   a. los miércoles, jueves y viernes   b. los lunes, miércoles y viernes
   c. los lunes, martes y jueves

4. Miguel necesita ir a (*needs to go to*) ___c___.
   a. la biblioteca   b. la residencia estudiantil   c. la librería

2 Identificar Indicate which person would make each statement. The names may be used more than once.

1. ¿Maru es compañera de ustedes? ___Marissa___
2. Mi mamá habla mucho. ___Maru___
3. El profesor Morales enseña la clase de química este semestre. ___Juan Carlos___
4. Mi diccionario está en casa de Felipe y Jimena. ___Marissa___
5. Necesito estudiar con Maru. ___Miguel___
6. Yo tomo clase de computación los martes por la tarde. ___Juan Carlos___

MARU
JUAN CARLOS
MARISSA
MIGUEL

NOTA CULTURAL
Maru is a shortened version of the name **María Eugenia**. Other popular "combination names" in Spanish are **Juanjo (Juan José)** and **Maite (María Teresa)**.

3 Completar These sentences are similar to things said in the **Fotonovela**. Complete each sentence with the correct word(s).

| Castillo de Chapultepec | estudiar | miércoles |
| clase | inglés | tarea |

1. Marissa, éste es el ___Castillo de Chapultepec___.
2. Felipe tiene (*has*) el diccionario porque (*because*) necesita practicar ___inglés___.
3. A Juan Carlos le gusta mucho la ___tarea___.
4. Hay clase de economía los lunes y ___miércoles___.
5. Miguel está con Maru para ___estudiar___.

NOTA CULTURAL
The **Castillo de Chapultepec** is one of Mexico City's most historic landmarks. Constructed in 1785, it was the residence of emperors and presidents. It has been open to the public since 1944 and now houses the National Museum of History.

4 Preguntas personales Interview a classmate about his/her classes. *Answers will vary.*

1. ¿Cuántas clases tomas?
2. ¿Qué clases tomas los martes?
3. ¿Qué clases tomas los viernes?
4. ¿En qué clase hay más chicos?
5. ¿En qué clase hay más chicas?
6. ¿Te gusta la clase de español?

Practice more at vhlcentral.com.

TEACHING OPTIONS

Small Groups Have students work in small groups to create a skit in which a radio reporter asks local students where they are from, which classes they are taking, and which classes they like. Encourage students to use the phrases in **Expresiones útiles** as much as possible. Have one or two groups role-play their skit for the class.

EXPANSION

Extra Practice Have students close their books and complete these statements with information from the **Fotonovela**. You may slowly read aloud the sentences or write them on the board. Ex: **1. Tomo cuatro _____: español, historia, literatura y geografía. (clases) 2. Y Miguel, ¿cuándo _____? (regresa) 3. Dos _____ son 64 pesos. (boletos) 4. ¿Dónde _____ tu diccionario? (está)**

Pronunciación
Spanish vowels

a   **e**   **i**   **o**   **u**

Spanish vowels are never silent; they are always pronounced in a short, crisp way without the glide sounds used in English.

| Álex | clase | nada | encantada |

The letter **a** is pronounced like the *a* in *father*, but shorter.

| el | ene | mesa | elefante |

The letter **e** is pronounced like the *e* in *they*, but shorter.

| Inés | chica | tiza | señorita |

The letter **i** sounds like the *ee* in *beet*, but shorter.

| hola | con | libro | don Francisco |

The letter **o** is pronounced like the *o* in *tone*, but shorter.

| uno | regular | saludos | gusto |

The letter **u** sounds like the *oo* in *room*, but shorter.

Práctica Practice the vowels by saying the names of these places in Spain.
1. Madrid
2. Alicante
3. Tenerife
4. Toledo
5. Barcelona
6. Granada
7. Burgos
8. La Coruña

Oraciones Read the sentences aloud, focusing on the vowels.
1. Hola. Me llamo Ramiro Morgado.
2. Estudio arte en la Universidad de Salamanca.
3. Tomo también literatura y contabilidad.
4. Ay, tengo clase en cinco minutos. ¡Nos vemos!

Refranes Practice the vowels by reading these sayings aloud.

Del dicho al hecho hay un gran trecho.¹

Cada loco con su tema.²

¹ Easier said than done. ² To each his own.

AYUDA

Although **hay** and **ay** are pronounced identically, they do not have the same meaning. As you learned in **Lección 1**, **hay** is a verb form that means *there is/are*. **Hay veinte libros.** (*There are twenty books.*) **¡Ay!** is an exclamation expressing pain, shock, or affliction: *Ouch!; Oh, my!*

Section Goals

In **Cultura**, students will:
- learn how Mexican students choose their program of study to determine their career or university-level studies
- learn school-related terms
- read about the **Instituto Nacional Francisco Menéndez**
- read about Latin American school systems

Communication 1.1, 1.2
Cultures 2.1, 2.2
Connections 3.1, 3.2
Comparisons 4.2

Student Resources
Cuaderno para hispanohablantes, p. 20
Supersite: Activities

Global Awareness
Students will gain perspectives on the Spanish-speaking world to develop respect and openness to others.

En detalle

Antes de leer Ask students about how they choose their classes. Who or what influences their choices?

Lectura
- Explain that students often choose their high school based on its programs.
- In Mexico, **preparatoria** is optional, but all students are legally required to finish **escuela secundaria**.

Después de leer Ask students what they think of the Mexican school system and how it differs from that of the U.S.

1 Expansion Give students these sentences as items 9–10: 9. Students in Mexico take courses in foreign languages every year. (**Cierto**.) 10. Students enrolled in **Ciencias Biológicas** are not expected to continue studying. (**Falso**.)

cultura

Lección 2

EN DETALLE

Additional Reading

La escuela secundaria

Manuel, a 15-year-old student in Mexico, is taking an intense third level course focused on **la química**. This is a typical part of the studies for his grade. **Escuela secundaria** (*secondary school*), which in Mexico begins after six years of **escuela primaria** (*primary school*), has three grades for students between the ages of 12 and 15.

Students like Manuel must study courses in mathematics, science, Spanish, foreign languages (English or French), music, and more every year. After that, students choose a **plan de estudio** (*program of study*) in **preparatoria**, the three years (or two, depending on the program) of school after

escuela secundaria and before university studies. The program of study that students choose requires them to study specific **materias** that are needed in preparation for their future career.

Some **bachilleratos** (*high school degrees*) are **terminales**, which means that when students graduate they are prepared with all of the skills and requirements to begin their field of work.

These students are not expected to continue studying. Some **modalidades** (*programs of study*) that are terminal include:
- **Educación Tecnológica Agropecuaria** (*Agriculture and Fishing*)
- **Comercio y Administración** (*Commerce, for administrative work*)

Other programs are designed for students who plan to continue their studies in a **carrera universitaria** (*college major*). Some programs that prepare students for university studies are:
- **Ciencias Biológicas**
- **Ciencias Contables, Económicas y Bancarias** (*Economic and Banking Sciences*)
- **Música y Arte**

Each program has courses that are designed for a specific career. This means that although all high school students may take a mathematics course, the type of mathematics studied varies according to the needs of each degree.

La escuela y la universidad
Some Mexican high schools are designed and managed by universities as well as by the Secretary of Education. One university that directs such schools is the **Universidad Nacional Autónoma de México (UNAM)**, Mexico's largest university.

ACTIVIDADES

1 ¿Cierto o falso? Indicate whether each statement is **cierto** or **falso**. Correct the false statements.

1. High schools are specialized in certain areas of study. **Cierto**.
2. Students in Mexico cannot study art in school. **Falso. Música y arte is a preparatoria program of study.**
3. Students do not need to complete primary school before going to **escuela secundaria**. **Falso. Students must complete primary school as a prerequisite for escuela secundaria.**
4. The length of high school **planes de estudio** in Mexico varies between two and three years. **Cierto**.
5. Students need to go to college to study to do administrative work. **Falso. Comercio y Administración is a terminal program of study.**
6. All students must take the same mathematics courses at the high school level. **Falso. Mathematics courses differ depending on the program of study a student follows.**
7. **La escuela secundaria** is for students from the ages of 16 to 18 years old. **Falso. Escuela secundaria primarily serves students who are 12 to 15 years old, followed by the preparatoria.**
8. All students in Mexico complete university studies. **Falso. Some students do not study beyond preparatoria.**

TEACHING OPTIONS

Small Groups In groups of three, have students discuss their favorite course in which they are currently enrolled. Ask them to write several sentences in Spanish about why they like the course and whether or not it is a **curso electivo** (*elective*).

PRE-AP*

Presentational Speaking with Cultural Comparison Ask student pairs to decide whether or not they would prefer to study in a school program similar to Manuel's program in Mexico. Ask them to explain their choice based on the aspects included in the reading, such as programs of study, courses offered, and future plans. Tally their choices and make a bar graph of the results to hang in the classroom.

En la clase

ASÍ SE DICE
Clases y exámenes

aprobar	to pass
el colegio/la escuela	school
la escuela secundaria/ la preparatoria (Méx.)/ el liceo (Ven.)/ el instituto (Esp.)	high school
el examen parcial	midterm exam
el horario	schedule
la matrícula	inscription (to school)
reprobar	to fail
sacar buenas/ malas notas	to get good/ bad grades

EL MUNDO HISPANO
La escuela en Latinoamérica

- **In Latin America**, public secondary schools are free of charge. Private schools, however, can be quite costly. At **la Escuela Campo Alegre** in Venezuela, annual tuition is about $25,000 a year.
- **Argentina** and **Chile** are the two Latin American countries with the most years of required schooling at 13 years each.
- **In Chile**, students begin the school year in March and finish in December. Of course—Chile lies south of the equator, so while it is winter in the United States, Chilean students are on their summer break!

PERFIL
El INFRAMEN

La ciudad de San Salvador

The **Instituto Nacional Francisco Menéndez (INFRAMEN)** is the largest public high school in El Salvador. So it should be: it is named after General Francisco Menéndez, an ex-president of the country who was the founder of **enseñanza secundaria** (*secondary studies*) for the entire country! The 1,900 students at the INFRAMEN can choose to complete one of four kinds of diplomas: general studies, health care, tourism, and business. The institution has changed locales (and even cities) many times since it was founded in 1885 and is currently located in the capital city of San Salvador. Students at the INFRAMEN begin their school year in mid January and finish in early November.

Conexión Internet

How do dress codes vary in schools across Latin America?

Go to **vhlcentral.com** to find more cultural information related to this **Cultura** section.

ACTIVIDADES

2 Comprensión Complete these sentences.
1. The INFRAMEN was founded in ___1885___.
2. The programs of study available in the INFRAMEN are _general studies, health care, tourism, and business_.
3. There are ___1,900___ students in the INFRAMEN.
4. General Francisco Menéndez was a ___president___ of El Salvador.
5. El ___horario___ is a student's schedule.

3 ¡A estudiar! All students have classes they like and classes they don't. What are your favorite classes? Which are your least favorite? With a partner, discuss what you like and don't like about your classes and make a short list of what could be done to improve the classes you don't like.
Answers will vary.

Practice more at **vhlcentral.com**.

EXPANSION

Extra Practice Ask students to reread **En detalle, El mundo hispano,** and **Perfil** and choose in which country they would like to study if they were to be an exchange student for a year of high school. Ask them to write a paragraph explaining their choice.

TEACHING OPTIONS

Game Play a game of Hangman. Begin by choosing a word from the **Así se dice** list and draw a space for each letter on the board. Draw a noose above the spaces. Then ask students to guess letters. Write each correct letter in its corresponding space and each incorrect letter next to the noose. For each incorrect letter, draw a part of the body hanging from the noose. In order to win, students must guess the word before the body is complete.

Así se dice
- Model the pronunciation and have students repeat.
- Additional words include **el calendario escolar** (*school calendar*), **el desarrollo** (*development*), **la destreza** (*skill*).
- Practice simple sentences using the terms.

Perfil Many graduates of the **INFRAMEN** go on to complete university studies and post-graduate degrees. **Dr. Alberto Chiquillo Alas,** who serves on the board of directors of the **Comisión de Acreditación de la Calidad de la Educación Superior** (*Accrediting Commission of Higher Education* in El Salvador), graduated from the **INFRAMEN** as **Primer Bachiller de la República,** or valedictorian of the entire nation!

El mundo hispano Have students compare and contrast the information with data about similar topics in the U.S. education system. Ask students where they would attend college in the U.S. if all universities were free.

21st Century Skills

Information and Media Literacy: Conexión Internet Students access and critically evaluate information from the Internet.

2 Expansion For additional practice, give students these items: 6. In Chile and Argentina, students have to complete _____ years of school. (13) 7. Seasons in Chile are opposite those in the U.S. because it is south of the _____. (equator)

3 Expansion Have students work in pairs to design a poster inviting other students to take Spanish classes at their school. Tell students to make the poster visually enticing, using the vocabulary they have studied in class.

Section Goals

In **Estructura 2.1**, students will learn:
- the present tense of regular -ar verbs
- the formation of negative sentences
- the verb **gustar**

 Communication 1.1
Comparisons 4.1

Student Resources
Cuaderno de práctica y actividades comunicativas, pp. 35–37
Cuaderno para hispanohablantes, pp. 21–22
Supersite: Activities, *eCuaderno*

Teacher Resources
Workbook TE; Grammar Slides; Audio Activities MP3s; Audio Script; Testing Program Quizzes; Activity Pack; Middle School Activity Pack

Teaching Tips
- Check students' progress through comprehensible input. Point out that students have been using verbs and verb constructions from the start: **¿Cómo te llamas?**, **hay**, **ser**, and so forth. Ask a student: **¿Qué clases tomas?** Model student answer as **Yo tomo…** Then ask another student: **¿Qué clases toma ____? ____ toma ____.**
- Explain that, because the verb endings indicate the person speaking or spoken about, subject pronouns are usually optional in Spanish.
- Remind students that **vosotros/as** forms will not be practiced actively in **DESCUBRE**.
- Model the pronunciation of each infinitive and have students repeat it after you.

---

2 estructura

Lección 2

2.1 Present tense of -ar verbs

 Tutorial

ANTE TODO In order to talk about activities, you need to use verbs. Verbs express actions or states of being. In English and Spanish, the infinitive is the base form of the verb. In English, the infinitive is preceded by the word *to*: *to study, to be*. The infinitive in Spanish is a one-word form and can be recognized by its endings: **-ar**, **-er**, or **-ir**.

-ar verb	**-er verb**	**-ir verb**
estudiar | *to study*	comer | *to eat*	escribir | *to write*

▶ In this lesson, you will learn the forms of regular **-ar** verbs.

The verb estudiar (*to study*)

SINGULAR FORMS	yo	estudi**o**	*I study*
	tú	estudi**as**	*you* (fam.) *study*
	Ud./él/ella	estudi**a**	*you* (form.) *study; he/she studies*
PLURAL FORMS	nosotros/as	estudi**amos**	*we study*
	vosotros/as	estudi**áis**	*you* (fam.) *study*
	Uds./ellos/ellas	estudi**an**	*you* (form.) *study; they study*

Juan Carlos estudia ciencias ambientales.

Y tú, ¿qué estudias, Miguel?

▶ To create the forms of most regular verbs in Spanish, drop the infinitive endings (**-ar, -er, -ir**). You then add to the stem the endings that correspond to the different subject pronouns. This diagram will help you visualize the process by which verb forms are created.

Conjugation of -ar verbs

INFINITIVE	VERB STEM	CONJUGATED FORM
estudi**ar**	estudi-	yo estudi**o**
bail**ar**	bail-	tú bail**as**
trabaj**ar**	trabaj-	nosotros trabaj**amos**

EXPANSION

Extra Practice Do a pattern practice drill. Write an infinitive from the list of common **-ar** verbs on page 51 on the board and ask individual students to provide conjugations for the subject pronouns and names you suggest. Reverse the activity by saying a conjugated form and asking students to give the corresponding subject pronoun. Allow multiple answers for the third-person singular and plural.

EXPANSION

Extra Practice Ask questions, using **estudiar, bailar,** and **trabajar**. Students should answer in complete sentences. Ask additional questions to get more information. Ex: —____, ¿trabajas? —Sí, trabajo. —¿Dónde trabajas? —Trabajo en ____. • —¿Quién baila los sábados? —Yo bailo los sábados. —¿Bailas merengue? • —¿Estudian mucho ustedes? —¿Quién estudia más? —¿Cuántas horas estudias los lunes? ¿Y los sábados?

50 Teacher's Edition • Lesson Two

En la clase   cincuenta y uno   **51**

Common -ar verbs

bailar	to dance	estudiar	to study
buscar	to look for	explicar	to explain
caminar	to walk	hablar	to talk; to speak
cantar	to sing	llegar	to arrive
cenar	to have dinner	llevar	to carry
comprar	to buy	mirar	to look (at); to watch
contestar	to answer	necesitar (+ *inf.*)	to need
conversar	to converse, to chat	practicar	to practice
desayunar	to have breakfast	preguntar	to ask (a question)
descansar	to rest	preparar	to prepare
desear (+ *inf.*)	to desire; to wish	regresar	to return
dibujar	to draw	terminar	to end; to finish
enseñar	to teach	tomar	to take; to drink
escuchar	to listen (to)	trabajar	to work
esperar (+ *inf.*)	to wait (for); to hope	viajar	to travel

▶ **¡Atención!** Unless referring to a person, the Spanish verbs **buscar, escuchar, esperar,** and **mirar** do not need to be followed by prepositions as do their English equivalents.

Busco la tarea.
I'm looking for the homework.

Espero el autobús.
I'm waiting for the bus.

Escucho la música.
I'm listening to the music.

Miro la pizarra.
I'm looking at the blackboard.

COMPARE & CONTRAST

English uses three sets of forms to talk about the present: (1) the simple present (*Paco works*), (2) the present progressive (*Paco is working*), and (3) the emphatic present (*Paco does work*). In Spanish, the simple present can be used in all three cases.

Paco **trabaja** en la cafetería.
1. Paco *works* in the cafeteria.
2. Paco *is working* in the cafeteria.
3. Paco *does work* in the cafeteria.

In Spanish, the present tense is also sometimes used to express future action.

Marina **viaja** a Madrid mañana.
1. Marina *travels* to Madrid tomorrow.
2. Marina *will travel* to Madrid tomorrow.
3. Marina *is traveling* to Madrid tomorrow.

▶ When two verbs are used together with no change of subject, the second verb is generally in the infinitive. To make a sentence negative in Spanish, the word **no** is placed before the conjugated verb. In this case, **no** means *not*.

Deseo hablar con el señor Díaz.
I want to speak with Mr. Díaz.

Alicia **no** desea bailar ahora.
Alicia doesn't want to dance now.

Teaching Tips

- Model clarification/contrast sentences. Ask several students: **¿Dónde desayunas?** Then, pointing to two students who answered differently, ask the class: **¿Dónde desayunan? (Él desayuna en la cafetería y ella desayuna en casa.)** Then show how to use subject pronouns to give emphasis. Ex: —____, ¿te gusta bailar? —No, no me gusta bailar. —____ no baila. Yo bailo.
- Point out the position of subjects and subject pronouns with regard to the verbs in affirmative and negative sentences.
- Stress that subject pronouns (**yo, tú**...) are never used with **gustar**. They appear in the grammar explanation only for guidance.
- Point out that, just as subject pronouns can be used for clarification or emphasis, students should use the prepositional phrases **a mí, a ti**, etc., with the verb **gustar** to clarify or give emphasis. Also, point out the written accent on **mí** and the lack of an accent on **ti**.
- Point out that, even when two or more infinitives are used, the form remains singular: **gusta**.
- Divide the board or an overhead transparency into two columns. On the left side, list the indirect object pronouns (**me, te**...). On the right side, provide a mix of infinitives and plural and singular nouns, and have students supply **gusta** or **gustan** for each one. Then call on volunteers to combine elements from each column to form sentences. Emphasize that there are no impossible combinations.
- Write the headings **Les gusta** and **No les gusta** on the board. Have the class brainstorm likes and dislikes among the students at your school, including classes, pastimes, music, and movies. Use the lists to form statements and questions.

Spanish speakers often omit subject pronouns because the verb endings indicate who the subject is. In Spanish, subject pronouns are used for emphasis, clarification, or contrast.

—¿Qué enseñan?
What do they teach?

—**Ella** enseña arte y **él** enseña física.
She teaches art, and he teaches physics.

—¿Quién desea trabajar hoy?
Who wants to work today?

—**Yo** no deseo trabajar hoy.
I don't want to work today.

The verb gustar

Gustar is different from other **-ar** verbs. To express your likes and dislikes, use the expression **(no) me gusta** + **el/la** + [*singular noun*] or **(no) me gustan** + **los/las** + [*plural noun*]. Note: You may use the phrase **a mí** for emphasis, but never the subject pronoun **yo**.

Me gusta la música clásica.
I like classical music.

Me gustan las clases de español y biología.
I like Spanish and biology classes.

A mí me gustan las artes.
I like the arts.

A mí no me gusta el programa.
I don't like the program.

To talk about what you like and don't like to do, use **(no) me gusta** + [*infinitive(s)*]. Note that the singular **gusta** is always used, even with more than one infinitive.

No me gusta viajar en autobús.
I don't like to travel by bus.

Me gusta cantar y **bailar.**
I like to sing and dance.

To ask a classmate about likes and dislikes, use the pronoun **te** instead of **me**. Note: You may use **a ti** for emphasis, but never the subject pronoun **tú**.

—¿**Te gusta la geografía**?
Do you like geography?

—Sí, me gusta. Y a ti, ¿te gusta el inglés?
Yes, I like it. And you, do you like English?

You can use this same structure to talk about other people by using the pronouns **nos**, **le**, and **les**. Unless your instructor tells you otherwise, only the **me** and **te** forms will appear on test materials until **Lección 7**.

Nos gusta dibujar. (nosotros)
We like to draw.

Nos gustan las clases de español e inglés. (nosotros)
We like Spanish class and English class.

No le gusta trabajar. (usted, él, ella)
You don't like to work. He/She doesn't like to work.

Les gusta el arte. (ustedes, ellos, ellas)
You like art. They like art.

¡ATENCIÓN!

Note that **gustar** does not behave like other **-ar** verbs. You must study its use carefully and pay attention to prepositions, pronouns, and agreement.

AYUDA

Use the construction **a** + [*name/pronoun*] to clarify to whom you are referring. This construction is not always necessary.

A Gabriela le gusta bailar.

A Sara y a él les gustan los animales.

¡INTÉNTALO! Provide the present tense forms of these verbs. The first items have been done for you.

hablar
1. Yo <u>hablo</u> español.
2. Ellos <u>hablan</u> español.
3. Inés <u>habla</u> español.
4. Nosotras <u>hablamos</u> español.
5. Tú <u>hablas</u> español.

gustar
1. <u>Me gusta</u> el café. (a mí)
2. ¿<u>Te gustan</u> las clases? (a ti)
3. No <u>te gusta</u> el café. (a ti)
4. No <u>me gustan</u> las clases. (a mí)
5. No <u>me gusta</u> el café. (a mí)

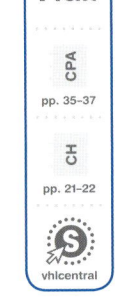

TEACHING OPTIONS

Video Show the **Fotonovela** again and stop the video where appropriate to discuss how certain verbs were used and to ask comprehension questions.

Pairs Write five word pairs (mix of infinitives and plural and singular nouns) on the board. Ex: **la Coca-Cola/la Pepsi** Have student pairs take turns asking each other what they like better: **¿Qué te gusta más...?** Then have them write a summary of what each of them likes and share it with the class.

Game Divide the class into two teams. Call on one team member at a time, alternating between teams. Give an **-ar** verb in its infinitive form and name a subject pronoun. The team member should say the corresponding present tense verb form. Give one point per correct answer. Deduct one point for each wrong answer. The team with the most points at the end wins.

En la clase

cincuenta y tres 53

Práctica

1 Completar Complete the conversation with the appropriate forms of the verbs.

JUAN ¡Hola, Linda! ¿Qué tal las clases?
LINDA Bien. (1) **Tomo** (Tomar) tres clases… química, biología y computación.
Y tú, ¿cuántas clases (2) **tomas** (tomar)?
JUAN (3) **Tomo** (Tomar) tres también… biología, arte y literatura.
El doctor Cárdenas (4) **enseña** (enseñar) la clase de biología.
LINDA ¿Ah, sí? Lily, Alberto y yo (5) **tomamos** (tomar) biología a las diez con la profesora Garza.
JUAN ¿(6) **Estudian** (Estudiar) mucho ustedes?
LINDA Sí, porque hay muchos exámenes. Alberto y yo (7) **necesitamos** (necesitar) estudiar dos horas todos los días (*every day*).

2 Oraciones Form sentences using the words provided. Remember to conjugate the verbs and add any other necessary words.

1. ustedes / practicar / vocabulario Ustedes practican el vocabulario.
2. ¿preparar (tú) / tarea? ¿Preparas la tarea?
3. clase de español / terminar / once La clase de español termina a las once.
4. ¿qué / buscar / ustedes? ¿Qué buscan ustedes?
5. (nosotros) buscar / pluma Buscamos una pluma.
6. (yo) comprar / calculadora Compro una calculadora.

3 Gustos Read what these people do. Then use the information in parentheses to tell what they like.

> **modelo**
> Yo enseño en la universidad. (las clases) Me gustan las clases.

1. Tú deseas mirar cuadros (*paintings*) de Picasso. (el arte) Te gusta el arte.
2. Soy estudiante de economía. (estudiar) Me gusta estudiar.
3. Tú estudias italiano y español. (las lenguas extranjeras) Te gustan las lenguas extranjeras.
4. No descansas los sábados. (cantar y bailar) Te gusta cantar y bailar.
5. Busco una computadora. (la computación) Me gusta la computación.

4 Actividades Get together with a classmate and take turns asking each other if you do these activities. Which activities does your partner like? Which do you both like? Answers will vary.

> **modelo**
> tomar el autobús
> **Estudiante 1:** ¿Tomas el autobús?
> **Estudiante 2:** Sí, tomo el autobús, pero (*but*) no me gusta./ No, no tomo el autobús.

bailar merengue	dibujar en clase	mirar la televisión
cantar bien	escuchar música rock	practicar el español
conversar con amigos	estudiar física	viajar a Europa

AYUDA

The Spanish **no** translates to both *no* and *not* in English. In negative answers to questions, you will need to use **no** twice:
¿Estudias geografía?
No, no estudio geografía.

Practice more at vhlcentral.com.

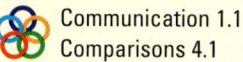
Communication 1.1
Comparisons 4.1

1 Teaching Tip To simplify, guide the class to first identify the subject and verb ending for each item.

1 Expansion Go over the answers quickly as a class. Then ask volunteers to role-play the dialogue.

2 Teaching Tip Point out that students will need to conjugate the verbs and add missing articles and other words to complete these dehydrated sentences. Tell them that subject pronouns in parentheses are not necessary in the completed sentences. Model completion of the first sentence for the class.

2 Expansion Give these dehydrated sentences to the class as items 7–10: **7.** (yo) desear / practicar / verbos / hoy (Deseo practicar los verbos hoy.) **8.** mi amigo / regresar / lunes (Mi amigo regresa el lunes.) **9.** ella / cantar / y / bailar / muy bien (Ella canta y baila muy bien.) **10.** jóvenes / necesitar / descansar / ahora (Los jóvenes necesitan descansar ahora.)

3 Teaching Tip To simplify, start by reading the model aloud. Then ask students why **me** is used in the answer (the first-person singular is used in the example sentence) and why **gustan** is needed (**las clases** is plural). Have students identify the indirect object pronoun and choose **gusta** or **gustan** for each item, then complete the activity.

3 Expansion If you wish to practice other forms, repeat the activity, providing different subjects for each item. Ex:
1. Deseamos mirar cuadros de Picasso. (Nos gusta el arte.)

4 Teaching Tip Before beginning, give a 2–3 minute oral rapid-response drill. Provide infinitives and subjects, and call on students to give the conjugated form.

TEACHING OPTIONS

Pairs Have individual students write five dehydrated sentences and exchange them with a partner, who will complete them. After pairs have completed their sentences, ask volunteers to share some of their dehydrated sentences. Write them on the board and have the class "rehydrate" them.

TEACHING OPTIONS

Game Divide the class into two teams. Prepare brief descriptions of easily recognizable people, using -ar verbs. Write each name on a card, and give each team a set of names. Then read the descriptions aloud. The first team to hold up the correct name earns a point. Ex: **Ella canta en inglés y en español, baila muy bien y viaja a muchos países. (Jennifer López)**

Estructura 53

Comunicación

5 **Describir** With a partner, use the given verbs to ask and answer questions about what you see in the pictures. Answers will vary.

modelo
enseñar, explicar
Estudiante 1: ¿Qué enseña la profesora?
Estudiante 2: Enseña química.
Estudiante 1: ¿Explica la lección?
Estudiante 2: Sí, explica la lección.

1. caminar, hablar, llevar

2. buscar, descansar, estudiar

3. dibujar, cantar, escuchar

4. llevar, tomar, viajar

6 **Charadas** In groups of three, play a game of charades using the verbs in the word bank. For example, if someone is studying, you say "**Estudias.**" The first person to guess correctly acts out the next charade. Answers will vary.

| bailar | cantar | descansar | enseñar | mirar |
| caminar | conversar | dibujar | escuchar | preguntar |

Síntesis

7 **Conversación** Pretend that you and a classmate are friends who have not seen each other at school for a few days. Have a conversation in which you catch up on things. Mention how you're feeling, what classes you're taking, what days and times you have classes, and which classes you like and don't like. Answers will vary.

En la clase   cincuenta y cinco   **55**

2.2 Forming questions in Spanish Tutorial

ANTE TODO There are three basic ways to ask questions in Spanish. Can you guess what they are by looking at the photos and photo captions on this page?

Te gusta mucho la tarea, ¿no?

¿Hablas con tu mamá?

¿Estudia Maru?

AYUDA

With a partner, take turns saying the example statements and questions on this page out loud. Your pitch indicates whether you are making a statement or asking a question. Then take turns making up statements of your own and turning them into questions, using all three methods.

▶ One way to form a question is to raise the pitch of your voice at the end of a declarative sentence. When writing any question in Spanish, be sure to use an upside-down question mark (¿) at the beginning and a regular question mark (?) at the end of the sentence.

Statement	Question
Ustedes trabajan los sábados.	¿Ustedes trabajan los sábados?
You work on Saturdays.	*Do you work on Saturdays?*
Carlota busca un mapa.	¿Carlota busca un mapa?
Carlota is looking for a map.	*Is Carlota looking for a map?*

▶ You can also form a question by inverting the order of the subject and the verb of a declarative statement. The subject may even be placed at the end of the sentence.

Statement	Question
SUBJECT VERB	VERB SUBJECT
Ustedes trabajan los sábados.	¿**Trabajan ustedes** los sábados?
You work on Saturdays.	*Do you work on Saturdays?*
SUBJECT VERB	VERB SUBJECT
Carlota regresa a las seis.	¿**Regresa** a las seis **Carlota**?
Carlota returns at six.	*Does Carlota return at six?*

AYUDA

With negative statements, only the tag ¿**verdad?** may be used.

Statement
Ustedes **no** trabajan los sábados.
You don't work on Saturdays.

Question
Ustedes **no** trabajan los sábados, ¿**verdad?**
You don't work on Saturdays, right?

▶ Questions can also be formed by adding the tags ¿**no?** or ¿**verdad?** at the end of a statement.

Statement	Question
Ustedes trabajan los sábados.	Ustedes trabajan los sábados, ¿**no?**
You work on Saturdays.	*You work on Saturdays, don't you?*
Carlota regresa a las seis.	Carlota regresa a las seis, ¿**verdad?**
Carlota returns at six.	*Carlota returns at six, right?*

Teaching Tips

- Model pronunciation by asking questions. Ex: **¿Cómo estás? ¿Cuál es tu clase favorita?**
- Point out written accent marks on interrogative words.
- Explain that **¿qué?** and **¿cuál?** are not used interchangeably. The word **¿qué?** generally precedes a noun while **¿cuál?** is typically used with a verb. Compare and contrast the following: **¿Qué clase te gusta? ¿Cuál es tu clase favorita?** Write similar questions on the board but leave out the interrogative word. Ask students to tell whether **¿qué?** or **¿cuál?** is used for each.
- Point out **¿cuáles?** and **¿quiénes?** and give examples for each.
- Clarify singular/plural and masculine/feminine variants for **¿cuánto/a?** and **¿cuántos/as?** Ex: **¿Cuánta tarea hay? ¿Cuántos libros hay?**
- Model the pronunciation of example sentences, asking similar questions of students. Ex: ___, **¿dónde trabajas?** Ask other students to verify their classmates' answers. Ex: ____ **trabaja en** ____.
- Explain that the answer to the question **¿por qué?** is **porque**.
- Point out that a question such as **¿Caminan a clase?** has several answers: **Sí, caminamos a clase. No, no caminamos a clase. No, tomamos el autobús.**

Question words

Interrogative words

¿Adónde?	Where (to)?	¿De dónde?	From where?
¿Cómo?	How?	¿Dónde?	Where?
¿Cuál?, ¿Cuáles?	Which?; Which one(s)?	¿Por qué?	Why?
¿Cuándo?	When?	¿Qué?	What?; Which?
¿Cuánto/a?	How much?	¿Quién?	Who?
¿Cuántos/as?	How many?	¿Quiénes?	Who (plural)?

▶ To ask a question that requires more than a *yes* or *no* answer, use an interrogative word.

¿Cuál de ellos estudia en la biblioteca?
Which one of them studies in the library?

¿Adónde caminamos?
Where are we walking to?

¿Cuántos estudiantes hablan español?
How many students speak Spanish?

¿Por qué necesitas hablar con ella?
Why do you need to talk to her?

¿Dónde trabaja Ricardo?
Where does Ricardo work?

¿Quién enseña la clase de arte?
Who teaches the art class?

¿Qué clases tomas?
What classes are you taking?

¿Cuánta tarea hay?
How much homework is there?

▶ When pronouncing this type of question, the pitch of your voice falls at the end of the sentence.

¿Cómo llegas a clase?
How do you get to class?

¿Por qué necesitas estudiar?
Why do you need to study?

▶ Notice the difference between **¿por qué?**, which is written as two words and has an accent, and **porque**, which is written as one word without an accent.

¿Por qué estudias español?
Why do you study Spanish?

¡Porque es divertido!
Because it's fun!

▶ In Spanish **no** can mean both *no* and *not*. Therefore, when answering a yes/no question in the negative, you need to use **no** twice.

¿Caminan a clase?
Do you walk to class?

No, no caminamos a clase.
No, we do not walk to class.

 **¡INTÉNTALO!** Make questions out of these statements. Use intonation in column 1 and the tag **¿no?** in column 2. The first item has been done for you.

Statement	Intonation	Tag question
1. Hablas inglés.	¿Hablas inglés?	Hablas inglés, ¿no?
2. Trabajamos mañana.	¿Trabajamos mañana?	Trabajamos mañana, ¿no?
3. Ustedes desean bailar.	¿Ustedes desean bailar?	Ustedes desean bailar, ¿no?
4. Raúl estudia mucho.	¿Raúl estudia mucho?	Raúl estudia mucho, ¿no?
5. Enseño a las nueve.	¿Enseño a las nueve?	Enseño a las nueve, ¿no?
6. Luz mira la televisión.	¿Luz mira la televisión?	Luz mira la televisión, ¿no?

recursos

vText

CPA
pp. 38–40

CH
pp. 23–24

vhlcentral

TEACHING OPTIONS

Video Show the **Fotonovela** again. Stop the video where appropriate to discuss how certain questions, including tag questions, are formed. Have students focus on characters' rising and falling intonation in questions and statements.

Pairs Give pairs of students five minutes to write original questions using as many interrogative words as they can. Can any group come up with questions using all the interrogative words?

DIFFERENTIATION

Heritage Speakers Ask heritage speakers to give original statements and questions at random. Have the rest of the class determine whether each sentence is a statement or a question.

Práctica

1 Preguntas Change these sentences into questions by inverting the word order.

modelo
Ernesto habla con su compañero de clase.
¿Habla Ernesto con su compañero de clase? /
¿Habla con su compañero de clase Ernesto?

1. La profesora Cruz prepara la prueba.
   ¿Prepara la profesora Cruz la prueba? / ¿Prepara la prueba la profesora Cruz?
2. Sandra y yo necesitamos estudiar.
   ¿Necesitamos Sandra y yo estudiar? / ¿Necesitamos estudiar Sandra y yo?
3. Los chicos practican el vocabulario.
   ¿Practican los chicos el vocabulario? / ¿Practican el vocabulario los chicos?
4. Jaime termina la tarea.
   ¿Termina Jaime la tarea? / ¿Termina la tarea Jaime?
5. Tú trabajas en la biblioteca. ¿Trabajas tú en la biblioteca? / ¿Trabajas en la biblioteca tú?

2 Completar Irene and Manolo are chatting in the library. Complete their conversation with the appropriate questions. *Answers will vary.*

IRENE Hola, Manolo. (1) ¿Cómo estás?/¿Qué tal?
MANOLO Bien, gracias. (2) ¿Y tú?
IRENE Muy bien. (3) ¿Qué hora es?
MANOLO Son las nueve.
IRENE (4) ¿Qué estudias?
MANOLO Estudio historia.
IRENE (5) ¿Por qué?
MANOLO Porque hay un examen mañana.
IRENE (6) ¿Te gusta la clase?
MANOLO Sí, me gusta mucho la clase.
IRENE (7) ¿Quién enseña la clase?
MANOLO El profesor Padilla enseña la clase.
IRENE (8) ¿Tomas psicología este semestre?
MANOLO No, no tomo psicología este semestre.
IRENE (9) ¿A qué hora regresas a la casa?
MANOLO Regreso a la casa a las tres y media.
IRENE (10) ¿Deseas tomar una soda?
MANOLO No, no deseo tomar una soda. ¡Deseo estudiar!

3 Dos profesores In pairs, create a dialogue, similar to the one in **Actividad 2**, between two teachers, Mr. Padilla and his colleague Ms. Martínez. Use question words. *Answers will vary.*

modelo
Señor Padilla: ¿Qué enseñas este semestre?
Señora Martínez: Enseño dos cursos de sociología.

Comunicación

4 Encuesta Your teacher will give you a worksheet. Change the categories in the first column into questions, then use them to survey your classmates. Find at least one person for each category. Be prepared to report the results of your survey to the class. *Answers will vary.*

5 Un juego In groups of four or five, play a game (**un juego**) of Jeopardy®. Each person has to write two clues. Then take turns reading the clues and guessing the questions. The person who guesses correctly reads the next clue. *Answers will vary.*

Es algo que...	Es un lugar donde...	Es una persona que...
It's something that...	*It's a place where...*	*It's a person that...*

modelo

Estudiante 1: Es un lugar donde estudiamos.
Estudiante 2: ¿Qué es la biblioteca?

Estudiante 1: Es algo que escuchamos.
Estudiante 2: ¿Qué es la música?

Estudiante 1: Es un director de España.
Estudiante 2: ¿Quién es Pedro Almodóvar?

NOTA CULTURAL
Pedro Almodóvar is a film director from Spain. His films are full of both humor and melodrama, and their controversial subject matter has often sparked great debate. His 1999 film **Todo sobre mi madre** (*All About My Mother*) received the Oscar for Best Foreign Film, followed by **Hable con ella**, which won the Oscar for Best Original Screenplay in 2002. **Volver** (2006) and **Los abrazos rotos** (2009) garnered numerous nominations and awards. His eighteenth film, **La piel que habito**, was released in 2011.

6 El nuevo estudiante Imagine you are a transfer student and today is your first day of Spanish class. Ask your partner questions to find out all you can about the class, your classmates, and the school. Then switch roles. *Answers will vary.*

modelo

Estudiante 1: Hola, me llamo Samuel. ¿Cómo te llamas?
Estudiante 2: Me llamo Laura.
Estudiante 1: ¿Quiénes son ellos?
Estudiante 2: Son Melanie y Lucas.
Estudiante 1: Y el profesor, ¿de dónde es?
Estudiante 2: Es de California.
Estudiante 1: En la escuela hay cursos de ciencias, ¿verdad?
Estudiante 2: Sí, hay clases de biología, química y física.
Estudiante 1: ¿Cuántos exámenes hay en esta clase?
Estudiante 2: Hay dos.

Síntesis

7 Entrevista Imagine that you are a reporter for the school newspaper. Write five questions about student life at your school and use them to interview two classmates. Be prepared to report your findings to the class. *Answers will vary.*

2.3 Present tense of estar  Tutorial

ANTE TODO In **Lección 1**, you learned how to conjugate and use the verb **ser** *(to be)*. You will now learn a second verb which means *to be*, the verb **estar**. Although **estar** ends in **-ar**, it does not follow the pattern of regular **-ar** verbs. The **yo** form (**estoy**) is irregular. Also, all forms have an accented **á** except the **yo** and **nosotros/as** forms.

The verb estar (to be)

SINGULAR FORMS	yo	est**oy**	*I am*
	tú	est**ás**	*you* (fam.) *are*
	Ud./él/ella	est**á**	*you* (form.) *are; he/she is*
PLURAL FORMS	nosotros/as	est**amos**	*we are*
	vosotros/as	est**áis**	*you* (fam.) *are*
	Uds./ellos/ellas	est**án**	*you* (form.) *are; they are*

¡Estamos en Perú!

María está en la biblioteca.

COMPARE & CONTRAST

Compare the uses of the verb **estar** to those of the verb **ser**.

Uses of estar

Location
Estoy en casa.
I am at home.

Marissa **está** al lado de Felipe.
Marissa is next to Felipe.

Health
Juan Carlos **está** enfermo hoy.
Juan Carlos is sick today.

Well-being
—¿Cómo **estás**, Jimena?
How are you, Jimena?

—**Estoy** muy bien, gracias.
I'm very well, thank you.

Uses of ser

Identity
Hola, **soy** Maru.
Hello, I'm Maru.

Occupation
Soy estudiante.
I'm a student.

Origin
—¿**Eres** de México?
Are you from Mexico?

—Sí, **soy** de México.
Yes, I'm from Mexico.

Telling time
Son las cuatro.
It's four o'clock.

CONSULTA
To review the forms of **ser**, see **Estructura 1.3**, pp. 19–21.

AYUDA
Use **la casa** to express *the house*, but **en casa** to express *at home*.

Teaching Tips

- Explain that prepositions typically indicate where one thing or person is in relation to another thing or person: *near, far, on, between, below.*
- Point out that **estar** is used in the model sentences to indicate presence or existence in a place.
- Take a book or other object and place it in various locations in relation to your desk or a student's. Ask individual students about its location. Ex: **¿Dónde está el libro? ¿Está cerca o lejos del escritorio de ____? ¿Qué objeto está al lado/a la izquierda del libro?** Work through various locations, eliciting all of the prepositions of location.
- Ask where students are in relation to one another. Ex: **____, ¿dónde está ____? Está al lado (a la derecha/izquierda, delante, detrás) de ____.**
- Describe students' locations in relation to each other. Ex: **Esta persona está lejos de ____. Está delante de ____. Está al lado de ____** ... Have the class call out the student you identify. Ex: **Es ____.** Then have students describe other students' locations for a partner to guess.

▶ **Estar** is often used with certain prepositions and adverbs to describe the location of a person or an object.

Prepositions and adverbs often used with **estar**

al lado de	next to; beside	**delante de**	in front of
a la derecha de	to the right of	**detrás de**	behind
a la izquierda de	to the left of	**en**	in; on
allá	over there	**encima de**	on top of
allí	there	**entre**	between; among
cerca de	near	**lejos de**	far from
con	with	**sin**	without
debajo de	below	**sobre**	on; over

La tiza **está al lado de** la pluma.
The chalk is next to the pen.

Los libros **están encima del** escritorio.
The books are on top of the desk.

El laboratorio **está cerca de** la clase.
The lab is near the classroom.

Maribel **está delante de** José.
Maribel is in front of José.

La maleta **está allí**.
The suitcase is over there.

El estadio no **está lejos de** la librería.
The stadium isn't far from the bookstore.

El mapa **está entre** la pizarra y la puerta.
The map is between the blackboard and the door.

Los estudiantes **están en** la clase.
The students are in class.

La calculadora **está sobre** la mesa.
The calculator is on the table.

Los turistas **están allá**.
The tourists are over there.

Estamos lejos de casa.

La biblioteca está al lado de la librería.

¡INTÉNTALO! Provide the present tense forms of **estar**.

1. Ustedes __están__ en la clase.
2. José __está__ en la biblioteca.
3. Yo __estoy__ bien, gracias.
4. Nosotras __estamos__ en la cafetería.
5. Tú __estás__ en el laboratorio.
6. Elena __está__ en la librería.
7. Ellas __están__ en la clase.
8. Ana y yo __estamos__ en la clase.
9. ¿Cómo __está__ usted?
10. Javier y Maribel __están__ en el estadio.
11. Nosotros __estamos__ en la cafetería.
12. Yo __estoy__ en el laboratorio.
13. Carmen y María __están__ enfermas.
14. Tú __estás__ en la clase.

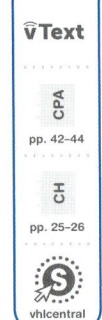

recursos

vText

CPA
pp. 42–44

CH
pp. 25–26

vhlcentral

EXPANSION

Extra Practice Name various places at your school and ask students to describe their location in relation to other buildings. Model sample sentences so students will know how to answer. You may wish to write **el aula de...** on the board and explain its meaning.

TEACHING OPTIONS

TPR Have students remain seated. One student holds a ball. Identify another student by his or her location with reference to other students. Ex: **Es la persona a la derecha de ____.** The student with the ball has to throw it to the student you described. That student must then toss the ball to the next person you identify.

Práctica

1 Completar Daniela has just returned home from school. Complete this conversation with the appropriate forms of **ser** or **estar**.

MAMÁ Hola, Daniela. ¿Cómo (1) _estás_ ?
DANIELA Hola, mamá. (2) _Estoy_ bien. ¿Dónde (3) _está_ papá? ¡Ya (*Already*) (4) _son_ las seis de la tarde!
MAMÁ No (5) _está_ aquí. (6) _Está_ en la oficina.
DANIELA Y Andrés y Margarita, ¿dónde (7) _están_ ellos?
MAMÁ (8) _Están_ en el restaurante La Palma con Martín.
DANIELA ¿Quién (9) _es_ Martín?
MAMÁ (10) _Es_ un compañero de clase. (11) _Es_ de México.
DANIELA Ah. Y el restaurante La Palma, ¿dónde (12) _está_ ?
MAMÁ (13) _Está_ cerca de la Plaza Mayor, en San Modesto.
DANIELA Gracias, mamá. Voy (*I'm going*) al restaurante. ¡Hasta pronto!

2 Escoger Choose the preposition that best completes each sentence.

1. La pluma está (encima de / detrás de) la mesa. _encima de_
2. La ventana está (a la izquierda de / debajo de) la puerta. _a la izquierda de_
3. La pizarra está (debajo de / delante de) los estudiantes. _delante de_
4. Las sillas están (encima de / detrás de) los escritorios. _detrás de_
5. Los estudiantes llevan los libros (en / sobre) la mochila. _en_
6. La biblioteca está (sobre / al lado de) la residencia estudiantil. _al lado de_
7. España está (cerca de / lejos de) Puerto Rico. _lejos de_
8. México está (cerca de / lejos de) los Estados Unidos. _cerca de_
9. Felipe trabaja (con / en) Ricardo en la cafetería. _con_

3 Buscar Imagine that you are in a school supply store and can't find various items. Ask the clerk (your partner) about the location of five items in the drawing. Then switch roles. _Answers will vary._

modelo
Estudiante 1: ¿Dónde están los diccionarios?
Estudiante 2: Los diccionarios están debajo de los libros de literatura.

Practice more at vhlcentral.com.

Comunicación

4 **¿Dónde estás...?** With a partner, take turns asking where you are at these times. *Answers will vary.*

modelo
lunes / 10:00 a.m.
Estudiante 1: ¿Dónde estás los lunes a las diez de la mañana?
Estudiante 2: Estoy en la clase de español.

1. sábados / 6:00 a.m.
2. miércoles / 9:15 a.m.
3. lunes / 11:10 a.m.
4. jueves / 12:30 a.m.
5. viernes / 2:25 p.m.
6. martes / 3:50 p.m.
7. jueves / 5:45 p.m.
8. miércoles / 8:20 p.m.

5 **La ciudad universitaria** You are visiting your older sister, who is an exchange student at a Spanish university. Tell a classmate which buildings you are looking for and ask for their location relative to where you are. *Answers will vary.*

modelo
Estudiante 1: ¿Está lejos la Facultad de Medicina?
Estudiante 2: No, está cerca. Está a la izquierda de la Facultad de Administración de Empresas.

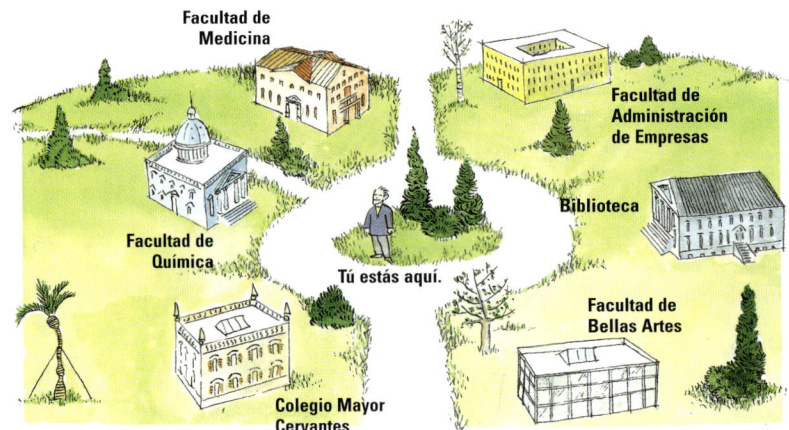

¡LENGUA VIVA!

La Facultad (*School*) de Filosofía y Letras includes departments such as language, literature, philosophy, history, and linguistics. Fine arts can be studied in la Facultad de Bellas Artes. In Spain the business school is sometimes called la Facultad de Administración de Empresas. Residencias estudiantiles are referred to as colegios mayores.

Síntesis

6 **Entrevista** In groups of three, ask each other these questions. *Answers will vary.*

1. ¿Cómo estás?
2. ¿Dónde tomas la clase de inglés/arte/biología/computación?
3. ¿Dónde está tu (*your*) padre ahora?
4. ¿Cuántos estudiantes hay en tu clase de historia/literatura/música/matemáticas?
5. ¿Quién(es) no está(n) en la clase hoy?
6. ¿A qué hora terminan tus clases los lunes?
7. ¿Estudias mucho?
8. ¿Cuántas horas estudias para (*for*) una prueba?

2.4 Numbers 31 and higher

ANTE TODO You have already learned numbers 0–30. Now you will learn the rest of the numbers.

Numbers 31–100

▶ Numbers 31–99 follow the same basic pattern as 21–29.

Numbers 31–100

31	treinta y uno	40	cuarenta	50	cincuenta
32	treinta y dos	41	cuarenta y uno	51	cincuenta y uno
33	treinta y tres	42	cuarenta y dos	52	cincuenta y dos
34	treinta y cuatro	43	cuarenta y tres	60	sesenta
35	treinta y cinco	44	cuarenta y cuatro	63	sesenta y tres
36	treinta y seis	45	cuarenta y cinco	64	sesenta y cuatro
37	treinta y siete	46	cuarenta y seis	70	setenta
38	treinta y ocho	47	cuarenta y siete	80	ochenta
39	treinta y nueve	48	cuarenta y ocho	90	noventa
		49	cuarenta y nueve	100	cien, ciento

▶ **Y** is used in most numbers from **31** through **99**. Unlike numbers 21–29, these numbers must be written as three separate words.

Hay **noventa y dos** exámenes.
There are ninety-two exams.

Hay **cuarenta y dos** estudiantes.
There are forty-two students.

Hay cuarenta y siete estudiantes en la clase de geografía.

Cien menos sesenta y cuatro son treinta y seis pesos de cambio.

▶ With numbers that end in **uno** (31, 41, etc.), **uno** becomes **un** before a masculine noun and **una** before a feminine noun.

Hay **treinta y un** chicos.
There are thirty-one guys.

Hay **treinta y una** chicas.
There are thirty-one girls.

▶ **Cien** is used before nouns and in counting. The words **un**, **una**, and **uno** are never used before **cien** in Spanish. Use **cientos** to say *hundreds*.

Hay **cien** libros y **cien** sillas.
There are one hundred books and one hundred chairs.

¿Cuántos libros hay? **Cientos.**
How many books are there? Hundreds.

EXPANSION

Extra Practice Give simple math problems (addition and subtraction) with numbers 31 and higher. Include numbers 0–30 as well, for a balanced review. Remind students that **más** = *plus*, **menos** = *minus*, and **es/son** = *equals*.

Extra Practice Write the beginning of a series of numbers on the board and have students continue the sequence.
Ex: **45, 50, 55…** or **77, 80, 83, 86…**

DIFFERENTIATION

Heritage Speakers Add an auditory aspect to this grammar presentation. Ask heritage speakers to give the house or apartment number where they live (they do not have to give the street name). Ask them to give the addresses in tens (**1471 = catorce setenta y uno**). Have volunteers write the numbers they say on the board.

Section Goal

In **Estructura 2.4**, students will be introduced to numbers 31 and higher.

Communication 1.1
Comparisons 4.1

Student Resources
Cuaderno de práctica y actividades comunicativas, pp. 45–51
Cuaderno para hispanohablantes, pp. 27–28
Supersite: Activities, *eCuaderno*

Teacher Resources
Workbook TE; Grammar Slides; Audio Activities MP3s; Audio Script; Testing Program Quizzes; Activity Pack; Middle School Activity Pack

Teaching Tips
- Review 0–30 by having the class count with you. When you reach 30, ask individual students to count through 39. Count 40 yourself and have students continue counting through 100.
- Write on the board numbers not included in the chart: 56, 68, 72, and so forth. Ask students to say the number in Spanish.
- Drill numbers 31–100 counting in sequences of twos and threes. Point to individuals at random and have them supply the next number in the series. Keep a brisk pace.
- Emphasize that from 31 to 99, numbers that don't end in 0 are written as three words (**treinta y nueve**).
- Remind students that **uno** changes to **un** and **una**, as in **veintiún** and **veintiuna**.
- Bring in a newspaper or magazine ad that shows phone numbers and prices. Call on volunteers to read the numbers aloud.

Teaching Tips

- Write these phrases on the board: **cuatrocientos estudiantes, novecientas personas, dos mil libros, once millones de turistas.** Help students deduce the meanings of the numbers.
- Write numbers on the board and call on volunteers to read them aloud.
- To practice agreement, write numbers from 101 to 999 followed by various nouns and have students read them aloud.
- To make sure that students do not say **un mil** for *one thousand*, list **1.000, 2.000, 3.000,** and **4.000** on the board. Have the class call out the numbers as you point to them randomly in rapid succession. Repeat this process for **cien mil**. Then emphasize that **un** is used with **millón**.
- Slowly dictate pairs of large numbers for students to write on separate pieces of paper. When finished writing, students should hold up the larger number. Ex: You say **seiscientos cincuenta y ocho mil, ciento catorce; quinientos setenta y siete mil, novecientos treinta y seis;** students hold up **658.114; 577.936**.

¡Lengua viva! Point out how dates are expressed in Spanish and have volunteers read aloud the examples in **LENGUA VIVA**. Then provide word groups that describe famous historical events. Ex: **Cristóbal Colón, las Américas; Neil Armstrong, la luna.** Have students state the year that they associate with each one. Ex: **Mil cuatrocientos y dos.**

---

64   sesenta y cuatro   Lección 2

Numbers 101 and higher

▶ As shown in the chart, Spanish traditionally uses a period to indicate thousands and millions, rather than a comma as used in English.

Numbers 101 and higher

101	ciento uno	1.000	mil
200	doscientos/as	1.100	mil cien
300	trescientos/as	2.000	dos mil
400	cuatrocientos/as	5.000	cinco mil
500	quinientos/as	100.000	cien mil
600	seiscientos/as	200.000	doscientos/as mil
700	setecientos/as	550.000	quinientos/as cincuenta mil
800	ochocientos/as	1.000.000	un millón (de)
900	novecientos/as	8.000.000	ocho millones (de)

▶ Notice that you should use **ciento**, not **cien**, to count numbers over 100.

    110 = **ciento diez**   118 = **ciento dieciocho**   150 = **ciento cincuenta**

▶ The numbers 200 through 999 agree in gender with the nouns they modify.

    324 plum**as**   605 libr**os**
    trescient**as** veinticuatro plum**as**   seiscient**os** cinco libr**os**

Hay tres mil quinient**os** libr**os** en la biblioteca.

▶ The word **mil**, which can mean *a thousand* and *one thousand*, is not usually used in the plural form to refer to an exact number, but it can be used to express the idea of *a lot*, *many*, or *thousands*. **Cientos** can also be used to express *hundreds* in this manner.

    Hay **miles** de personas en el estadio.
    There are thousands of people in the stadium.

▶ To express a complex number (including years), string together all of its components.

    55.422   cincuenta y cinco mil cuatrocientos veintidós

¡INTÉNTALO!
Give the Spanish equivalent of each number. The first item has been done for you.

1. 102   *ciento dos*
2. 5.000.000   *cinco millones*
3. 201   *doscientos uno*
4. 76   *setenta y seis*
5. 92   *noventa y dos*
6. 550.300   *quinientos cincuenta mil trescientos*
7. 235   *doscientos treinta y cinco*
8. 79   *setenta y nueve*
9. 113   *ciento trece*
10. 88   *ochenta y ocho*
11. 17.123   *diecisiete mil ciento veintitrés*
12. 497   *cuatrocientos noventa y siete*

¡LENGUA VIVA!

In Spanish, years are not expressed as pairs of two-digit numbers as they are in English (1979, *nineteen seventy-nine*): **1776, mil setecientos setenta y seis; 1945, mil novecientos cuarenta y cinco; 2015, dos mil quince.**

¡ATENCIÓN!

When **millón** or **millones** is used before a noun, the word **de** is placed between the two: **1.000.000 hombres = un millón de hombres 12.000.000 casas = doce millones de casas**

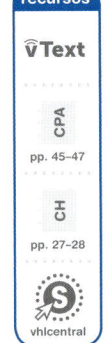

recursos

vText

CPA
pp. 45–47

CH
pp. 27–28

vhlcentral

TEACHING OPTIONS

TPR Write number patterns on cards (one number per card) and distribute them among the class. Begin a number chain by calling out **the first three numbers in the pattern. Ex: veinticinco, cincuenta, setenta y cinco.** The students holding these cards have five seconds to get up and stand in front of the class. The rest of the class continues by calling out the numbers in the pattern for the students to join the chain. Continue until the chain is broken or complete; then begin a new pattern.

TEACHING OPTIONS

Pairs Ask students to create a list of nine items containing three numerals in the hundreds, three in the thousands, and three in the millions; each numeral should be followed by a masculine or feminine noun. Have students exchange lists with a classmate, who will read the items aloud. Partners should listen for the correct number and gender agreement. Ex: **204 personas (doscientas cuatro personas)**

64   Teacher's Edition • Lesson Two

Práctica y Comunicación

1 Baloncesto Provide these basketball scores in Spanish.

1. Ohio State 76, Michigan 65
2. Florida 92, Florida State 104
3. Stanford 78, UCLA 89
4. Purdue 81, Indiana 78
5. Princeton 67, Harvard 55
6. Duke 115, Virginia 121

1. setenta y seis, sesenta y cinco
2. noventa y dos, ciento cuatro
3. setenta y ocho, ochenta y nueve
4. ochenta y uno, setenta y ocho
5. sesenta y siete, cincuenta y cinco
6. ciento quince, ciento veintiuno

2 Completar Complete these sequences of numbers.

1. 50, 150, 250 … 1.050 trescientos cincuenta, cuatrocientos cincuenta, quinientos cincuenta, seiscientos cincuenta, setecientos cincuenta, ochocientos cincuenta, novecientos cincuenta
2. 5.000, 20.000, 35.000 … 95.000 cincuenta mil, sesenta y cinco mil, ochenta mil
3. 100.000, 200.000, 300.000 … 1.000.000 cuatrocientos mil, quinientos mil, seiscientos mil, setecientos mil, ochocientos mil, novecientos mil
4. 100.000.000, 90.000.000, 80.000.000 … 0 setenta millones, sesenta millones, cincuenta millones, cuarenta millones, treinta millones, veinte millones, diez millones

3 Resolver In pairs, take turns reading the math problems aloud for your partner to solve.

AYUDA
+ → más
− → menos
= → son

modelo
200 + 300 =
Estudiante 1: Doscientos más trescientos son…
Estudiante 2: … quinientos.

1. 1.000 + 753 = Mil más setecientos cincuenta y tres son mil setecientos cincuenta y tres.
2. 1.000.000 − 30.000 = Un millón menos treinta mil son novecientos setenta mil.
3. 10.000 + 555 = Diez mil más quinientos cincuenta y cinco son diez mil quinientos cincuenta y cinco.
4. 15 + 150 = Quince más ciento cincuenta son ciento sesenta y cinco.
5. 100.000 + 205.000 = Cien mil más doscientos cinco mil son trescientos cinco mil.
6. 29.000 − 10.000 = Veintinueve mil menos diez mil son diecinueve mil.

4 Entrevista Find out the telephone numbers and e-mail addresses of four classmates. Answers will vary.

AYUDA
arroba at (@)
punto dot (.)

modelo
Estudiante 1: ¿Cuál es tu (your) número de teléfono?
Estudiante 2: Es el 635-19-51.
Estudiante 1: ¿Y tu dirección de correo electrónico?
Estudiante 2: Es a-Smith-arroba-pe-ele-punto-e-de-u. (asmith@pl.edu)

Síntesis

5 ¿A qué distancia…? Your teacher will give you and a partner incomplete charts that indicate the distances between Madrid and various locations. Fill in the missing information on your chart by asking your partner questions. Answers will vary.

modelo
Estudiante 1: ¿A qué distancia está Arganda del Rey?
Estudiante 2: Está a veintisiete kilómetros de Madrid.

Section Goal

In **Recapitulación**, students will review the grammar concepts from this lesson.

Student Resources
Supersite: Activities

1 Teaching Tips
- To simplify, ask students to identify the infinitive of the verb in each row.
- Complete this activity orally as a class. Write each form on the board as students call them out.

1 Expansion Ask students to provide the third-person singular (**Ud./él/ella**) conjugations.

2 Expansion
- Ask students to write five more numbers above 31. Have them read the numbers to a partner, who will jot them down. Remind students to check each other's answers.
- To challenge students, have them complete the activity and then say what they can buy with that amount of money. Model the first item for the class. Ex: **Con 49 dólares, compro una mochila.**

3 Teaching Tips
- Remind students that all question words should carry accent marks.
- Remind students that verbs in Spanish do not require subject pronouns; they are used for emphasis or clarification.

---

66 sesenta y seis   Lección 2

Recapitulación

 Diagnostics

Review the grammar concepts you have learned in this lesson by completing these activities.

1 Completar Complete the chart with the correct verb forms. **24 pts.**

yo	tú	nosotros	ellas
compro	compras	compramos	compran
deseo	**deseas**	deseamos	desean
miro	miras	**miramos**	miran
pregunto	preguntas	preguntamos	**preguntan**

2 Números Write these numbers in Spanish. **16 pts.**

modelo
645: seiscientos cuarenta y cinco

1. **49:** cuarenta y nueve
2. **97:** noventa y siete
3. **113:** ciento trece
4. **632:** seiscientos treinta y dos
5. **1.781:** mil setecientos ochenta y uno
6. **3.558:** tres mil quinientos cincuenta y ocho
7. **1.006.015:** un millón seis mil quince
8. **67.224.370:** sesenta y siete millones doscientos veinticuatro mil trescientos setenta

3 Preguntas Write questions for these answers. **12 pts.**

1. —¿ De dónde es _____ Patricia?
   —Patricia es de Colombia.
2. —¿ Quién es _____ él?
   —Él es mi amigo (*friend*).
3. —¿ Cuántas lenguas hablas _____ (tú)?
   —Hablo dos lenguas.
4. —¿ Qué desean (tomar) _____ (ustedes)?
   —Deseamos tomar café.
5. —¿ Por qué tomas biología _____?
   —Tomo biología porque me gustan las ciencias.
6. —¿ Cuándo descansa Camilo _____?
   —Camilo descansa por las mañanas.

RESUMEN GRAMATICAL

2.1 Present tense of -ar verbs pp. 50–52

estudiar	
estudi**o**	estudi**amos**
estudi**as**	estudi**áis**
estudi**a**	estudi**an**

The verb gustar

(no) me gusta + el/la + [*singular noun*]
(no) me gustan + los/las + [*plural noun*]
(no) me gusta + [*infinitive(s)*]

Note: You may use **a mí** for emphasis, but never **yo**.

To ask a classmate about likes and dislikes, use **te** instead of **me**, but never **tú**.

¿Te gusta la historia?

2.2 Forming questions in Spanish pp. 55–56

▶ ¿Ustedes trabajan los sábados?
▶ ¿Trabajan ustedes los sábados?
▶ Ustedes trabajan los sábados, ¿verdad?/¿no?

Interrogative words

¿Adónde?	¿Cuánto/a?	¿Por qué?
¿Cómo?	¿Cuántos/as?	¿Qué?
¿Cuál(es)?	¿De dónde?	¿Quién(es)?
¿Cuándo?	¿Dónde?	

2.3 Present tense of estar pp. 59–60

▶ estar: est**oy**, est**ás**, est**á**, est**amos**, est**áis**, est**án**

2.4 Numbers 31 and higher pp. 63–64

31	treinta y uno	101	ciento uno
32	treinta y dos	200	doscientos/as
(and so on)		500	quinientos/as
40	cuarenta	700	setecientos/as
50	cincuenta	900	novecientos/as
60	sesenta	1.000	mil
70	setenta	2.000	dos mil
80	ochenta	5.100	cinco mil cien
90	noventa	100.000	cien mil
100	cien, ciento	1.000.000	un millón (de)

EXPANSION

Pairs Have students create ten questions using the interrogative words from **Estructura 2.2**. Remind students that **¿Cuánto/a?** and **¿Cuántos/as?** should modify their corresponding nouns. Then have students exchange papers with a classmate and answer the questions. Finally, have pairs work together to review the answers. Have them write sentences using **nosotros/as** about any items they have in common.

EXPANSION

Extra Practice On the board, write a list of landmarks (libraries, parks, churches, restaurants, hotels, and so forth) in the community. Have students create sentences describing the location of the landmarks. Ex: **El Hotel Plaza está al lado de la biblioteca. Está cerca de la catedral y delante de Sebastian's Café.**

En la clase

sesenta y siete 67

4 **Al teléfono** Complete this telephone conversation with the correct forms of the verb **estar**. `16 pts.`

MARÍA TERESA Hola, señora López. (1) ¿__Está__ Elisa en casa?
SRA. LÓPEZ Hola, ¿quién es?
MARÍA TERESA Soy María Teresa. Elisa y yo (2) __estamos__ en la misma (*same*) clase de literatura.
SRA. LÓPEZ ¡Ah, María Teresa! ¿Cómo (3) __estás__?
MARÍA TERESA (4) __Estoy__ muy bien, gracias. Y usted, ¿cómo (5) __está__?
SRA. LÓPEZ Bien, gracias. Pues, no, Elisa no (6) __está__ en casa. Ella y su hermano (*her brother*) (7) __están__ en la Biblioteca Cervantes.
MARÍA TERESA ¿Cervantes?
SRA. LÓPEZ Es la biblioteca que (8) __está__ al lado del café Bambú.
MARÍA TERESA ¡Ah, sí! Gracias, señora López.
SRA. LÓPEZ Hasta luego, María Teresa.

5 **¿Qué te gusta?** Write a paragraph of at least five sentences stating what you like and don't like about your school. If possible, explain your likes and dislikes. `32 pts.`
Answers will vary.

Me gusta la clase de música porque no hay muchos exámenes. No me gusta estudiar en la cafetería...

6 **Canción** Use the appropriate forms of the verb **gustar** to complete the beginning of a popular song by Manu Chao. `2 EXTRA points!`

" Me __gustan__ los aviones°,
me gustas tú,
me __gusta__ viajar,
me gustas tú,
me gusta la mañana,
me gustas tú. "

aviones *airplanes*

TEACHING OPTIONS

Pairs Write **más, menos, multiplicado por,** and **dividido por** on the board. Model a few simple problems using numbers 31 and higher. Ex: **Cien mil trescientos menos diez mil son noventa mil trescientos. Mil dividido por veinte son cincuenta.** Then ask students to write two math problems of each type for a classmate to solve. Have partners verify each other's work.

TEACHING OPTIONS

Small Groups Tell students to think of a famous person and write five statements about their likes and dislikes from that person's point of view. Tell them to progressively give more clues to the person's identity and to end with **¿Quién soy?** Then, in small groups, have students read their statements aloud for their partners to guess. Have them respond to the guesses with more hints or information as necessary.

---

4 Expansion Ask student pairs to write a brief phone conversation based on the one in **Actividad 4**. Have volunteers role-play their dialogues for the class.

5 Teaching Tips
- Before writing their paragraphs, have students brainstorm a list of words or phrases related to middle or high school life.
- Remind students of when to use **gusta** versus **gustan**. Write a few example sentences on the board.
- Have students exchange papers with a partner to peer-edit each other's paragraphs.

6 Teaching Tip Point out the form **gustas** in lines 2, 4, and 6, and ask students to guess the translation of the phrase **me gustas** (*I like you*; literally, *you are pleasing to me*). Tell students that **me gustas** and **le gustas** are not used as much as their English counterparts. Most often they are used to express romantic sentiments.

6 Expansion **Manu Chao** (born 1961) is a French singer of Spanish origin. In the 80s, he and his brother started the band **Mano Negra**. Since the band's breakup in 1995, he has led a successful solo career. His music, which draws on diverse influences such as punk, ska, reggae, salsa, and Algerian raï, is popular throughout Europe and Latin America. **Chao** often mixes several languages in one song.

Estructura 67

2 adelante

Lección 2

Section Goals

In **Lectura**, students will:
- learn to use text formats to predict content
- read documents in Spanish

Communication 1.1, 1.2, 1.3
Cultures 2.1, 2.2
Connections 3.1, 3.2
Comparisons 4.2

Student Resources
Cuaderno para hispanohablantes, pp. 29–30
Supersite: Activities

 Pre-AP*

Interpretive Reading: Estrategia
Introduce the strategy. Point out that many documents have easily identifiable formats that can help readers predict content. Have students look at the document in the **Estrategia** box and ask them to name the recognizable elements:
- days of the week
- time
- classes

Ask what kind of document it is (a student's weekly schedule).

Examinar el texto Ask students what type of information is contained in **¡Español en Madrid!** (It is a brochure for an intensive Spanish-language summer program.) Discuss elements of the recognizable format that helped them predict the content, such as headings, list of courses, and course schedule with dates.

Correspondencias Go over the answers as a class or assign pairs of students to work together to check each other's answers.

Lectura  Audio: Reading / Additional Reading

Antes de leer

Estrategia
Predicting Content through Formats

Recognizing the format of a document can help you to predict its content. For instance, invitations, greeting cards, and classified ads follow an easily identifiable format, which usually gives you a general idea of the information they contain. Look at the text and identify it based on its format.

	lunes	martes	miércoles	jueves	viernes
8:30	biología		biología		biología
9:00		historia		historia	
9:30	inglés		inglés		inglés
10:00					
10:30					
11:00					
12:00					
12:30					
1:00					
2:00	arte		arte		arte

If you guessed that this is a page from a student's schedule, you are correct. You can now infer that the document contains information about a student's weekly schedule, including days, times, and activities.

Cognados
With a classmate, make a list of the cognates in the document entitled *¡Español en Madrid!* and guess their English meanings. What do cognates reveal about the content of the document?

Examinar el texto
Look at the format of the document. What type of text is it? What information do you expect to find in this type of document?

recursos

pp. 29–30 / vhlcentral

¡ESPAÑOL EN MADRID!

UAE

Programa de Cursos Intensivos de Español
Universidad Autónoma Española

Después de leer

Correspondencias
Match each item in Column B with the correct word in Column A. Two items will not be used.

A
1. profesores **f**
2. vivienda **h**
3. Madrid **d**
4. número de teléfono **a**
5. Español 2B **c**
6. número de fax **g**

B
a. (34) 91 779 4500
b. (34) 91 779 0210
c. 23 junio–30 julio
d. capital cultural de Europa
e. 23 junio–22 julio
f. especializados en enseñar español como lengua extranjera
g. (34) 91 779 4623
h. familias españolas

EXPANSION

Extra Practice For homework, ask students to write a weekly schedule (**horario semanal**) of a friend or family member. Ask them to label the days of the week in Spanish and add notes for that person's appointments and activities as well. In class, ask students questions about the schedules they wrote. Ex: ¿Qué clase toma _____ hoy? ¿Trabaja _____ mañana? ¿Cuántos días trabaja _____ esta semana?

DIFFERENTIATION

Heritage Speakers Ask heritage speakers who have attended or know about a school in the Spanish-speaking world to describe their schedule there, comparing and contrasting it with their schedule now. Invite them to make other comparisons between U.S. or Canadian institutions and those in the Spanish-speaking world.

68 Teacher's Edition • Lesson Two

En la clase

Universidad Autónoma Española

Madrid, la capital cultural de Europa, y la UAE te ofrecen cursos intensivos de verano° para aprender° español como nunca antes°.

Cursos	Empieza°	Termina
Español 1A	16 junio	22 julio
Español 1B	23 junio	30 julio
Español 1C	30 junio	10 agosto
Español 2A	16 junio	22 julio
Español 2B	23 junio	30 julio
Español 3A	16 junio	22 julio
Español 3B	23 junio	30 julio

¿Dónde?
En el campus de la UAE, edificio° de la Facultad de Filosofía y Letras.

¿Quiénes son los profesores?
Son todos hablantes nativos del español y catedráticos° de la UAE especializados en enseñar el español como lengua extranjera.

¿Qué niveles se ofrecen?
Se ofrecen tres niveles° básicos:
1. Español Elemental, A, B y C
2. Español Intermedio, A y B
3. Español Avanzado, A y B

Viviendas
Para estudiantes extranjeros se ofrece vivienda° con familias españolas.

¿Cuándo?
Este verano desde° el 16 de junio hasta el 10 de agosto. Los cursos tienen una duración de 6 semanas.

Información
Para mayor información, sirvan comunicarse con la siguiente° oficina:

Universidad Autónoma Española
Programa de Español como Lengua Extranjera
Ctra. Villalba, Km. 32, 28049 Madrid, España
Tel. (34) 91 779 4500, **Fax** (34) 91 779 4623
www.uae.es

verano summer   aprender to learn   nunca antes never before   edificio building   catedráticos professors   niveles levels   vivienda housing   desde from   Empieza Begins   siguiente following

¿Cierto o falso?

Indicate whether each statement is **cierto** or **falso**. Then correct the false statements.

1. La Universidad Autónoma Española ofrece (*offers*) cursos intensivos de italiano. — Falso
   Ofrece cursos intensivos de español.
2. La lengua nativa de los profesores del programa es el inglés. — Falso
   La lengua nativa de los profesores es el español.
3. Los cursos de español son en la Facultad de Ciencias. — Falso
   Son en la Facultad de Filosofía y Letras.
4. Los estudiantes pueden vivir (*can live*) con familias españolas. — Cierto
5. La universidad que ofrece los cursos intensivos está en Salamanca. — Falso
   Está en Madrid.
6. Español 2A termina en agosto. — Falso
   Termina en julio.
7. Si deseas información sobre (*about*) los cursos intensivos de español, puedes llamar al (34) 91 779 4500. — Cierto
8. Español 1B empieza en julio. — Falso
   Empieza en junio.

Practice more at vhlcentral.com.

Section Goals

In **Escritura**, students will:
- brainstorm and organize their ideas for writing
- write a description of themselves
- incorporate lesson vocabulary and structures

 Communication 1.3

Student Resources
Cuaderno de práctica y actividades comunicativas, pp. 52–53
Cuaderno para hispanohablantes, pp. 31–32
Supersite: Activities, *eCuaderno*

Teacher Resources
Workbook TE

 Pre-AP*

Interpretative Reading: Estrategia
Discuss information students might want to include in a self-description. Quickly review structures students will include in their writing, such as **me gusta** and **no me gusta** as well as the first-person singular of several verbs, for example: **soy, estoy, tomo, trabajo, estudio.**

Tema Copy on the board the description for Alicia Roberts, leaving blanks where her name, courses, and preferences appear. Add the sentences **Me gusta _____.** and **No me gusta _____.** Model completing the description orally with your information and then ask volunteers to complete it with their information.

 **Pre-AP***

Presentational Writing: Estrategia
Remind students that the audience for this description is Spanish-speaking teens. Encourage them to think of likes and dislikes that they might have in common.

Escritura

Estrategia
Brainstorming

How do you find ideas to write about? In the early stages of writing, brainstorming can help you generate ideas on a specific topic. You should spend ten to fifteen minutes brainstorming and jotting down any ideas about the topic.
Whenever possible, try to write your ideas in Spanish. Express your ideas in single words or phrases, and jot them down in any order. While brainstorming, don't worry about whether your ideas are good or bad. Selecting and organizing ideas should be the second stage of your writing. Remember that the more ideas you write down while you're brainstorming, the more options you'll have to choose from later when you start to organize your ideas.

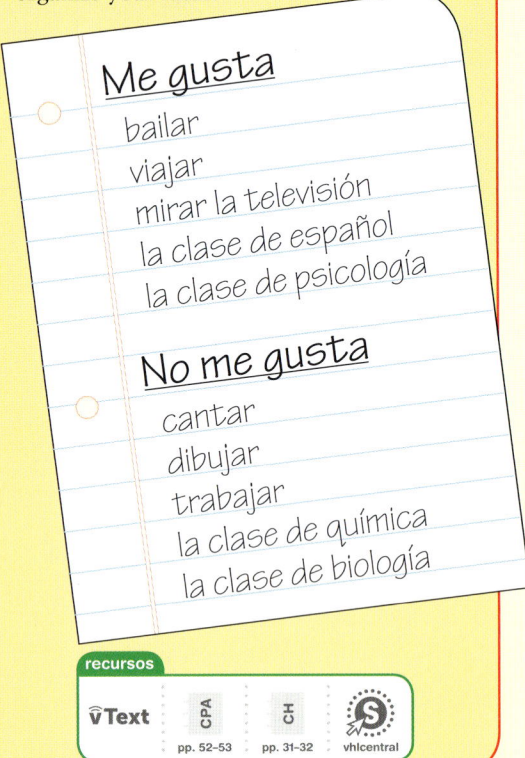

Me gusta
- bailar
- viajar
- mirar la televisión
- la clase de español
- la clase de psicología

No me gusta
- cantar
- dibujar
- trabajar
- la clase de química
- la clase de biología

recursos
vText pp. 52–53 | CPA | CH pp. 31–32 | vhlcentral

Tema
Una descripción

Write a description of yourself to post in a chat room on a website in order to meet Spanish-speaking people. Include this information in your description:

▶ your name, where you are from, and a photo (optional) of yourself
▶ where you go to school
▶ the courses you are taking
▶ where you work (if you have a job)
▶ some of your likes and dislikes

¡Hola! Me llamo Alicia Roberts. Estudio matemáticas y economía. Me gusta dibujar, cantar y viajar.

EVALUATION: Descripción

Criteria	Scale
Content	1 2 3 4 5
Organization	1 2 3 4 5
Use of vocabulary	1 2 3 4 5
Grammatical accuracy	1 2 3 4 5

Scoring	
Excellent	18–20 points
Good	14–17 points
Satisfactory	10–13 points
Unsatisfactory	< 10 points

Escuchar  Audio

Estrategia
Listening for cognates

You already know that cognates are words that have similar spellings and meanings in two or more languages: for example, *group* and **grupo** or *stereo* and **estéreo**. Listen for cognates to increase your comprehension of spoken Spanish.

 To help you practice this strategy, you will now listen to two sentences. Make a list of all the cognates you hear.

Preparación

Based on the photograph, who do you think Armando and Julia are? What do you think they are talking about? Answers will vary.

Ahora escucha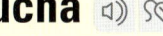

Now you are going to hear Armando and Julia's conversation. Make a list of the cognates they use.

Armando	Julia
clases, biología	semestre, astronomía
antropología, filosofía	geología, italiano
japonés, italiano	cálculo, hora, clase
cálculo, profesora	profesora

Based on your knowledge of cognates, decide whether the following statements are **cierto** or **falso**.

	Cierto	Falso
1. Armando y Julia hablan de la familia.	○	●
2. Armando y Julia toman una clase de matemáticas.	●	○
3. Julia toma clases de ciencias.	●	○
4. Armando estudia lenguas extranjeras.	●	○
5. Julia toma una clase de religión.	○	●

 Practice more at vhlcentral.com.

Comprensión

Preguntas
Answer these questions about Armando and Julia's conversation.
1. ¿Qué clases toma Armando?
   Toma antropología, filosofía, japonés, italiano y cálculo.
2. ¿Qué clases toma Julia?
   Toma astronomía, geología, italiano y cálculo.

Seleccionar
Choose the answer that best completes each sentence.
1. Armando toma ___b___ clases en la universidad.
   a. cuatro   b. cinco   c. seis
2. Julia toma dos clases de ___c___.
   a. matemáticas   b. lengua   c. ciencias
3. Armando toma italiano y ___b___.
   a. astronomía   b. japonés   c. geología
4. Armando y Julia estudian ___c___ los martes y jueves.
   a. filosofía   b. matemáticas   c. italiano

Preguntas personales   Answers will vary.
1. ¿Cuántas clases tomas tú este semestre?
2. ¿Qué clases tomas este semestre?
3. ¿Qué clases te gustan y qué clases no te gustan?

J: ¿A qué hora es tu clase de italiano?
A: A las nueve, con la profesora Menotti.

J: Yo también tomo italiano los martes y jueves con la profesora Menotti, pero a las once.

Section Goals

In **En pantalla**, students will:
- read about the seasons in Chile
- watch a television commercial for **Jumbo**, a Chilean superstore chain

Communication 1.1, 1.2, 1.3
Cultures 2.1, 2.2
Connections 3.2
Comparisons 4.2

Student Resources
Supersite: *En pantalla* video, Activities

Teacher Resources
Transcript & Translation

Calendarios Check comprehension: 1. What is the weather like in the southern hemisphere when it is cold and snowy in North America? 2. How long is summer in Chile? 3. What months are included in Chile's scholastic calendar?

 TELL Connection

Learning Tools 3
Why: Students need to understand the perspectives behind practices of target cultures. *What:* Short authentic clips—especially those that use humor—provide visual as well as spoken clues to experiences and perspectives.

 Pre-AP*

Audiovisual Interpretive Communication
Antes de ver strategy
Show the clip without sound to focus students' attention on the concept being presented. Ask: What can observation alone allow them to predict about its content and purpose?

Comprensión To challenge students, have them write a list in Spanish of objects they see as they watch the ad.

 Video: TV Clip

Anuncio de **Jumbo**

Viejito Pascuero°...

Preparación
Answer the following questions in English. *Answers will vary.*
1. For what occasions do you give and get gifts?
2. When did you get a very special or needed gift? What was the gift?

Calendarios
During the months of cold weather and snow in North America, the southern hemisphere enjoys warm weather and longer days. Since Chile's summer lasts from December to February, school vacation coincides with these months. In Chile, the school year starts in early March and finishes toward the end of December. All schools, from preschools to universities, observe this scholastic calendar, with only a few days' variation between institutions.

Viejito Pascuero *Santa Claus (Chile)*

Vocabulario útil

ahorrar	to save (money)
Navidad	Christmas
pedirte	to ask you
quería	I wanted
te preocupa	it worries you

Comprensión
Answer the following questions, using both English and Spanish as directed.
1. In the video, what was the young boy doing? *Writing a letter to Santa Claus.*
2. Who else is in the video? How do you know who he is? *His father. The boy says, "Papá."*
3. What did the boy ask? Give both the Spanish and the English equivalent. *He asked "¿Cómo se escribe mountain bike?" In English: How do you spell "mountain bike"?*
4. What answer was he given? Give both the Spanish and the English equivalent. *He was told "mochila." In English: "backpack."*

 ### Aplicación
With a partner, describe your school calendar and vacations. Then research and describe the same for a Spanish-speaking culture. Include the following elements: at what age students start school, the first and last days of the school year, and the dates of school vacations. Present your descriptions to the class, comparing the two as you present. *Answers will vary.*

Conversación
With a partner, take turns asking for something and being sure of the spelling. Each of you should ask for four different things. Follow the model. *Answers will vary.*

modelo
Estudiante 1: ¿Qué quieres?
Estudiante 2: Quiero un diccionario.
Estudiante 1: ¿Cómo se escribe "diccionario"?
Estudiante 2: D-I-C-C-I-O-N-A-R-I-O

 Practice more at vhlcentral.com.

 recursos / vText / vhlcentral

---

EXPANSION

Culture Note Latin American supermarkets differ from those in the U.S.; they are similar to a Wal-Mart superstore. **Jumbo** is an **hipermercado** that sells groceries, televisions, clothing, and school supplies.

Culture Note The idea of Santa Claus differs throughout the Spanish-speaking world. In Chile, he is referred to as **Viejito Pascuero** or **Viejo Pascuero**. In other countries, such as

HERITAGE SPEAKERS

Colombia, young people expect gifts from **El Niño Jesús**. In Spain and Argentina, **Los Reyes Magos** deliver gifts on January 6.
Heritage Speakers Ask heritage speakers in the class to describe a typical school experience in their culture. Which aspects do they find to be significantly different from the experience of their current school and classmates? Which do they find to be similar? Why might these differences and similarities exist?

En la clase · setenta y tres · 73

  Video: *Flash cultura*

Los estudios

Mexican author and diplomat Octavio Paz (March 31, 1914–April 19, 1998) studied both law and literature at the **Universidad Nacional Autónoma de México** (**UNAM**), but after graduating he immersed himself in the art of writing. An incredibly prolific writer of novels, poetry, and essays, Paz solidified his prestige as Mexico's preeminent author with his 1950 book ***El laberinto de la soledad***, a fundamental study of Mexican identity. Among the many awards he received in his lifetime are the **Premio Miguel de Cervantes** (1981) and Nobel Prize for Literature (1990). Paz foremost considered himself a poet and affirmed that poetry constitutes "**la religión secreta de la edad° moderna.**"

Vocabulario útil

¿Cuál es tu materia favorita?	What is your favorite subject?
¿Cuántos años tienes?	How old are you?
¿Qué estudias?	What do you study?
el/la alumno/a	student
la carrera (de medicina)	(medical) degree program, major
derecho	law
reconocido	well-known

Preparación

What is the name of your school? What classes are you taking this semester? Answers will vary.

Emparejar

Match the first part of the sentence in the left column with the appropriate ending in the right column.

1. En la UNAM no hay c
2. México, D.F. es d
3. La UNAM es a
4. La UNAM ofrece (*offers*) b

a. una universidad muy grande.
b. 74 carreras de estudio.
c. residencias estudiantiles.
d. la ciudad más grande (*biggest*) de Hispanoamérica.

edad *age* ¿Conoces a algún...? *Do you know any...?* que dé *that teaches*

—¿Qué estudias?
—Ciencias de la comunicación.

Estudio derecho en la UNAM.

¿Conoces a algún° profesor famoso que dé° clases... en la UNAM?

Practice more at vhlcentral.com.

Section Goal

In **Panorama**, students will read about the geography and culture of Spain.

Communication 1.3
Cultures 2.1, 2.2
Connections 3.1, 3.2
Comparisons 4.2

Student Resources
Cuaderno de práctica y actividades comunicativas, pp. 56–59
Supersite: *Panorama cultural* video, Activities, *eCuaderno*

Teacher Resources
Workbook TE; Digital Image Bank; Video Script & Translation

 21st Century Skills

Global Awareness
Students will gain perspectives on the Spanish-speaking world to develop respect and openness to others and to interact appropriately and effectively with citizens of Spanish-speaking cultures.

Teaching Tips
- Use the map to find the places mentioned. Explain that the Canary Islands are located in the Atlantic Ocean, off the northwestern coast of Africa.
- Use the **Lección 2 Panorama** Digital Image Bank to support this presentation.

El país en cifras After students have read **Idiomas**, associate the regional languages with the larger map by asking questions such as: ¿Hablan catalán en Barcelona? ¿Qué idioma hablan en Madrid?

¡Increíble pero cierto! Spain has many festivals rooted in Catholic tradition. Among the most famous is **Semana Santa** (*Holy Week*), which is celebrated annually with great reverence and pageantry.

2 panorama

España

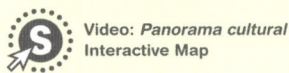
Video: *Panorama cultural*
Interactive Map

El país en cifras

- **Área:** 505.370 km² (kilómetros cuadrados) o 195.124 millas cuadradas°, incluyendo las islas Baleares y las islas Canarias
- **Población:** 47.043.000
- **Capital:** Madrid—6.213.000
- **Ciudades° principales:** Barcelona—5.029.000, Valencia—812.000, Sevilla, Zaragoza
- **Moneda°:** euro
- **Idiomas°:** español o castellano, catalán, gallego, valenciano, euskera

Regiones lingüísticas

Bandera de España

Españoles célebres
- **Miguel de Cervantes,** escritor° (1547–1616)
- **Pedro Almodóvar,** director de cine° (1949–)
- **Rosa Montero,** escritora y periodista° (1951–)
- **Fernando Alonso,** corredor de autos° (1981–)
- **Paz Vega,** actriz° (1976–)
- **Severo Ochoa,** Premio Nobel de Medicina, 1959; doctor y científico (1905–1993)

millas cuadradas *square miles* Ciudades *Cities* Moneda *Currency* Idiomas *Languages* escritor *writer* cine *film* periodista *reporter* corredor de autos *race car driver* actriz *actress* pueblo *town* Cada año *Every year* Durante todo un día *All day long* se tiran *throw at each other* varias toneladas *many tons*

¡Increíble pero cierto!
En Buñol, un pueblo° de Valencia, la producción de tomates es un recurso económico muy importante. Cada año° se celebra el festival de *La Tomatina*. Durante todo un día°, miles de personas se tiran° tomates. Llegan turistas de todo el país, y se usan varias toneladas° de tomates.

Lección 2

La Sagrada Familia en Barcelona

Plaza Mayor en Madrid

El baile flamenco

recursos
vText | CPA pp. 56–59 | vhlcentral

DIFFERENTIATION

Heritage Speakers **Paella**, the national dish of Spain, is the ancestor of the popular Latin American dish **arroz con pollo**. Ask heritage speakers if they know of any dishes traditional in their families that have their roots in Spanish cuisine. Invite them to describe the dish to the class.

EXPANSION

Variación léxica Tell students that they may also see the word **eusquera** spelled **euskera** and **euskara**. The letter **k** is used in Spanish only in words of foreign origin. **Euskera** is the Basque name of the Basque language, which linguists believe is unrelated to any other known language. The spelling students see on this page (**eusquera**) follows the principles of Spanish orthography. The Spanish name for *Basque* is **vascuence** or **vasco**.

Gastronomía • José Andrés

José Andrés es un chef español famoso internacionalmente°. Le gusta combinar platos° tradicionales de España con las técnicas de cocina más innovadoras°. Andrés vive° en Washington, DC, es dueño° de varios restaurantes en los EE.UU. y presenta° un programa en PBS. También° ha estado° en *Late Show with David Letterman* y *Top Chef*.

Cultura • La diversidad

La riqueza° cultural y lingüística de España refleja la combinación de las diversas culturas que han habitado° en su territorio durante siglos°. El español es la lengua oficial del país, pero también son oficiales el catalán, el gallego, el euskera y el valenciano.

Póster en catalán

Artes • Velázquez y el Prado

Las meninas, Diego Velázquez, 1656

El Prado, en Madrid, es uno de los museos más famosos del mundo°. En el Prado hay pinturas° importantes de Botticelli, de El Greco y de los españoles Goya y Velázquez. *Las meninas* es la obra° más conocida° de Diego Velázquez, pintor° oficial de la corte real° durante el siglo° XVII.

Comida • La paella

La paella es uno de los platos más típicos de España. Siempre se prepara° con arroz° y azafrán°, pero hay diferentes recetas°. La paella valenciana, por ejemplo, es de pollo° y conejo°, y la paella marinera es de mariscos°.

La costa de Ibiza

¿Qué aprendiste? Completa las oraciones con la información adecuada.

1. El chef español __José Andrés__ es muy famoso.
2. El arroz y el azafrán son ingredientes básicos de la __paella__.
3. El Prado está en __Madrid__.
4. __Las meninas__ es una pintura famosa de Diego Velázquez.
5. El chef José Andrés tiene un __programa__ de televisión en PBS.
6. El gallego es una de las lenguas oficiales de __España__.

Conexión Internet Investiga estos temas en **vhlcentral.com**.

1. Busca información sobre la Universidad de Salamanca u otra universidad española. ¿Qué cursos ofrece (*does it offer*)?
2. Busca información sobre un español o una española célebre (por ejemplo, un[a] político/a, un actor, una actriz, un[a] artista). ¿De qué parte de España es y por qué es célebre?

internacionalmente internationally *platos* dishes *más innovadoras* most innovative *vive* lives *dueño* owner *presenta* he hosts *También* Also *ha estado* he has been *riqueza* richness *han habitado* have lived *durante siglos* for centuries *mundo* world *pinturas* paintings *obra* work *más conocida* best-known *pintor* painter *corte real* royal court *siglo* century *Siempre se prepara* It is always prepared *arroz* rice *azafrán* saffron *recetas* recipes *pollo* chicken *conejo* rabbit *mariscos* seafood

EXPANSION

Variación léxica Regional cultures and languages have remained strong in Spain, despite efforts made in the past to suppress them in the name of national unity. The language that has come to be called *Spanish*, **español**, is the language of the region of north central Spain called **Castilla**. Because Spain was unified under the Kingdom of Castile at the end of the Middle Ages, the language of Castile, **castellano**, became the principal language of government, business, and literature. Even today one is likely to hear Spanish speakers refer to Spanish as **castellano** or **español**. Efforts to suppress the regional languages, though often harsh, were ineffective, and after the death of the dictator **Francisco Franco** and the return of power to regional governing bodies, the regional languages of Spain were given co-official status.

2 vocabulario

Student Resources
Cuaderno de práctica y actividades comunicativas, p. 47
Supersite: Activities, *eCuaderno*

Teacher Resources
Workbook TE; Textbook and Testing Audio MP3s; Testing Audio Script; Testing Program Tests

21st Century Skills
Creativity and Innovation
Ask students to prepare a list of the three products or perspectives they learned about in this lesson to share with the class. You may ask them to focus specifically on the **Cultura** and **Panorama** sections.

21st Century Skills
Leadership and Responsibility Extension Project
As a class, have students decide on three questions they want to ask the partner class related to the topic of the lesson they have just completed. Based on the responses they receive, work as a class to explain to the Spanish-speaking partners one aspect of their responses that surprised the class and why

  My Vocabulary

La clase

el/la compañero/a de clase	classmate
el/la compañero/a de cuarto	roommate
el/la estudiante	student
el/la profesor(a)	teacher
el borrador	eraser
la calculadora	calculator
el escritorio	desk
el libro	book
el mapa	map
la mesa	table
la mochila	backpack
el papel	paper
la papelera	wastebasket
la pizarra	blackboard
la pluma	pen
la puerta	door
el reloj	clock; watch
la silla	seat
la tiza	chalk
la ventana	window
la biblioteca	library
la cafetería	cafeteria
la casa	house; home
el estadio	stadium
el laboratorio	laboratory
la librería	bookstore
la residencia estudiantil	dormitory
la universidad	university; college
la clase	class
el curso, la materia	course
la especialización	major
el examen	test; exam
el horario	schedule
la prueba	test; quiz
el semestre	semester
la tarea	homework
el trimestre	trimester; quarter

recursos
 vText   CPA p. 47 vhlcentral

Las materias

la administración de empresas	business administration
el arte	art
la biología	biology
las ciencias	sciences
la computación	computer science
la contabilidad	accounting
la economía	economics
el español	Spanish
la física	physics
la geografía	geography
la historia	history
las humanidades	humanities
el inglés	English
las lenguas extranjeras	foreign languages
la literatura	literature
las matemáticas	mathematics
la música	music
el periodismo	journalism
la psicología	psychology
la química	chemistry
la sociología	sociology

Preposiciones

al lado de	next to; beside
a la derecha de	to the right of
a la izquierda de	to the left of
allá	over there
allí	there
cerca de	near
con	with
debajo de	below; under
delante de	in front of
detrás de	behind
en	in; on
encima de	on top of
entre	between; among
lejos de	far from
sin	without
sobre	on; over

Palabras adicionales

¿Adónde?	Where (to)?
ahora	now
¿Cuál?, ¿Cuáles?	Which?; Which one(s)?
¿Por qué?	Why?
porque	because

Verbos

bailar	to dance
buscar	to look for
caminar	to walk
cantar	to sing
cenar	to have dinner
comprar	to buy
contestar	to answer
conversar	to converse, to chat
desayunar	to have breakfast
descansar	to rest
desear	to wish; to desire
dibujar	to draw
enseñar	to teach
escuchar la radio/música	to listen (to) the radio/music
esperar (+ *inf.*)	to wait (for); to hope
estar	to be
estudiar	to study
explicar	to explain
gustar	to like
hablar	to talk; to speak
llegar	to arrive
llevar	to carry
mirar	to look (at); to watch
necesitar (+ *inf.*)	to need
practicar	to practice
preguntar	to ask (a question)
preparar	to prepare
regresar	to return
terminar	to end; to finish
tomar	to take; to drink
trabajar	to work
viajar	to travel

Los días de la semana

¿Cuándo?	When?
¿Qué día es hoy?	What day is it?
Hoy es…	Today is…
la semana	week
lunes	Monday
martes	Tuesday
miércoles	Wednesday
jueves	Thursday
viernes	Friday
sábado	Saturday
domingo	Sunday

Numbers 31 and higher	See pages 63–64.
Expresiones útiles	See page 45.

La familia

3

Communicative Goals
I will be able to:
- Talk about my family and friends
- Describe people and things
- Express possession

pages 78–81
- The family
- Identifying people
- Professions and occupations

contextos

pages 82–85
The Díaz family spends Sunday afternoon in Xochimilco. Marissa meets the extended family and answers questions about her own family. The group has a picnic and takes a boat ride through the canals.

fotonovela

pages 86–87
- Surnames and families in the Spanish-speaking world
- Spain's Royal Family

cultura

pages 88–105
- Descriptive adjectives
- Possessive adjectives
- Present tense of -er and -ir verbs
- Present tense of tener and venir
- Recapitulación

estructura

pages 106–113
Lectura: A brief article about families
Escritura: A letter to a friend
Escuchar: A conversation between friends
En pantalla
Flash cultura
Panorama: Ecuador

adelante

A PRIMERA VISTA
- ¿Cuántas personas hay en la foto?
- ¿La mujer está a la izquierda o a la derecha?
- ¿Está el hombre al lado de la mujer?
- ¿Conversan ellos? ¿Trabajan? ¿Viajan? ¿Caminan?

Lesson Goals
In **Lección 3**, students will be introduced to the following:
- terms for family relationships
- names of various professions
- surnames and families in the Spanish-speaking world
- Spain's Royal Family
- descriptive adjectives
- possessive adjectives
- the present tense of common regular -er and -ir verbs
- the present tense of **tener** and **venir**
- context clues to unlock meaning of unfamiliar words
- using idea maps when writing
- how to write a friendly letter
- strategies for asking clarification in oral communication
- a television commercial for **Pentel**
- a video about two Ecuadorian families
- geographical and cultural information about Ecuador

 21st Century Skills

Initiative and Self-Direction
Students can monitor their progress online using the Supersite activities and assessments.

A primera vista Here are some additional questions: **¿Cuántas personas hay en tu familia? ¿De qué conversas con ellos? ¿Viajas mucho con ellos?**

 TELL Connection

Performance and Feedback 3
Why: Students take responsibility for monitoring their own performance and proficiency goals. *What:* Hand out the I Can Worksheets available on the Supersite.

SUPPORT FOR BACKWARD DESIGN

Lección 3 Essential Questions
1. How do people describe their families and family members?
2. How do people talk about how they spend their time?
3. How are a person's surnames determined in the Spanish-speaking world?

Lección 3 Integrated Performance Assessment
Before teaching this chapter, review the Integrated Performance Assessment (IPA) and its accompanying scoring rubric provided in the Testing Program. Use the IPA to assess students' progress toward proficiency targets at the end of the chapter.
IPA Context: You and a classmate are spending Spring vacation in a Spanish-speaking country, and the coordinator of the trip needs to place you with host families. You are going to read about six different people. Decide which person is the best host for your classmate. Then, present your recommendation to the class, describing your classmate and explaining your choice of host.

 Voice boards on the Supersite allow you and your students to record and share up to five minutes of audio. Use voice boards for presentations, oral assessments, discussions, directions, etc.

Section Goals

In **Contextos**, students will learn and practice:
- terms for family relationships
- names of professions

Communication 1.2
Comparisons 4.1

Student Resources
Cuaderno de práctica y actividades comunicativas, pp. 61–63
Cuaderno para hispanohablantes, pp. 33–34
Supersite: Activities, eCuaderno

Teacher Resources
Workbook TE; Digital Image Bank; Textbook and Audio Activities MP3s; Audio Scripts; Testing Program Quizzes; Activity Pack; Middle School Activity Pack

Teaching Tips
- Use the Digital Image Bank to support this presentation.
- Point out plural family terms and explain that the masculine plural forms can refer to mixed groups of males and females:
  los hermanos *brothers; siblings; brothers and sisters*
  los primos *male cousins; male and female cousins*
  los sobrinos *nephews; nieces and nephews*
  los tíos *uncles; aunts and uncles*
- Introduce the vocabulary. Ask: **¿Cómo se llama tu hermano?** Ask another student: **¿Cómo se llama el hermano de ____?** Work your way through various family relationships.
- Point out that the family tree is drawn from the point of view of **José Miguel Pérez Santoro**. Have students refer to the family tree as you ask questions. Ex: **¿Cómo se llama la madre de Víctor?**

---

3 contextos

Lección 3

La familia

  My Vocabulary Tutorials

La familia de José Miguel Pérez Santoro

Más vocabulario	
los abuelos	grandparents
el/la bisabuelo/a	great-grandfather/great-grandmother
el/la gemelo/a	twin
el/la hermanastro/a	stepbrother/stepsister
el/la hijastro/a	stepson/stepdaughter
la madrastra	stepmother
el medio hermano/la media hermana	half-brother/half-sister
el padrastro	stepfather
los padres	parents
los parientes	relatives
el/la cuñado/a	brother-in-law/sister-in-law
la nuera	daughter-in-law
el/la suegro/a	father-in-law/mother-in-law
el yerno	son-in-law
el/la amigo/a	friend
el apellido	last name
la gente	people
el/la muchacho/a	boy/girl
el/la niño/a	child
el/la novio/a	boyfriend/girlfriend
la persona	person
el/la artista	artist
el/la ingeniero/a	engineer
el/la doctor(a), el/la médico/a	doctor; physician
el/la periodista	journalist
el/la programador(a)	computer programmer

Variación léxica

madre ↔ mamá, mami (*colloquial*)
padre ↔ papá, papi (*colloquial*)
muchacho/a ↔ chico/a

Juan Santoro Sánchez
mi abuelo (*my grandfather*)

Ernesto Santoro González
mi tío (*uncle*)
hijo (*son*) de Juan y Socorro

Marina Gutiérrez de Santoro
mi tía (*aunt*)
esposa (*wife*) de Ernesto

Silvia Socorro Santoro Gutiérrez
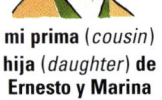
mi prima (*cousin*)
hija (*daughter*) de Ernesto y Marina

Héctor Manuel Santoro Gutiérrez
mi primo (*cousin*)
nieto (*grandson*) de Juan y Socorro

Carmen Santoro Gutiérrez
mi prima
hija de Ernesto y Marina

¡LENGUA VIVA!
In Spanish-speaking countries, it is common for people to go by both their first name and middle name, such as **José Miguel** or **María Teresa**. You will learn more about names and naming conventions on p. 86.

recursos
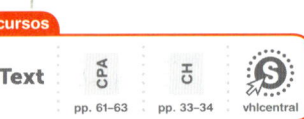
vText | CPA pp. 61–63 | CH pp. 33–34 | vhlcentral

EXPANSION
Extra Practice Draw your own family tree on the board and ask students questions about it. Ex: **¿Es ____ mi tío o mi abuelo? ¿Cómo se llama mi madre? ____ es el primo de ____, ¿verdad? ¿____ es el sobrino o el hermano de ____? ¿Quién es el cuñado de ____?** Help students identify the relationships between members. Encourage them to ask you questions.

DIFFERENTIATION
Heritage Speakers Ask heritage speakers to tell the class any other terms they use to refer to members of their families. These may include terms of endearment. Ask them to tell where these terms are used. Possible responses: **nene/a, guagua, m'hijo/a, chamaco/a, chaval(a), cuñis, tata, viejo/a, cielo, cariño, corazón.**

La familia

setenta y nueve | **79** | Communication 1.1

Socorro González de Santoro

mi abuela (*my grandmother*)

Mirta Santoro de Pérez
mi madre (*mother*)
hija de Juan y Socorro

Rubén Ernesto Pérez Gómez
mi padre (*father*)
esposo de mi madre

José Miguel Pérez Santoro
hijo de Rubén y de Mirta

Beatriz Alicia Pérez de Morales
mi hermana (*sister*)

Felipe Morales Zapata
esposo (*husband*) de Beatriz Alicia

Víctor Miguel Morales Pérez
mi sobrino (*nephew*)
hermano (*brother*) de Anita

Anita Morales Pérez
mi sobrina (*niece*)
nieta (*granddaughter*) de mis padres

los hijos (*children*) de Beatriz Alicia y de Felipe

Práctica

1 Escuchar Listen to each statement made by José Miguel Pérez Santoro, then indicate whether it is **cierto** or **falso**, based on his family tree.

	Cierto	Falso		Cierto	Falso
1.	●	○	6.	●	○
2.	●	○	7.	●	○
3.	○	●	8.	○	●
4.	●	○	9.	○	●
5.	○	●	10.	●	○

2 Personas Indicate each word that you hear mentioned in the narration.

1. _____ cuñado   4. ✔ niño   7. _____ ingeniera
2. ✔ tía   5. ✔ esposo   8. ✔ primo
3. ✔ periodista   6. ✔ abuelos

3 Emparejar Match the letter of each phrase with the correct description. Two items will not be used.

1. Mi hermano programa las computadoras. c
2. Son los padres de mi esposo. e
3. Son los hijos de mis (*my*) tíos. h
4. Mi tía trabaja en un hospital. a
5. Es el hijo de mi madrastra y el hijastro de mi padre. b
6. Es el esposo de mi hija. l
7. Es el hijo de mi hermana. k
8. Mi primo dibuja y pinta mucho. i
9. Mi hermanastra enseña en la universidad. j
10. Mi padre trabaja con planos (*blueprints*). d

a. Es médica.
b. Es mi hermanastro.
c. Es programador.
d. Es ingeniero.
e. Son mis suegros.
f. Es mi novio.
g. Es mi padrastro.
h. Son mis primos.
i. Es artista.
j. Es profesora.
k. Es mi sobrino.
l. Es mi yerno.

4 Definiciones Define these family terms in Spanish.

modelo
hijastro Es el hijo de mi esposo/a, pero no es mi hijo.

1. abuela   5. suegra
2. bisabuelo   6. cuñado
3. tío   7. nietos
4. primas   8. medio hermano

1. la madre de mi madre/padre
2. el abuelo de mi madre/padre
3. el hermano de mi madre/padre
4. las hijas de mis tíos/as
5. la madre de mi esposo/a
6. el esposo de mi hermana
7. los hijos de mis hijos
8. el hijo de mi padre/madre pero no de mi madre/padre

TEACHING OPTIONS

TPR Make a "living" family tree. Assign students different roles as family members and have students write down the term assigned to them on a sheet of paper. Arrange students as in a family tree and ask questions about relationships. Ex: ¿Quién es la madre de ____? ¿Cómo se llama el tío de ____?

TEACHING OPTIONS

Game Have students state the relationship between people on José Miguel's family tree; have their classmates guess which person they are describing. Ex: **Es la hermana de Ernesto y su padre es Juan. (Mirta) Héctor Manuel es su hermano y Beatriz Alicia es su prima. (Carmen o Silvia)** Take turns until each member of the class or group has stated a relationship.

---

1 Expansion To challenge students, write the false statements on the board and have students correct them by referring to the family tree.

1 Script 1. Beatriz Alicia es mi hermana. 2. Rubén es el abuelo de Víctor Miguel. 3. Silvia es mi sobrina. 4. Mirta y Rubén son los tíos de Héctor Manuel. 5. Anita es mi prima. 6. Ernesto es el hermano de mi madre. 7. Soy el tío de Anita. 8. Víctor Miguel es mi nieto. 9. Carmen, Beatriz Alicia y Marina son los nietos de Juan y Socorro. 10. El hijo de Juan y Socorro es el tío de Beatriz Alicia.
Teacher Resources DVD

2 Teaching Tips
- To simplify, read through the list as a class before playing the audio. Remind students to focus only on these words as they listen.
- Tell students that the words, if they appear in the narration, will not follow the sequence in the list.

2 Script Julia y Daniel son mis abuelos. Ellos viven en Montreal con mi tía Leti, que es periodista, y con mi primo César. César es un niño muy bueno y dibuja muy bien. Hoy voy a hablar por teléfono con todos ellos y con el esposo de Leti. Él es de Canadá.
Teacher Resources DVD

3 Expansion After students finish, ask volunteers to provide complete sentences combining elements from the numbered and lettered lists. Ex: **Los padres de mi esposo son mis suegros. Mis primos son los hijos de mis tíos.**

4 Expansion Have student pairs write five additional definitions following the pattern of those in the activity.

Contextos 79

5 Teaching Tips

- To challenge students, ask them to provide other possible responses for items 2, 4, 5, and 8. Ex: **2. esposos 4. tío/sobrino, hijastro/padrastro 5. niños, muchachos, amigos, primos, chicos, hermanastros, medios hermanos 8. bisabuelo, tío, padre, cuñado, padrastro**
- Ask the class questions about the photos and captions in the textbook. Ex: **¿Quién es artista? (Elena Vargas Soto es artista.) ¿Trabaja Irene? (Sí, es ingeniera.)**

5 Expansion Have pairs of students create an additional sentence for each photo. Ask one student to write sentences for the first four photos and the other student to write sentences for the remainder. Then have them exchange papers and check each other's work.

---

5 Escoger Complete the description of each photo using words you have learned in **Contextos**.

Some answers will vary.

1. La __familia__ de Sara es grande.

2. Héctor y Lupita son __novios__.

3. Maira Díaz es __periodista__.

4. Rubén habla con su __hijo/padre__.

5. Los dos __hermanos__ están en el parque.

6. Irene es __ingeniera__.

7. Elena Vargas Soto es __artista__.

8. Don Armando es el __abuelo__ de Martín.

Practice more at vhlcentral.com.

EXPANSION

Extra Practice Add an additional visual aspect to this vocabulary practice. Ask students to bring in a family-related photo of their own or a photo from the Internet or a magazine. Have them write a fill-in-the-blank sentence to go with it. Working in pairs, have them guess what is happening in each other's photo and complete the sentence.

TEACHING OPTIONS

Pairs In pairs, have students take turns assuming the identity of a person pictured in **Actividad 5** and making statements using **gustar** and **-ar** verbs. Encourage them to be creative. (Ex: **Me gusta cenar con mi novio.**) Their partner will try to guess the person's identity (**Eres Lupita.**).

Comunicación

6 Una familia With a classmate, identify the members in the family tree by asking questions about how each family member is related to Graciela Vargas García.

modelo
Estudiante 1: ¿Quién es Beatriz Pardo de Vargas?
Estudiante 2: Es la abuela de Graciela.

CONSULTA
To see the cities where these family members live, look at the map in **Panorama** on p. 112.

Family tree labels:
- David Vargas Olmedo — de Quito — abuelo
- Beatriz Pardo de Vargas — de Ibarra — abuela
- Carlos Antonio López Ríos — de Cuenca — tío
- Lupe Vargas de López — de Quito — tía
- Juan Vargas Pardo — de Quito — padre
- María Susana García de Vargas — de Guayaquil — madre
- Ernesto López Vargas — de Loja — primo
- Ramón Vargas García — de Machala — hermano
- Graciela Vargas García — de Machala

Now take turns asking each other these questions. Then invent three original questions.

1. ¿Cómo se llama el primo de Graciela? Se llama Ernesto López Vargas.
2. ¿Cómo se llama la hija de David y de Beatriz? Se llama Lupe Vargas de López.
3. ¿De dónde es María Susana? Es de Guayaquil.
4. ¿De dónde son Ramón y Graciela? Son de Machala.
5. ¿Cómo se llama el yerno de David y de Beatriz? Se llama Carlos Antonio López Ríos.
6. ¿De dónde es Carlos Antonio? Es de Cuenca.
7. ¿De dónde es Ernesto? Es de Loja.
8. ¿Cuáles son los apellidos del sobrino de Lupe? Son Vargas García.

7 Preguntas personales With a classmate, take turns asking each other these questions.
Answers will vary.

1. ¿Cuántas personas hay en tu familia?
2. ¿Cómo se llaman tus padres? ¿De dónde son? ¿Dónde trabajan?
3. ¿Cuántos hermanos tienes? ¿Cómo se llaman? ¿Dónde estudian o trabajan?
4. ¿Cuántos primos tienes? ¿Cuáles son los apellidos de ellos? ¿Cuántos son niños y cuántos son adultos? ¿Hay más chicos o más chicas en tu familia?
5. ¿Quién es tu pariente favorito?
6. ¿Tienes un(a) mejor amigo/a? ¿Cómo se llama?

AYUDA
tu *your* (sing.)
tus *your* (plural)
mi *my* (sing.)
mis *my* (plural)
tienes *you have*
tengo *I have*

Section Goals

In **Fotonovela**, students will:
- receive comprehensible input from free-flowing discourse
- learn functional phrases for talking about their families

Communication 1.2
Cultures 2.1, 2.2

Student Resources
Cuaderno de práctica y actividades comunicativas, pp. 64–65
Supersite: *Fotonovela* video, Activities, *eCuaderno*

Teacher Resources
Workbook TE; Video Script & Translation

Video Recap: Lección 2
Before doing this **Fotonovela** section, review the previous one with these questions:
1. ¿Quién estudia historia del arte? (Miguel estudia historia del arte.) 2. ¿Quién toma cuatro clases? (Marissa toma cuatro clases.) 3. ¿Qué necesita comprar Miguel? (Necesita comprar unos libros.) 4. ¿Qué enseña el profesor Morales? (Enseña la clase de química.)

Video Synopsis
The **Díaz** family spends Sunday afternoon in **Xochimilco**. **Marissa** meets some of the extended family and answers questions about her own family. The group has a picnic and the women take a boat ride through the canals. **Carolina** makes arrangements for **Marissa** and her friends to travel to **Mérida**.

Teaching Tips
- Ask students to read the title, glance at the video stills, and predict what they think the episode will be about.
- Hand out the *Antes de ver el video* and the *Mientras ves el video* activities from the **Cuaderno de práctica y actividades comunicativas** and go over the **Antes de ver** questions before starting the **Fotonovela**.

3 fotonovela

Lección 3

Un domingo en familia

Marissa pasa el día en Xochimilco con la familia Díaz.

PERSONAJES  FELIPE TÍA NAYELI

Video: *Fotonovela*

JIMENA Hola, tía Nayeli.
TÍA NAYELI ¡Hola, Jimena! ¿Cómo estás?
JIMENA Bien, gracias. Y, ¿dónde están mis primas?
TÍA NAYELI No sé. ¿Dónde están mis hijas? ¡Ah!

MARISSA ¡Qué bonitas son tus hijas! Y ¡qué simpáticas!

FELIPE Soy guapo y delgado.
JIMENA Ay, ¡por favor! Eres gordo, antipático y muy feo.

MARISSA Tía Nayeli, ¿cuántos años tienen tus hijas?
TÍA NAYELI Marta tiene ocho años y Valentina, doce.

SRA. DÍAZ Chicas, ¿compartimos una trajinera?
MARISSA ¡Claro que sí! ¡Qué bonitas son!
SRA. DÍAZ ¿Vienes, Jimena?
JIMENA No, gracias. Tengo que leer.

MARISSA Me gusta mucho este sitio. Tengo ganas de visitar otros lugares en México.
SRA. DÍAZ ¡Debes viajar a Mérida!
TÍA NAYELI ¡Sí, con tus amigos! Debes visitar a Ana María, la hermana de Roberto y de Ramón.

TEACHING OPTIONS

Un domingo en familia Before viewing the **Un domingo en familia** episode of the **Fotonovela**, ask students to brainstorm a list of what they might see and hear in an episode in which the characters find out about each other's families. Then play the episode once without sound and have the class create a plot summary based on visual clues. Next, show the segment with sound and have the class correct any mistaken guesses and fill in any gaps in the plot summary. Ask comprehension questions as a follow-up.

La familia

JIMENA   MARTA   VALENTINA   SRA. DÍAZ   TÍO RAMÓN   SR. DÍAZ   MARISSA

TÍO RAMÓN ¿Tienes una familia grande, Marissa?

MARISSA Tengo dos hermanos mayores, Zack y Jennifer, y un hermano menor, Adam.

MARISSA La verdad, mi familia es pequeña.

SRA. DÍAZ ¿Pequeña? Yo soy hija única. Bueno, y ¿qué más? ¿Tienes novio?

MARISSA No. Tengo mala suerte con los novios.

(*La Sra. Díaz habla por teléfono con la tía Ana María.*)

SRA. DÍAZ ¡Qué bien! Excelente. Sí, la próxima semana. Muchísimas gracias.

MARISSA ¡Gracias, Sra. Díaz!
SRA. DÍAZ Tía Ana María.
MARISSA Tía Ana María.
SRA. DÍAZ ¡Un beso, chau!
MARISSA Bye!

Expresiones útiles

Talking about your family
¿Tienes una familia grande?
Do you have a big family?
Tengo dos hermanos mayores y un hermano menor.
I have two older siblings and a younger brother.
La verdad, mi familia es pequeña.
The truth is, my family is small.
¿Pequeña? Yo soy hija única.
Small? I'm an only child.

Describing people
¡Qué bonitas son tus hijas! Y ¡qué simpáticas!
Your daughters are so pretty! And so nice!
Soy guapo y delgado.
I'm handsome and slim.
¡Por favor! Eres gordo, antipático y muy feo.
Please! You're fat, unpleasant, and very ugly.

Talking about plans
¿Compartimos una trajinera?
Shall we share a trajinera?
¡Claro que sí! ¡Qué bonitas son!
Of course! They're so pretty!
¿Vienes, Jimena?
Are you coming, Jimena?
No, gracias. Tengo que leer.
No, thanks. I have to read.

Saying how old people are
¿Cuántos años tienen tus hijas?
How old are your daughters?
Marta tiene ocho años y Valentina, doce.
Marta is eight and Valentina twelve.

Additional vocabulary
ensayo *essay*
pobrecito/a *poor thing*
próxima *next*
sitio *place*
todavía *still*
trajinera *type of barge*

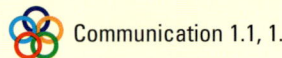

Communication 1.1, 1.2

1 Expansion Give these true/false statements to the class as items 7–10: **7. Jimena dice que Felipe es feo. (Cierto.) 8. Marissa tiene novio. (Falso. Tiene mala suerte con los novios.) 9. Valentina tiene una hermana menor. (Cierto.) 10. Jimena no comparte la trajinera porque tiene que asistir a clase. (Falso. Tiene que leer.)**

2 Expansion Sra. Díaz is the only person not associated with a statement. Ask students to look at the **Fotonovela** captions and **Expresiones útiles** on pages 82–83 and invent a statement for her. Remind them not to use her exact words. Ex: **Hablo por teléfono con mi cuñada.**

Nota cultural In the 19th century, the **chinampas** fulfilled agricultural purposes. At that time, **trajineras** were used to transport crops from the islands of **Xochimilco** to markets in Mexico City.

3 Expansion Have pairs who wrote about the same family exchange papers and compare their descriptions. Ask them to share the differences with the class.

4 Teaching Tip Model the activity by providing answers based on your own family.

4 Expansion Ask volunteers to share their partner's answers with the class.

4 Virtual Chat You can also assign activity 4 on the Supersite. Students record individual responses that appear in your gradebook.

84 Teacher's Edition • Lesson Three

---

84 ochenta y cuatro   Lección 3

¿Qué pasó?

1 ¿Cierto o falso? Indicate whether each sentence is **cierto** or **falso**. Correct the false statements.

		Cierto	Falso	
1.	Marissa dice que (*says that*) tiene una familia grande.	○	●	Marissa dice que tiene una familia pequeña.
2.	La Sra. Díaz tiene dos hermanos.	○	●	La señora Díaz es hija única.
3.	Marissa no tiene novio.	●	○	
4.	Valentina tiene veinte años.	○	●	Valentina tiene doce años.
5.	Marissa comparte una trajinera con la Sra. Díaz y la tía Nayeli.	●	○	
6.	A Marissa le gusta mucho Xochimilco.	●	○	

NOTA CULTURAL

Xochimilco is famous for its system of canals and **chinampas**, or artificial islands, which have been used for agricultural purposes since Pre-Hispanic times. In 1987, UNESCO declared **Xochimilco** a World Heritage Site.

2 Identificar Indicate which person would make each statement. The names may be used more than once. **¡Ojo!** One name will not be used.

1. Felipe es antipático y feo.   Jimena
2. Mis hermanos se llaman Jennifer, Adam y Zack.   Marissa
3. ¡Soy un joven muy guapo!   Felipe
4. Mis hijas tienen ocho y doce años.   tía Nayeli
5. ¡Qué bonitas son las trajineras!   Marissa
6. Ana María es la hermana de Ramón y Roberto.   tía Nayeli
7. No puedo (*I can't*) compartir una trajinera porque tengo que leer.   Jimena
8. Tus hijas son bonitas y simpáticas, tía Nayeli.   Marissa

SRA. DÍAZ   JIMENA

MARISSA   FELIPE

TÍA NAYELI

NOTA CULTURAL

Trajineras are large passenger barges that you can rent in **Xochimilco**. Each boat is named and decorated and has a table and chairs so passengers can picnic while they ride.

3 Escribir In pairs, choose Marissa, Sra. Díaz, or tía Nayeli and write a brief description of her family. Be creative! Answers will vary.

MARISSA

SRA. DÍAZ

TÍA NAYELI

Marissa es de los EE.UU. ¿Cómo es su familia?

La Sra. Díaz es de Cuba. ¿Cómo es su familia?

La tía Nayeli es de México. ¿Cómo es su familia?

4 Conversar With a partner, use these questions to talk about your families. Answers will vary.

1. ¿Cuántos años tienes?
2. ¿Tienes una familia grande?
3. ¿Tienes hermanos o hermanas?
4. ¿Cuántos años tiene tu abuelo (tu hermana, tu primo, etc.)?
5. ¿De dónde son tus padres?

Practice more at vhlcentral.com.

AYUDA

Here are some expressions to help you talk about age.
Yo tengo… años.
I am… years old.
Mi abuelo tiene… años.
My grandfather is… years old.

PRE-AP*

Interpersonal Speaking Ask volunteers to ad-lib the **Fotonovela** episode for the class. Assure them that it is not necessary to memorize the script or stick strictly to its content. They should try to get the general meaning across with the vocabulary and expressions they know, and they also should feel free to be creative. Give students time to prepare.

TEACHING OPTIONS

Small Groups Have groups of three interview each other about their families. Assign one person as the interviewer, one the interviewee, and the third person as the note taker. At three-minute intervals, have students switch roles. When everyone has been interviewed, have students report back to the class.

Pronunciación

Diphthongs and linking

herm**a**n**o**   **ni**ñ**a**   **cu**ñ**a**d**o**

In Spanish, **a**, **e**, and **o** are considered strong vowels. The weak vowels are **i** and **u**.

ru**i**d**o**   **par**i**e**nt**e**s   **per**i**o**d**i**st**a**

A diphthong is a combination of two weak vowels or of a strong vowel and a weak vowel. Diphthongs are pronounced as a single syllable.

mi hijo   **una clas**e **e**xcelente

Two identical vowel sounds that appear together are pronounced like one long vowel.

la abuela

con **N**atalia   **sus s**obrinos   **las s**illas

Two identical consonants together sound like a single consonant.

es ingeniera   **mis a**buelos   **sus hi**jos

A consonant at the end of a word is linked with the vowel at the beginning of the next word.

mi hermano   **su e**sposa   **nuestro a**migo

A vowel at the end of a word is linked with the vowel at the beginning of the next word.

Práctica Say these words aloud, focusing on the diphthongs.

1. historia
2. nieto
3. parientes
4. novia
5. residencia
6. prueba
7. puerta
8. ciencias
9. lenguas
10. estudiar
11. izquierda
12. ecuatoriano

Oraciones Read these sentences aloud to practice diphthongs and linking words.

1. Hola. Me llamo Anita Amaral. Soy del Ecuador.
2. Somos seis en mi familia.
3. Tengo dos hermanos y una hermana.
4. Mi papá es del Ecuador y mi mamá es de España.

Refranes Read these sayings aloud to practice diphthongs and linking sounds.

Cuando una puerta se cierra, otra se abre.[1]

Hablando del rey de Roma, por la puerta se asoma.[2]

[1] When one door closes, another opens. [2] Speak of the devil and he will appear.

Section Goals

In **Cultura**, students will:
- read about surnames and families in the Spanish-speaking world
- learn terms related to family and friends
- read about Spain's Royal Family
- read about average household size

 Communication 1.1, 1.2
Cultures 2.1, 2.2
Connections 3.1, 3.2
Comparisons 4.2

Student Resources
Cuaderno para hispanohablantes, p. 36
Supersite: Activities

 21st Century Skills

Global Awareness
Students will gain perspectives on the Spanish-speaking world to develop respect and openness to others and to interact appropriately and effectively with citizens of Spanish-speaking cultures.

En detalle
Antes de leer Have students brainstorm a list of famous Spanish speakers with two last names (Ex: **Gael García Bernal**).

Lectura
- Gabriel García Márquez was a Nobel Prize-winning writer from Colombia. Rodrigo García Barcha is a TV and film director (*In Treatment, Albert Nobbs*). Another son, Gonzalo García Barcha (not pictured), is an artist and graphic designer for film.
- Point out that **de** can be an indicator of ancestral origin (Ex: **Ramón del Valle**). In the case of Juan Carlos de Borbón (page 87), **de** refers to the House of Bourbon, a European royal dynasty.

Después de leer Have students say their names using this naming convention.

Lección 3

EN DETALLE

Additional Reading

¿Cómo te llamas?

In the Spanish-speaking world, it is common to have two last names: one paternal and one maternal. In some cases, the conjunctions **de** or **y** are used to connect the two last names. For example, in the name **Juan Martínez de Velasco**, *Martínez* is the paternal surname (**el apellido paterno**), and *Velasco* is the maternal surname (**el apellido materno**); **de** simply links the two. This convention of using two last names (**doble apellido**) is a European tradition that Spaniards brought to the Americas. It continues to be practiced in many countries, including Chile, Colombia, Mexico, Peru, and Venezuela. There are exceptions, however; in Argentina, the prevailing custom is for children to inherit only the father's last name.

When a woman marries in a country where two last names are used, legally she retains her two maiden surnames. However, socially she may take her husband's paternal surname in place of her inherited maternal surname. For example, **Mercedes Barcha Pardo**, wife of Colombian writer **Gabriel García Márquez**,

 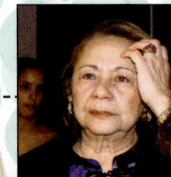

Gabriel García Márquez Mercedes Barcha Pardo

Rodrigo García Barcha

might use the names **Mercedes Barcha García** or **Mercedes Barcha de García** in social situations (although officially her name remains **Mercedes Barcha Pardo**). Adopting a husband's last name for social purposes, though widespread, is only legally recognized in Ecuador and Peru.

Regardless of the surnames the mother uses, most parents do not break tradition upon naming their children; they maintain the father's first surname followed by the mother's first surname, as in the name **Rodrigo García Barcha**. However, one should note that both surnames come from the grandfathers, and therefore all **apellidos** are effectively paternal.

Hijos en la casa

In Spanish-speaking countries, family and society place very little pressure on young adults to live on their own (**independizarse**), and children often live with their parents well into their thirties. For example, about 60% of Spaniards under 34 years of age live at home with their parents. This delay in moving out is both cultural and economic—lack of job security or low wages coupled with a high cost of living may make it impractical for young adults to live independently before they marry.

ACTIVIDADES

1 **¿Cierto o falso?** Indicate whether these statements are **cierto** or **falso**. Correct the false statements.

1. Most Spanish-speaking people have three last names. **Falso.** Most people have two last names.
2. Hispanic last names generally consist of the paternal last name followed by the maternal last name. **Cierto.**
3. It is common to see **de** or **y** used in a Hispanic last name. **Cierto.**
4. Someone from Argentina would most likely have two last names. **Falso.** They would use only the father's last name.
5. Generally, married women legally retain two maiden surnames. **Cierto.**
6. In social situations, a married woman often uses her husband's last name in place of her inherited paternal surname. **Falso.** She often uses it in place of her inherited maternal surname.
7. Adopting a husband's surname is only legally recognized in Peru and Ecuador. **Cierto.**
8. Hispanic last names are effectively a combination of the maternal surnames from the previous generation. **Falso.** They are a combination of the paternal surnames from the previous generation.

EXPANSION

Culture Note Explain that surnames began to be widely used in Europe in the Middle Ages, and that many refer to the person's profession, title, or place of origin. Ex: Tailor, Miller (professions); Carlson (son of Carl). Then explain that Hispanic surnames have similar roots. Ex: **Sastre, Zapatero, Herrero** (professions); **Fernández, Rodríguez** (the suffix **-ez** denotes "son of"); **Hidalgo, Conde, Abad** (titles); **Aragón, Villa, Castillo, de León** (places).

TEACHING OPTIONS

Large Group Write examples of Hispanic first and last names on the board. Then have students circulate around the room and introduce themselves to their classmates using a Hispanic last name. The other student must state their mother's and father's last names. Ex: **Soy Roberto Domínguez Trujillo. (Tu padre es el señor Domínguez y tu madre es la señora Trujillo.)**

La familia

ASÍ SE DICE
Familia y amigos

el/la bisnieto/a	great-grandson/daughter
el/la chamaco/a (Méx.); el/la chamo/a (Ven.); el/la chaval(a) (Esp.); el/la pibe/a (Arg.)	el/la muchacho/a
el/la colega (Esp.); mi cuate (Méx.); mi parcero/a (Col.); mi pana (Ven., P. Rico, Rep. Dom.)	el/la amigo/a *my pal; my buddy*
la madrina	godmother
el padrino	godfather
el/la tatarabuelo/a	great-great-grandfather/ great-great-grandmother

EL MUNDO HISPANO
Las familias

Although worldwide population trends show a decrease in average family size, households in many Spanish-speaking countries are still larger than their U.S. counterparts.

- **México** 4,0 personas
- **Colombia** 3,9 personas
- **Argentina** 3,6 personas
- **Uruguay** 3,0 personas
- **España** 2,9 personas
- **Estados Unidos** 2,6 personas

PERFIL
La familia real española

Undoubtedly, Spain's most famous family is **la familia real** (*Royal*). In 1962, then-prince **Juan Carlos de Borbón** married Princess **Sofía** of Greece. In the late 1970s, **el rey** (*King*) **Juan Carlos** and **la reina** (*Queen*) **Sofía** returned to Spain and helped transition the country to democracy after a forty-year dictatorship. The royal couple, who enjoys immense public support, has three children: **las infantas** (*Princesses*) **Elena** and **Cristina**, and a son, **Felipe**. In 2004, Felipe married **Letizia Ortiz Rocasolano**, a journalist and TV presenter. In June 2014, King Juan Carlos abdicated in favor of his son Felipe VI, who is now King of Spain. The king and queen have two daughters, **las infantas Leonor** (born in 2005) and **Sofía** (born in 2007).

Conexión Internet

What role do **padrinos** and **madrinas** have in today's Hispanic family?

Go to **vhlcentral.com** to find more cultural information related to this **Cultura** section.

ACTIVIDADES

2 Comprensión Complete these sentences.
1. Spain's royals were responsible for guiding in ___democracy___
2. In Spanish, your godmother is called ___la madrina___
3. Princess Leonor is the ___granddaughter___ of Queen Sofía.
4. Uruguay's average household has ___3,0___ people.
5. If a Venezuelan calls you **mi pana**, you are that person's ___friend___

3 Una familia famosa Create a genealogical tree of a famous family, using photos or drawings labeled with names and ages. Present the family tree to a classmate and explain who the people are and their relationships to each other.
Answers will vary.

Practice more at vhlcentral.com.

Section Goals

In **Estructura 3.1**, students will learn:
- forms, agreement, and position of adjectives ending in -o/-a, -e, or a consonant
- high-frequency descriptive adjectives and some adjectives of nationality

Communication 1.1
Comparisons 4.1

Student Resources
Cuaderno de práctica y actividades comunicativas, pp. 67–71
Cuaderno para hispanohablantes, pp. 37–38
Supersite: Activities, *eCuaderno*

Teacher Resources
Workbook TE; Grammar Slides; Audio Activities MP3s; Audio Script; Testing Program Quizzes; Activity Pack; Middle School Activity Pack

Teaching Tips
- Write these adjectives on the board: **ecuatoriana, alto, bonito, viejo, trabajador.** Ask what each means and say whether it is masculine or feminine.
- Work through the discussion of adjective forms point by point, writing examples on the board. Test comprehension by asking for the correct form of adjectives for nouns you suggest. Remind students that grammatical gender does not necessarily reflect actual gender.
- Drill gender by pointing to individuals and asking the class to supply the correct form. Ex: (Pointing to male student) **¿Guapo o guapa?** (Pointing to female) **¿Simpático o simpática?** Then use adjectives ending in **-e**. Point to a male and say **inteligente**, then point to a female and have students provide the correct form. Continue with plurals.

---

3 estructura

Lección 3

3.1 Descriptive adjectives

ANTE TODO Adjectives are words that describe people, places, and things. In Spanish, descriptive adjectives are used with the verb **ser** to point out characteristics such as nationality, size, color, shape, personality, and appearance.

Forms and agreement of adjectives

> **COMPARE & CONTRAST**
>
> In English, the forms of descriptive adjectives do not change to reflect the gender (masculine/feminine) and number (singular/plural) of the noun or pronoun they describe.
>
>   *Juan is **nice**.*   *Elena is **nice**.*   *They are **nice**.*
>
> In Spanish, the forms of descriptive adjectives agree in gender and/or number with the nouns or pronouns they describe.
>
>   Juan es simpátic**o**.   Elena es simpátic**a**.   Ellos son simpátic**os**.

▶ Adjectives that end in **-o** have four different forms. The feminine singular is formed by changing the **-o** to **-a**. The plural is formed by adding **-s** to the singular forms.

Masculine		Feminine	
SINGULAR	PLURAL	SINGULAR	PLURAL
el muchach**o** alt**o**	los muchach**os** alt**os**	la muchach**a** alt**a**	las muchach**as** alt**as**

¡Qué bonitas son tus hijas, tía Nayeli!

Felipe es gordo, antipático y muy feo.

▶ Adjectives that end in **-e** or a consonant have the same masculine and feminine forms.

Masculine		Feminine	
SINGULAR	PLURAL	SINGULAR	PLURAL
el chico inteligent**e**	los chicos inteligent**es**	la chica inteligent**e**	las chicas inteligent**es**
el examen difíci**l**	los exámenes difíci**les**	la clase difíci**l**	las clases difíci**les**

▶ Adjectives that end in **-or** are variable in both gender and number.

Masculine		Feminine	
SINGULAR	PLURAL	SINGULAR	PLURAL
el hombre trabajad**or**	los hombres trabajad**ores**	la mujer trabajad**ora**	las mujeres trabajad**oras**

EXPANSION

Extra Practice Have pairs of students write sentences using adjectives such as **inteligente, alto, joven.** When they have finished, ask volunteers to dictate their sentences to you while you write them on the board. After you have written a sentence and corrected any errors, ask volunteers to suggest a sentence that uses the antonym of the adjective.

EXPANSION

Variación léxica Clarify that the adjective **americano/a** applies to all inhabitants of North and South America, not just citizens of the United States. Residents of the United States usually are referred to with the adjective **norteamericano/a**. In more formal contexts, such as official documents, the adjective **estadounidense** is used.

La familia

ochenta y nueve

AYUDA

Many adjectives are cognates, that is, words that share similar spellings and meanings in Spanish and English. A cognate can be a noun like **profesor** or a descriptive adjective like **interesante**.

¡ATENCIÓN!

Note that **joven** takes an accent in its plural form. **Los jóvenes estudian mucho.**

▶ Adjectives that refer to nouns of different genders use the masculine plural form.

Manuel es alt**o**.   Lola es alt**a**.   Manuel y Lola son alt**os**.

Common adjectives

alto/a	tall	gordo/a	fat	moreno/a	brunet(te)
antipático/a	unpleasant	grande	big; large	mucho/a	much; many; a lot of
bajo/a	short (in height)	guapo/a	good-looking		
		importante	important	pelirrojo/a	red-haired
bonito/a	pretty	inteligente	intelligent	pequeño/a	small
bueno/a	good	interesante	interesting	rubio/a	blond(e)
delgado/a	thin; slender	joven	young	simpático/a	nice; likeable
difícil	hard; difficult	(jóvenes)		tonto/a	silly; foolish
fácil	easy	malo/a	bad	trabajador(a)	hard-working
feo/a	ugly	mismo/a	same	viejo/a	old

Colors

amarillo/a	yellow	negro/a	black
azul	blue	rojo/a	red
blanco/a	white	verde	green

Some adjectives of nationality

alemán, alemana	German	francés, francesa	French
argentino/a	Argentine	inglés, inglesa	English
canadiense	Canadian	italiano/a	Italian
chino/a	Chinese	japonés, japonesa	Japanese
costarricense	Costa Rican	mexicano/a	Mexican
cubano/a	Cuban	norteamericano/a	(North) American
ecuatoriano/a	Ecuadorian	puertorriqueño/a	Puerto Rican
español(a)	Spanish	ruso/a	Russian
estadounidense	from the U.S.		

▶ In Spanish, country names are capitalized, but adjectives of nationality are **not**.

▶ Adjectives of nationality that end in a consonant form the feminine by adding **-a**.

japoné**s** ⟶ japone**sa**   españo**l** ⟶ españo**la**

¡ATENCIÓN!

Note that adjectives with an accent on the last syllable drop the accent in the feminine and plural forms.
inglés → inglesa
alemán → alemanes

▶ Adjectives of color and nationality are formed like other descriptive adjectives.

Masculine

SINGULAR: argentin**o** / azul / verde
PLURAL: argentin**os** / azul**es** / verde**s**

Feminine

SINGULAR: argentin**a** / azul / verde
PLURAL: argentin**as** / azul**es** / verde**s**

Teaching Tips

- Point out that when referring to people, **bonito/a** can only be used for females, but **guapo/a** can be used for both males and females. Some heritage speakers may use **moreno/a** to refer to someone with dark skin, and **rubio/a** for someone with light brown hair.
- Use pictures or names of celebrities to teach descriptive adjectives in semantic pairs. Ex: **¿Marc Gasol es alto o bajo? (Es alto.) ¿Salma Hayek es fea? (No, es bonita.) ¿Los candidatos son inteligentes o tontos? (Son inteligentes.)**
- Explain that these color words are adjectives and agree in number and gender with the nouns they modify, except for **azul** and **verde**, which only change in number.
- Point to objects in the classroom and have students describe them using color words. Ex: **una pluma roja, unos cuadernos negros**. Then make statements about objects and have students identify them. Ex: **Está al lado del escritorio de Laura. (Es una mochila verde.)**
- Use names of celebrities to practice adjectives of nationality. Ex: **David Beckham, ¿es canadiense? (No, es inglés.) Hillary Clinton, ¿es francesa? (No, es norteamericana.)**
- Point out that adjectives of nationality also can be used as nouns. Ex: **La chica rusa es guapa. La rusa es guapa.** Like adjectives, nouns of nationality are not capitalized.
- You may want to add to the list of nationalities. Ex: **¿Cate Blanchett es australiana? (Sí, es australiana.) ¿Cuáles son las formas plurales de *australiano*? (australianos/australianas)**

TEACHING OPTIONS

Pairs If the majority of your students are **norteamericanos**, have pairs ask each other their family's origin. Write **¿Cuál es el origen de tu familia?** and **Mi familia es de origen…** on the board. Brainstorm other adjectives of nationality as necessary (Ex: **galés, indígena, nigeriano, polaco**). Point out that since **el origen** is masculine and singular, any adjectives they use will be as well.

TEACHING OPTIONS

TPR Create two sets of note cards with a city and a corresponding adjective of nationality. Shuffle the cards and distribute them. Have students circulate around the room to find the person who shares their nationality. Ex: **¿De dónde eres? Soy de Managua. Soy nicaragüense**. Then students should arrange themselves in a "map," finding their place by asking other pairs' nationality (**¿De dónde son ustedes? Somos panameños.**).

Position of adjectives

▶ Descriptive adjectives and adjectives of nationality generally follow the nouns they modify.

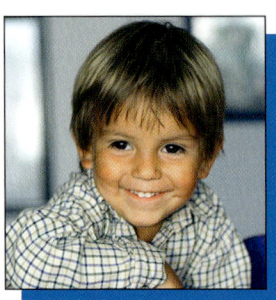

El niño **rubio** es de España.
The blond boy is from Spain.

La mujer **española** habla inglés.
The Spanish woman speaks English.

▶ Unlike descriptive adjectives, adjectives of quantity precede the modified noun.

Hay **muchos** libros en la biblioteca.
There are many books in the library.

Hablo con **dos** turistas puertorriqueños.
I am talking with two Puerto Rican tourists.

▶ **Bueno/a** and **malo/a** can appear before or after a noun. When placed before a masculine singular noun, the forms are shortened: **bueno** → **buen**; **malo** → **mal**.

Joaquín es un **buen** amigo.
Joaquín es un amigo **bueno**.
→ *Joaquín is a good friend.*

Hoy es un **mal** día.
Hoy es un día **malo**.
→ *Today is a bad day.*

▶ When **grande** appears before a singular noun, it is shortened to **gran,** and the meaning of the word changes: **gran** = *great* and **grande** = *big, large*.

Don Francisco es un **gran** hombre.
Don Francisco is a great man.

La familia de Inés es **grande**.
Inés' family is large.

¡LENGUA VIVA!
Like **bueno** and **grande**, **santo** (*saint*) is also shortened before masculine nouns (unless they begin with **To-** or **Do-**): **San Francisco, San José** (but: **Santo Tomás, Santo Domingo**). **Santa** is used with names of female saints: **Santa Bárbara, Santa Clara**.

¡INTÉNTALO! Provide the appropriate forms of the adjectives.

simpático
1. Mi hermano es _simpático_.
2. La profesora Martínez es _simpática_.
3. Rosa y Teresa son _simpáticas_.
4. Nosotros somos _simpáticos_.

alemán
1. Hans es _alemán_.
2. Mis primas son _alemanas_.
3. Marcus y yo somos _alemanes_.
4. Mi tía es _alemana_.

azul
1. La calculadora es _azul_.
2. El papel es _azul_.
3. Las maletas son _azules_.
4. Los libros son _azules_.

guapo
1. Su esposo es _guapo_.
2. Mis sobrinas son _guapas_.
3. Los padres de ella son _guapos_.
4. Marta es _guapa_.

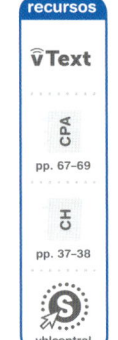

recursos
vText
CPA pp. 67–69
CH pp. 37–38
vhlcentral

La familia

Práctica

1 Emparejar Find the words in column B that are the opposite of the words in column A. One word in B will not be used.

A		B
1. guapo	d	a. delgado
2. moreno	f	b. pequeño
3. alto	h	c. verde
4. gordo	a	d. feo
5. joven	e	e. viejo
6. grande	b	f. rubio
7. blanco	g	g. negro
		h. bajo

2 Completar Indicate the nationalities of these people by selecting the correct adjectives and changing their forms when necessary.

1. Penélope Cruz es _española_.
2. Alfonso Cuarón es un gran director de cine de México; es _mexicano_.
3. Ellen Page y Avril Lavigne son _canadienses_.
4. Giorgio Armani es un diseñador de modas (*fashion designer*) _italiano_.
5. Daisy Fuentes es de La Habana, Cuba; ella es _cubana_.
6. Emma Watson y Daniel Radcliffe son actores _ingleses_.
7. Heidi Klum y Boris Becker son _alemanes_.
8. Apolo Anton Ohno y Shaun White son _estadounidenses_.

NOTA CULTURAL

Alfonso Cuarón (1961–) became the first Mexican winner of the Best Director Academy Award for his film *Gravity* (2013).

3 Describir Describe the drawing using as many adjectives as possible. *Some answers will vary.*

1. Susana Romero Barcos es _delgada, rubia, alta_.
2. Tomás Romero Barcos es _pelirrojo, inteligente, gordo_.
3. Tomás y su (*his*) padre, Carlos, son _pelirrojos, gordos_.
4. Los libros de Tomás son de color _amarillo, azul y rojo_.
5. Carlos Romero Sandoval es _bajo, gordo, pelirrojo_.
6. Alberto Romero Pereda es _viejo, bajo, gordo_.
7. Los dos hermanos son _jóvenes_.
8. Susana y su (*her*) madre, Josefina, son _altas, delgadas, rubias_.

4 ¿Cómo son? Now, look at the drawing in Activity 1 and form sentences that describe Jorge and Marcos and their houses. *Answers will vary.*

modelo
La casa de Marcos es azul.

Practice more at vhlcentral.com.

EXPANSION

Extra Practice Have students write brief descriptions of themselves: where they are from, what they study, their personalities, and what they look like. Collect the descriptions, shuffle them, and read a few of them to the class. Have the class guess who wrote each description.
Heritage Speakers Ask heritage speakers to use adjectives of nationality to describe their family's origin.

EXPANSION

Extra Practice Add an auditory aspect to this grammar practice. Prepare short descriptions of five easily recognizable people. Write their names on the board in random order. Then read your descriptions and have students match each one to the appropriate name. Ex: **Son hermanas. Son jóvenes, morenas y atléticas. Practican el tenis todos los días.** (Venus y Serena Williams)

Communication 1.1
Comparisons 4.1

1 Expansion Ask volunteers to create sentences describing famous people, using an adjective from column A and its opposite from B. Ex: **Barack Obama no es gordo; es delgado. Taylor Swift no es morena; es rubia.**

2 Teaching Tip To simplify, guide students in first identifying the gender and number of the subject for each sentence.

2 Expansion Ask pairs of students to write four original statements modeled on the activity. Have them leave a blank where the adjectives of nationality should go. Ask each pair to exchange its sentences with another pair, who will fill in the adjectives.

3 Teaching Tip To challenge students, ask them to provide all possible answers for each item. Ex: **1. delgada, rubia, joven, alta, bonita, guapa**

3 Expansion
- Have students say what each person in the drawing is not. Ex: **Susana no es vieja. Tomás no es moreno.**
- Have students ask each other questions about the family relationships shown in the illustration. Ex: —¿**Tomás Romero Barcos es el hijo de Alberto Romero Pereda?** —**No, Tomás es el hijo de Carlos Romero Sandoval.**

4 Expansion Have students convert their sentences to cloze items and exchange papers with a partner, who will complete the sentences.

Comunicación

5 **¿Cómo es?** With a partner, take turns describing each item on the list. Tell your partner whether you agree (**Estoy de acuerdo**) or disagree (**No estoy de acuerdo**) with their descriptions.
Answers will vary.

> **modelo**
> San Francisco
> **Estudiante 1:** San Francisco es una ciudad (*city*) muy bonita.
> **Estudiante 2:** No estoy de acuerdo. Es muy fea.

1. Nueva York
2. Steve Carell
3. las canciones (*songs*) de Taylor Swift
4. el presidente de los Estados Unidos
5. Steven Spielberg
6. la primera dama (*first lady*) de los Estados Unidos
7. el/la profesor(a) de español
8. las personas de Los Ángeles
9. las flores de primavera (*spring*)
10. mi clase de español

AYUDA

Here is some information to help you complete the descriptions:
- Steve Carell es actor de cine y de televisión.
- Taylor Swift es cantante.
- Steven Spielberg es director de cine.

6 **Perfil personal** Write a personal profile for your school newspaper. Describe yourself and your ideal best friend. Then compare your profile with a classmate's. How are you similar and how are you different? Are you looking for the same things in a best friend?
Answers will vary.

SOY ALTA, morena y bonita. Soy cubana, de Holguín. Me gusta mucho el arte. Busco una amiga similar. Mi amiga ideal es alta, morena, inteligente y muy simpática.

Síntesis

7 **Diferencias** Your teacher will give you and a partner each a drawing of a family. Describe your version of the drawing to your partner in order to find at least five differences between your picture and your partner's.
Answers will vary.

> **modelo**
> **Estudiante 1:** Susana, la madre, es rubia.
> **Estudiante 2:** No, la madre es morena.

recursos
vText
CPA
pp. 70–71

La familia

3.2 Possessive adjectives Tutorial

ANTE TODO Possessive adjectives, like descriptive adjectives, are words that are used to qualify people, places, or things. Possessive adjectives express the quality of ownership or possession.

Forms of possessive adjectives

SINGULAR FORMS	PLURAL FORMS	
mi	mis	my
tu	tus	your (fam.)
su	sus	his, her, its, your (form.)
nuestro/a	nuestros/as	our
vuestro/a	vuestros/as	your (fam.)
su	sus	their, your (form.)

COMPARE & CONTRAST

In English, possessive adjectives are invariable; that is, they do not agree in gender and number with the nouns they modify. Spanish possessive adjectives, however, do agree in number with the nouns they modify.

my cousin	*my* cousins	*my* aunt	*my* aunts
mi primo	**mis** primos	**mi** tía	**mis** tías

The forms **nuestro** and **vuestro** agree in both gender and number with the nouns they modify.

| nuestr**o** prim**o** | nuestr**os** prim**os** | nuestr**a** tí**a** | nuestr**as** tí**as** |

▶ Possessive adjectives are always placed before the nouns they modify.

—¿Está **tu** novio aquí?
Is your boyfriend here?

—No, **mi** novio está en la biblioteca.
No, my boyfriend is in the library.

▶ Because **su** and **sus** have multiple meanings (*your, his, her, their, its*), you can avoid confusion by using this construction instead: [*article*] + [*noun*] + **de** + [*subject pronoun*].

sus parientes ◀ los parientes **de él/ella** — *his/her* relatives
los parientes **de Ud./Uds.** — *your* relatives
los parientes **de ellos/ellas** — *their* relatives

AYUDA
Look at the context, focusing on nouns and pronouns, to help you determine the meaning of **su(s)**.

¡INTÉNTALO! 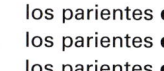 Provide the appropriate form of each possessive adjective.

Singular
1. Es ___mi___ (*my*) libro.
2. ___Mi___ (*My*) familia es ecuatoriana.
3. ___Tu___ (*Your,* fam.) novio es italiano.
4. ___Nuestro___ (*Our*) profesor es español.
5. Es ___su___ (*her*) reloj.
6. Es ___tu___ (*your,* fam.) mochila.
7. Es ___su___ (*your,* form.) maleta.
8. ___Su___ (*Their*) casa es amarilla.

Plural
1. ___Sus___ (*Her*) primos son franceses.
2. ___Nuestros___ (*Our*) cuadernos son verdes.
3. Son ___sus___ (*their*) lápices.
4. ___Sus___ (*Their*) nietos son japoneses.
5. Son ___nuestras___ (*our*) plumas.
6. Son ___mis___ (*my*) papeles.
7. ___Mis___ (*My*) amigas son inglesas.
8. Son ___sus___ (*his*) cuadernos.

Práctica

1 La familia de Manolo
Complete each sentence with the correct possessive adjective from the options in parentheses. Use the subject of each sentence as a guide.

1. Me llamo Manolo, y __mi__ (nuestro, mi, sus) hermano es Federico.
2. __Nuestra__ (Nuestra, Sus, Mis) madre Silvia es profesora y enseña química.
3. Ella admira a __sus__ (tu, nuestro, sus) estudiantes porque trabajan mucho.
4. Yo estudio en la misma escuela, pero no tomo clases con __mi__ (mi, nuestras, tus) madre.
5. Federico trabaja en una oficina con __nuestro__ (mis, tu, nuestro) padre.
6. __Su__ (Mi, Su, Tu) oficina está en el centro de la Ciudad de México.
7. Javier y Óscar son __mis__ (mis, mi, sus) tíos de Oaxaca.
8. ¿Y tú? ¿Cómo es __tu__ (mi, su, tu) familia?

AYUDA
Remember that possessive adjectives don't agree in number or gender with the *owner* of an item, but rather with the item(s) or person(s) they describe.

2 Clarificar
Clarify each sentence with a prepositional phrase. Follow the model.

modelo
Su hermana es muy bonita. (ella)
La hermana de ella es muy bonita.

1. Su casa es muy grande. (ellos) — La casa de ellos es muy grande.
2. ¿Cómo se llama su hermano? (ellas) — ¿Cómo se llama el hermano de ellas?
3. Sus padres trabajan en el centro. (ella) — Los padres de ella trabajan en el centro.
4. Sus abuelos son muy simpáticos. (él) — Los abuelos de él son muy simpáticos.
5. Maribel es su prima. (ella) — Maribel es la prima de ella.
6. Su primo lee los libros. (ellos) — El primo de ellos lee los libros.

3 ¿Dónde está?
With a partner, imagine that you can't remember where you put some of the belongings you see in the pictures. Your partner will help you by reminding you where your things are. Take turns playing each role. *Answers will vary.*

modelo
Estudiante 1: ¿Dónde está mi mochila?
Estudiante 2: Tu mochila está encima del escritorio.

1.   2.   3.
4.   5.   6.

CONSULTA
For a list of useful prepositions, refer to the table *Prepositions often used with estar*, in **Estructura 2.3**, p. 60.

Comunicación

4 Describir With a partner, take turns describing the people and places listed below. Make note of any similarities and be prepared to share them with the class. Answers will vary.

modelo

la biblioteca de su escuela
La biblioteca de nuestra escuela es muy grande. Hay muchos libros en la biblioteca. Mis amigos y yo estudiamos en la biblioteca.

1. tu profesor favorito
2. tu profesora favorita
3. su clase de español
4. la biblioteca de su escuela
5. tus padres
6. tus abuelos
7. tu mejor (*best*) amigo
8. tu mejor amiga
9. su escuela
10. tu país de origen

5 Una familia famosa Assume the identity of a member of a famous family, real or fictional (the Obamas, Clintons, Bushes, Kardashians, Simpsons, etc.), and write a description of "your" family. Be sure not to use any names! Then, in small groups, take turns reading the descriptions aloud. The other group members may ask follow-up questions to help them identify the famous person. Answers will vary.

modelo

Estudiante 1: Soy periodista. Mi esposo es el rey de un país. Tengo dos hijas.
Estudiante 2: ¿Eres española?
Estudiante 1: Sí.
Estudiante 3: ¿Eres Letizia Ortiz Rocasolano, la reina de España?
Estudiante 1: Sí.

Síntesis

6 Describe a tu familia Get together with two classmates and describe your family to them in several sentences (**Mi padre es alto y moreno. Mi madre es delgada y muy bonita. Mis hermanos son...**). They will work together to try to repeat your description (**Su padre es alto y moreno. Su madre...**). If they forget any details, they can ask you questions (**¿Es alto tu hermano?**). Alternate roles until all of you have described your families. Answers will vary.

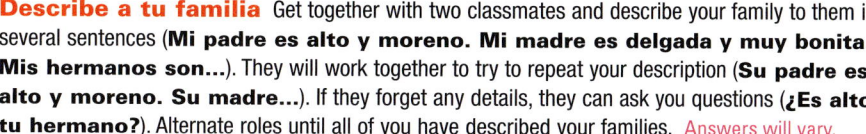

EXPANSION

Extra Practice Have students work in small groups to prepare a description of a famous person, such as a politician, a movie star, or a sports figure, and his or her extended family. Tell them to feel free to invent family members as necessary. Have groups present their descriptions to the class.

DIFFERENTIATION

Heritage Speakers Ask heritage speakers to describe their families' home countries (**países de origen**) for the class. As they are giving their descriptions, ask questions that elicit more information. Clarify for the class any unfamiliar words and expressions they may use.

Section Goals

In **Estructura 3.3**, students will learn:
- the present-tense forms of regular **-er** and **-ir** verbs
- some high-frequency regular **-er** and **-ir** verbs

Communication 1.1
Comparisons 4.1

Student Resources
Cuaderno de práctica y actividades comunicativas, pp. 75–80
Cuaderno para hispanohablantes, pp. 41–42
Supersite: Activities, eCuaderno

Teacher Resources
Workbook TE; Grammar Slides; Audio Activities MP3s; Audio Script; Testing Program Quizzes; Activity Pack; Middle School Activity Pack

Teaching Tips
- Review the present tense of **-ar** verbs. Write **trabajo** on the board and ask for the corresponding subject pronoun. **(yo)** Continue until you have the entire paradigm. Underline the endings, pointing out the characteristic vowel (**-a-**) where it appears and the personal endings.
- Ask questions and make statements that use the verb **comer** to elicit all the present-tense forms. Ex: **¿Comes en la cafetería o en un restaurante? Yo no como en la cafetería. ¿Come ____ en casa?** As you elicit responses, write just the verbs on the board until you have the complete conjugation. Repeat the process with **escribir**. Ex: **¿Quién escribe muchos mensajes de texto? ¿A quién escribes?** When you have a complete paradigm of both verbs, contrast it with the paradigm of **trabajar**.

---

96   noventa y seis   **Lección 3**

3.3 Present tense of -er and -ir verbs

ANTE TODO   In **Lección 2,** you learned how to form the present tense of regular **-ar** verbs. You also learned about the importance of verb forms, which change to show who is performing the action. The chart below shows the forms from two other important groups, **-er** verbs and **-ir** verbs.

Present tense of -er and -ir verbs

		comer (to eat)	**escrib**ir (to write)
SINGULAR FORMS	yo	com**o**	escrib**o**
	tú	com**es**	escrib**es**
	Ud./él/ella	com**e**	escrib**e**
PLURAL FORMS	nosotros/as	com**emos**	escrib**imos**
	vosotros/as	com**éis**	escrib**ís**
	Uds./ellos/ellas	com**en**	escrib**en**

▶ **-Er** and **-ir** verbs have very similar endings. Study the preceding chart to detect the patterns that make it easier for you to use them to communicate in Spanish.

Felipe y su tío comen.

Jimena lee.

▶ Like **-ar** verbs, the **yo** forms of **-er** and **-ir** verbs end in **-o.**
    Yo com**o**.   Yo escrib**o**.

▶ Except for the **yo** form, all of the verb endings for **-er** verbs begin with **-e.**

    -es   -emos   -en
    -e   -éis

▶ **-Er** and **-ir** verbs have the exact same endings, except in the **nosotros/as** and **vosotros/as** forms.

    nosotros ◀ com**emos**   vosotros ◀ com**éis**
                 escrib**imos**   escrib**ís**

Tutorial

CONSULTA
To review the conjugation of **-ar** verbs, see **Estructura 2.1,** p. 50.

AYUDA
Here are some tips on learning Spanish verbs:
1) Learn to identify the verb's stem, to which all endings attach.
2) Memorize the endings that go with each verb and verb tense.
3) As often as possible, practice using different forms of each verb in speech and writing.
4) Devote extra time to learning irregular verbs, such as **ser** and **estar**.

DIFFERENTIATION

Heritage Speakers Have heritage speakers make statements about themselves or their family members, using different verbs from the chart on page 97. Some statements should be true and others should be false. Have the class guess which statements are true and encourage them to ask follow-up questions.

TEACHING OPTIONS

Game Divide the class into two teams. Name an infinitive and a subject pronoun (Ex: **creer/yo**) and have a member of team A give the appropriate conjugation. If the student answers correctly, team A gets one point. If he or she is incorrect, give a member of team B the same items. If that student doesn't know the answer, say the correct form and start over with a new infinitive and subject pronoun. The team with the most points at the end wins.

La familia

noventa y siete 97

Common -er and -ir verbs

-er verbs		-ir verbs	
aprender (a + *inf.*)	to learn	abrir	to open
beber	to drink	asistir (a)	to attend
comer	to eat	compartir	to share
comprender	to understand	decidir (+ *inf.*)	to decide
correr	to run	describir	to describe
creer (en)	to believe (in)	escribir	to write
deber (+ *inf.*)	should; must; ought to	recibir	to receive
leer	to read	vivir	to live

Ellos **corren** en el parque.

Él **escribe** una carta.

¡INTÉNTALO! Provide the appropriate present tense forms of these verbs.

correr
1. Graciela _corre_.
2. Tú _corres_.
3. Yo _corro_.
4. Sara y Ana _corren_.
5. Usted _corre_.
6. Ustedes _corren_.
7. La gente _corre_.
8. Marcos y yo _corremos_.

abrir
1. Ellos _abren_ la puerta.
2. Carolina _abre_ la maleta.
3. Yo _abro_ las ventanas.
4. Nosotras _abrimos_ los libros.
5. Usted _abre_ el cuaderno.
6. Tú _abres_ la ventana.
7. Ustedes _abren_ las maletas.
8. Los muchachos _abren_ los cuadernos.

aprender
1. Él _aprende_ español.
2. Maribel y yo _aprendemos_ inglés.
3. Tú _aprendes_ japonés.
4. Tú y tu hermanastra _aprenden_ francés.
5. Mi hijo _aprende_ chino.
6. Yo _aprendo_ alemán.
7. Usted _aprende_ inglés.
8. Nosotros _aprendemos_ italiano.

recursos
vText
CPA pp. 75–77
CH pp. 41–42
vhlcentral

EXPANSION

Video Replay the **Fotonovela**. Have students listen for **-er/-ir** verbs and write down those they hear. Afterward, write the verbs on the board and ask their meanings. Have students write original sentences using each verb.

EXPANSION

Extra Practice Have students answer questions about their Spanish class. Have them answer in complete sentences. Ex: ¿Ustedes estudian mucho para la clase de español o deben estudiar más? Leen las lecciones, ¿no? Escriben mucho en clase, ¿verdad? ¿Comen sándwiches en clase? ¿Beben café? Comprenden el libro, ¿no? Pairs may ask each other these questions by changing the verbs to the **tú** form.

Teaching Tips
- Point out the characteristic vowel (**-e-**) of **-er** verbs. Help students see that all the present-tense endings of regular **-er/-ir** verbs are the same except for the **nosotros/as** and **vosotros/as** forms.
- Reinforce **-er/-ir** endings and introduce the verbs by asking the class questions. First, ask a series of questions with a single verb until you have elicited all of its present-tense forms. Have students answer with complete sentences. Ex: ¿**Aprenden ustedes historia en nuestra clase? ¿Aprendes álgebra en tu clase de matemáticas? ¿Qué aprenden ____ y ____ en la clase de computación? Aprendo mucho cuando leo, ¿verdad?** Then, ask questions using all the verbs at random.
- Prepare a series of sentences about students and professors using the verbs on this page, but do not include the subjects. Have students write **estudiante** and **profesor** on separate sheets of paper. Read each sentence aloud and have students hold up **estudiante** if it refers to a student, **profesor** if it refers to a professor, or both pieces of paper if it can relate to either person. Ex: **No vive en una residencia estudiantil.** (students hold up **profesor**) **Aprende los verbos.** (students hold up **estudiante**) **Hoy decide comer en la cafetería.** (students hold up both papers)
- Ask questions based on the photos. Ex: ¿**Quiénes corren en el parque en la foto? ¿Ustedes corren? ¿Dónde corren? ¿A quién creen que escribe el chico? ¿A quién escriben ustedes?**
- Ask students to write a description of things they routinely do in Spanish class or in any of their other classes. Encourage them to use as many **-er/-ir** verbs that they can.

Estructura 97

Communication 1.1
Comparisons 4.1

1 Expansion
- As a class, come up with the questions that would elicit the statements in this activity. Ex: ¿Dónde viven tú y tu familia? ¿Cuántos libros tienes? ¿Por qué tienes muchos libros? ¿Cómo es tu hermano Alfredo? ¿Cuándo asiste Alfredo a sus clases? ¿Cuándo corren ustedes? ¿Qué comen tus padres los domingos? ¿Cuánto deben comer tus padres?
- Have small groups describe the family pictured here. Ask the groups to invent each person's name, using Hispanic naming conventions, and include a physical description, place of origin, and the family relationship to the other people in the photo.

2 Teaching Tip To simplify, guide students in classifying the infinitives as **-er** or **-ir**. Then help them identify the subject for each verb and the appropriate verb ending. Finally, aid students in identifying any missing words.

2 Expansion Have pairs create two additional dehydrated sentences for another pair to write out.

3 Teaching Tip To challenge students, add these words to the list: **aprender historia japonesa, comer más *sushi*, escribir más cartas, describir sus experiencias.**

3 Expansion Have students imagine that they are studying for the summer in a Spanish-speaking country. Using the verbs in the word bank as a guide, have them write an e-mail to a friend back home. Tell students to state four things they are doing, three things they and their classmates are doing, and two things that they should be doing.

98   Teacher's Edition • Lesson Three

---

noventa y ocho   Lección 3

Práctica

1 Completar Complete Susana's sentences about her family with the correct forms of the verbs in parentheses. One of the verbs will remain in the infinitive.

1. Mi familia y yo __vivimos__ (vivir) en Mérida, Yucatán.
2. Tengo muchos libros. Me gusta __leer__ (leer).
3. Mi hermano Alfredo es muy inteligente. Alfredo __asiste__ (asistir) a clases los lunes, miércoles y viernes.
4. Los martes y jueves Alfredo y yo __corremos__ (correr) en el Parque del Centenario.
5. Mis padres __comen__ (comer) mucha lasaña los domingos y se quedan dormidos (*they fall asleep*).
6. Yo __creo__ (creer) que (*that*) mis padres deben comer menos (*less*).

2 Oraciones Juan is talking about what he and his friends do after school. Form complete sentences by adding any other necessary elements.

> **modelo**
> yo / correr / amigos / lunes y miércoles
> Yo corro con mis amigos los lunes y miércoles.

1. Manuela / asistir / clase / yoga   Manuela asiste a la clase de yoga.
2. Eugenio / abrir / correo electrónico (*e-mail*)   Eugenio abre su correo electrónico.
3. Isabel y yo / leer / biblioteca   Isabel y yo leemos en la biblioteca.
4. Sofía y Roberto / aprender / hablar / inglés   Sofía y Roberto aprenden a hablar inglés.
5. tú / comer / cafetería / escuela   Tú comes en la cafetería de la escuela.
6. mi novia y yo / compartir / libro de historia   Mi novia y yo compartimos el libro de historia.

3 Consejos Mario and his family are spending a year abroad to learn Japanese. In pairs, use the words below to say what he and/or his family members are doing or should do to adjust to life in Japan. Then, create one more sentence using a verb not on the list.   Answers will vary.

> **modelo**
> recibir libros / deber practicar japonés
> **Estudiante 1:** Mario y su esposa reciben muchos libros en japonés.
> **Estudiante 2:** Los hijos deben practicar japonés.

aprender japonés	decidir explorar el país
asistir a clases	escribir listas de palabras en japonés
beber té (*tea*)	leer novelas japonesas
deber comer cosas nuevas	vivir con una familia japonesa
¿?	¿?

Practice more at vhlcentral.com.

TEACHING OPTIONS

Pairs Have pairs of students role-play an interview with a movie star. Allow sufficient time to plan and practice; they can review previous lesson vocabulary if needed. After completing the activity, ask a few pairs to introduce their characters and perform the interview for the class.
TPR Create a list of phrases similar to those in **Actividad 3**, but change the context to a Spanish-speaking country. In

DIFFERENTIATION

groups of three, have students act out the activities for their classmates to guess.
Heritage Speakers Have heritage speakers brainstorm a list of things that an exchange student in a Spanish-speaking country might want to do. Have them base their list on **Actividad 3** using as many **-er/-ir** verbs as they can. Then have the rest of the class write complete sentences based on the list.

La familia   noventa y nueve **99**

Comunicación

4 Entrevista With a classmate, use these questions to interview each other. Be prepared to report the results of your interviews to the class. *Answers will vary.*

1. ¿Dónde comes al mediodía? ¿Comes mucho?
2. ¿Cuándo asistes a tus clases?
3. ¿Cuál es tu clase favorita? ¿Por qué?
4. ¿Dónde vives?
5. ¿Con quién vives?
6. ¿Qué cursos debes tomar el próximo (*next*) semestre?
7. ¿Lees el periódico (*newspaper*)? ¿Qué periódico lees y cuándo?
8. ¿Recibes muchos mensajes de texto (*text messages*)? ¿De quién(es)?
9. ¿Escribes poemas?
10. ¿Crees en fantasmas (*ghosts*)?

5 Encuesta Your teacher will give you a worksheet. Walk around the class and ask a different classmate each question about his/her family members. Be prepared to report the results of your survey to the class. *Answers will vary.*

Actividades	Miembros de la familia
1. vivir en una casa	los padres de Alicia
2. beber café	
3. correr todos los días (*every day*)	
4. comer mucho en restaurantes	
5. recibir mucho correo electrónico (*e-mail*)	
6. comprender tres lenguas	
7. deber estudiar más (*more*)	
8. leer muchos libros	

Síntesis

6 Horario Your teacher will give you and a partner incomplete versions of Alicia's schedule. Fill in the missing information on the schedule by talking to your partner. Be prepared to reconstruct Alicia's complete schedule with the class. *Answers will vary.*

modelo
Estudiante 1: A las ocho, Alicia corre.
Estudiante 2: ¡Ah, sí! (*Writes down information.*) A las nueve, ella...

TEACHING OPTIONS

Small Groups Have small groups talk about their favorite classes and teachers. They should describe the classes and the teachers and indicate why they like them. They should also mention what days and times they attend each class. Ask a few volunteers to present a summary of their conversation.

EXPANSION

Extra Practice Add an auditory aspect to this grammar practice. Use these sentences as a dictation. Read each twice, pausing after each time for students to write. **1. Mi hermana Juana y yo vivimos en Quito. 2. Ella asiste a la universidad y yo asisto a una escuela cerca de casa. 3. Juana es estudiante de literatura y lee mucho. 4. A mí me gusta la computación y aprendo a programar computadoras.**

Communication 1.1
Comparisons 4.1

4 Teaching Tip Students should complete their interviews before switching roles.

21st Century Skills

4 Technology Literacy Ask students to prepare a digital presentation to show the trends of the whole class for this activity.

4 Virtual Chat You can also assign activity 4 on the Supersite. Students record individual responses that appear in your gradebook.

5 Teaching Tips
- Model one or two items. Then distribute the Communication Activities worksheets from the Activity Pack.
- The activity can also be done in pairs. Have students change the heading of the second column to **¿Sí o no?** and ask each other the same questions about themselves.

5 Expansion Find out how the items apply to the class. Record the results on the board. Ask: **¿Quiénes viven en una casa?**

Communication 1.1

6 Teaching Tip Divide the class into pairs and distribute the worksheets from the Activity Pack that correspond to this activity. Give students ten minutes to complete this activity.

6 Expansion
- Ask questions based on **Alicia's** schedule. Ex: **¿Qué hace Alicia a las nueve?** (**Ella desayuna.**)
- Have volunteers take turns reading aloud **Alicia's** schedule. Then have them write their own schedules using as many **-er/-ir** verbs as they can.

Estructura **99**

Section Goals	100 cien Lección 3

Section Goals

In **Estructura 3.4**, students will:
- learn the present tense forms of **tener** and **venir**
- learn several common expressions with **tener**

Communication 1.1
Comparisons 4.1

Student Resources
Cuaderno de práctica y actividades comunicativas, pp. 81–83
Cuaderno para hispanohablantes, pp. 43–44
Supersite: Activities, eCuaderno

Teacher Resources
Workbook TE; Grammar Slides; Audio Activities MP3s; Audio Script; Testing Program Quizzes; Activity Pack; Middle School Activity Pack

Teaching Tips
- Model **tener** by asking volunteers questions. Ex: **¿Tienes una familia grande? ¿Tienes hermanos? ¿Cuántos tíos tiene ____? ¿Tienes muchos primos?** Point out that students have been using forms of **tener** since the beginning of the lesson.
- Point out that the **yo** form of **tener** is irregular and ends in **-go**. Begin a paradigm for **tener** by writing **tengo** on the board. Ask volunteers questions that elicit **tengo** such as: **Tengo una pluma, ¿quién tiene un lápiz?**
- Write **tienes, tiene, tienen** in the paradigm. Point out that in the **tú, usted,** and **ustedes** forms, the **-e-** of the verb stem changes to **-ie-**.
- Write **tenemos** in the paradigm and point out that this form is regular.
- Follow the same procedure to present **venir**. Have students give you the **nosotros** forms of **beber** and **escribir** for comparison.

3.4 Present tense of tener and venir

 Tutorial

ANTE TODO   The verbs **tener** (*to have*) and **venir** (*to come*) are among the most frequently used in Spanish. Because most of their forms are irregular, you will have to learn each one individually.

▶ The endings are the same as those of regular **-er** and **-ir** verbs, except for the **yo** forms, which are irregular: **tengo, vengo.**

▶ In the **tú, Ud.,** and **Uds.** forms, the **e** of the stem changes to **ie**, as shown below.

INFINITIVE	VERB STEM	VERB FORM
tener	→ ten- →	tú t**ie**nes
		Ud./él/ella t**ie**ne
		Uds./ellos/ellas t**ie**nen
venir	→ ven- →	tú v**ie**nes
		Ud./él/ella v**ie**ne
		Uds./ellos/ellas v**ie**nen

AYUDA

Use what you already know about regular **-er** and **-ir** verbs to identify the irregularities in **tener** and **venir.**

1) Which verb forms use a regular stem? Which use an irregular stem?

2) Which verb forms use the regular endings? Which use irregular endings?

¿Tienes una familia grande, Marissa?

No, tengo una familia pequeña.

▶ Only the **nosotros** and **vosotros** forms are regular. Compare them to the forms of **comer** and **escribir** that you learned on page 96.

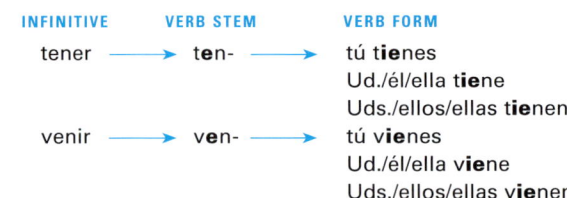

	tener	comer	venir	escribir
nosotros/as	ten**emos**	com**emos**	ven**imos**	escrib**imos**
vosotros/as	ten**éis**	com**éis**	ven**ís**	escrib**ís**

TEACHING OPTIONS

Pairs Have students work in pairs to create a short conversation in which they use forms of **tener, venir,** and other **-er/-ir** verbs they know. Tell them their conversations should involve the family and should include some descriptions of family members. Have pairs role-play their conversations for the class.

EXPANSION

Extra Practice For further practice with the conjugation of **tener** and **venir**, first write a sentence on the board and have students say it. Then say a new subject and have students repeat the sentence, substituting the new subject and making all necessary changes. Ex: **Yo tengo una familia grande.** (Ernesto y yo, usted, tú, ellos) **Claudia y Pilar vienen a la clase de historia.** (nosotras, Ernesto, ustedes, tú)

La familia

▶ In certain idiomatic or set expressions in Spanish, you use the construction **tener** + [*noun*] to express *to be* + [*adjective*]. This chart contains a list of the most common expressions with **tener**.

Expressions with tener

tener… años	*to be… years old*	**tener (mucha) prisa**	*to be in a (big) hurry*
tener (mucho) calor	*to be (very) hot*	**tener razón**	*to be right*
tener (mucho) cuidado	*to be (very) careful*	**no tener razón**	*to be wrong*
tener (mucho) frío	*to be (very) cold*	**tener (mucha) sed**	*to be (very) thirsty*
tener (mucha) hambre	*to be (very) hungry*	**tener (mucho) sueño**	*to be (very) sleepy*
tener (mucho) miedo (de)	*to be (very) afraid/ scared (of)*	**tener (mucha) suerte**	*to be (very) lucky*

—¿**Tienen** hambre ustedes? —Sí, y **tenemos** sed también.
Are you hungry? *Yes, and we're thirsty, too.*

▶ To express an obligation, use **tener que** (*to have to*) + [*infinitive*].

—¿Qué **tienes que** estudiar hoy? —**Tengo que** estudiar biología.
What do you have to study today? *I have to study biology.*

▶ To ask people if they feel like doing something, use **tener ganas de** (*to feel like*) + [*infinitive*].

—¿**Tienes ganas de** comer? —No, **tengo ganas de** dormir.
Do you feel like eating? *No, I feel like sleeping.*

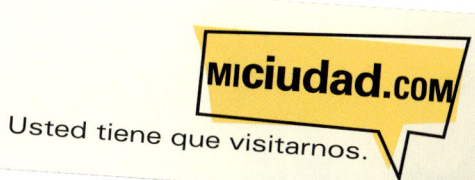
Usted tiene que visitarnos.

¡INTÉNTALO!  Provide the appropriate forms of **tener** and **venir**.

tener
1. Ellos __tienen__ dos hermanos.
2. Yo __tengo__ una hermana.
3. El artista __tiene__ tres primos.
4. Nosotros __tenemos__ diez tíos.
5. Eva y Diana __tienen__ un sobrino.
6. Usted __tiene__ cinco nietos.
7. Tú __tienes__ dos hermanastras.
8. Ustedes __tienen__ cuatro hijos.
9. Ella __tiene__ una hija.

venir
1. Mis padres __vienen__ de México.
2. Tú __vienes__ de España.
3. Nosotras __venimos__ de Cuba.
4. Pepe __viene__ de Italia.
5. Yo __vengo__ de Francia.
6. Ustedes __vienen__ de Canadá.
7. Alfonso y yo __venimos__ de Portugal.
8. Ellos __vienen__ de Alemania.
9. Usted __viene__ de Venezuela.

Práctica

1 Emparejar Find the expression in column B that best matches an item in column A. Then, come up with a new item that corresponds with the leftover expression in column B.

A
1. el Polo Norte — c
2. una sauna — a
3. la comida salada (*salty food*) — b
4. una persona muy inteligente — d
5. un abuelo — g
6. una dieta — f

B
a. tener calor
b. tener sed
c. tener frío
d. tener razón
e. tener ganas de
f. tener hambre
g. tener 75 años

2 Completar Complete the sentences with the correct forms of **tener** or **venir**.

1. Hoy nosotros __tenemos__ una reunión familiar (*family reunion*).
2. Yo __vengo__ en autobús del aeropuerto (*airport*) de Quito.
3. Todos mis parientes __vienen__, excepto mi tío Manolo y su esposa.
4. Ellos no __tienen__ ganas de venir porque viven en Portoviejo.
5. Mi prima Susana y su novio no __vienen__ hasta las ocho porque ella __tiene__ que trabajar.
6. En las fiestas, mi hermana siempre (*always*) __viene__ muy tarde (*late*).
7. Nosotros __tenemos__ mucha suerte porque las reuniones son divertidas (*fun*).
8. Mi madre cree que mis sobrinos son muy simpáticos. Creo que ella __tiene__ razón.

3 Describir Describe what these people are doing or feeling, using an expression with **tener**.

1. Tiene (mucha) prisa.

2. Tiene (mucho) calor.

3. Tiene veintiún años.

4. Tienen (mucha) hambre.

5. Tienen (mucho) frío.

6. Tiene (mucha) sed.

Practice more at vhlcentral.com.

Comunicación

4 ¿Sí o no? Indicate whether these statements apply to you by checking either **Sí** or **No**.

Answers will vary.

	Sí	No
1. Mi padre tiene 50 años.	○	○
2. Mis amigos vienen a mi casa todos los días (*every day*).	○	○
3. Vengo a clase a tiempo (*on time*).	○	○
4. Tengo hambre.	○	○
5. Tengo dos computadoras.	○	○
6. Tengo sed.	○	○
7. Tengo que estudiar los domingos.	○	○
8. Tengo una familia grande.	○	○

Now interview a classmate by transforming each statement into a question. Be prepared to report the results of your interview to the class. Answers will vary.

modelo
Estudiante 1: ¿Tiene tu padre 50 años?
Estudiante 2: No, no tiene 50 años. Tiene 40.

5 Preguntas With a classmate, ask each other these questions. Answers will vary.

1. ¿Tienes que estudiar hoy?
2. ¿Cuántos años tienes? ¿Y tus hermanos/as?
3. ¿Cuándo vienes a la clase de español?
4. ¿Cuándo vienen tus amigos a tu casa o apartamento?
5. ¿De qué tienes miedo? ¿Por qué?
6. ¿Qué tienes ganas de hacer esta noche (*tonight*)?

6 Conversación Use an expression with **tener** to hint at what's on your mind. Your partner will ask questions to find out why you feel that way. If your partner cannot guess what's on your mind after three attempts, tell him/her. Then switch roles. Answers will vary.

modelo
Estudiante 1: Tengo miedo.
Estudiante 2: ¿Tienes que hablar en público?
Estudiante 1: No.
Estudiante 2: ¿Tienes un examen hoy?
Estudiante 1: Sí, y no tengo tiempo para estudiar.

Síntesis

7 Minidrama Act out this situation with a partner: you are introducing your best friend to your extended family. To avoid any surprises before you go, talk about who is coming and what each family member is like. Switch roles. Answers will vary.

TEACHING OPTIONS

Small Groups Have small groups prepare skits in which one person takes a few friends to a family reunion. The first person should make polite introductions and tell the people he or she is introducing a few facts about each other. All the people involved should attempt to make small talk.

TEACHING OPTIONS

Pairs Give pairs of students five minutes to write a conversation in which they use as many **tener** expressions as they can in a logical manner. Have the top three pairs perform their conversations for the class.

Communication 1.1
Comparisons 4.1

5 Teaching Tip You may want to provide additional vocabulary for item 5.

5 Virtual Chat You can also assign activity 5 on the Supersite. Students record individual responses that appear in your gradebook.

6 Teaching Tip Model the activity by giving an expression with **tener**. Ex: **Tengo mucha prisa.** Encourage students to guess the reason, using **tener** and **venir**. If they guess incorrectly, give them more specific clues. Ex: **Tengo mucho que hacer hoy. Es un día especial. (Viene un amigo a la casa.)**

Communication 1.1

Pre-AP*

7 Interpersonal Speaking Before doing **Síntesis,** have students quickly review this material: family vocabulary on pages 78–79; descriptive adjectives on pages 88–90; possessive adjectives on page 93; and the forms of **tener** and **venir** on pages 100–101.

21st Century Skills

7 Productivity and Accountability Provide students with the oral testing rubric found in the Teacher Resources on the Supersite. Ask them to keep these strategies in mind as they prepare their oral exchanges.

7 Partner Chat You can also assign activity 7 on the Supersite. Students work in pairs to record the activity online. The pair's recorded conversation will appear in your gradebook.

Section Goal

In **Recapitulación**, students will review the grammar concepts from this lesson.

Student Resources
Supersite: Activities

1 Teaching Tips
- To add an auditory aspect to the activity, have students read their answers aloud, emphasizing the adjective ending sounds -a(s) and -o(s).
- Remind students that some adjectives have the same masculine and feminine forms.

1 Expansion
Ask students to rewrite the sentences to convey an opposite or different meaning. Ex: **1. Mi tía es francesa. Vive en París. 2. Mi primo no es moreno, es rubio.**

2 Teaching Tip
Remind students that possessive adjectives agree in number (and in gender for **nuestro/a** and **vuestro/a**) with the nouns they modify, not with the subject. Therefore, in item 1, even though **Esteban y Julio** is a plural subject, **su** is singular to agree with **tía**.

2 Expansion
Have students rewrite the sentences using different subjects. Encourage them to add an additional sentence to each item using any of the -er/-ir verbs they have learned in this lesson. Ex: **Yo tengo una tía. Es mi tía. Ella vive en Nueva York.**

3 Teaching Tip
To simplify, have students circle the subject and underline the verb before forming the sentences.

3 Expansion
Have pairs create two additional dehydrated sentences for another pair to write out.

Recapitulación

RESUMEN GRAMATICAL

Diagnostics

Review the grammar concepts you have learned in this lesson by completing these activities.

1 Adjetivos Complete each sentence with the appropriate adjective. Change the form of the adjective as necessary for gender/number agreement. **12 pts.**

| antipático | interesante | mexicano |
| difícil | joven | moreno |

1. Mi tía es _mexicana_. Vive en Guadalajara.
2. Mi primo no es rubio, es _moreno_.
3. Mi amigo cree que la clase no es fácil; es _difícil_.
4. Los libros son _interesantes_; me gustan mucho.
5. Mis hermanos son _antipáticos_; no tienen muchos amigos.
6. Las gemelas tienen nueve años. Son _jóvenes_.

2 Completar For each set of sentences, provide the appropriate form of the verb **tener** and the possessive adjective. Follow the model. **24 pts.**

modelo
Él **tiene** un libro. Es **su** libro.

1. Esteban y Julio _tienen_ una tía. Es _su_ tía.
2. Yo _tengo_ muchos amigos. Son _mis_ amigos.
3. Tú _tienes_ tres primas. Son _tus_ primas.
4. María y tú _tienen_ un hermano. Es _su_ hermano.
5. Nosotras _tenemos_ unas mochilas. Son _nuestras_ mochilas.
6. Usted _tiene_ dos sobrinos. Son _sus_ sobrinos.

3 Oraciones Arrange the words in the correct order to form complete logical sentences. ¡Ojo! Don't forget to conjugate the verbs. **10 pts.**

1. libros / unos / tener / interesantes / tú / muy
   Tú tienes unos libros muy interesantes.
2. dos / leer / fáciles / compañera / tu / lecciones
   Tu compañera lee dos lecciones fáciles.
3. mi / francés / ser / amigo / buen / Hugo
   Hugo es mi buen amigo francés./Mi buen amigo francés es Hugo.
4. ser / simpáticas / dos / personas / nosotras
   Nosotras somos dos personas simpáticas.
5. a / clases / menores / mismas / sus / asistir / hermanos / las
   Sus hermanos menores asisten a las mismas clases.

3.1 Descriptive adjectives pp. 88–90

Forms and agreement of adjectives

	Masculine		Feminine	
	Singular	Plural	Singular	Plural
	alt**o**	alt**os**	alt**a**	alt**as**
	inteligent**e**	inteligent**es**	inteligent**e**	inteligent**es**
	trabajad**or**	trabajad**ores**	trabajad**ora**	trabajad**oras**

▶ Descriptive adjectives follow the noun:
   el chico rubio
▶ Adjectives of color and nationality also follow the noun:
   la mujer española, el cuaderno azul
▶ Adjectives of quantity precede the noun:
   muchos libros, dos turistas
▶ When placed before a singular masculine noun, these adjectives are shortened:
   bueno → buen   malo → mal
▶ When placed before a singular noun, **grande** is shortened to **gran**.

3.2 Possessive adjectives p. 93

Singular		Plural	
mi	nuestro/a	mis	nuestros/as
tu	vuestro/a	tus	vuestros/as
su	su	sus	sus

3.3 Present tense of -er and -ir verbs pp. 96–97

com**er**		escrib**ir**	
com**o**	com**emos**	escrib**o**	escrib**imos**
com**es**	com**éis**	escrib**es**	escrib**ís**
com**e**	com**en**	escrib**e**	escrib**en**

3.4 Present tense of tener and venir pp. 100–101

tener		venir	
ten**go**	tenemos	ven**go**	venimos
t**ie**nes	tenéis	v**ie**nes	venís
t**ie**ne	t**ie**nen	v**ie**ne	v**ie**nen

TEACHING OPTIONS

TPR Make sets of cards containing -er and -ir infinitives that are easy to act out. Divide the class into groups of five. Have students take turns drawing a card and acting out the verb for the group. Once someone has correctly guessed the verb, the group members must take turns providing the conjugated forms.

EXPANSION

Extra Practice To add a visual aspect to this grammar review, bring in magazine or newspaper photos of people and places. Have students describe the people and places using descriptive adjectives.

La familia

4 Carta
Complete this letter with the appropriate forms of the verbs in the word list. Not all verbs will be used. **20 pts.**

abrir	correr	recibir
asistir	creer	tener
compartir	escribir	venir
comprender	leer	vivir

Hola, Ángel:

¿Qué tal? (Yo) (1) **Escribo** esta carta (*this letter*) en la biblioteca. Todos los días (2) **vengo** aquí y (3) **leo** un buen libro. Yo (4) **creo** que es importante leer por diversión. Mi amigo José Luis no (5) **comprende** por qué me gusta leer. Él sólo (6) **abre/lee** los libros de texto. Pero nosotros (7) **compartimos** unos intereses. Por ejemplo, los dos somos atléticos; por las mañanas nosotros (8) **corremos**. También nos gustan las ciencias; por las tardes (9) **asistimos** a nuestra clase de biología. Y tú, ¿cómo estás? ¿(Tú) (10) **Tienes** trabajo (*work*)?

5 Su familia
Write a brief description of a friend's family. Describe the family members using vocabulary and structures from this lesson. Write at least five sentences. **34 pts.**

Answers will vary.

modelo
La familia de mi amiga Gabriela es grande. Ella tiene tres hermanos y una hermana. Su hermana mayor es periodista...

6 Proverbio
Complete this proverb with the correct forms of the verbs in parentheses. **4 EXTRA points!**

"Dos andares° **tiene** (*tener*) el dinero°, **viene** (*venir*) despacio° y se va° ligero°."

andares *speeds* dinero *money* despacio *slowly*
se va *it leaves* ligero *quickly*

3 adelante

Lección 3

Section Goals

In **Lectura**, students will:
- learn to use context clues in reading
- read context-rich selections about Hispanic families

 Communication 1.1, 1.2, 1.3
Cultures 2.1, 2.2
Connections 3.1, 3.2
Comparisons 4.2

Student Resources
Cuaderno para hispanohablantes, pp. 45–46
Supersite: Activities

 Pre-AP*

Interpretive Reading: Estrategia
Tell students that they can often infer the meaning of an unfamiliar Spanish word by looking at the word's context and by using common sense. Context clues include synonyms, antonyms, clarifications, definitions, and additional details.
Have students read the sentence **Ayer fui a ver a mi tía abuela, la hermana de mi abuela** from the letter. Point out that the meaning of **tía abuela** can be inferred from its similarity to the known word **abuela** and from the clarification that follows (**la hermana de mi abuela**).

Examinar el texto Have students read Paragraph 1 silently, without looking up the glossed words. Point out the phrase **salgo a pasear** and ask a volunteer to explain how the context might give clues to the meaning. Afterward, point out that **salgo** is the first-person singular form of **salir** (*to go out*). Tell students they will learn all the forms of **salir** in **Lección 4**.

Examinar el formato Guide students to see that the photos and captions reveal that the paragraphs are about several different families.

Lectura  Audio: Reading
Additional Reading

Antes de leer

Estrategia
Guessing meaning from context

As you read in Spanish, you'll often come across words you haven't learned. You can guess what they mean by looking at the surrounding words and sentences. Look at the following text and guess what **tía abuela** means, based on the context.

¡Hola, Claudia!
  ¿Qué hay de nuevo?
¿Sabes qué? Ayer fui a ver a mi tía abuela, la hermana de mi abuela. Tiene 85 años, pero es muy independiente. Vive en un apartamento en Quito con su prima Lorena, quien también tiene 85 años.

If you guessed *great-aunt*, you are correct, and you can conclude from this word and the format clues that this is a letter about someone's visit with his or her great-aunt.

Examinar el texto
Quickly read through the paragraphs and find two or three words you don't know. Using the context as your guide, guess what these words mean. Then glance at the paragraphs where these words appear and try to predict what the paragraphs are about.

Examinar el formato
Look at the format of the reading. What clues do the captions, photos, and layout give you about its content?

recursos
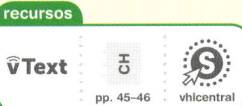
vText CH pp. 45–46 vhlcentral

Gente... Las familias

1. Me llamo Armando y tengo setenta años pero no me considero viejo. Tengo seis nietas y un nieto. Vivo con mi hija y tengo la oportunidad de pasar mucho tiempo con ella y con mi nieto. Por las tardes salgo a pasear° por el parque con él y por la noche le leo cuentos°.

Armando. Tiene seis nietas y un nieto.

2. Mi prima Victoria y yo nos llevamos muy bien. Estudiamos juntas° en la universidad y compartimos un apartamento. Ella es muy inteligente y me ayuda° con los estudios. Además°, es muy simpática y generosa. Si no tengo dinero°, ¡ella me lo presta!

Diana. Vive con su prima.

3. Me llamo Ramona y soy paraguaya, aunque° ahora vivo en los Estados Unidos. Tengo tres hijos, uno de nueve años, uno de doce y el mayor de quince. Es difícil a veces, pero mi esposo y yo tratamos° de ayudarlos y comprenderlos siempre°.

Ramona. Sus hijos son muy importantes para ella.

EXPANSION

Extra Practice Ask students to use the paragraphs in **Gente… Las familias** as models for writing paragraphs about their families, but from the perspective of another family member (e.g., their mother). Have volunteers read their paragraphs aloud.

EXPANSION

Extra Practice Use these items, each of which contains an unfamiliar word or phrase, to practice using context clues. **1. Mi tío Daniel es maestro en una escuela secundaria; enseña ciencias. 2. No, Daniel no es antipático, ¡es un cariño! 3. Por favor, ¿tienes un boli o un lápiz? Te escribo su número de teléfono.**

La familia

4. Tengo mucha suerte. Aunque mis padres están divorciados, tengo una familia muy unida. Tengo dos hermanos y dos hermanas. Me gusta hablar y salir a fiestas con ellos. Ahora tengo novio en la universidad y él no conoce a mis hermanos. ¡Espero que se lleven bien!

Ana María. Su familia es muy unida.

5. Antes quería° tener hermanos, pero ya no° es tan importante. Ser hijo único tiene muchas ventajas°: no tengo que compartir mis cosas con hermanos, no hay discusiones° y, como soy nieto único también, ¡mis abuelos piensan° que soy perfecto!

Fernando. Es hijo único.

6. No tengo ni esposa ni hijos. Pero tengo un sobrino, el hijo de mi hermano, que es muy especial para mí. Se llama Benjamín y tiene diez años. Es un muchacho muy simpático. Siempre tiene hambre y por lo tanto vamos° frecuentemente a comer hamburguesas. Nos gusta también ir al cine° a ver películas de acción. Hablamos de todo. ¡Creo que ser tío es mejor que ser padre!

Santiago. Cree que ser tío es divertido.

salgo a pasear *I go take a walk* cuentos *stories* juntas *together*
me ayuda *she helps me* Además *Besides* dinero *money* aunque *although*
tratamos *we try* siempre *always* quería *I wanted* ya no *no longer*
ventajas *advantages* discusiones *arguments* piensan *think* vamos *we go*
ir al cine *to go to the movies*

Después de leer

Emparejar

Glance at the paragraphs and see how the words and phrases in column A are used in context. Then find their definitions in column B.

A		B
1. me lo presta	d	a. the oldest
2. nos llevamos bien	h	b. movies
3. no conoce	g	c. the youngest
4. películas	b	d. loans it to me
5. mejor que	j	e. borrows it from me
6. el mayor	a	f. we see each other
		g. doesn't know
		h. we get along
		i. portraits
		j. better than

Seleccionar

Choose the sentence that best summarizes each paragraph.

1. Párrafo 1 a
   a. Me gusta mucho ser abuelo.
   b. No hablo mucho con mi nieto.
   c. No tengo nietos.
2. Párrafo 2 c
   a. Mi prima es antipática.
   b. Mi prima no es muy trabajadora.
   c. Mi prima y yo somos muy buenas amigas.
3. Párrafo 3 a
   a. Tener hijos es un gran sacrificio, pero es muy bonito también.
   b. No comprendo a mis hijos.
   c. Mi esposo y yo no tenemos hijos.
4. Párrafo 4 c
   a. No hablo mucho con mis hermanos.
   b. Comparto mis cosas con mis hermanos.
   c. Mis hermanos y yo somos como (*like*) amigos.
5. Párrafo 5 a
   a. Me gusta ser hijo único.
   b. Tengo hermanos y hermanas.
   c. Vivo con mis abuelos.
6. Párrafo 6 b
   a. Mi sobrino tiene diez años.
   b. Me gusta mucho ser tío.
   c. Mi esposa y yo no tenemos hijos.

Practice more at vhlcentral.com.

Section Goals

In **Escritura**, students will:
- learn to write a friendly letter in Spanish
- integrate vocabulary and structures taught in **Lección 3** and before

 Communication 1.3

Student Resources
Cuaderno de práctica y actividades comunicativas, pp. 84–85
Cuaderno para hispanohablantes, pp. 47–48
Supersite: Activities, eCuaderno

Teacher Resources
Workbook TE

 TELL Connection

Learning Experience 5
Why and *What:* Students need strategies (e.g. Idea Maps) and tools (e.g. Salutations) to stay in the target language.

 Pre-AP*

Interpersonal Writing: Estrategia
Have students create their idea maps in Spanish. Some students may find it helpful to use note cards to create their idea maps.

Tema
- Point out that the salutation **Estimado/a** is more formal than **Querido/a**, which is more familiar. Also explain that **Un abrazo** is less familiar in Spanish than its English translation.
- Point out that **Estimado/a** and **Querido/a** are adjectives and thus change in gender and number. Write salutations on the board and have students supply the correct form:
   ____ **Señora Martínez:** (Estimada)
   ____ **Allison:** (Querida)
   ____ **padres:** (Queridos)
- Point out the use of the colon (**dos puntos**), which is used instead of a comma.

108 Teacher's Edition • Lesson Three

---

108 ciento ocho — Lección 3

Escritura

Estrategia
Using idea maps

How do you organize ideas for a first draft? Often, the organization of ideas represents the most challenging part of the process. Idea maps are useful for organizing pertinent information. Here is an example of an idea map you can use:

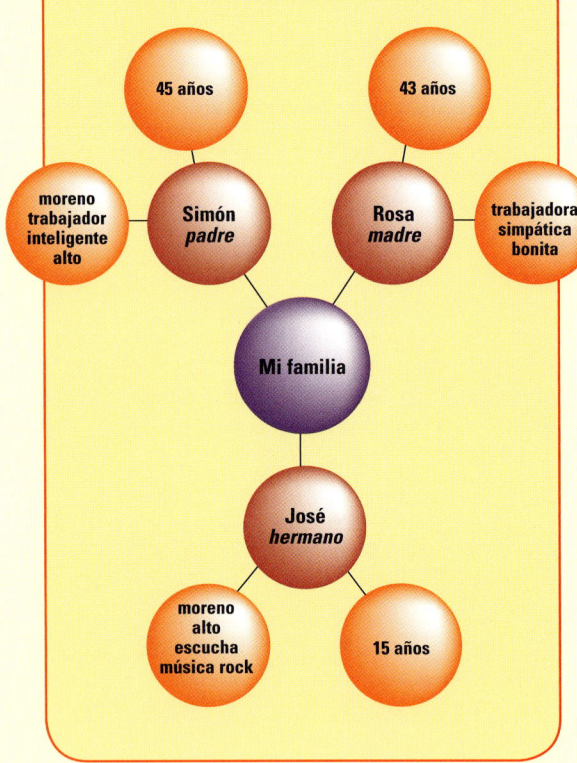

MAPA DE IDEAS

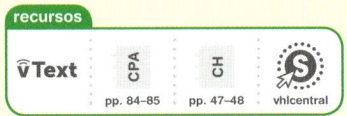

recursos — vText pp. 84–85 — CPA pp. 47–48 — CH vhlcentral

Tema

Escribir un mensaje electrónico

A friend you met in a chat room for Spanish speakers wants to know about your family. Using some of the verbs and adjectives you have learned in this lesson, write a brief e-mail describing your family or an imaginary family, including:

▶ Names and relationships
▶ Physical characteristics
▶ Hobbies and interests

Here are some useful expressions for writing a letter or e-mail in Spanish:

Salutations

Estimado/a Julio/Julia:	Dear Julio/Julia,
Querido/a Miguel/Ana María:	Dear Miguel/Ana María,

Closings

Un abrazo,	A hug,
Abrazos,	Hugs,
Cariños,	Much love,
¡Hasta pronto!	See you soon!
¡Hasta la próxima semana!	See you next week!

EVALUATION: Mensaje electrónico

Criteria	Scale
Appropriate salutations/closings	1 2 3 4 5
Appropriate details	1 2 3 4 5
Organization	1 2 3 4 5
Accuracy	1 2 3 4 5

Scoring	
Excellent	18–20 points
Good	14–17 points
Satisfactory	10–13 points
Unsatisfactory	< 10 points

La familia

Escuchar  Audio

> ### Estrategia
> **Asking for repetition/ Replaying the recording**
>
> Sometimes it is difficult to understand what people say, especially in a noisy environment. During a conversation, you can ask someone to repeat by saying **¿Cómo?** (*What?*) or **¿Perdón?** (*Pardon me?*). In class, you can ask your teacher to repeat by saying **Repita, por favor** (*Repeat, please*). If you don't understand a recorded activity, you can simply replay it.
>
> To help you practice this strategy, you will listen to a short paragraph. Ask your professor to repeat it or replay the recording, and then summarize what you heard.

Preparación

Based on the photograph, where do you think Cristina and Laura are? What do you think Laura is saying to Cristina?

Ahora escucha

Now you are going to hear Laura and Cristina's conversation. Use **R** to indicate which adjectives describe Cristina's boyfriend, Rafael. Use **E** for adjectives that describe Laura's boyfriend, Esteban. Some adjectives will not be used.

____ rubio	_E_ interesante
____ feo	____ antipático
_R_ alto	_R_ inteligente
_E_ trabajador	_R_ moreno
_E_ un poco gordo	____ viejo

Comprensión

Identificar

Which person would make each statement: Cristina or Laura?

	Cristina	Laura
1. Mi novio habla sólo de fútbol y de béisbol.	●	○
2. Tengo un novio muy interesante y simpático.	○	●
3. Mi novio es alto y moreno.	●	○
4. Mi novio trabaja mucho.	○	●
5. Mi amiga no tiene buena suerte con los muchachos.	○	●
6. El novio de mi amiga es un poco gordo, pero guapo.	●	○

¿Cierto o falso?

Indicate whether each sentence is **cierto** or **falso**, then correct the false statements.

	Cierto	Falso
1. Esteban es un chico interesante y simpático.	●	○
2. Laura tiene mala suerte con los chicos. *Cristina tiene mala suerte con los chicos.*	○	●
3. Rafael es muy interesante. *Esteban es muy interesante.*	○	●
4. Laura y su novio hablan de muchas cosas.	●	○

Practice more at **vhlcentral.com**.

---

también… pero es que no lo encuentro muy interesante.
L: ¿Cómo?
C: No es muy interesante. Sólo habla del fútbol y del béisbol. No me gusta hablar del fútbol las veinticuatro horas al día. No comprendo a los muchachos.
C: ¿Cómo es tu novio, Laura?

L: Esteban es muy simpático. Es un poco gordo, pero creo que es muy guapo. También es muy trabajador.
C: ¿Es interesante?
L: Sí. Hablamos dos o tres horas cada día. Hablamos de muchas cosas… las clases, los amigos… de todo.
C: ¡Qué bien! Siempre tengo mala suerte con los novios.

---

ciento nueve **109**

Section Goals

In **Escuchar**, students will:
- listen to and summarize a short paragraph
- learn strategies for asking for clarification in oral communication
- answer questions based on the content of a recorded conversation

 Communication 1.2

> **Student Resources**
> Supersite: Activities
>
> **Teacher Resources**
> Textbook and Audio Activities MP3s, Audio Scripts

 21st Century Skills

Critical Thinking and Problem Solving
Students practice aural comprehension as a tool to negotiate meaning in Spanish.

Estrategia
Script La familia de María Dolores es muy grande. Tiene dos hermanos y tres hermanas. Su familia vive en España. Pero la familia de Alberto es muy pequeña. No tiene hermanos ni hermanas. Alberto y sus padres viven en el Ecuador.

Teaching Tip Have students look at the photo and describe what they see. Guide them to guess where they think **Cristina** and **Laura** are and what they are talking about.

Ahora escucha
Script LAURA: ¿Qué hay de nuevo, Cristina?
CRISTINA: No mucho… sólo problemas con mi novio.
L: ¿Perdón?
C: No hay mucho de nuevo… sólo problemas con mi novio, Rafael.
L: ¿Qué les pasa?
C: Bueno, Rafael es alto y moreno… es muy guapo. Y es buena gente. Es inteligente

(Script continues at far left in the bottom panels.)

Adelante **109**

Section Goals

In **En pantalla**, students will:
- read about dating in the Spanish-speaking world
- watch a television commercial for **Pentel**

Communication 1.1, 1.2, 1.3
Cultures 2.1, 2.2
Connections 3.2
Comparisons 4.2

Student Resources
Supersite: *En pantalla* video, Activities

Teacher Resources
Transcript & Translation

 TELL Connection

Environment 1
Why: Students need a safe learning environment. *What:* Visual representations of **Aplicación** adjectives support positive perceptions of both students and target cultures.

Un beso Check comprehension: 1. Does the American concept of dating exist in the Hispanic world? 2. What kind of pressures might be associated with "being on a date"?

 Pre-AP*

Audiovisual Interpretive Communication
Antes de ver Strategy
- Read through the **Vocabulario útil** with the students.
- Remind students that linguistic cues like adjective agreement can be important clues to meaning.

Aplicación Whether the ad is print or video, have students provide lots of visual support for the product. Encourage students to use short, clear sentences and phrases that focus on the key adjectives.

110 Teacher's Edition • Lesson Three

 Video: TV Clip

Anuncio de **Pentel**

Eres una buena chica.

Preparación
Answer these questions in English. *Answers will vary.*

1. How do you and your friends communicate most effectively? Talking? Texting? In other ways?
2. If you have to give a friend bad news, how do you go about it? How hard or easy is it to tell someone something difficult? Why?

Un beso
The American concept of dating does not exist in the same way in the Spanish-speaking world. In many countries like Mexico, Spain, and Argentina, young people spend most of their time in groups of friends, learning about each other without pairing off right away. This approach means that young people can develop relationships without the social or psychological pressures and expectations of "being on a date." Relationships for young people develop just like in the rest of the world, but perhaps this approach allows for more spontaneity and less "labeling."

Vocabulario útil

has sido	you have been
te sorprenda	it catches you by surprise
quiero que me dejes	I want you to let me
por muy bajo que te parezca	however low it seems to you
Gracias por haberme querido escuchar.	Thank you for having wanted to listen to me.
que me dejes	that you leave me
haberme querido	having loved me
vida	life

Comprensión
Label the adjectives **a** (**el chico**) or **b** (**la chica**), based on what you see in the video.

_a_ 1. bajo/a
_b_ 2. bueno/a
_a_ 3. feo/a
_b_ 4. maravilloso/a *wonderful*
_a_ 5. tonto/a

Conversación
Talk with a classmate about these questions.

1. In the video, what did the young woman expect at the beginning? In what way did her experience differ from her expectation? How did she transform her experience from a negative to a positive one for herself?
2. How did the young man describe himself in the letter? The young woman? Why do you think he wrote in this way?

1. In the beginning, she expected a loving note. In fact, her boyfriend was breaking up with her. She edited the letter to make it a positive message about herself.

Aplicación
Work in small groups to create an ad for a product, using specific adjectives from this chapter to develop a positive message and image. Present the ad to the class, and discuss afterward which ads seem most effective in promoting the product, and why.
Answers will vary.

 Practice more at vhlcentral.com.

 recursos vText vhlcentral

2. He described himself using negative adjectives, while describing her using positive ones. Answers to the final question will vary.

EXPANSION

Culture Note The **Pentel** Company has been in business for 70 years, and is best known for the invention of the rollerball pen. A Japanese company by origin, **Pentel** now has offices and headquarters all over the world, including in Mexico and Panama.

EXPANSION

Extra Practice Point out that **Juan** ends the letter with **Un beso**. Ask students to name other ways for closing a letter that they learned in **Escritura**. Ex: **Abrazos**

Extra Practice Ask additional questions. Ex: What advice would you give this girl? Is the ad effective? Why or why not?

La familia

  Video: Flash cultura

La familia

If a Spanish-speaking friend told you he was going to a **reunión familiar**, what type of event would you picture? Most likely, your friend would not be referring to an annual event reuniting family members from far-flung cities. In Hispanic culture, family gatherings are much more frequent and relaxed, and thus do not require intensive planning or juggling of schedules. Some families gather every Sunday afternoon to enjoy a leisurely meal; others may prefer to hold get-togethers on a Saturday evening, with food, music, and dancing. In any case, gatherings tend to be laid-back events in which family members spend hours chatting, sharing stories, and telling jokes.

Vocabulario útil

el Día de la Madre	Mother's Day
estamos celebrando	we are celebrating
familia grande y feliz	a big, happy family
familia numerosa	a large family
hacer (algo) juntos	to do (something) together
el patio interior	courtyard
pelear	to fight
reuniones familiares	family gatherings, reunions

Preparación
What is a "typical family" like where you live? Is there such a thing? What members of a family usually live together?
Answers will vary.

Completar
Complete this paragraph with the correct options.

Los Valdivieso y los Bolaños son dos ejemplos de familias en Ecuador. Los Valdivieso son una familia (1) __numerosa__ (difícil/numerosa). Viven en una casa (2) __grande__ (grande/buena). En el patio, hacen (*they have*) muchas reuniones (3) __familiares__ (familiares/con amigos). Los Bolaños son una familia pequeña. Ellos comen (4) __juntos__ (separados/juntos) y preparan canelazo, una bebida (*drink*) típica ecuatoriana.

tan *so*

—Érica, ¿y cómo se llaman tus padres?
—Mi mamá, Lorena y mi papá, Miguel.

¡Qué familia tan° grande tiene!

Te presento a la familia Bolaños.

 Practice more at vhlcentral.com.

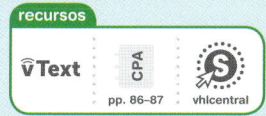

Section Goal

In **Panorama**, students will receive comprehensible input by reading about the geography and culture of Ecuador.

Communication 1.3
Cultures 2.1, 2.2
Connections 3.1, 3.2
Comparisons 4.2

Student Resources
Cuaderno de práctica y actividades comunicativas, pp. 88–91
Supersite: *Panorama cultural* video, Activities, eCuaderno

Teacher Resources
Workbook TE; Digital Image Bank; Video Script & Translation

21st Century Skills

Global Awareness
Students will gain perspectives on the Spanish-speaking world to develop respect and openness to others and to interact appropriately and effectively with citizens of Spanish-speaking cultures.

Teaching Tips
- Have students examine the map of Ecuador and look at the call-out photos and read the captions. Encourage students to mention anything they may know about Ecuador.
- Use the **Lección 3 Panorama** Digital Image Bank to support this presentation.

El país en cifras Point out that in September 2000, the U.S. dollar became the official currency of Ecuador.

¡Increíble pero cierto!
Mt. St. Helens in Washington and **Cotopaxi** in Ecuador are just two of a chain of volcanoes that stretches along the entire Pacific coast of North and South America, from Mt. McKinley in Alaska to **Monte Sarmiento** in the **Tierra del Fuego** of southern Chile.

---

3 panorama

Ecuador

Video: *Panorama cultural*
Interactive Map

El país en cifras

- **Área:** 283.560 km2 (109.483 millas2), incluyendo las islas Galápagos, aproximadamente el área de Colorado
- **Población:** 15.439.000
- **Capital:** Quito—1.622.000
- **Ciudades° principales:** Guayaquil—2.634.000, Cuenca, Machala, Portoviejo
- **Moneda:** dólar estadounidense
- **Idiomas:** español (oficial), quichua

La lengua oficial de Ecuador es el español, pero también se hablan° otras° lenguas en el país. Aproximadamente unos 4.000.000 de ecuatorianos hablan lenguas indígenas; la mayoría° de ellos habla quichua. El quichua es el dialecto ecuatoriano del quechua, la lengua de los incas.

Bandera de Ecuador

Ecuatorianos célebres
- **Francisco Eugenio De Santa Cruz y Espejo,** médico, periodista y patriota (1747–1795)
- **Juan León Mera,** novelista (1832–1894)
- **Eduardo Kingman,** pintor° (1913–1998)
- **Rosalía Arteaga,** abogada°, política y ex vicepresidenta (1956–)
- **Iván Vallejo Ricafuerte,** montañista (1959–)

Ciudades *cities* se hablan *are spoken* otras *other* mayoría *majority* pintor *painter* abogada *lawyer* sur *south* mundo *world* pies *feet* dos veces más alto que *twice as tall as*

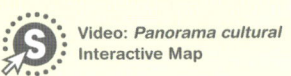

Las islas Galápagos
COLOMBIA
Indígenas del Amazonas
Río Esmeraldas
• Ibarra
Quito
Océano Pacífico
Volcán Cotopaxi
Río Napo
Portoviejo
Río Daule
Volcán Tungurahua
Río Pastaza
Guayaquil
Volcán Chimborazo
Cuenca
Muchos indígenas de Ecuador hablan quichua.
Machala
La ciudad de Quito y la Cordillera de los Andes
• Loja
PERÚ
Catedral de Guayaquil

recursos
vText | CPA pp. 88–91 | vhlcentral

¡Increíble pero cierto!
El volcán Cotopaxi, situado a unos 60 kilómetros al sur° de Quito, es considerado el volcán activo más alto del mundo°. Tiene una altura de 5.897 metros (19.340 pies°). Es dos veces más alto que° el monte Santa Elena (2.550 metros o 9.215 pies) en el estado de Washington.

DIFFERENTIATION

Heritage Speakers If a heritage speaker is of Ecuadorian origin or has visited Ecuador, ask him or her to share some of his or her favorite experiences there. Encourage the rest of the class to ask follow-up questions, and if a particular topic piques their interest, to find out more online.

EXPANSION

Language Notes Remind students that **km2** is the abbreviation for **kilómetros cuadrados** and that **millas2** is the abbreviation for **millas cuadradas**. Ask a volunteer to explain why **kilómetros** takes **cuadrados** and **millas** takes **cuadradas**.

La familia

Lugares • Las islas Galápagos

Muchas personas vienen de lejos a visitar las islas Galápagos porque son un verdadero tesoro° ecológico. Aquí Charles Darwin estudió° las especies que inspiraron° sus ideas sobre la evolución. Como las Galápagos están lejos del continente, sus plantas y animales son únicos. Las islas son famosas por sus tortugas° gigantes.

Artes • Oswaldo Guayasamín

Oswaldo Guayasamín fue° uno de los artistas latinoamericanos más famosos del mundo. Fue escultor° y muralista. Su expresivo estilo viene del cubismo y sus temas preferidos son la injusticia y la pobreza° sufridas° por los indígenas de su país.

Madre y niño en azul, 1986, Oswaldo Guayasamín

Deportes • El *trekking*

El sistema montañoso de los Andes cruza° y divide Ecuador en varias regiones. La Sierra, que tiene volcanes, grandes valles y una variedad increíble de plantas y animales, es perfecta para el *trekking*. Muchos turistas visitan Ecuador cada° año para hacer° *trekking* y escalar montañas°.

Lugares • Latitud 0

Hay un monumento en Ecuador, a unos 22 kilómetros (14 millas) de Quito, donde los visitantes están en el hemisferio norte y el hemisferio sur a la vez°. Este monumento se llama la Mitad del Mundo° y es un destino turístico muy popular.

Explosión del volcán Tungurahua

¿Qué aprendiste? Completa las oraciones con la información correcta.
1. La ciudad más grande (*biggest*) de Ecuador es ___Guayaquil___.
2. La capital de Ecuador es ___Quito___.
3. Unos 4.000.000 de ecuatorianos hablan ___lenguas indígenas___.
4. Darwin estudió el proceso de la evolución en ___las islas Galápagos___.
5. Dos temas del arte de ___Guayasamín___ son la pobreza y la ___injusticia___.
6. Un monumento muy popular es ___la Mitad del Mundo___.
7. La Sierra es un lugar perfecto para el ___trekking___.
8. El volcán ___Cotopaxi___ es el volcán activo más alto del mundo.

Conexión Internet Investiga estos temas en **vhlcentral.com**.
1. Busca información sobre una ciudad de Ecuador. ¿Te gustaría (*Would you like*) visitar la ciudad? ¿Por qué?
2. Haz una lista de tres animales o plantas que viven sólo en las islas Galápagos. ¿Dónde hay animales o plantas similares?

verdadero tesoro *true treasure* **estudió** *studied* **inspiraron** *inspired* **tortugas** *tortoises* **fue** *was* **escultor** *sculptor* **pobreza** *poverty* **sufridas** *suffered* **cruza** *crosses* **cada** *every* **hacer** *to do* **escalar montañas** *to climb mountains* **a la vez** *at the same time* **Mitad del Mundo** *Equatorial Line Monument (lit. Midpoint of the World)*

vocabulario

Student Resources
Cuaderno de práctica y actividades comunicativas, p. 83
Supersite: Activities, *eCuaderno*

Teacher Resources
Workbook TE; Textbook and Testing Audio MP3s; Testing Audio Script; Testing Program Tests

21st Century Skills

Creativity and Innovation
Ask students to prepare a list of the three products or perspectives they learned about in this lesson to share with the class. You may ask them to focus specifically on the **Cultura** and **Panorama** sections.

21st Century Skills

Leadership and Responsibility Extension Project
As a class, have students decide on three questions they want to ask the partner class related to the topic of the lesson they have just completed. Based on the responses they receive, work as a class to explain to the Spanish-speaking partners one aspect of their responses that surprised the class and why.

  My Vocabulary

La familia

el/la abuelo/a	grandfather/grandmother
los abuelos	grandparents
el apellido	last name
el/la bisabuelo/a	great-grandfather/great-grandmother
el/la cuñado/a	brother-in-law/sister-in-law
el/la esposo/a	husband/wife; spouse
la familia	family
el/la gemelo/a	twin
el/la hermanastro/a	stepbrother/stepsister
el/la hermano/a	brother/sister
el/la hijastro/a	stepson/stepdaughter
el/la hijo/a	son/daughter
los hijos	children
la madrastra	stepmother
la madre	mother
el/la medio/a hermano/a	half-brother/half-sister
el/la nieto/a	grandson/granddaughter
la nuera	daughter-in-law
el padrastro	stepfather
el padre	father
los padres	parents
los parientes	relatives
el/la primo/a	cousin
el/la sobrino/a	nephew/niece
el/la suegro/a	father-in-law/mother-in-law
el/la tío/a	uncle/aunt
el yerno	son-in-law

Otras personas

el/la amigo/a	friend
la gente	people
el/la muchacho/a	boy/girl
el/la niño/a	child
el/la novio/a	boyfriend/girlfriend
la persona	person

Profesiones

el/la artista	artist
el/la doctor(a), el/la médico/a	doctor; physician
el/la ingeniero/a	engineer
el/la periodista	journalist
el/la programador(a)	computer programmer

Adjetivos

alto/a	tall
antipático/a	unpleasant
bajo/a	short (in height)
bonito/a	pretty
buen, bueno/a	good
delgado/a	thin; slender
difícil	difficult; hard
fácil	easy
feo/a	ugly
gordo/a	fat
gran, grande	big; large
guapo/a	good-looking
importante	important
inteligente	intelligent
interesante	interesting
joven (sing.), jóvenes (pl.)	young
mal, malo/a	bad
mismo/a	same
moreno/a	brunet(te)
mucho/a	much; many; a lot of
pelirrojo/a	red-haired
pequeño/a	small
rubio/a	blond(e)
simpático/a	nice; likeable
tonto/a	silly; foolish
trabajador(a)	hard-working
viejo/a	old

Colores

amarillo/a	yellow
azul	blue
blanco/a	white
negro/a	black
rojo/a	red
verde	green

Nacionalidades

alemán, alemana	German
argentino/a	Argentine
canadiense	Canadian
chino/a	Chinese
costarricense	Costa Rican
cubano/a	Cuban
ecuatoriano/a	Ecuadorian
español(a)	Spanish
estadounidense	from the U.S.
francés, francesa	French
inglés, inglesa	English
italiano/a	Italian
japonés, japonesa	Japanese
mexicano/a	Mexican
norteamericano/a	(North) American
puertorriqueño/a	Puerto Rican
ruso/a	Russian

Verbos

abrir	to open
aprender (a + *inf.*)	to learn
asistir (a)	to attend
beber	to drink
comer	to eat
compartir	to share
comprender	to understand
correr	to run
creer (en)	to believe (in)
deber (+ *inf.*)	should; must; ought to
decidir (+ *inf.*)	to decide
describir	to describe
escribir	to write
leer	to read
recibir	to receive
tener	to have
venir	to come
vivir	to live

Possessive adjectives	See page 93.
Expressions with *tener*	See page 101.
Expresiones útiles	See page 83.

recursos

  p. 83 vhlcentral

Los pasatiempos

4

Communicative Goals

I will be able to:
- Talk about pastimes, weekend activities, and sports
- Make plans and invitations

contextos
pages 116–119
- Pastimes
- Sports
- Places in the city

fotonovela
pages 120–123
The friends spend the day exploring Mérida and the surrounding area. Maru, Jimena, and Miguel take Marissa to a **cenote**; Felipe and Juan Carlos join Felipe's cousins for soccer and lunch.

cultura
pages 124–125
- Soccer rivalries
- Miguel Cabrera and Paola Espinosa

estructura
pages 126–141
- Present tense of **ir**
- Stem-changing verbs: e:ie; o:ue
- Stem-changing verbs: e:i
- Verbs with irregular **yo** forms
- Recapitulación

adelante
pages 142–149
Lectura: Popular sports in Latin America
Escritura: A pamphlet about activities in your area
Escuchar: A conversation about pastimes
En pantalla
Flash cultura
Panorama: México

A PRIMERA VISTA
- ¿Es esta persona un atleta o un artista?
- ¿En qué tiene interés, en el ciclismo o en el tenis?
- ¿Es viejo? ¿Es delgado?
- ¿Tiene frío o calor?

Lesson Goals
In **Lección 4**, students will be introduced to the following:
- names of sports and other pastimes
- names of places in a city
- soccer rivalries
- baseball player **Miguel Cabrera** and diver **Paola Espinosa**
- present tense of **ir**
- the contraction **al**
- **ir a** + [*infinitive*]
- present tense of common stem-changing verbs
- verbs with irregular **yo** forms
- predicting content from visual elements
- using a Spanish-English dictionary
- writing an events pamphlet
- listening for the gist
- a television commercial for **Totofútbol**, an electronic lottery based on soccer match results
- a video about soccer in Spain
- cultural, historical, economic, and geographic information about Mexico

21st Century Skills

Initiative and Self-Direction
Students can monitor their progress online using the Supersite activities and assessments.

A primera vista Ask these additional questions based on the photo: ¿Te gusta practicar deportes? ¿Crees que son importantes los pasatiempos?

TELL Connection

Performance and Feedback 3
Why: Students take responsibility for monitoring their own performance and proficiency goals. *What:* Hand out the I Can Worksheets available on the Supersite.

SUPPORT FOR BACKWARD DESIGN

Lección 4 Essential Questions
1. How do people talk about pastimes, weekend activities, and sports?
2. How do people make plans and extend invitations?
3. What sports and sports figures are popular in the Spanish-speaking world?

Lección 4 Integrated Performance Assessment
Before teaching this chapter, review the Integrated Performance Assessment (IPA) and its accompanying scoring rubric provided in the Testing Program. Use the IPA to assess students' progress toward proficiency targets at the end of the chapter.
IPA Context: Your school is having an election for student council, and you need to decide what attributes are important in the person you elect. You are going to listen to two people describe themselves. Then, you and a partner will talk about the characteristics that would make each of them a better candidate. Finally, you will describe the characteristics of your ideal candidate to the class.

 Voice boards on the Supersite allow you and your students to record and share up to five minutes of audio. Use voice boards for presentations, oral assessments, discussions, directions, etc.

4 contextos
Lección 4

Section Goals
In **Contextos**, students will learn and practice:
- names of sports and other pastimes
- names of places in a city

Communication 1.2
Comparisons 4.1

Student Resources
Cuaderno de práctica y actividades comunicativas, pp. 95–99
Cuaderno para hispanohablantes, pp. 49–50
Supersite: Activities, eCuaderno

Teacher Resources
Workbook TE; Digital Image Bank; Textbook and Audio Activities MP3s; Audio Scripts; Testing Program Quizzes; Activity Pack; Middle School Activity Pack

Teaching Tips
- Write **practicar un deporte** on the board and explain what it means. Ask: **¿Qué deportes practicas?** Offer some cognates as suggestions: **¿Practicas el béisbol? ¿El vóleibol? ¿El tenis? ¿El golf?** After the student answers, ask another student: **¿Qué deporte practica ____?**
- Use the **Lección 4 Contextos** Digital Image Bank to support this presentation.
- Ask true/false questions about the illustration. Ex: **¿Cierto o falso? Una chica nada en la piscina. (Falso. Es un chico.)** Next, name famous athletes and have students name the sports they play. Ex: **¿Qué deporte practica Roger Federer?**
- Point out that, except for the **nosotros/as** and **vosotros/as** forms, all present tense forms of **esquiar** carry an accent over the **i**: **esquío, esquías, esquía, esquían.**

Los pasatiempos

My Vocabulary Tutorials

Más vocabulario

el béisbol	baseball
el ciclismo	cycling
el esquí (acuático)	(water) skiing
el fútbol americano	football
el golf	golf
el hockey	hockey
la natación	swimming
el tenis	tennis
el vóleibol	volleyball
el equipo	team
el parque	park
el partido	game; match
la plaza	city or town square
andar en patineta	to skateboard
bucear	to scuba dive
escalar montañas (*f., pl.*)	to climb mountains
esquiar	to ski
ganar	to win
ir de excursión	to go on a hike
practicar deportes (*m., pl.*)	to play sports
escribir una carta/ un mensaje electrónico	to write a letter/ an e-mail
leer correo electrónico	to read e-mail
leer una revista	to read a magazine
deportivo/a	sports-related

Variación léxica

piscina ↔ pileta (*Arg.*); alberca (*Méx.*)
baloncesto ↔ básquetbol (*Amér. L.*)
béisbol ↔ pelota (*P. Rico, Rep. Dom.*)

recursos
vText — CPA pp. 95–97 — CH pp. 49–50 — vhlcentral

Lee el periódico. (leer)
Pasea en bicicleta. (pasear)
la pelota
el fútbol
la jugadora
Visitan el monumento. (visitar)
Pasean. (pasear)
Toma el sol. (tomar)
Nada. (nadar)
la piscina
PARQUE MUNICIPAL

TEACHING OPTIONS
Pairs Ask students to write down in Spanish their three favorite sports or leisure activities. Have students pair up and share the information using complete sentences. Ex: **Me gusta practicar la natación. Es un deporte divertido. Nado en mi piscina. ¿Qué deportes practicas?** As a class, call on individuals to report their partners' favorite pastimes. Partners will confirm or correct the information.

EXPANSION
Variación léxica Point out that many sports in Spanish are referred to by names derived from English (**básquetbol, béisbol, fútbol**), including many in **Más vocabulario: el golf, el hockey, el vóleibol**. Ask students to guess the meaning of these activities (be sure to use Spanish pronunciation): **el footing** (*jogging*), **el camping, el surf(ing), el windsurf.**

Práctica

1 **Escuchar** Indicate the letter of the activity in Column B that best corresponds to each statement you hear. Two items in Column B will not be used.

A
1. _b_
2. _d_
3. _f_
4. _c_
5. _g_
6. _h_

B
a. leer correo electrónico
b. tomar el sol
c. pasear en bicicleta
d. ir a un partido de fútbol americano
e. escribir una carta
f. practicar muchos deportes
g. nadar
h. ir de excursión

2 **Ordenar** Order these activities according to what you hear in the narration.

_5_ a. pasear en bicicleta
_1_ b. nadar
_4_ c. leer una revista
_3_ d. tomar el sol
_6_ e. practicar deportes
_2_ f. patinar en línea

3 **¿Cierto o falso?** Indicate whether each statement is **cierto** or **falso** based on the illustration.

	Cierto	Falso
1. Un hombre nada en la piscina.	✓	○
2. Un hombre lee una revista.	○	✓
3. Un chico pasea en bicicleta.	✓	○
4. Dos muchachos esquían.	○	✓
5. Una mujer y dos niños visitan un monumento.	✓	○
6. Un hombre bucea.	○	✓
7. Hay un equipo de hockey.	○	✓
8. Una mujer toma el sol.	✓	○

4 **Clasificar** Fill in the chart below with as many terms from **Contextos** as you can. Answers will vary.

Actividades	Deportes	Personas

Patina en línea. (patinar)

el jugador

el baloncesto

EXPANSION

Extra Practice Add an auditory aspect to this vocabulary practice. Prepare short descriptions of different places you need to visit using the vocabulary from the chapter. Read each description aloud and have students name an appropriate location. Ex: **Necesito estudiar en un lugar tranquilo. También deseo leer una revista y unos periódicos. Aquí la gente no debe comer ni beber ni hablar por teléfono. (la biblioteca)**

TEACHING OPTIONS

Game Play a modified version of **20 Preguntas**. Ask a volunteer to choose an activity, person, or place from the illustration or **Más vocabulario** that other students will take turns guessing by asking yes/no questions. Limit the attempts to ten questions, after which the volunteer will reveal the item. You may need to provide some phrases on the board.

 Communication 1.1

1 Teaching Tip Have students check their answers with a partner before going over **Actividad 1** with the class.

1 Script 1. No me gusta nadar pero paso mucho tiempo al lado de la piscina. 2. Alicia y yo vamos al estadio a las cuatro. Creemos que nuestro equipo va a ganar. 3. Me gusta patinar en línea, esquiar y practicar el tenis. 4. El ciclismo es mi deporte favorito. 5. Me gusta mucho la natación. Paso mucho tiempo en la piscina. 6. Mi hermana es una gran excursionista.
Teacher Resources DVD

2 Teaching Tips
- To simplify, prepare the class for listening by having students read the list aloud.
- Ask students if the verbs in the list are conjugated or if they are infinitives. Tell them that the verbs they hear in the audio recording may be in the infinitive or conjugated form.

2 Script Hoy es sábado y mis amigos y yo estamos en el parque. Todos tenemos pasatiempos diferentes. Clara y Daniel nadan en la piscina. Luis patina en línea. Sergio y Paco toman el sol. Dalia lee una revista. Rosa y yo paseamos en bicicleta. Y tú, ¿practicas deportes?
Teacher Resources DVD

3 Expansion Ask students to write three additional true/false sentences based on the illustration. Have volunteers read sentences aloud for the rest of the class to answer.

4 Expansion Ask students to write three sentences using the words they listed in each category. You can cue students in order to elicit more responses. Ex: ¿Qué es la natación? (La natación es un deporte.)

En el centro

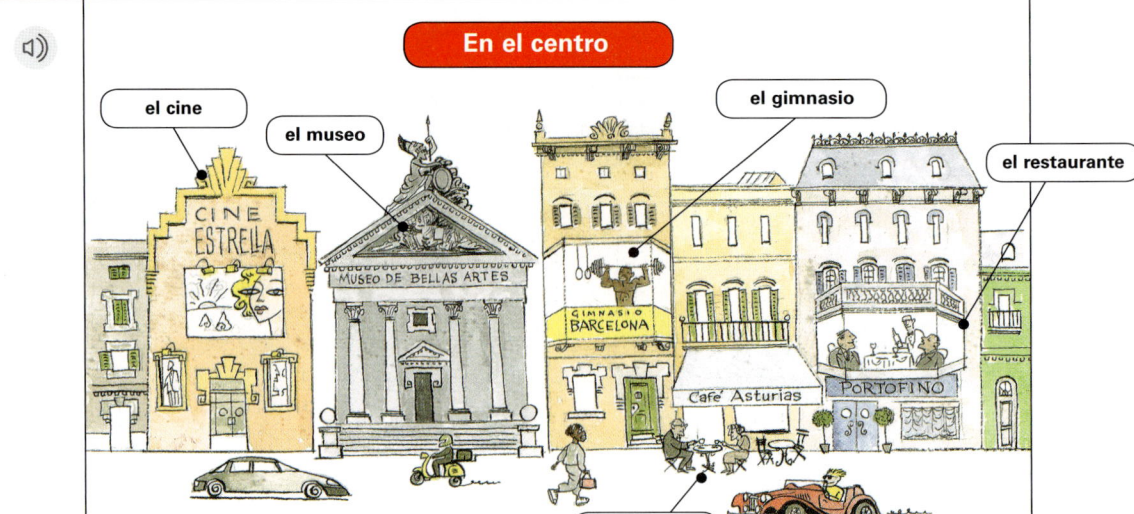

- el cine
- el museo
- el gimnasio
- el restaurante
- el café

Más vocabulario

la diversión	fun activity; entertainment; recreation
el fin de semana	weekend
el pasatiempo	pastime; hobby
los ratos libres	spare (free) time
el videojuego	video game
la iglesia	church
el lugar	place
ver películas (f., pl.)	to watch movies
favorito/a	favorite

5 **Identificar** Identify the place where these activities would take place.

modelo
Esquiamos. *Es una montaña.*

1. Tomamos una limonada. *Es un café./Es un restaurante.*
2. Vemos una película. *Es un cine.*
3. Nadamos y tomamos el sol. *Es una piscina./Es un parque.*
4. Hay muchos monumentos. *Es un parque.*
5. Comemos tacos y fajitas. *Es un restaurante.*
6. Miramos pinturas (*paintings*) de Diego Rivera y Frida Kahlo. *Es un museo.*
7. Hay mucho tráfico. *Es el centro.*
8. Practicamos deportes. *Es un gimnasio./Es un parque.*

6 **Preguntar** Ask a classmate what he or she does in the places mentioned below. Your classmate will respond using verbs from the word bank. *Answers will vary.*

modelo
una plaza
Estudiante 1: *¿Qué haces (do you do) cuando estás en una plaza?*
Estudiante 2: *Camino por la plaza y miro a las personas.*

beber	escalar	mirar	practicar
caminar	escribir	nadar	tomar
correr	leer	patinar	visitar

1. una biblioteca
2. un estadio
3. una plaza
4. una piscina
5. las montañas
6. un parque
7. un café
8. un museo

Practice more at vhlcentral.com.

Los pasatiempos

Comunicación

7 Crucigrama Your instructor will give you and your partner an incomplete crossword puzzle. Yours has the words your partner needs and vice versa. In order to complete the puzzle, take turns giving each other clues, using definitions, examples, and phrases. *Answers will vary.*

modelo
2 horizontal: Es un deporte que practicamos en la piscina.
6 vertical: Es un mensaje que escribimos con lápiz o con pluma.

8 Entrevista In pairs, take turns asking and answering these questions. *Answers will vary.*

1. ¿Hay un café cerca de la escuela? ¿Dónde está?
2. ¿Cuál es tu restaurante favorito?
3. ¿Te gusta viajar y visitar monumentos? ¿Por qué?
4. ¿Te gusta ir al cine los fines de semana?
5. ¿Cuáles son tus películas favoritas?
6. ¿Te gusta practicar deportes?
7. ¿Cuáles son tus deportes favoritos? ¿Por qué?
8. ¿Cuáles son tus pasatiempos favoritos?

CONSULTA
To review the verb **gustar**, see **Estructura 2.1**, p. 52.

9 Conversación Using the words and expressions provided, work with a partner to prepare a short conversation about pastimes. *Answers will vary.*

¿a qué hora?   ¿con quién(es)?   ¿dónde?
¿cómo?   ¿cuándo?   ¿qué?

modelo
Estudiante 1: ¿Cuándo patinas en línea?
Estudiante 2: Patino en línea los domingos. Y tú, ¿patinas en línea?
Estudiante 1: No, no me gusta patinar en línea. Me gusta practicar el béisbol.

10 Pasatiempos In pairs, tell each other what pastimes three of your friends and family members enjoy. Be prepared to share with the class any pastimes they have in common. *Answers will vary.*

modelo
Estudiante 1: Mi hermana pasea mucho en bicicleta, pero mis padres practican la natación. Mi hermano no nada, pero visita muchos museos.
Estudiante 2: Mi primo lee muchas revistas, pero no practica muchos deportes. Mis tíos esquían y practican el golf...

TEACHING OPTIONS

Large Group Have students write down six activities they enjoy and then circulate around the room to collect signatures from others who enjoy the same activities (¿**Te gusta…? Firma aquí, por favor.**). Ask volunteers to report back to the class.

TEACHING OPTIONS

Game Ask students to take out a piece of paper and anonymously write a set of activities that best corresponds to their interests. Collect and shuffle the slips of paper. Divide the class into two teams. Pull out and read aloud each slip of paper, and have the teams take turns guessing the student's identity.

Communication 1.1, 1.2

7 Teaching Tips
- Distribute the Communication Activity worksheets from the Activity Pack that correspond to this activity.
- Model the different ways that students can give clues. Write **el gimnasio** on the board. Then write: **Es un lugar donde la gente corre. (definición) / En nuestra ciudad hay uno que se llama Excel Fitness. (ejemplo) / un lugar para practicar deportes (frase)** The person receiving the clue should use the letter spaces to figure out the answer.

7 Expansion In pairs, have students create another type of word puzzle, such as a word search. Tell them to use the lesson vocabulary.

8 Teaching Tip Before beginning the activity, review the verb **gustar**.

8 Expansion Have the same pairs ask each other additional questions. Have volunteers share their mini-conversations with the class.

8 Virtual Chat You can also assign activity 8 on the Supersite. Students record individual responses that appear in your gradebook.

9 Teaching Tip After students have asked and answered questions, ask volunteers to report their partners' activities back to the class. The partners should verify the information and provide at least one additional detail.

10 Expansion Ask volunteers to share any pastimes they and their partners, friends, and families have in common. Ask for a show of hands to find out which activities are most popular and where they do them.

Contextos 119

Section Goals

In **Fotonovela**, students will:
- receive comprehensible input from free-flowing discourse
- learn functional phrases for making invitations and plans, and talking about pastimes

Communication 1.2
Cultures 2.1, 2.2

Student Resources
Cuaderno de práctica y actividades comunicativas,
pp. 100–101
Supersite: *Fotonovela* video, Activities, *eCuaderno*

Teacher Resources
Workbook TE; Video Script & Translation

Video Recap: Lección 3
Before doing this **Fotonovela** section, review the previous episode with this activity.
1. Marta y Valentina son las _____ de Jimena y Felipe. (primas) 2. Marissa tiene _____ hermanos y una hermana. (dos) 3. _____ es hija única. (la Sra. Díaz) 4. Las mujeres comparten una _____. (trajinera) 5. Marissa tiene planes para visitar a _____. (tía Ana María)

Video Synopsis The friends have arrived at **tía Ana María's** house in **Mérida**. **Juan Carlos** and **Felipe** head off to play soccer with **Felipe's** cousins, **Eduardo** and **Pablo**. Meanwhile, **Maru, Miguel,** and **Jimena** take **Marissa** to explore a **cenote**.

Teaching Tips
- Hand out the **Antes de ver el video** and the **Mientras ves el video** activities from the **Cuaderno de práctica y actividades comunicativas** and go over the **Antes de ver** questions before starting the **Fotonovela**.
- Have students quickly glance over the **Fotonovela** captions and make a list of the cognates they find. Then, ask them to predict what this episode is about.

4 fotonovela

Lección 4

Fútbol, cenotes y mole

Maru, Miguel, Jimena y Marissa visitan un cenote, mientras Felipe y Juan Carlos van a un partido de fútbol.

PERSONAJES  MIGUEL PABLO

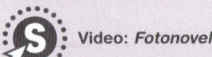 Video: *Fotonovela*

MIGUEL Buenos días a todos.
TÍA ANA MARÍA Hola, Miguel. Maru, ¿qué van a hacer hoy?
MARU Miguel y yo vamos a llevar a Marissa a un cenote.

MARISSA ¿No vamos a nadar? ¿Qué es un cenote?
MIGUEL Sí, sí vamos a nadar. Un cenote... difícil de explicar. Es una piscina natural en un hueco profundo.
MARU ¡Ya vas a ver! Seguro que te va a gustar.

ANA MARÍA Marissa, ¿qué te gusta hacer? ¿Escalar montañas? ¿Ir de excursión?
MARISSA Sí, me gusta ir de excursión y practicar el esquí acuático. Y usted, ¿qué prefiere hacer en sus ratos libres?

FELIPE ¿Recuerdas el restaurante del mole?
EDUARDO ¿Qué restaurante?
JIMENA El mole de mi tía Ana María es mi favorito.
MARU Chicos, ya es hora. ¡Vamos!

(más tarde, en el parque)
PABLO No puede ser. ¡Cinco a uno!
FELIPE ¡Vamos a jugar! Si perdemos, compramos el almuerzo. Y si ganamos...
EDUARDO ¡Empezamos!

(mientras tanto, en el cenote)
MARISSA ¿Hay muchos cenotes en México?
MIGUEL Sólo en la península de Yucatán.
MARISSA ¡Vamos a nadar!

TEACHING OPTIONS

Fútbol, cenotes y mole Play the last half of the **Fútbol, cenotes y mole** episode and have the class give you a description of what they saw. Write their observations on the board, pointing out any incorrect information. Repeat this process to allow the class to pick up more details of the plot.

Then ask students to use the information they have accumulated to guess what happened at the beginning of the episode. Write their guesses on the board. Then play the entire episode and, through discussion, help the class summarize the plot.

Los pasatiempos

ciento veintiuno **121**

ANA MARÍA **MARU** **MARISSA** **EDUARDO** **FELIPE** **JUAN CARLOS** **JIMENA** **DON GUILLERMO**

4

PABLO Mi mamá tiene muchos pasatiempos y actividades.
EDUARDO Sí. Ella nada y juega al tenis y al golf.
PABLO Va al cine y a los museos.
ANA MARÍA Sí, salgo mucho los fines de semana.

5

(unos minutos después)
EDUARDO Hay un partido de fútbol en el parque. ¿Quieren ir conmigo?
PABLO Y conmigo. Si no consigo más jugadores, nuestro equipo va a perder.

9

(Los chicos visitan a don Guillermo, un vendedor de paletas heladas.)
JUAN CARLOS Don Guillermo, ¿dónde podemos conseguir un buen mole?
FELIPE Eduardo y Pablo van a pagar el almuerzo. Y yo voy a pedir un montón de comida.

10

FELIPE Sí, éste es el restaurante. Recuerdo la comida.
EDUARDO Oye, Pablo... No tengo...
PABLO No te preocupes, hermanito.
FELIPE ¿Qué buscas? (muestra la cartera de Pablo) ¿Esto?

recursos

pp. 100–101   vhlcentral

Expresiones útiles

Making invitations
Hay un partido de fútbol en el parque. ¿Quieren ir conmigo?
There's a soccer game in the park. Do you want to come with me?
¡Yo puedo jugar!
I can play!
Mmm... no quiero.
Hmm... I don't want to.
Lo siento, pero no puedo.
I'm sorry, but I can't.
¡Vamos a nadar!
Let's go swimming!
Sí, vamos.
Yes, let's go.

Making plans
¿Qué van a hacer hoy?
What are you going to do today?
Vamos a llevar a Marissa a un cenote.
We are taking Marissa to a cenote.
Vamos a comprar unas paletas heladas.
We're going to buy some popsicles.
Vamos a jugar. Si perdemos, compramos el almuerzo.
Let's play. If we lose, we'll buy lunch.

Talking about pastimes
¿Qué te gusta hacer? ¿Escalar montañas? ¿Ir de excursión?
What do you like to do? Mountain climbing? Hiking?
Sí, me gusta ir de excursión y practicar esquí acuático.
Yes, I like hiking and water skiing.
Y usted, ¿qué prefiere hacer en sus ratos libres?
And you, what do you like to do in your free time?
Salgo mucho los fines de semana.
I go out a lot on the weekends.
Voy al cine y a los museos.
I go to the movies and to museums.

Additional vocabulary
la cartera *wallet*
el hueco *hole*
un montón de *a lot of*
el/la aficionado/a *fan*

EXPANSION

Extra Pairs Ask students to write six true/false statements about the **Fotonovela** episode. Have them exchange papers with a classmate, who will complete the activity, correcting any false information.

TEACHING OPTIONS

Large Groups Go through the **Expresiones útiles** as a class. Then have students stand and form a circle. Call out a question or statement from **Expresiones útiles** and toss a ball to a student. He or she must respond appropriately and toss the ball back to you.

Expresiones útiles
- Point out the written accents in the words **fútbol**, **sí**, **¿Qué?**, and **excursión**. Explain that accents indicate a stressed syllable in a word. Remind students that all question words have accent marks. Tell students that they will learn more about word stress and accent marks in **Pronunciación**.
- Mention that **Vamos**, **van**, and **Voy** are present-tense forms of the verb **ir**. Point out that **ir a** is used with an infinitive to tell what is going to happen. Ask: **¿Qué vas a hacer esta noche? ¿Por qué no vamos al parque?** Explain that **quiero**, **quieren**, and **siento** are forms of **querer** and **sentir**, which undergo a stem change from **e** to **ie** in certain forms. Tell students that they will learn more about these concepts in **Estructura**.
- Have students look for a few expressions used to talk about pastimes. Then ask a few questions. Ex: **¿Qué te gusta hacer en tus ratos libres? ¿Te gusta el fútbol?**

Teaching Tip Have the class read through the entire **Fotonovela**, with volunteers playing the various parts. Have students take turns playing the roles so that more students participate.

Nota cultural Traditionally, **mole** ingredients are ground on a flat slab of volcanic stone known as a **metate**, using a **mano**, or rounded grinding stone. The **metate** has been used for grinding grains (especially corn) and spices since pre-Columbian times, and although electric blenders and grinders have replaced many **metates** in Mexican homes, this utensil has experienced a resurgence. Many claim that using the **metate**, although time-consuming, gives dishes better flavor.

¿Qué pasó?

1 Escoger Choose the answer that best completes each sentence.

1. Marissa, Maru y Miguel desean ___a___.
   a. nadar   b. correr por el parque   c. leer el periódico
2. A Marissa le gusta ___c___.
   a. el tenis   b. el vóleibol   c. ir de excursión y practicar esquí acuático
3. A la tía Ana María le gusta ___b___.
   a. jugar al hockey   b. nadar y jugar al tenis y al golf   c. hacer ciclismo
4. Pablo y Eduardo pierden el partido de ___a___.
   a. fútbol   b. béisbol   c. baloncesto
5. Juan Carlos y Felipe desean ___c___.
   a. patinar   b. esquiar   c. comer mole

NOTA CULTURAL

Mole is a typical sauce in Mexican cuisine. It is made from pumpkin seeds, chile, and chocolate, and it is usually served with chicken, beef, or pork.

2 Identificar Identify the person who would make each statement.

1. A mí me gusta nadar, pero no sé qué es un cenote. ___Marissa___
2. Mamá va al cine y al museo en sus ratos libres. ___Pablo/Eduardo___
3. Yo voy a pedir mucha comida. ___Felipe___
4. ¿Quieren ir a jugar al fútbol con nosotros en el parque? ___Eduardo/Pablo___
5. Me gusta salir los fines de semana. ___tía Ana María___

MARISSA
FELIPE
EDUARDO
PABLO
TÍA ANA MARÍA

NOTA CULTURAL

Cenotes are deep, freshwater sinkholes found in caves throughout the Yucatán peninsula. They were formed in prehistoric times by the erosion and collapse of cave walls. The Mayan civilization considered the **cenotes** sacred, and performed rituals there. Today, they are popular destinations for swimming and diving.

3 Preguntas Answer the questions using the information from the **Fotonovela**.

1. ¿Qué van a hacer Miguel y Maru?
   Miguel y Maru van a llevar a Marissa a un cenote.
2. ¿Adónde van Felipe y Juan Carlos mientras sus amigos van al cenote?
   Felipe y Juan Carlos van a jugar al fútbol con Pablo y Eduardo.
3. ¿Quién gana el partido de fútbol?
   Felipe y Juan Carlos ganan el partido de fútbol.
4. ¿Quiénes van al cenote con Maru y Miguel?
   Marissa y Jimena van al cenote con Maru y Miguel.

4 Conversación With a partner, prepare a conversation in which you talk about pastimes and invite each other to do some activity together. Use these expressions and also look at **Expresiones útiles** on the previous page. Answers will vary.

| ¿A qué hora? (At) What time? | ¿Dónde? Where? | Nos vemos a las siete. See you at seven. |
| contigo with you | No puedo porque... I can't because... | |

▶ ¿Eres aficionado/a a...?
▶ ¿Te gusta...?
▶ ¿Por qué no...?
▶ ¿Quieres... conmigo?
▶ ¿Qué vas a hacer esta noche?

Pronunciación
Word stress and accent marks

| pe-**lí**-cu-la | e-di-**fi**-cio | v**er** | y**o** |

Every Spanish syllable contains at least one vowel. When two vowels are joined in the same syllable they form a **diphthong***. A **monosyllable** is a word formed by a single syllable.

| bi-blio-**te**-ca | vi-si-**tar** | **par**-que | **fút**-bol |

The syllable of a Spanish word that is pronounced most emphatically is the "stressed" syllable.

| pe-**lo**-ta | pis-**ci**-na | **ra**-tos | **ha**-blan |

Words that end in **n**, **s**, or a **vowel** are usually stressed on the next-to-last syllable.

| na-ta-**ción** | pa-**pá** | in-**glés** | Jo-**sé** |

If words that end in **n**, **s**, or a **vowel** are stressed on the last syllable, they must carry an accent mark on the stressed syllable.

| bai-**lar** | es-pa-**ñol** | u-ni-ver-si-**dad** | tra-ba-ja-**dor** |

Words that do *not* end in **n**, **s**, or a **vowel** are usually stressed on the last syllable.

| **béis**-bol | **lá**-piz | **ár**-bol | **Gó**-mez |

If words that do *not* end in **n**, **s**, or a **vowel** are stressed on the next-to-last syllable, they must carry an accent mark on the stressed syllable.

*The two vowels that form a diphthong are either both weak or one is weak and the other is strong.

Práctica Pronounce each word, stressing the correct syllable. Then give the word stress rule for each word.

1. profesor
2. Puebla
3. ¿Cuántos?
4. Mazatlán
5. examen
6. ¿Cómo?
7. niños
8. Guadalajara
9. programador
10. México
11. están
12. geografía

Oraciones Read the conversation aloud to practice word stress.

MARINA Hola, Carlos. ¿Qué tal?
CARLOS Bien. Oye, ¿a qué hora es el partido de fútbol?
MARINA Creo que es a las siete.
CARLOS ¿Quieres ir?
MARINA Lo siento, pero no puedo. Tengo que estudiar biología.

Refranes Read these sayings aloud to practice word stress.

En la unión está la fuerza.[2]

Quien ríe de último, ríe mejor.[1]

[1] He who laughs last, laughs the loudest.   [2] United we stand.

Section Goals

In **Cultura**, students will:
- read about soccer rivalries
- learn sports-related terms
- read about **Miguel Cabrera** and **Paola Espinosa**
- read about renowned athletes

Communication 1.1, 1.2
Cultures 2.1, 2.2
Connections 3.1, 3.2
Comparisons 4.2

Student Resources
Cuaderno para hispanohablantes, p. 52
Supersite: Activities

21st Century Skills

Global Awareness
Students will gain perspectives on the Spanish-speaking world to develop respect and openness to others and to interact appropriately and effectively with citizens of Spanish-speaking cultures.

En detalle

Antes de leer Have students predict the reading content based on the title and photos.

Lectura
- Use the map on page 74 to point out the locations of Barcelona and Madrid. Briefly explain that Spain's regional cultures (Basque, Catalan, Galician, etc.) were at odds with the authoritarian, centralized approach of Franco's regime, which banned the public use of regional languages. Point out that the nickname **Barça** is Catalan, which is why it has a cedilla to indicate a soft **c**.
- **Camp Nou** (Catalan for *New Field*) holds about 100,000 spectators and is the largest stadium in Europe. Madrid's **Estadio Santiago Bernabéu**, seats about 80,000.

Después de leer Ask students what facts in this reading are new or surprising to them.

---

4 cultura — Lección 4

EN DETALLE

Additional Reading

Real Madrid y Barça: rivalidad total

Soccer in Spain is a force to be reckoned with, and no two teams draw more attention than **Real Madrid** and the **Fútbol Club Barcelona**.

Rivalidades del fútbol	
Argentina:	Boca Juniors vs River Plate
México:	Águilas del América vs Chivas del Guadalajara
Chile:	Colo Colo vs Universidad de Chile
Guatemala:	Comunicaciones vs Municipal
Uruguay:	Peñarol vs Nacional
Colombia:	Millonarios vs Independiente Santa Fe

Whether the venue is Madrid's **Santiago Bernabéu** or Barcelona's **Camp Nou**, both cities become paralyzed by **fútbol** fever. A ticket to the actual game is always the hottest ticket in town.

The rivalry between **Real Madrid** and **Barça** is about more than soccer. As the two biggest, most powerful cities in Spain, Barcelona and Madrid are constantly compared to one another and have a natural rivalry. There is also a political component to the dynamic. Barcelona, with its distinct language and culture, has long struggled for increased autonomy from Madrid's centralized government. Under Francisco Franco's rule (1939–1975), when repression of the Catalan identity was at its height, a game between **Real Madrid** and **FC Barcelona** was wrapped up with all the symbolism of the regime versus the resistance, even though both teams suffered casualties in Spain's civil war and the subsequent Franco dictatorship.

Although the dictatorship is long over, the legacy of decades' worth of competition still transforms both cities into a frenzied, tense panic leading up to the game. Once the final score is announced, one of those cities transforms again, this time into the best party in the country.

ACTIVIDADES

1 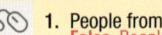 **¿Cierto o falso?** Indicate whether each statement is **cierto** or **falso**. Correct the false statements.

1. People from Spain don't like soccer. **Falso.** People from Spain like soccer very much.
2. Madrid and Barcelona are the most important cities in Spain. **Cierto.**
3. Santiago Bernabéu is a stadium in Barcelona. **Falso.** It is a stadium in Madrid.
4. The rivalry between Real Madrid and FC Barcelona is not only in soccer. **Cierto.**
5. Barcelona has resisted Madrid's centralized government. **Cierto.**
6. Only the FC Barcelona team was affected by the civil war. **Falso.** Both teams were affected by the civil war.
7. During Franco's regime, the Catalan culture thrived. **Falso.** Catalan culture was repressed during Franco's regime.
8. There are many famous rivalries between soccer teams in the Spanish-speaking world. **Cierto.**
9. River Plate is a popular team from Argentina. **Cierto.**
10. Comunicaciones and Peñarol are famous rivals in Guatemala. **Falso.** Comunicaciones and Municipal are important rivals in Guatemala.

TEACHING OPTIONS

Small Groups Have small groups choose famous soccer rivalries, then split up to research and create a web page for each of the rival teams. The pages should feature each team's colors, players, home stadium, official song, and other significant or interesting information. Have the groups present their rivals' web pages to the class.

EXPANSION

Culture Note Explain that sportscasters in the Spanish-speaking world are famous for their theatrical commentaries. One example is Andrés Cantor, who provides commentary for soccer matches on Spanish-language stations in the U.S. Each time a goal is scored, fans know they can hear a drawn-out bellow of ¡Gooooooool! Cantor's call, which can last for nearly thirty seconds, was made into a ringtone for cell phones in the U.S.

Los pasatiempos

ASÍ SE DICE
Los deportes

el/la árbitro/a	referee
el/la atleta	athlete
la bola; el balón	la pelota
el campeón/la campeona	champion
la carrera	race
competir	to compete
empatar	to draw; to tie
la medalla	medal
el/la mejor	the best
mundial	worldwide
el torneo	tournament

EL MUNDO HISPANO
Atletas importantes

World-renowned Hispanic athletes:

- **Rafael Nadal** (España) has won 14 Grand Slam singles titles and the 2008 Olympic gold medal in singles.
- **Lionel Andrés Messi** (Argentina) is one of the world's top soccer players. He plays for **FC Barcelona** and for the Argentine national team.
- **Mireia Belmonte García** (España), won two silver medals in swimming at the 2012 Olympics.
- **Lorena Ochoa** (México) was the top-ranked female golfer in the world when she retired in 2010 at the age of 28.

PERFILES
Miguel Cabrera y Paola Espinosa

Miguel Cabrera, considered one of the best hitters in baseball, now plays first base for the Detroit Tigers. Born in Venezuela in 1983, he made his Major League debut at the age of 20. Cabrera has been selected for both the National League and American League All-Star Teams. In 2012, he became the first player since 1967 to win the Triple Crown.

Mexican diver **Paola Milagros Espinosa Sánchez**, born in 1986, has competed in three Olympics (2004, 2008, and 2012). She and her partner Tatiana Ortiz took home a bronze medal in 2008. In 2012, she won a silver medal with partner Alejandra Orozco. She won three gold medals at the Pan American Games in 2007 and again in 2011.

Conexión Internet

¿Qué deportes son populares en los países hispanos?

Go to **vhlcentral.com** to find more cultural information related to this **Cultura** section.

ACTIVIDADES

2 Comprensión Write the name of the athlete described in each sentence.

1. Es un jugador de fútbol de Argentina. _Lionel Andrés Messi_
2. Es una chica que practica el golf. _Lorena Ochoa_
3. Es un jugador de béisbol de Venezuela. _Miguel Cabrera_
4. Es una mujer mexicana que practica un deporte en la piscina. _Paola Milagros Espinosa Sánchez_

3 ¿Quién es? Write a short paragraph describing an athlete that you like, but do not mention his or her name. What does he or she look like? What sport does he or she play? Where does he or she live? Read your description to the class to see if they can guess the identity of the athlete.
Answers will vary.

Practice more at **vhlcentral.com**.

recursos

vText

CH p. 52

vhlcentral

PRE-AP*

Presentational Speaking with Cultural Comparison For homework, ask students to research one of the athletes from **El mundo hispano**. They should write five sentences in Spanish about the athlete's life and career, and bring in a photo from the Internet. Tell them to do the same for an athlete from this country that practices the same sport. Then have them present their descriptions to the class.

DIFFERENTIATION

Heritage Speakers Ask heritage speakers to describe sports preferences in their families' countries of origin, especially ones that are not widely known in the United States, such as **jai-alai**. What well-known athletes in the U.S. are from their families' countries of origin?

Así se dice Model the pronunciation of each term and have students repeat it.

Perfiles
- Miguel Cabrera has played left field, right field, third base, and first base. In 2012, he led the American League with a .330 batting average, 44 home runs, and 139 runs batted in, which constitutes baseball's "Triple Crown." Cabrera was named the American League's Most Valuable Player in 2012 and 2013.
- Paola Espinosa's Olympic medals are in the 10m platform synchronized diving event. She won gold medals at the Pan American Games for individual and synchronized events.

El mundo hispano Have students write three true/false sentences about this section. Then have pairs take turns reading and correcting their statements.

21st Century Skills

Information and Media Literacy: Conexión Internet Students access and critically evaluate information from the Internet.

TELL Connection

Learning Experience 6
Why: Students need frequent cultural input. *What:* **Conexión Internet** contextualizes language-culture tasks.

2 Expansion Give students these sentences as items 5–6:
5. ____ es una mujer española que practica la natación. (Mireia Belmonte García)
6. El tenis es el deporte favorito de ____. (Rafael Nadal)

3 Teaching Tip In pairs, have students peer edit each other's paragraphs, paying close attention to gender agreement.

Section Goals

In **Estructura 4.1**, students will learn:
- the present tense of **ir**
- the contraction **al**
- **ir a** + [*infinitive*] to express future events
- **vamos a** to express *let's...*

Communication 1.1
Comparisons 4.1

Student Resources
Cuaderno de práctica y actividades comunicativas, pp. 103–106
Cuaderno para hispanohablantes, pp. 53–54
Supersite: Activities, *eCuaderno*

Teacher Resources
Workbook TE; Grammar Slides; Audio Activities MP3s; Audio Script; Testing Program Quizzes; Activity Pack; Middle School Activity Pack

Teaching Tips
- Write your next day's schedule on the board. Ex: **8:00—la biblioteca; 12:00—comer.** Explain what you are going to do, using the verb **ir.**
- Add a visual aspect to this grammar presentation. Write names of Spanish-speaking countries on construction paper, and pin up the papers at different points around the classroom in order to make a "map." Point to your destination "country," and as you act out flying there, ask students: **¿Adónde voy? (Va a Chile.)** Once there, act out an activity, asking: **¿Qué voy a hacer? (Va a esquiar.)**
- Practice **vamos a** to express the idea of *let's* by asking volunteers to suggest things to do. Ex: **Tengo hambre. (Vamos a la cafetería.)**

Ayuda Point out the difference in usage between **dónde** and **adónde**. Ask: **¿Adónde va el presidente para descansar? (Va a Camp David.) ¿Dónde está Camp David? (Está en Maryland.)**

---

4 estructura
Lección 4

4.1 Present tense of ir

 Tutorial

ANTE TODO The verb **ir** (*to go*) is irregular in the present tense. Note that, except for the **yo** form (**voy**) and the lack of a written accent on the **vosotros** form (**vais**), the endings are the same as those for regular present-tense **-ar** verbs.

The verb ir (*to go*)

Singular forms		Plural forms	
yo	**voy**	nosotros/as	**vamos**
tú	**vas**	vosotros/as	**vais**
Ud./él/ella	**va**	Uds./ellos/ellas	**van**

▶ **Ir** is often used with the preposition **a** (*to*). If **a** is followed by the definite article **el**, they combine to form the contraction **al**. If **a** is followed by the other definite articles (**la, las, los**), there is no contraction.

a + el = al

Voy **al** parque con Juan.
I'm going to the park with Juan.

Mis amigos van **a las** montañas.
My friends are going to the mountains.

CONSULTA
To review the contraction **de** + **el**, see **Estructura 1.3**, pp. 20–21.

▶ The construction **ir a** + [*infinitive*] is used to talk about actions that are going to happen in the future. It is equivalent to the English *to be going* + [*infinitive*].

Va a leer el periódico.
He is going to read the newspaper.

Van a pasear por el pueblo.
They are going to walk around town.

AYUDA
When asking a question that contains a form of the verb **ir**, remember to use **adónde**:
¿Adónde vas?
(To) Where are you going?

¡Voy a ir con ellos!

Ella va al cine y a los museos.

▶ **Vamos a** + [*infinitive*] can also express the idea of *let's* (*do something*).

Vamos a pasear.
Let's take a stroll.

¡Vamos a comer!
Let's eat!

¡INTÉNTALO! Provide the present tense forms of **ir**.

1. Ellos __van__.
2. Yo __voy__.
3. Tu novio __va__.
4. Adela __va__.
5. Mi prima y yo __vamos__.
6. Tú __vas__.
7. Ustedes __van__.
8. Nosotros __vamos__.
9. Usted __va__.
10. Nosotras __vamos__.
11. Miguel __va__.
12. Ellas __van__.

recursos
vText
CPA pp. 103–105
CH pp. 53–54
vhlcentral

TEACHING OPTIONS

TPR Invent gestures to act out the activities mentioned in **Lección 4**. Ex: **esquiar** (move arms and sway as if skiing), **patinar** (skate), **nadar** (move arms as if swimming). Signal individuals to gesture appropriately as you cue activities with **Vamos a**. Keep a brisk pace.

Pairs Have students form pairs and tell them they are going somewhere with a friend. On paper strips, write varying dollar amounts, ranging from three dollars to five thousand. Have each pair draw out a dollar amount at random and tell the class where they will go and what they will do with the money. Encourage creativity. Ex: **Tenemos seis dólares. Vamos a McDonald's para comer. Ella va a cenar, pero yo voy a beber agua porque no tenemos más dinero. / Tenemos cinco mil dólares. Vamos a cenar en París…**

Práctica

1 **¿Adónde van?** Everyone in your neighborhood is dashing off to various places. Say where they are going.

1. la señora Castillo / el centro — La señora Castillo va al centro.
2. las hermanas Gómez / la piscina — Las hermanas Gómez van a la piscina.
3. tu tío y tu papá / el partido de fútbol — Tu tío y tu papá van al partido de fútbol.
4. yo / el Museo de Arte Moderno — (Yo) Voy al Museo de Arte Moderno.
5. nosotros / el restaurante Miramar — (Nosotros) Vamos al restaurante Miramar.

2 **¿Qué van a hacer?** These sentences describe what several students in a high school hiking club are doing today. Use **ir a** + [*infinitive*] to say that they are also going to do the same activities tomorrow.

modelo
Martín y Rodolfo nadan en la piscina.
Van a nadar en la piscina mañana también.

1. Sara lee una revista. — Va a leer una revista mañana también.
2. Yo practico deportes. — Voy a practicar deportes mañana también.
3. Ustedes van de excursión. — Van a ir de excursión mañana también.
4. El presidente del club patina. — Va a patinar mañana también.
5. Tú tomas el sol. — Vas a tomar el sol mañana también.
6. Paseamos con nuestros amigos. — Vamos a pasear con nuestros amigos mañana también.

3 **Preguntas** With a partner, take turns asking and answering questions about where the people are going and what they are going to do there. *Some answers will vary.*

modelo
Estudiante 1: ¿Adónde va Estela?
Estudiante 2: Va a la Librería Sol.
Estudiante 1: Va a comprar un libro.

Estela

1. Álex y Miguel
¿Adónde van Álex y Miguel?
Van al parque. Van a…

2. mi amigo
¿Adónde va mi amigo?
Va al gimnasio. Va a…

3. tú
¿Adónde vas? Voy al partido de tenis. Voy a…

4. los estudiantes
¿Adónde van los estudiantes?
Van al estadio. Van a…

5. la profesora Torres
¿Adónde va la profesora Torres? Va a la Biblioteca Nacional. Va a…

6. ustedes
¿Adónde van ustedes? Vamos a la piscina. Vamos a…

Practice more at vhlcentral.com.

Communication 1.1
Comparisons 4.1

1 Teaching Tip To add a visual aspect to this exercise, bring in photos of people dressed for a particular activity. As you hold up each photo, have the class say where they are going, using the verb **ir**. Ex: Show a photo of a basketball player. (**Va al gimnasio./Va a un partido.**)

1 Expansion After completing the activity, extend each answer with **pero** and a different name or pronoun, and have students complete the sentence. Ex: **La señora Castillo va al centro, pero el señor Castillo… (va al trabajo).**

2 Expansion
- Show the same photos you used for **Actividad 1** and ask students to describe what the people are going to do. Ex: **Va a jugar al baloncesto.**
- Ask students about tomorrow's activities. Ex: **¿Qué van a hacer tus amigos mañana? ¿Qué va a hacer tu padre/madre mañana?**

3 Expansion Ask pairs to write a riddle using **ir a** + [*infinitive*]. Ex: **Ángela, Laura, Tomás y Manuel van a hacer cosas diferentes. Tomás va a nadar y Laura va a comer, pero no en casa. Uno de los chicos y una de las chicas van a ver una película. ¿Adónde van todos?** Then have pairs exchange papers to solve the riddles.

DIFFERENTIATION

Heritage Speakers Ask heritage speakers to write six sentences with the verb **ir** indicating places they go on weekends either by themselves or with friends and family. Ex: **Mi familia y yo vamos a visitar a mi abuela los domingos.** Share the descriptions with the class and ask comprehension questions.
Small Groups Divide the class into teams. Ask each team to write a brief description of a well-known fictional character's

TEACHING OPTIONS

activities for tomorrow, using the verb **ir**. Ex: **Mañana va a dormir de día. Va a pasear de noche. Va a buscar una muchacha bonita. La muchacha va a tener mucho miedo.** Have each team read their description aloud without naming the character. Teams can ask for and share more details about the person as needed. If another team correctly identifies the person (**Es Drácula.**), they receive one point. The team with the most points at the end wins.

Communication 1.1
Comparisons 4.1

4 Expansion Have students make the phrases negative and then provide a new appropriate ending. Ex: **Cuando no deseo descansar, voy al gimnasio.**

4 Partner Chat (Premium) You can also assign activity 4 on the Supersite. Students work in pairs to record the activity online. The pair's recorded conversation will appear in your gradebook.

5 Teaching Tip Model question formation. Ex: **1. ¿Vas a comer en un restaurante chino hoy?** Then distribute the Communication Activity worksheets from the Activity Pack that correspond to this activity. Allow students five minutes to fill out the surveys. Ask students to present their results to the class.

6 Teaching Tip Add a visual aspect to this activity. Ask students to use an idea map to brainstorm a trip they would like to take. Have them write **lugar** in the central circle, and in the surrounding ones: **ver, deportes, otras actividades, comida, compañeros/as.**

6 Partner Chat You can also assign activity 6 on the Supersite.

 Communication 1.1

7 Teaching Tips
• To simplify, have students make two columns on a sheet of paper. The first one should be headed **El fin de semana tengo que...** and the other **El fin de semana tengo ganas de...** Give students a few minutes to brainstorm their activities for the weekend.
• Before students begin the last step, brainstorm a list of expressions as a class. Ex: —**¿Quieres jugar al tenis conmigo?** —**Lo siento, pero no puedo./Sí, vamos.**

---

128 ciento veintiocho Lección 4

Comunicación

4 Situaciones Work with a partner and say where you and your friends go in these situations. *Answers will vary.*

1. Cuando deseo descansar...
2. Cuando mi mejor amigo/a tiene que estudiar...
3. Si mis compañeros de clase necesitan practicar el español...
4. Si deseo hablar con mis amigos...
5. Cuando tengo dinero (*money*)...
6. Cuando mis amigos y yo tenemos hambre...
7. En mis ratos libres...
8. Cuando mis amigos desean esquiar...
9. Si estoy de vacaciones...
10. Si tengo ganas de leer...

5 Encuesta Your teacher will give you a worksheet. Walk around the class and ask your classmates if they are going to do these activities today. Find one person to answer **Sí** and one to answer **No** for each item and note their names on the worksheet in the appropriate column. Be prepared to report your findings to the class. *Answers will vary.*

modelo
Tú: ¿Vas a leer el periódico hoy?
Ana: Sí, voy a leer el periódico hoy.
Luis: No, no voy a leer el periódico hoy.

recursos
vText
CPA p. 106

Actividades	Sí	No
1. comer en un restaurante chino		
2. leer el periódico	Ana	Luis
3. escribir un mensaje electrónico		
4. correr 20 kilómetros		
5. ver una película de terror		
6. pasear en bicicleta		

6 Entrevista Talk to two classmates in order to find out where they are going and what they are going to do on their next vacation. *Answers will vary.*

modelo
Estudiante 1: ¿Adónde vas de vacaciones (*on vacation*)?
Estudiante 2: Voy a Guadalajara con mi familia.
Estudiante 3: ¿Y qué van a hacer (*to do*) ustedes en Guadalajara?
Estudiante 2: Vamos a visitar unos monumentos y museos. ¿Y tú?

Síntesis

7 Planes Make a schedule of your activities for the weekend. Then, share with a partner. *Answers will vary.*

▶ For each day, list at least three things you have to do.
▶ For each day, list at least two things you will do for fun.
▶ Tell a classmate what your weekend schedule is like. He or she will write down what you say.
▶ Switch roles to see if you have any plans in common.
▶ Take turns asking each other to participate in some of the activities you listed.

TEACHING OPTIONS

Pairs Write these times on the board: **8:00 a.m., 12:00 p.m., 12:45 p.m., 4:00 p.m., 6:00 p.m., 10:00 p.m.** Have student pairs take turns reading a time and suggesting an appropriate activity or place. Ex: **E1: Son las ocho de la mañana. E2: Vamos a correr./Vamos al gimnasio.**
Game Divide the class into teams. Name a category (Ex: **lugares públicos**) and set a time limit of two minutes. The first team member will write down one answer on a piece of paper and pass it to the next person. The paper will continue to be passed from student to student until the two minutes are up. The team with the most words wins.
Video Show the **Fotonovela** episode again. Stop the video where appropriate to discuss how **ir** is used to express different ideas.

4.2 Stem-changing verbs: e:ie, o:ue Tutorial

ANTE TODO Stem-changing verbs deviate from the normal pattern of regular verbs. Note the spelling changes to the stem in the conjugations below.

INFINITIVE	VERB STEM	STEM CHANGE	CONJUGATED FORM
empezar	empez-	emp**iez**-	emp**ie**zo
volver	volv-	v**uelv**-	v**ue**lvo

▸ In many verbs, such as **empezar** (*to begin*), the stem vowel changes from **e** to **ie**. Note that the **nosotros/as** and **vosotros/as** forms don't have a stem change.

The verb empezar (e:ie) (to begin)

Singular forms		Plural forms	
yo	emp**ie**zo	nosotros/as	empezamos
tú	emp**ie**zas	vosotros/as	empezáis
Ud./él/ella	emp**ie**za	Uds./ellos/ellas	emp**ie**zan

Los chicos empiezan a hablar de su visita al cenote.

Ellos vuelven a comer en el restaurante.

▸ In many other verbs, such as **volver** (*to return*), the stem vowel changes from **o** to **ue**. The **nosotros/as** and **vosotros/as** forms have no stem change.

The verb volver (o:ue) (to return)

Singular forms		Plural forms	
yo	v**ue**lvo	nosotros/as	volvemos
tú	v**ue**lves	vosotros/as	volvéis
Ud./él/ella	v**ue**lve	Uds./ellos/ellas	v**ue**lven

▸ To help you identify stem-changing verbs, they will appear as follows throughout the text:

empezar (e:ie), volver (o:ue)

Common stem-changing verbs

e:ie		o:ue	
cerrar	to close	almorzar	to have lunch
comenzar (a + *inf.*)	to begin	contar	to count; to tell
empezar (a + *inf.*)	to begin	dormir	to sleep
entender	to understand	encontrar	to find
pensar	to think	mostrar	to show
perder	to lose; to miss	poder (+ *inf.*)	to be able to; can
preferir (+ *inf.*)	to prefer	recordar	to remember
querer (+ *inf.*)	to want; to love	volver	to return

▶ **Jugar** (*to play a sport or a game*) is the only Spanish verb that has a **u:ue** stem change. **Jugar** is followed by **a** + [*definite article*] when the name of a sport or game is mentioned.

Ella juega al tenis y al golf.

Los chicos juegan al fútbol.

▶ **Comenzar** and **empezar** require the preposition **a** when they are followed by an infinitive.

Comienzan a jugar a las siete.
They begin playing at seven.

Ana **empieza a** escribir una postal.
Ana is starting to write a postcard.

▶ **Pensar** + [*infinitive*] means *to plan* or *to intend to do something*. **Pensar en** means *to think about someone* or *something*.

¿**Piensan** ir al gimnasio?
Are you planning to go to the gym?

¿**En** qué **piensas**?
What are you thinking about?

¡LENGUA VIVA!

The verb **perder** can mean *to lose* or *to miss*, in the sense of "to miss a train."

Siempre **pierdo** mis llaves.
I always lose my keys.

Es importante no **perder** el autobús.
It's important not to miss the bus.

¡INTÉNTALO! Provide the present tense forms of these verbs.

cerrar (e:ie)
1. Ustedes _cierran_.
2. Tú _cierras_.
3. Nosotras _cerramos_.
4. Mi hermano _cierra_.
5. Yo _cierro_.
6. Usted _cierra_.
7. Los chicos _cierran_.
8. Ella _cierra_.

dormir (o:ue)
1. Mi abuela no _duerme_.
2. Yo no _duermo_.
3. Tú no _duermes_.
4. Mis hijos no _duermen_.
5. Usted no _duerme_.
6. Nosotros no _dormimos_.
7. Él no _duerme_.
8. Ustedes no _duermen_.

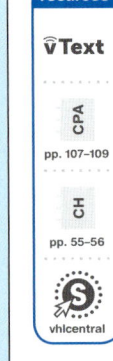

recursos

vText

CPA
pp. 107–109

CH
pp. 55–56

vhlcentral

Práctica

1 Completar Complete this conversation with the appropriate forms of the verbs. Then act it out with a partner.

PABLO Óscar, voy al centro ahora.
ÓSCAR ¿A qué hora (1) _piensas_ (pensar) volver? El partido de fútbol (2) _empieza_ (empezar) a las dos.
PABLO (3) _Vuelvo_ (Volver) a la una. (4) _Quiero_ (Querer) ver el partido.
ÓSCAR (5) ¿_Recuerdas_ (Recordar) que (*that*) nuestro equipo es muy bueno? (6) ¡_Puede_ (Poder) ganar!
PABLO No, (7) _pienso_ (pensar) que va a (8) _perder_ (perder). Los jugadores de Guadalajara son salvajes (*wild*) cuando (9) _juegan_ (jugar).

2 Preferencias With a partner, take turns asking and answering questions about what these people want to do, using the cues provided.

> **modelo**
> Guillermo: estudiar / pasear en bicicleta
> **Estudiante 1:** ¿Quiere estudiar Guillermo?
> **Estudiante 2:** No, prefiere pasear en bicicleta.

1. tú: trabajar / dormir
   ¿Quieres trabajar? No, prefiero dormir.
2. ustedes: mirar la televisión / jugar al dominó
   ¿Quieren ustedes mirar la televisión? No, preferimos jugar al dominó.
3. tus amigos: ir de excursión / descansar
   ¿Quieren ir de excursión tus amigos? No, mis amigos prefieren descansar.
4. tú: comer en la cafetería / ir a un restaurante
   ¿Quieres comer en la cafetería? No, prefiero ir a un restaurante.
5. Elisa: ver una película / leer una revista
   ¿Quiere ver una película Elisa? No, prefiere leer una revista.
6. María y su hermana: tomar el sol / practicar el esquí acuático
   ¿Quieren tomar el sol María y su hermana? No, prefieren practicar el esquí acuático.

NOTA CULTURAL
Dominó (*Dominoes*) is a popular pastime throughout Colombia, Venezuela, Central America, and the Spanish-speaking countries of the Caribbean. It's played both socially and competitively by people of all ages.

3 Describir Use a verb from the list to describe what these people are doing.

| almorzar | cerrar | contar | dormir | encontrar | mostrar |

1. las niñas Las niñas duermen. 2. yo (Yo) Cierro la ventana.   3. nosotros (Nosotros) Almorzamos.

4. tú (Tú) Encuentras/Muestras una maleta. 5. Pedro Pedro muestra una foto. 6. Teresa Teresa cuenta.

Practice more at vhlcentral.com.

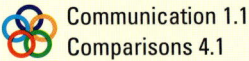

**Communication 1.1
Comparisons 4.1**

4 Teaching Tip Model the activity by asking questions about famous people. Ex: **¿Con qué frecuencia juega al fútbol americano Tom Brady?** Write the answers on the board.

4 Expansion After tallying results on the board, have students work in pairs to graph them. Have them refer to pages 142–143 for models.

4 Partner Chat (Premium) You can also assign activity 4 on the Supersite.

5 Teaching Tips
- Model the activity by stating two programs from the listing that you want to watch and asking the class to react.
- Remind students that the 24-hour clock is often used for schedules. Model a few of the program times. Then ask: **Quiero ver *Héroes* y mi amigo prefiere ver *Elsa y Fred*. ¿Hay un conflicto? (No.) ¿Por qué? (Porque *Héroes* es a las 15:00 y *Elsa y Fred* es a las 22:00.)** Give students the option of answering with the 12-hour clock.

5 Expansion Have students list their favorite TV programs. Then, have them talk with a partner and compare and contrast their TV preferences.

6 Teaching Tip Divide the class into pairs and distribute the Communication Activities worksheets from the Activity Pack.

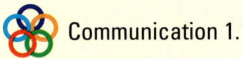
Communication 1.1

6 Expansion
- Ask questions based on the artwork. Ex: **¿Dónde empiezan el día? (en el café)**
- Have volunteers take turns completing the information in the puzzle. Then have students invent their own stories, using stem-changing verbs, about what happens to the same group of tourists.

132 Teacher's Edition • Lesson Four

---

132   ciento treinta y dos   Lección 4

Comunicación

4 Frecuencia In pairs, take turns using the verbs from the list and other stem-changing verbs you know to tell your partner which activities you do daily (**todos los días**), which you do once a month (**una vez al mes**), and which you do once a year (**una vez al año**). Record your partner's responses in the chart so that you can report back to class. *Answers will vary.*

modelo
Estudiante 1: Yo recuerdo a mis abuelos todos los días.
Estudiante 2: Yo pierdo uno de mis libros una vez al año.

cerrar	perder
dormir	poder
empezar	preferir
encontrar	querer
jugar	recordar
¿?	¿?

todos los días	una vez al mes	una vez al año

5 En la televisión Read the television listings for Saturday. In pairs, write a conversation between two siblings arguing about what to watch. Be creative and be prepared to act out your conversation for the class. *Answers will vary.*

modelo
Hermano: Podemos ver la Copa Mundial.
Hermana: ¡No, no quiero ver la Copa Mundial! Prefiero ver...

	13:00	14:00	15:00	16:00	17:00	18:00	19:00	20:00	21:00	22:00	23:00
7	Copa Mundial (*World Cup*) de fútbol			República Deportiva		Campeonato (*Championship*) Mundial de Vóleibol: México-Argentina				Torneo de Natación	
8	Abierto (*Open*) Mexicano de Tenis: Santiago González (México) vs. Nicolás Almagro (España). Semifinales			Campeonato de baloncesto: Los Correcaminos de Tampico vs. los Santos de San Luis				Aficionados al buceo		Cozumel: Aventuras	
12	Yo soy Betty, la fea		Héroes		Hermanos y hermanas			Película: Sin nombre		Película: El coronel no tiene quien le escriba	
13	El padrastro		60 Minutos			El esquí acuático			Patinaje artístico		
17	Biografías: La artista Frida Kahlo		Música de la semana			Entrevista del día: Iker Casillas y su pasión por el fútbol			Cine de la noche: Elsa y Fred		

NOTA CULTURAL
Iker Casillas Fernández is a famous goalkeeper for **Real Madrid**. A native of Madrid, he is among the best goalkeepers of his generation.

Síntesis

6 Situación Your teacher will give you and your partner each a partially illustrated itinerary of a city tour. Complete the itineraries by asking each other questions using the verbs in the captions and vocabulary you have learned. *Answers will vary.*

modelo
Estudiante 1: Por la mañana, empiezan en el café.
Estudiante 2: Y luego...

recursos
vText
CPA
pp. 110–111

TEACHING OPTIONS

Small Groups Have students choose their favorite pastime and work in small groups with other students who have chosen that same activity. Have each group write six sentences about the activity, using a different stem-changing verb in each.

TEACHING OPTIONS

Pairs Ask students to write incomplete dehydrated sentences (only subjects and infinitives) about people and groups at school. Ex: **el equipo de béisbol / perder / ¿?** Then have them exchange papers with a classmate, who will form a complete sentence by conjugating the verb and inventing an appropriate ending. Ask volunteers to write sentences on the board.

4.3 Stem-changing verbs: e:i

ANTE TODO You've already seen that many verbs in Spanish change their stem vowel when conjugated. There is a third kind of stem-vowel change in some verbs, such as **pedir** (*to ask for; to request*). In these verbs, the stressed vowel in the stem changes from **e** to **i**, as shown in the diagram.

INFINITIVE	VERB STEM	STEM CHANGE	CONJUGATED FORM
pedir	p**e**d-	p**i**d-	p**i**do

▸ As with other stem-changing verbs you have learned, there is no stem change in the **nosotros/as** or **vosotros/as** forms in the present tense.

The verb **pedir** (e:i) (*to ask for; to request*)

Singular forms
- yo — pido
- tú — pides
- Ud./él/ella — pide

Plural forms
- nosotros/as — pedimos
- vosotros/as — pedís
- Uds./ellos/ellas — piden

▸ To help you identify verbs with the **e:i** stem change, they will appear as follows throughout the text:

pedir (e:i)

▸ These are the most common **e:i** stem-changing verbs:

conseguir	decir	repetir	seguir
to get; to obtain	*to say; to tell*	*to repeat*	*to follow; to continue; to keep (doing something)*

Pido favores cuando es necesario.
I ask for favors when it's necessary.

Sigue con su tarea.
He continues with his homework.

Javier **dice** la verdad.
Javier is telling the truth.

Consiguen ver buenas películas.
They get to see good movies.

▸ **¡Atención!** The verb **decir** is irregular in its **yo** form: **yo digo**.

▸ The **yo** forms of **seguir** and **conseguir** have a spelling change in addition to the stem change **e:i**.

Sigo su plan.
I'm following their plan.

Consigo novelas en la librería.
I get novels at the bookstore.

¡INTÉNTALO! Provide the correct forms of the verbs.

repetir (e:i)
1. Arturo y Eva __repiten__.
2. Yo __repito__.
3. Nosotros __repetimos__.
4. Julia __repite__.
5. Sofía y yo __repetimos__.

decir (e:i)
1. Yo __digo__.
2. Él __dice__.
3. Tú __dices__.
4. Usted __dice__.
5. Ellas __dicen__.

seguir (e:i)
1. Yo __sigo__.
2. Nosotros __seguimos__.
3. Tú __sigues__.
4. Los chicos __siguen__.
5. Usted __sigue__.

¡LENGUA VIVA!
As you learned in **Lección 2**, **preguntar** means *to ask a question*. **Pedir**, however, means *to ask for something*.
Ella me pregunta cuántos años tengo. *She asks me how old I am.*
Él me pide ayuda. *He asks me for help.*

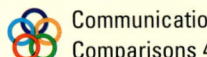

Communication 1.1
Comparisons 4.1

1 Expansion Have students use **conseguir, decir, pedir, repetir,** and **seguir** to write sentences about their own family members. Then have them exchange papers with a partner for peer editing.

Nota cultural Have students research **el Bosque de Chapultepec** in the library or on the Internet and bring a photo of the park to class. Ask them to share one new fact they learned about the park.

2 Teaching Tips
• Before beginning the activity, point out that not all verbs in column B have an **e:i** stem change. Have students identify those that do not (**poder, dormir, perder**).
• In pairs, have students decide which activities in column B are characteristic of a good student. Ex: **Un buen estudiante repite el vocabulario.**

2 Expansion In pairs, have students read their sentences aloud. Their partner must decide if each one is true or false.

3 Teaching Tip Remind students that their partners may guess information that is true, but not necessarily what they wrote for **Actividad 2**.

4 Teaching Tips
• Distribute the Communication Activity worksheets from the Activity Pack that correspond to this activity.
• As you check answers, ask follow-up questions so that students provide more details.

134   Teacher's Edition • Lesson Four

---

134   ciento treinta y cuatro   Lección 4

Práctica

1 Completar Complete these sentences with the correct form of the verb provided.

1. Cuando mi familia pasea por la ciudad, mi madre siempre (*always*) va a un café y ___pide___ (pedir) una soda.
2. Pero mi padre ___dice___ (decir) que perdemos mucho tiempo. Tiene prisa por llegar al Bosque de Chapultepec.
3. Mi padre tiene suerte, porque él siempre ___consigue___ (conseguir) lo que (*that which*) desea.
4. Cuando llegamos al parque, mis hermanos y yo ___seguimos___ (seguir) conversando (*talking*) con nuestros padres.
5. Mis padres siempre ___repiten___ (repetir) la misma cosa: "Nosotros tomamos el sol aquí sin ustedes."
6. Yo siempre ___pido___ (pedir) permiso para volver a casa un poco más tarde porque me gusta mucho el parque.

2 Combinar Combine words from the columns to create sentences about yourself and people you know. Answers will vary.

A	B
yo	(no) pedir muchos favores
mi mejor (*best*) amigo/a	nunca (*never*) pedir perdón
mi familia	nunca seguir las instrucciones
mis amigos/as	siempre seguir las instrucciones
mis amigos/as y yo	conseguir libros en Internet
mis padres	repetir el vocabulario
mi hermano/a	poder hablar dos lenguas
mi profesor(a) de español	dormir hasta el mediodía
	siempre perder sus libros

3 Opiniones In pairs, take turns guessing how your partner completed the sentences from **Actividad 2**. If you guess incorrectly, your partner must supply the correct answer. Answers will vary.

modelo
Estudiante 1: Creo que tus padres consiguen libros en Internet.
Estudiante 2: ¡No! Mi hermana consigue libros en Internet.

4 ¿Quién? Your instructor will give you a worksheet. Talk to your classmates until you find one person who does each of the activities. Use **e:ie, o:ue,** and **e:i** stem-changing verbs. Answers will vary.

modelo
Tú: ¿Pides consejos con frecuencia?
Maira: No, no pido consejos con frecuencia.
Tú: ¿Pides consejos con frecuencia?
Lucas: Sí, pido consejos con frecuencia.

NOTA CULTURAL
A popular weekend destination for residents and tourists, **el Bosque de Chapultepec** is a beautiful park located in Mexico City. It occupies over 1.5 square miles and includes lakes, wooded areas, several museums, and a botanical garden. You may recognize this park from **Fotonovela, Lección 2**.

CONSULTA
To review possessive adjectives, see **Estructura 3.2**, p. 93.

recursos

vText

CPA p. 115

Practice more at vhlcentral.com.

TEACHING OPTIONS

Pairs Ask students to write four simple statements using **e:i** verbs. Then have them read their sentences to a partner, who will guess where the situation takes place. Ex: **Consigo libros para las clases. (Estás en la biblioteca.)** Then reverse the activity, allowing them to answer with verbs from **Estructura 4.2**.

TEACHING OPTIONS

Small Groups Explain to students that movie titles for English-language films are frequently not directly translated into Spanish and that titles may vary by country. Bring in a list of movie titles in Spanish. Ex: *X-Men: Primera generación* (*X-Men: First Class*); *Lo que el viento se llevó* (*Gone with the Wind*). In groups, have students guess the original English titles. Then ask them to state which movies they would prefer to watch.

Comunicación

5 **Las películas** Use these questions to interview a classmate. *Answers will vary.*

1. ¿Prefieres las películas románticas, las películas de acción o las películas de terror? ¿Por qué?
2. ¿Dónde consigues información sobre (*about*) cine y televisión?
3. ¿Dónde consigues las entradas (*tickets*) para ver una película?
4. Para decidir qué películas vas a ver, ¿sigues las recomendaciones de tus amigos? ¿Qué dicen tus amigos en general?
5. ¿Qué cines en tu comunidad muestran las mejores (*best*) películas?
6. ¿Vas a ver una película esta semana? ¿A qué hora empieza la película?

Síntesis

6 **El cine** In pairs, first scan the ad and jot down all the stem-changing verbs. Then answer the questions. Be prepared to share your answers with the class. *Answers will vary.*

1. ¿Qué palabras indican que *Gravity* es una película dramática?
2. ¿Cómo está el personaje (*character*) del póster? ¿Qué quiere hacer?
3. ¿Te gustan las películas como ésta (*this one*)? ¿Por qué?
4. Describe tu película favorita con los verbos de la **Lección 4**.

Ganadora de siete premios Óscar

Cuando todo comienza a fallar, ellos no pierden la esperanza.

Del director de Hijos de los hombres y Harry Potter y el prisionero de Azkaban

Un accidente espacial deja a Ryan Stone y Matt Kowalski atrapados en el espacio. Sólo quieren una cosa: seguir vivos.

¿Consiguen sobrevivir? ¿Vuelven finalmente a la Tierra?

Section Goal

In **Estructura 4.4,** students will learn verbs with irregular **yo** forms.

 Communication 1.1
Comparisons 4.1

Student Resources
Cuaderno de práctica y actividades comunicativas, pp. 116–118
Cuaderno para hispanohablantes, pp. 59–60
Supersite: Activities, *eCuaderno*

Teacher Resources
Workbook TE; Grammar Slides; Audio Activities MP3s; Audio Script; Testing Program Quizzes; Activity Pack; Middle School Activity Pack

Teaching Tips
- Quickly review the present tense of **decir, tener,** and **venir,** pointing out the **-go** ending of the **yo** forms.
- Ask specific students questions to elicit the **yo** forms of the verbs. Ex: **Alicia, ¿haces la tarea en casa o en la biblioteca? (Hago la tarea en la biblioteca.) ¿Traes un diccionario a clase? (Sí, traigo un diccionario a clase.)** As students respond, write the verbs on the board until you have listed all the irregular **yo** forms.
- Go over the uses of **salir.** Model an additional example of each use.
- You may want to tell students that in many Latin American countries (e.g., Mexico, Venezuela, Colombia, and Peru), the verb **prender** is used to express *to turn on an electrical device or appliance.*

---

136 ciento treinta y seis • **Lección 4**

4.4 Verbs with irregular yo forms

 Tutorial

ANTE TODO In Spanish, several verbs have irregular **yo** forms in the present tense. You have already seen three verbs with the **-go** ending in the **yo** form: **decir → digo, tener → tengo,** and **venir → vengo.**

▶ Here are some common expressions with **decir.**

decir la verdad
to tell the truth

decir mentiras
to tell lies

decir que
to say that

decir la respuesta
to say the answer

▶ The verb **hacer** is often used to ask questions about what someone does. Note that when answering, **hacer** is frequently replaced with another, more specific action verb.

Verbs with irregular yo forms

	hacer (to do; to make)	poner (to put; to place)	salir (to leave)	suponer (to suppose)	traer (to bring)
SINGULAR FORMS	hago haces hace	pongo pones pone	salgo sales sale	supongo supones supone	traigo traes trae
PLURAL FORMS	hacemos hacéis hacen	ponemos ponéis ponen	salimos salís salen	suponemos suponéis suponen	traemos traéis traen

Salgo mucho los fines de semana.

Yo no salgo, yo hago la tarea y veo películas en la televisión.

▶ **Poner** can also mean *to turn on* a household appliance.

Carlos **pone** la radio.
Carlos turns on the radio.

María **pone** la televisión.
María turns on the television.

▶ **Salir de** is used to indicate that someone is leaving a particular place.

Hoy **salgo del** hospital.
Today I leave the hospital.

Sale de la clase a las cuatro.
He leaves class at four.

TEACHING OPTIONS

TPR Have students act out actions as you make statements with irregular **yo** forms. Ex: **Hago la tarea.** (Students imitate writing their homework.) **Pongo la radio.** (They imitate turning on a radio.)
Game Divide the class into teams of three. Each team has a piece of paper. Call out an infinitive and a person. Ex: **traer / primera persona plural.** Each team has to compose a sentence, with

TEACHING OPTIONS

each member writing one part. The first team member thinks of an appropriate subject or proper name and writes it down (Ex: **nosotras**). The second writes the correct form of the verb (Ex: **traemos**). The third completes the sentence in a logical way (Ex: **el libro**). The first team to write a logical and correct sentence wins. Team members should rotate positions each time a new verb is given.

Los pasatiempos

▶ **Salir para** is used to indicate someone's destination.

Mañana **salgo para** México.
Tomorrow I leave for Mexico.

Hoy **salen para** España.
Today they leave for Spain.

▶ **Salir con** means *to leave with someone or something*, or *to date someone*.

Alberto **sale con** su mochila.
Alberto is leaving with his backpack.

Margarita **sale con** Guillermo.
Margarita is going out with Guillermo.

The verbs ver and oír

▶ The verb **ver** (*to see*) has an irregular **yo** form. The other forms of **ver** are regular.

The verb ver (to see)

Singular forms		Plural forms	
yo	veo	nosotros/as	vemos
tú	ves	vosotros/as	veis
Ud./él/ella	ve	Uds./ellos/ellas	ven

▶ The verb **oír** (*to hear*) has an irregular **yo** form and the spelling change **i:y** in the **tú**, **usted/él/ella**, and **ustedes/ellos/ellas** forms. The **nosotros/as** and **vosotros/as** forms have an accent mark.

The verb oír (to hear)

Singular forms		Plural forms	
yo	oigo	nosotros/as	oímos
tú	oyes	vosotros/as	oís
Ud./él/ella	oye	Uds./ellos/ellas	oyen

▶ While most commonly translated as *to hear*, **oír** is also used in contexts where English would use *to listen*.

Oigo a unas personas en la otra sala.
I hear some people in the other room.

¿**Oyes** la radio por la mañana?
Do you listen to the radio in the morning?

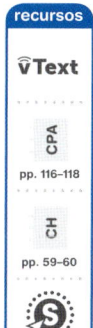

¡INTÉNTALO! Provide the appropriate forms of these verbs.

1. salir — Isabel **sale**. Nosotros **salimos**. Yo **salgo**.
2. ver — Yo **veo**. Uds. **ven**. Tú **ves**.
3. poner — Rita y yo **ponemos**. Yo **pongo**. Los niños **ponen**.
4. hacer — Yo **hago**. Tú **haces**. Ud. **hace**.
5. oír — Él **oye**. Nosotros **oímos**. Yo **oigo**.
6. traer — Ellas **traen**. Yo **traigo**. Tú **traes**.
7. suponer — Yo **supongo**. Mi amigo **supone**. Nosotras **suponemos**.

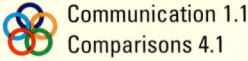

Communication 1.1
Comparisons 4.1

1 Teaching Tip Quickly review the new verbs with irregular **yo** forms. Then, ask pairs to complete and role-play the conversation.

1 Expansion In pairs, have students write a conversation between David and Luisa as they are waiting for the movie to start. Have volunteers act out their conversations for the class.

2 Teaching Tip To simplify, lead the class to identify key words in each sentence. Then have students choose the infinitive that best fits with the key words and name any missing words for each item. After students complete the activity individually, have volunteers write the sentences on the board.

2 Expansion
- Change the subjects of the dehydrated sentences in the activity and have students write or say aloud the new sentences.
- Ask students to form questions that would elicit the statements in **Actividad 2**. Ex: **¿Qué hago antes de salir?**
- Have students write three sentences, each using a verb from **Estructura 4.4**. Then ask them to copy their sentences onto a sheet of paper in dehydrated form, following the model of **Actividad 2**. Students should exchange papers with a partner, who writes the complete sentences. Finally, have partners check each other's work.

3 Expansion Use magazine pictures which elicit the target verbs to extend the activity. Encourage students to add further descriptions if they can.

138   Teacher's Edition • Lesson Four

---

138   ciento treinta y ocho   Lección 4

Práctica

1 Completar Complete this conversation with the appropriate forms of the verbs. Then act it out with a partner.

ERNESTO David, ¿qué (1) **haces** (hacer) hoy?
DAVID Ahora estudio biología, pero esta noche (2) **salgo** (salir) con Luisa. Vamos al cine. (3) **Dice(n)** (Decir) que la nueva (*new*) película de Almodóvar es buena.
ERNESTO ¿Y Diana? ¿Qué (4) **hace** (hacer) ella?
DAVID (5) **Sale** (Salir) a comer con sus padres.
ERNESTO ¿Qué (6) **hacen** (hacer) Andrés y Javier?
DAVID Tienen que (7) **hacer** (hacer) las maletas. (8) **Salen** (Salir) para Monterrey mañana.
ERNESTO Pues, ¿qué (9) **hago** (hacer) yo?
DAVID (10) **Supongo** (Suponer) que puedes estudiar o (11) **ver** (ver) la televisión.
ERNESTO No quiero estudiar. Mejor (12) **pongo** (poner) la televisión. Mi programa favorito empieza en unos minutos.

2 Oraciones Form sentences using the cues provided and verbs from **Estructura 4.4**.

modelo
tú / _____ / cosas / en / su lugar / antes de (*before*) / salir
Tú *pones las cosas en su lugar antes de salir.*

1. mis amigos / _____ / conmigo / centro   Mis amigos salen conmigo al centro.
2. tú / _____ / mentiras / pero / yo / _____ / verdad   Tú dices mentiras, pero yo digo la verdad.
3. Alberto / _____ / música del café Pasatiempos   Alberto oye la música del café Pasatiempos.
4. yo / no / _____ / muchas películas   Yo no veo muchas películas.
5. domingo / nosotros / _____ / mucha / tarea   El domingo, nosotros hacemos mucha tarea.
6. si / yo / _____ / que / yo / querer / ir / cine / mis amigos / ir / también   Si yo digo que quiero ir al cine, mis amigos van también.

3 Describir Use the verbs from **Estructura 4.4** to describe what these people are doing.

1. Fernán   Fernán pone la mochila en el escritorio/trae una mochila.

2. los aficionados   Los aficionados salen del estadio/para sus casas.

3. yo   Yo traigo/salgo con una cámara.

4. nosotros   Nosotros vemos el monumento.

5. la señora Vargas   La señora Vargas no oye bien.

6. el estudiante   El estudiante hace su tarea.

Practice more at **vhlcentral.com**.

TEACHING OPTIONS

Small Groups Ask students to write three sentences about themselves: two should be true and one should be false. Then, in groups of four, have students share their sentences with the group, who must decide whether that person **dice la verdad** or **dice una mentira**. Survey the class to find out who was successful at stumping their classmates.

EXPANSION

Extra Practice Have students use five of the target verbs from **Estructura 4.4** to write sentences about their habits that others may find somewhat unusual. Ex: **Traigo doce bolígrafos en la mochila. Hago la tarea en un café del centro. No pongo la televisión hasta las diez de la noche.**

Comunicación

4 **Tu rutina** In pairs, take turns asking each other these questions. Answers will vary.
1. ¿Qué traes a clase?
2. ¿Quiénes traen un diccionario a clase? ¿Por qué traen un diccionario?
3. ¿A qué hora sales de tu casa por la mañana? ¿A qué hora salen tus hermanos/as o tus padres?
4. ¿Dónde pones tus libros cuando regresas de clase? ¿Siempre (*Always*) pones tus cosas en su lugar?
5. ¿Qué prefieres hacer, oír la radio o ver la televisión?
6. ¿Oyes música cuando estudias?
7. ¿Ves películas en casa o prefieres ir al cine?
8. ¿Haces mucha tarea los fines de semana?
9. ¿Sales con tus amigos los fines de semana? ¿A qué hora? ¿Qué hacen?
10. ¿Te gusta ver deportes en la televisión o prefieres ver otros programas? ¿Cuáles?

5 **Charadas** In groups, play a game of charades. Each person should think of two phrases containing the verbs **hacer, oír, poner, salir, traer,** or **ver**. The first person to guess correctly acts out the next charade. Answers will vary.

6 **Entrevista** You are doing a market research report on lifestyles. Interview a classmate to find out when he or she goes out with these people and what they do for entertainment. Answers will vary.

▸ los/las amigos/as
▸ los/las hermanos/as
▸ los padres
▸ otros parientes

Síntesis

7 **Situación** Imagine that you are speaking with a member of your family or your best friend. With a partner, prepare a conversation using these cues. Answers will vary.

Estudiante 1	Estudiante 2
Ask your partner what he or she is doing.	Tell your partner that you are watching TV.
Say what you suppose he or she is watching.	Say that you like the show _____. Ask if he or she wants to watch.
Say no, because you are going out with friends and tell where you are going.	Say you think it's a good idea, and ask what your partner and his or her friends are doing there.
Say what you are going to do, and ask your partner whether he or she wants to come along.	Say no and tell your partner what you prefer to do.

TEACHING OPTIONS

Pairs Have pairs of students role-play an awful first date. Students should write their script first, then present it to the class. Encourage students to use descriptive adjectives as well as the new verbs learned in **Estructura 4.4**.

DIFFERENTIATION

Heritage Speakers Ask heritage speakers to talk about a social custom in their cultural community. Remind them to use familiar vocabulary and simple sentences. Have the rest of the class ask follow-up questions.

Recapitulación

Review the grammar concepts you have learned in this lesson by completing these activities.

1 Completar Complete the chart with the correct verb forms. 30 pts.

Infinitive	yo	nosotros/as	ellos/as
volver	**vuelvo**	volvemos	vuelven
comenzar	comienzo	**comenzamos**	comienzan
hacer	hago	**hacemos**	**hacen**
ir	voy	vamos	van
jugar	**juego**	jugamos	juegan
repetir	repito	repetimos	**repiten**

2 Un día típico Complete the paragraph with the appropriate forms of the stem-changing verbs in the word list. Not all verbs will be used. Some may be used more than once. 20 pts.

almorzar	ir	salir
cerrar	jugar	seguir
empezar	mostrar	ver
hacer	querer	volver

¡Hola! Me llamo Cecilia y vivo en Puerto Vallarta, México. ¿Cómo es un día típico en mi vida (*life*)? Por la mañana como con mis padres y juntos (*together*) (1) _vemos_ las noticias (*news*) en la televisión. A las siete y media, (yo) (2) _salgo_ de mi casa y tomo el autobús. Me gusta llegar temprano (*early*) a la escuela porque siempre (*always*) (3) _veo_ a mis amigos en la cafetería. Conversamos y planeamos lo que (4) _queremos_ hacer cada (*each*) día. A las ocho y cuarto, mi amiga Sandra y yo (5) _vamos_ al laboratorio de lenguas. La clase de francés (6) _empieza_ a las ocho y media. ¡Es mi clase favorita! A las doce y media (yo) (7) _almuerzo_ en la cafetería con mis amigos. Después (*Afterwards*), yo (8) _sigo_ con mis clases. Por las tardes, mis amigos (9) _vuelven_ a sus casas, pero yo (10) _juego_ al vóleibol con mi amigo Tomás.

RESUMEN GRAMATICAL

4.1 Present tense of ir *p. 126*

yo	voy	nosotros	vamos
tú	vas	vosotros	vais
él	va	ellas	van

▸ **ir a** + [*infinitive*] = *to be going* + [*infinitive*]
▸ **a + el = al**
▸ **vamos a** + [*infinitive*] = *let's* (*do something*)

4.2 Stem-changing verbs e:ie, o:ue, u:ue *pp. 129–130*

	empezar	volver	jugar
yo	emp**ie**zo	v**ue**lvo	j**ue**go
tú	emp**ie**zas	v**ue**lves	j**ue**gas
él	emp**ie**za	v**ue**lve	j**ue**ga
nos.	empezamos	volvemos	jugamos
vos.	empezáis	volvéis	jugáis
ellas	emp**ie**zan	v**ue**lven	j**ue**gan

▸ Other **e:ie** verbs: **cerrar, comenzar, entender, pensar, perder, preferir, querer**
▸ Other **o:ue** verbs: **almorzar, contar, dormir, encontrar, mostrar, poder, recordar**

4.3 Stem-changing verbs e:i *p. 133*

	pedir		
yo	p**i**do	nos.	pedimos
tú	p**i**des	vos.	pedís
él	p**i**de	ellas	p**i**den

▸ Other **e:i** verbs: **conseguir, decir, repetir, seguir**

4.4 Verbs with irregular yo forms *pp. 136–137*

hacer	poner	salir	suponer	traer
hago	pongo	salgo	supongo	traigo

▸ **ver: veo,** ves, ve, vemos, veis, ven
▸ **oír: oigo,** oyes, oye, oímos, oís, oyen

Los pasatiempos

3 Oraciones Arrange the cues provided in the correct order to form complete sentences. Make all necessary changes. **14 pts.**

1. tarea / los / hacer / sábados / nosotros / la
   Los sábados nosotros hacemos la tarea./Nosotros hacemos la tarea los sábados.
2. en / pizza / Andrés / una / restaurante / el / pedir
   Andrés pide una pizza en el restaurante.
3. a / ? / museo / ir / ¿ / el / (tú)
   ¿(Tú) Vas al museo?
4. de / oír / amigos / bien / los / no / Elena
   Los amigos de Elena no oyen bien.
5. libros / traer / yo / clase / mis / a
   Yo traigo mis libros a clase.
6. película / ver / en / Jorge y Carlos / pensar / cine / una / el
   Jorge y Carlos piensan ver una película en el cine.
7. unos / escribir / Mariana / electrónicos / querer / mensajes
   Mariana quiere escribir unos mensajes electrónicos.

4 Escribir Write a short paragraph about what you do on a typical day. Use at least six of the verbs you have learned in this lesson. You can use the paragraph on the opposite page (**Actividad 2**) as a model. **36 pts.** Answers will vary.

Un día típico

Hola, me llamo Julia y vivo en Vancouver, Canadá. Por la mañana, yo...

5 Adivinanza Complete the rhyme with the appropriate forms of the correct verbs from the list. **4 EXTRA points!**

contar	poder
oír	suponer

"Si no ___puedes___ dormir
y el sueño deseas,
lo vas a conseguir
si ___cuentas___ ovejas°."

ovejas *sheep*

Section Goals

In **Lectura**, students will:
- learn the strategy of predicting content from visual elements in reading matter
- read a magazine article containing graphs and charts

Communication 1.1, 1.2, 1.3
Cultures 2.1, 2.2
Connections 3.1, 3.2
Comparisons 4.2

Student Resources
Cuaderno para hispanohablantes, pp. 61–62
Supersite: Activities

 Pre-AP*

Interpretive Reading:
Estrategia Tell students that they can infer a great deal of information about the content of an article by surveying the graphic elements included in it. When students survey an article for its graphic elements, they should look for such things as:
- headlines or headings
- bylines
- photos
- photo captions
- graphs and tables

Examinar el texto Give students two minutes to take a look at the visual clues in the article and write down all the ideas the clues suggest.

Contestar After going over students' responses, ask them to discuss the accuracy of their predictions from **Examinar el texto**.

---

4 adelante

Lección 4

Lectura

 Audio: Reading Additional Reading

Antes de leer

Estrategia
Predicting content from visuals

When you are reading in Spanish, be sure to look for visual clues that will orient you to the content and purpose of what you are reading. Photos and illustrations, for example, will often give you a good idea of the main points that the reading covers. You may also encounter very helpful visuals that are used to summarize large amounts of data in a way that is easy to comprehend; these include bar graphs, pie charts, flow charts, lists of percentages, and other sorts of diagrams.

Examinar el texto
Take a quick look at the visual elements of the magazine article in order to generate a list of ideas about its content. Then compare your list with a classmate's. Are they the same or are they different? Discuss they and make any changes needed to produce a final list of ideas.

Contestar
Read the list of ideas you wrote in **Examinar el texto**, and look again at the visual elements of the magazine article. Then answer these questions:

1. Who is the woman in the photo, and what is her role?
   María Úrsula Echevarría is the author of the article.
2. What is the article about?
   The article is about sports in the Hispanic world.
3. What is the subject of the pie chart?
   The most popular sports among college students
4. What is the subject of the bar graph?
   Hispanic countries in world soccer championships

recursos
vText pp. 61–62 | CH | vhlcentral

---

por María Úrsula Echevarría

El fútbol es el deporte más popular en el mundo° hispano, según° una encuesta° reciente realizada entre jóvenes universitarios. Mucha gente practica este deporte y tiene un equipo de fútbol favorito. Cada cuatro años se realiza la Copa Mundial°. Argentina y Uruguay han ganado° este campeonato° más de una vez°. Los aficionados siguen los partidos de fútbol en casa por tele y en muchos otros lugares como bares, restaurantes, estadios y clubes deportivos. Los jóvenes juegan al fútbol con sus amigos en parques y gimnasios.

Países hispanos en campeonatos mundiales de fútbol (1930–2014)

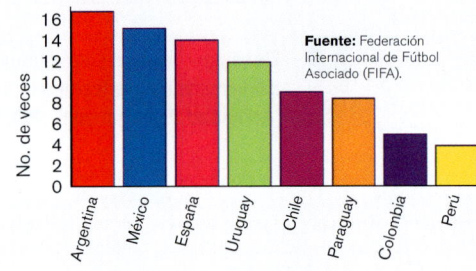

Fuente: Federación Internacional de Fútbol Asociado (FIFA).

Pero, por supuesto°, en los países de habla hispana también hay otros deportes populares. ¿Qué deporte sigue al fútbol en estos países? Bueno, ¡depende del país y de otros factores!

Después de leer

Evaluación y predicción

Which of the following sporting events would be most popular among the college students surveyed? Rate them from one (most popular) to five (least popular). Which would be the most popular at your school? Answers will vary.

_____ 1. la Copa Mundial de Fútbol
_____ 2. los Juegos Olímpicos
_____ 3. el Campeonato de Wimbledon
_____ 4. la Serie Mundial de Béisbol
_____ 5. el Tour de Francia

EXPANSION

Variación léxica Remind students that the term **fútbol** in the Hispanic world refers to soccer, and that in the English-speaking world outside of the United States and Canada, soccer is called *football*. The game known as *football* in the U.S. and Canada is known as **fútbol americano** in the Spanish-speaking world.

EXPANSION

Extra Practice Ask questions that require students to refer to the article. Model the use of the definite article with percentages. ¿Qué porcentaje prefiere el fútbol? (el 69 por ciento) ¿Qué porcentaje prefiere el vóleibol? (el 2 por ciento)

Los pasatiempos

ciento cuarenta y tres 143

No sólo el fútbol

En Colombia, el béisbol también es muy popular después del fútbol, aunque° esto varía según la región del país. En la costa del norte de Colombia, el béisbol es una pasión. Y el ciclismo también es un deporte que los colombianos siguen con mucho interés.

Donde el béisbol es más popular
En los países del Caribe, el béisbol es el deporte predominante. Éste es el caso en Puerto Rico, Cuba y la República Dominicana. Los niños empiezan a jugar cuando son muy pequeños. En Puerto Rico y la República Dominicana, la gente también quiere participar en otros deportes, como el baloncesto, o ver los partidos en la tele. Y para los espectadores aficionados del Caribe, el boxeo es número dos.

Deportes más populares

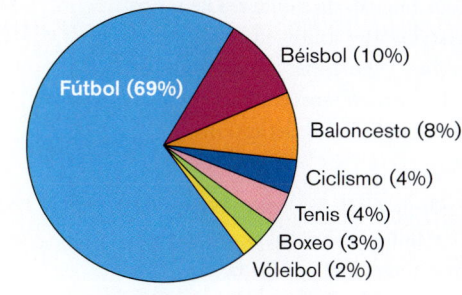

Donde el fútbol es más popular
En México, el béisbol es el segundo° deporte más popular después° del fútbol. Pero en Argentina, después del fútbol, el rugby tiene mucha importancia. En Perú a la gente le gusta mucho ver partidos de vóleibol. ¿Y en España? Muchas personas prefieren el baloncesto, el tenis y el ciclismo.

---

mundo *world* según *according to* encuesta *survey* se realiza la Copa Mundial *the World Cup is held* han ganado *have won* campeonato *championship* más de una vez *more than once* por supuesto *of course* segundo *second* después *after* aunque *although*

¿Cierto o falso?
Indicate whether each sentence is **cierto** or **falso**, then correct the false statements.

	Cierto	Falso
1. El vóleibol es el segundo deporte más popular en México. Es el béisbol.	○	●
2. En España a la gente le gustan varios deportes como el baloncesto y el ciclismo.	●	○
3. En la costa del norte de Colombia, el tenis es una pasión. El béisbol es una pasión.	○	●
4. En el Caribe, el deporte más popular es el béisbol.	●	○

Preguntas
Answer these questions in Spanish. Answers will vary.
1. ¿Dónde ven el fútbol los aficionados? Y tú, ¿cómo ves tus deportes favoritos?
2. ¿Te gusta el fútbol? ¿Por qué?
3. ¿Miras la Copa Mundial en la televisión?
4. ¿Qué deportes miras en la televisión?
5. En tu opinión, ¿cuáles son los tres deportes más populares en tu escuela? ¿En tu comunidad? ¿En tu país?
6. ¿Practicas deportes en tus ratos libres?

 Practice more at vhlcentral.com.

Escritura

Estrategia
Using a dictionary

A common mistake made by beginning language learners is to embrace the dictionary as the ultimate resource for reading, writing, and speaking. While it is true that the dictionary is a useful tool that can provide valuable information about vocabulary, using the dictionary correctly requires that you understand the elements of each entry.

If you glance at a Spanish-English dictionary, you will notice that its format is similar to that of an English dictionary. The word is listed first, usually followed by its pronunciation. Then come the definitions, organized by parts of speech. Sometimes the most frequently used definitions are listed first.

To find the best word for your needs, you should refer to the abbreviations and the explanatory notes that appear next to the entries. For example, imagine that you are writing about your pastimes. You want to write, "I want to buy a new racket for my match tomorrow," but you don't know the Spanish word for "racket." In the dictionary, you may find an entry like this:

> **racket** *s* **1.** alboroto; **2.** raqueta (*dep.*)

The abbreviation key at the front of the dictionary says that *s* corresponds to **sustantivo** (*noun*). Then, the first word you see is **alboroto**. The definition of **alboroto** is *noise* or *racket*, so **alboroto** is probably not the word you're looking for. The second word is **raqueta**, followed by the abbreviation *dep.*, which stands for **deportes**. This indicates that the word **raqueta** is the best choice for your needs.

Tema

Escribir un folleto

Choose one topic to write a pamphlet.

1. You are on the Homecoming Committee at your school this year. Create a pamphlet that lists events for Friday night, Saturday, and Sunday. Include a brief description of each event and its time and location. Include activities for different age groups, since some alumni will bring their families.

2. You are on the Freshman Student Orientation Committee and are in charge of creating a pamphlet for new students that describes the sports offered at your school. Write the flyer, including a variety of activities.

3. You volunteer at your community's recreation center. It is your job to market your community to potential residents. Write a brief pamphlet that describes the recreational opportunities your community provides, the areas where the activities take place, and the costs, if any. Be sure to include activities that will appeal to singles as well as couples and families; you should include activities for all age groups and for both men and women.

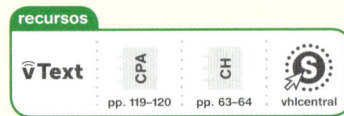

EVALUATION: Folleto

Criteria	Scale
Appropriate details	1 2 3 4
Organization	1 2 3 4
Use of vocabulary	1 2 3 4
Grammatical accuracy	1 2 3 4
Mechanics	1 2 3 4

Scoring	
Excellent	18–20 points
Good	14–17 points
Satisfactory	10–13 points
Unsatisfactory	< 10 points

Escuchar  Audio

Estrategia
Listening for the gist

Listening for the general idea, or gist, can help you follow what someone is saying even if you can't hear or understand some of the words. When you listen for the gist, you simply try to capture the essence of what you hear without focusing on individual words.

To help you practice this strategy, you will listen to a paragraph made up of three sentences. Jot down a brief summary of what you hear.

Preparación

Based on the photo, what do you think Anabela is like? Do you and Anabela have similar interests?

Ahora escucha

You will hear first José talking, then Anabela. As you listen, check off each person's favorite activities.

Pasatiempos favoritos de José

1. ✓ leer el correo electrónico
2. ___ jugar al béisbol
3. ✓ ver películas de acción
4. ✓ ir al café
5. ✓ ir a partidos de béisbol
6. ✓ ver películas románticas
7. ✓ dormir la siesta
8. ✓ escribir mensajes electrónicos

Pasatiempos favoritos de Anabela

9. ✓ esquiar
10. ✓ nadar
11. ✓ practicar el ciclismo
12. ✓ jugar al golf
13. ___ jugar al baloncesto
14. ___ ir a ver partidos de tenis
15. ✓ escalar montañas
16. ___ ver televisión

Comprensión

Preguntas

Answer these questions about José's and Anabela's pastimes.
1. ¿Quién practica más deportes? Anabela
2. ¿Quién piensa que es importante descansar? José
3. ¿A qué deporte es aficionado José? Le gusta el béisbol.
4. ¿Por qué Anabela no practica el baloncesto? Ella no es alta.
5. ¿Qué películas le gustan a la novia de José? Le gustan las películas de romance.
6. ¿Cuál es el deporte favorito de Anabela? el ciclismo

Seleccionar

Which person do these statements best describe?
1. Le gusta practicar deportes. Anabela
2. Prefiere las películas de acción. José
3. Le gustan las computadoras. José
4. Le gusta nadar. Anabela
5. Siempre (*Always*) duerme una siesta por la tarde. José
6. Quiere ir de vacaciones a las montañas. Anabela

Practice more at vhlcentral.com.

recursos

Anuncio de Totofútbol

Por eso° esperaban que yo fuera° el mejor de todos°.

Preparación
Answer these questions in English. *Answers will vary.*
1. What role do sports play in your life? Which sports do you enjoy? Why?
2. Is there a sport you enjoy with other members of your family? With a group of friends? Is there a special season for that sport?

Más que un juego
In many Spanish-speaking countries, soccer isn't just a game; it's a way of life. Many countries have professional and amateur leagues, and soccer is even played in the streets. Every four years, during the World Cup, even those who aren't big fans of the sport find it impossible not to get swept up in "soccer fever." During the month-long Cup, companies also get caught up in the soccer craze, conducting ad campaigns and offering promotions and all kinds of prizes.

Por eso *That's why* esperaban que yo fuera *they expected that I'd be* el mejor de todos *the best of all*

Vocabulario útil

cracks	stars, aces (sports)
Dios me hizo	God made me
jugando	playing
lo tuvo a Pelé de hijo	he was a better player than Pelé (coll. expr. Peru)
patito feo	ugly duckling
plata	money (S. America)

Comprensión
Indicate whether each statement is **cierto** or **falso**.

	Cierto	Falso
1. La familia juega al baloncesto.	○	●
2. No hay mujeres en el anuncio (*ad*).	○	●
3. La pareja tiene cinco hijos.	○	●
4. El hijo más joven es un mariachi.	●	○

Conversación
Answers will vary.
With a partner, discuss these questions in Spanish.
1. En el anuncio hay varios elementos culturales representativos de la cultura de los países hispanos. ¿Cuáles son?
2. ¿Qué otros elementos culturales de los países hispanos conocen (*do you know*)?

Aplicación
The habit of playing sports should be an important part of everyone's life. With two classmates, prepare an oral presentation for your community. The objective of your presentation is to encourage families and communities to promote the habit of playing sports among kids from an early age. Include illustrations in your presentation.
Answers will vary.

Los pasatiempos

Video: Flash cultura

¡Fútbol en España!

The rivalry between the teams **Real Madrid** and **FC Barcelona** is perhaps the fiercest in all of soccer—just imagine if they occupied the same city! Well, each team also has competing clubs within its respective city: Spain's capital has the **Club Atlético de Madrid**, and Barcelona is home to **Espanyol**. In fact, across the Spanish-speaking world, it is common for a city to have more than one professional team, often with strikingly dissimilar origins, identity, and fan base. For example, in Bogotá, the **Millonarios** were so named for the large sums spent on players, while the **Santa Fe** team is one of the most traditional in Colombian soccer. **River Plate** and **Boca Juniors**, who enjoy a famous rivalry, are just two of twenty-four clubs in Buenos Aires—the city with the most professional soccer teams in the world.

Vocabulario útil

afición	fans
celebran	they celebrate
preferido/a	favorite
rivalidad	rivalry
se junta con	it's tied up with

Preparación
What is the most popular sport at your school? What teams are your rivals? How do students celebrate a win?
Answers will vary.

Escoger
Select the correct answer.
1. Un partido entre el Barça y el Real Madrid es un __evento__ (deporte/evento) importante en toda España.
2. El Camp Nou es el __estadio__ (estadio/equipo) más grande (*largest*) de Europa.
3. Los aficionados __celebran__ (miran/celebran) las victorias de sus equipos en las calles (*streets*).
4. La rivalidad entre el Real Madrid y el Barça está relacionada con la __política__ (religión/política).

(*Hay mucha afición al fútbol en España.*)

¿Y cuál es vuestro jugador favorito?

—¿Y quién va a ganar?
—El Real Madrid.

Practice more at vhlcentral.com.

4 panorama

México

 Video: *Panorama cultural*
Interactive Map

El país en cifras

▶ **Área:** 1.972.550 km² (761.603 millas²), casi° tres veces° el área de Texas

La situación geográfica de México, al sur° de los Estados Unidos, ha influido en° la economía y la sociedad de los dos países. Una de las consecuencias es la emigración de la población mexicana al país vecino°. Hoy día, más de 33 millones de personas de ascendencia mexicana viven en los Estados Unidos.

▶ **Población:** 118.818.000
▶ **Capital:** México, D.F. (y su área metropolitana)—19.319.000
▶ **Ciudades principales:**
   Guadalajara—4.338.000,
   Monterrey—3.838.000,
   Puebla—2.278.000,
   Ciudad Juárez—1.321.000
▶ **Moneda:** peso mexicano
▶ **Idiomas:** español (oficial), náhuatl, otras lenguas indígenas

 Bandera de México

Mexicanos célebres

▶ **Benito Juárez,** héroe nacional (1806–1872)
▶ **Octavio Paz,** poeta (1914–1998)
▶ **Elena Poniatowska,** periodista y escritora (1932–)
▶ **Mario Molina,** Premio Nobel de Química, 1995; químico (1943–)
▶ **Paulina Rubio,** cantante (1971–)

casi *almost* veces *times* sur *south* ha influido en *has influenced* vecino *neighboring* se llenan de luz *get filled with light* flores *flowers* Muertos *Dead* se ríen *laugh* muerte *death* lo cual se refleja *which is reflected* calaveras de azúcar *sugar skulls* pan *bread* huesos *bones*

¡Increíble pero cierto!

Cada dos de noviembre los cementerios de México se llenan de luz°, música y flores°. El Día de Muertos° no es un evento triste; es una fiesta en honor a las personas muertas. En ese día, los mexicanos se ríen° de la muerte°, lo cual se refleja° en detalles como las calaveras de azúcar° y el pan° de muerto —pan en forma de huesos°.

Cabo San Lucas

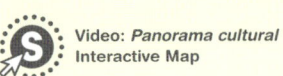
Autorretrato con mono (Self-portrait with monkey), 1938, Frida Kahlo

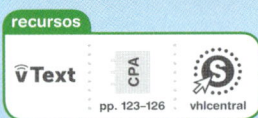
Artesanías en Taxco, Guerrero

Pirámide de Kukulcán en Chichén Itzá

recursos
vText   CPA pp. 123–126   vhlcentral

Los pasatiempos

Ciudades • México, D.F.

La Ciudad de México, fundada° en 1525, también se llama el D.F. o Distrito Federal. Muchos turistas e inmigrantes vienen a la ciudad porque es el centro cultural y económico del país. El crecimiento° de la población es de los más altos° del mundo°. El D.F. tiene una población mayor que las de Nueva York, Madrid o París.

Artes • Diego Rivera y Frida Kahlo

Frida Kahlo y Diego Rivera eran° artistas mexicanos muy famosos. Se casaron° en 1929. Los dos se interesaron° en las condiciones sociales de la gente indígena de su país. Puedes ver algunas° de sus obras° en el Museo de Arte Moderno de la Ciudad de México.

Historia • Los aztecas

Los aztecas dominaron° en México del siglo° XIV al siglo XVI. Sus canales, puentes° y pirámides con templos religiosos eran muy importantes. El fin del imperio azteca comenzó° con la llegada° de los españoles en 1519, pero la presencia azteca sigue hoy. La Ciudad de México está situada en la capital azteca de Tenochtitlán, y muchos turistas van a visitar sus ruinas.

Economía • La plata

México es el mayor productor de plata° del mundo. Estados como Zacatecas y Durango tienen ciudades fundadas cerca de los más grandes yacimientos° de plata del país. Estas ciudades fueron° en la época colonial unas de las más ricas e importantes. Hoy en día, aún° conservan mucho de su encanto° y esplendor.

Golfo de México
Península de Yucatán
Mérida
Cancún
Bahía de Campeche
Veracruz
Istmo de Tehuantepec
BELICE
GUATEMALA

¿Qué aprendiste? Responde a cada pregunta con una oración completa.

1. ¿Qué lenguas hablan los mexicanos?
   Los mexicanos hablan español y lenguas indígenas.
2. ¿Cómo es la población del D.F. en comparación con la de otras ciudades?
   La población del D.F. es mayor.
3. ¿En qué se interesaron Frida Kahlo y Diego Rivera? *Se interesaron en las condiciones sociales de la gente indígena de su país.*
4. Nombra algunas de las estructuras de la arquitectura azteca. *Hay canales, puentes y pirámides con templos religiosos.*
5. ¿Dónde está situada la capital de México? *Está situada en la capital azteca de Tenochtitlán.*
6. ¿Qué estados de México tienen los mayores yacimientos de plata? *Zacatecas y Durango tienen los mayores yacimientos de plata.*

Conexión Internet Investiga estos temas en **vhlcentral.com**.

1. Busca información sobre dos lugares de México. ¿Te gustaría (*Would you like*) vivir allí? ¿Por qué?
2. Busca información sobre dos artistas mexicanos. ¿Cómo se llaman sus obras más famosas?

fundada *founded* crecimiento *growth* más altos *highest* mundo *world* eran *were* Se casaron *They got married* se interesaron *were interested* algunas *some* obras *works* dominaron *dominated* siglo *century* puentes *bridges* comenzó *started* llegada *arrival* plata *silver* yacimientos *deposits* fueron *were* aún *still* encanto *charm*

Practice more at vhlcentral.com.

EXPANSION

Variación léxica Over 52 languages are spoken by indigenous communities in Mexico today; of these, Mayan languages are the most prevalent. Also, **náhuatl**, the language of the Aztecs, is spoken by a significant part of the population. Some **náhuatl** words have entered Mexican Spanish, such as **aguacate** (*avocado*), **guajolote** (*turkey*), **cacahuate** (*peanut*), **ejote** (*green bean*), **chile** (*chili pepper*), and **elote** (*corn*). Two food names of **náhuatl** origin that are now used in world languages are *tomato* and *chocolate*, as these foods are native to Mexico and were brought to Europe in the sixteenth century.

México, D.F. Mexicans usually refer to their capital as **México** or **el D.F.** The monument pictured here is **El Ángel de la Independencia**, located on the **Paseo de la Reforma** in el D.F.

Diego Rivera y Frida Kahlo Show students paintings by Rivera and Kahlo, and discuss the indigenous Mexican themes that dominate their works: Rivera's murals have largely proletarian and political messages, while Kahlo incorporated indigenous motifs in her portrayals of suffering.

Los aztecas Explain that the coat of arms on the Mexican flag represents an Aztec prophecy. Legend states that nomadic Aztecs wandered present-day Mexico in search of a place to establish a city. According to their gods, the precise location would be indicated by an eagle devouring a snake while perched atop a nopal cactus. The Aztecs saw this sign on an island in Lake Texcoco, where they founded Tenochtitlán.

La plata Taxco, in the state of Guerrero, is the home to the annual **Feria Nacional de la Plata**. Although Taxco has exploited its silver mines since pre-Columbian days, the city did not have a native silvermaking industry until American William Spratling founded his workshop there in the 1930s.

Conexión Internet Students will find supporting Internet activities and links at **vhlcentral.com**.

21st Century Skills

Information and Media Literacy: Conexión Internet Students access and critically evaluate information from the Internet.

Teaching Tip You can wrap up this section by playing the *Panorama cultural* video.

4 vocabulario

Student Resources
Cuaderno de práctica y actividades comunicativas, p. 118
Supersite: Activities, *eCuaderno*

Teacher Resources
Workbook TE; Textbook and Testing Audio MP3s; Testing Audio Script; Testing Program Tests

21st Century Skills

Creativity and Innovation
Ask students to prepare a list of the three products or perspectives they learned about in this lesson to share with the class. You may ask them to focus specifically on the **Cultura** and **Panorama** sections.

21st Century Skills

Leadership and Responsibility Extension Project
As a class, have students decide on three questions they want to ask the partner class related to the topic of the lesson they have just completed. Based on the responses they receive, work as a class to explain to the Spanish-speaking partners one aspect of their responses that surprised the class and why.

  My Vocabulary

Pasatiempos

andar en patineta	to skateboard
bucear	to scuba dive
escalar montañas (*f., pl.*)	to climb mountains
escribir una carta	to write a letter
escribir un mensaje electrónico	to write an e-mail
esquiar	to ski
ganar	to win
ir de excursión	to go on a hike
leer correo electrónico	to read e-mail
leer un periódico	to read a newspaper
leer una revista	to read a magazine
nadar	to swim
pasear	to take a walk; to stroll
pasear en bicicleta	to ride a bicycle
patinar (en línea)	to (inline) skate
practicar deportes (*m., pl.*)	to play sports
tomar el sol	to sunbathe
ver películas (*f., pl.*)	to watch movies
visitar monumentos (*m., pl.*)	to visit monuments
la diversión	fun activity; entertainment; recreation
el fin de semana	weekend
el pasatiempo	pastime; hobby
los ratos libres	spare (free) time
el videojuego	video game

Deportes

el baloncesto	basketball
el béisbol	baseball
el ciclismo	cycling
el equipo	team
el esquí (acuático)	(water) skiing
el fútbol	soccer
el fútbol americano	football
el golf	golf
el hockey	hockey
el/la jugador(a)	player
la natación	swimming
el partido	game; match
la pelota	ball
el tenis	tennis
el vóleibol	volleyball

Adjetivos

deportivo/a	sports-related
favorito/a	favorite

Lugares

el café	café
el centro	downtown
el cine	movie theater
el gimnasio	gymnasium
la iglesia	church
el lugar	place
el museo	museum
el parque	park
la piscina	swimming pool
la plaza	city or town square
el restaurante	restaurant

Verbos

almorzar (o:ue)	to have lunch
cerrar (e:ie)	to close
comenzar (e:ie)	to begin
conseguir (e:i)	to get; to obtain
contar (o:ue)	to count; to tell
decir (e:i)	to say; to tell
dormir (o:ue)	to sleep
empezar (e:ie)	to begin
encontrar (o:ue)	to find
entender (e:ie)	to understand
hacer	to do; to make
ir	to go
jugar (u:ue)	to play (a sport or a game)
mostrar (o:ue)	to show
oír	to hear
pedir (e:i)	to ask for; to request
pensar (e:ie)	to think
pensar (+ *inf.*)	to intend
pensar en	to think about
perder (e:ie)	to lose; to miss
poder (o:ue)	to be able to; can
poner	to put; to place
preferir (e:ie)	to prefer
querer (e:ie)	to want; to love
recordar (o:ue)	to remember
repetir (e:i)	to repeat
salir	to leave
seguir (e:i)	to follow; to continue
suponer	to suppose
traer	to bring
ver	to see
volver (o:ue)	to return

Decir **expressions**	See page 136.
Expresiones útiles	See page 121.

recursos

p. 118   vhlcentral

Consulta

Apéndice A
Glossary of Grammatical Terms — pages 152–155

Apéndice B
Verb Conjugation Tables — pages 156–165

Vocabulario
Spanish–English — pages 166–176
English–Spanish — pages 177–187

References — pages 188–199

Índice — pages 200–201

Credits — page 202

Glossary of Grammatical Terms

ADJECTIVE A word that modifies, or describes, a noun or pronoun.

>muchos libros
>*many books*
>
>un hombre rico
>*a rich man*
>
>las mujeres altas
>*the tall women*

Demonstrative adjective An adjective that specifies which noun a speaker is referring to.

>esta fiesta
>*this party*
>
>ese chico
>*that boy*
>
>aquellas flores
>*those flowers*

Possessive adjective An adjective that indicates ownership or possession.

>mi mejor vestido
>*my best dress*
>
>Éste es mi hermano.
>*This is my brother.*

Stressed possessive adjective A possessive adjective that emphasizes the owner or possessor.

>Es un libro mío.
>*It's my book./It's a book of mine.*
>
>Es amiga tuya; yo no la conozco.
>*She's a friend of yours; I don't know her.*

ADVERB A word that modifies, or describes, a verb, adjective, or other adverb.

>Pancho escribe rápidamente.
>*Pancho writes quickly.*
>
>Este cuadro es muy bonito.
>*This picture is very pretty.*

ARTICLE A word that points out a noun in either a specific or a non-specific way.

Definite article An article that points out a noun in a specific way.

>el libro
>*the book*
>
>la maleta
>*the suitcase*
>
>los diccionarios
>*the dictionaries*
>
>las palabras
>*the words*

Indefinite article An article that points out a noun in a general, non-specific way.

>un lápiz
>*a pencil*
>
>una computadora
>*a computer*
>
>unos pájaros
>*some birds*
>
>unas escuelas
>*some schools*

CLAUSE A group of words that contains both a conjugated verb and a subject, either expressed or implied.

Main (or Independent) clause A clause that can stand alone as a complete sentence.

>Pienso ir a cenar pronto.
>*I plan to go to dinner soon.*

Subordinate (or Dependent) clause A clause that does not express a complete thought and therefore cannot stand alone as a sentence.

>Trabajo en la cafetería porque necesito dinero para la escuela.
>*I work in the cafeteria because I need money for school.*

COMPARATIVE A construction used with an adjective or adverb to express a comparison between two people, places, or things.

>Este programa es más interesante que el otro.
>*This program is more interesting than the other one.*
>
>Tomás no es tan alto como Alberto.
>*Tomás is not as tall as Alberto.*

CONJUGATION A set of the forms of a verb for a specific tense or mood or the process by which these verb forms are presented.

>Preterite conjugation of cantar:
>canté   cantamos
>cantaste   cantasteis
>cantó   cantaron

CONJUNCTION A word used to connect words, clauses, or phrases.

>Susana es de Cuba y Pedro es de España.
>*Susana is from Cuba and Pedro is from Spain.*
>
>No quiero estudiar pero tengo que hacerlo.
>*I don't want to study, but I have to.*

Glossary of Grammatical Terms

CONTRACTION The joining of two words into one. The only contractions in Spanish are **al** and **del**.

Mi hermano fue **al** concierto ayer.
*My brother went **to the** concert yesterday.*

Saqué dinero **del** banco.
*I took money **from the** bank.*

DIRECT OBJECT A noun or pronoun that directly receives the action of the verb.

Tomás lee **el libro**.   **La** pagó ayer.
*Tomás reads **the book**.   She paid **it** yesterday.*

GENDER The grammatical categorizing of certain kinds of words, such as nouns and pronouns, as masculine, feminine, or neuter.

Masculine
articles el, un
pronouns él, lo, mío, éste, ése, aquél
adjective simpático

Feminine
articles la, una
pronouns ella, la, mía, ésta, ésa, aquélla
adjective simpática

IMPERSONAL EXPRESSION A third-person expression with no expressed or specific subject.

Es muy importante.   Llueve mucho.
It's very important.   It's raining hard.

Aquí **se habla** español.
*Spanish **is spoken** here.*

INDIRECT OBJECT A noun or pronoun that receives the action of the verb indirectly; the object, often a living being, to or for whom an action is performed.

Eduardo **le** dio un libro **a Linda**.
*Eduardo gave a book **to Linda**.*

La profesora **me** puso una C en el examen.
*The professor gave **me** a C on the test.*

INFINITIVE The basic form of a verb. Infinitives in Spanish end in **-ar**, **-er**, or **-ir**.

hablar   correr   abrir
to speak   to run   to open

INTERROGATIVE An adjective or pronoun used to ask a question.

¿**Quién** habla?   ¿**Cuántos** compraste?
***Who** is speaking?   **How many** did you buy?*

¿**Qué** piensas hacer hoy?
***What** do you plan to do today?*

INVERSION Changing the word order of a sentence, often to form a question.

Statement: Elena pagó la cuenta del restaurante.

Inversion: ¿Pagó Elena la cuenta del restaurante?

MOOD A grammatical distinction of verbs that indicates whether the verb is intended to make a statement or command or to express a doubt, emotion, or condition contrary to fact.

Imperative mood Verb forms used to make commands.

Di la verdad.   **Caminen** ustedes conmigo.
***Tell** the truth.   **Walk** with me.*

¡**Comamos** ahora!
***Let's eat** now!*

Indicative mood Verb forms used to state facts, actions, and states considered to be real.

Sé que **tienes** el dinero.
*I know that **you have** the money.*

Subjunctive mood Verb forms used principally in subordinate (dependent) clauses to express wishes, desires, emotions, doubts, and certain conditions, such as contrary-to-fact situations.

Prefieren que **hables** en español.
*They prefer that **you speak** in Spanish.*

Dudo que Luis **tenga** el dinero necesario.
*I doubt that Luis **has** the necessary money.*

NOUN A word that identifies people, animals, places, things, and ideas.

hombre	gato
man	*cat*
México	casa
Mexico	*house*
libertad	libro
freedom	*book*

NUMBER A grammatical term that refers to singular or plural. Nouns in Spanish and English have number. Other parts of a sentence, such as adjectives, articles, and verbs, can also have number.

Singular	Plural
una cosa *a thing*	unas cosas *some things*
el profesor *the professor*	los profesores *the professors*

NUMBERS Words that represent amounts.

Cardinal numbers Words that show specific amounts.

cinco minutos
five minutes

el año dos mil veintitrés
the year 2023

Ordinal numbers Words that indicate the order of a noun in a series.

el **cuarto** jugador   la **décima** hora
*the **fourth** player*   *the **tenth** hour*

PAST PARTICIPLE A past form of the verb used in compound tenses. The past participle may also be used as an adjective, but it must then agree in number and gender with the word it modifies.

Han **buscado** por todas partes.
*They have **searched** everywhere.*

Yo no había **estudiado** para el examen.
*I hadn't **studied** for the exam.*

Hay una **ventana abierta** en la sala.
*There is an **open window** in the living room.*

PERSON The form of the verb or pronoun that indicates the speaker, the one spoken to, or the one spoken about. In Spanish, as in English, there are three persons: first, second, and third.

Person	Singular	Plural
1st	yo *I*	nosotros/as *we*
2nd	tú, Ud. *you*	vosotros/as, Uds. *you*
3rd	él, ella *he, she*	ellos, ellas *they*

PREPOSITION A word or words that describe(s) the relationship, most often in time or space, between two other words.

Anita es **de** California.
*Anita is **from** California.*

La chaqueta está **en** el carro.
*The jacket is **in** the car.*

Marta se peinó **antes de** salir.
*Marta combed her hair **before** going out.*

PRESENT PARTICIPLE In English, a verb form that ends in *-ing*. In Spanish, the present participle ends in **-ndo**, and is often used with **estar** to form a progressive tense.

Mi hermana está **hablando** por teléfono ahora mismo.
*My sister is **talking** on the phone right now.*

PRONOUN A word that takes the place of a noun or nouns.

Demonstrative pronoun A pronoun that takes the place of a specific noun.

Quiero **ésta**.
*I want **this one**.*

¿Vas a comprar **ése**?
*Are you going to buy **that one**?*

Juan prefirió **aquéllos**.
*Juan preferred **those** (over there).*

Object pronoun A pronoun that functions as a direct or indirect object of the verb.

Te digo la verdad.
*I'm telling **you** the truth.*

Me lo trajo Juan.
*Juan brought **it** to **me**.*

Reflexive pronoun A pronoun that indicates that the action of a verb is performed by the subject on itself. These pronouns are often expressed in English with *-self: myself, yourself*, etc.

Yo **me** bañé antes de salir.
*I bathed (**myself**) before going out.*

Elena **se** acostó a las once y media.
*Elena **went to bed** at eleven-thirty.*

Glossary of Grammatical Terms

Relative pronoun A pronoun that connects a subordinate clause to a main clause.

El chico **que** nos escribió viene a visitar mañana.
*The boy **who** wrote us is coming to visit tomorrow.*

Ya sé **lo que** tenemos que hacer.
*I already know **what** we have to do.*

Subject pronoun A pronoun that replaces the name or title of a person or thing, and acts as the subject of a verb.

Tú debes estudiar más.
***You** should study more.*

Él llegó primero.
***He** arrived first.*

SUBJECT A noun or pronoun that performs the action of a verb and is often implied by the verb.

María va al supermercado.
***María** goes to the supermarket.*

(**Ellos**) Trabajan mucho.
***They** work hard.*

Esos **libros** son muy caros.
*Those **books** are very expensive.*

SUPERLATIVE A word or construction used with an adjective or adverb to express the highest or lowest degree of a specific quality among three or more people, places, or things.

De todas mis clases, ésta es la **más interesante**.
*Of all my classes, this is the **most interesting**.*

Raúl es el **menos simpático** de los chicos.
*Raúl is the **least pleasant** of the boys.*

TENSE A set of verb forms that indicates the time of an action or state: past, present, or future.

Compound tense A two-word tense made up of an auxiliary verb and a present or past participle. In Spanish, there are two auxiliary verbs: **estar** and **haber**.

En este momento, **estoy estudiando**.
*At this time, **I am studying**.*

El paquete no **ha llegado** todavía.
*The package **has** not **arrived** yet.*

Simple tense A tense expressed by a single verb form.

María **estaba** enferma anoche.
*María **was** sick last night.*

Juana **hablará** con su mamá mañana.
*Juana **will speak** with her mom tomorrow.*

VERB A word that expresses actions or states-of-being.

Auxiliary verb A verb used with a present or past participle to form a compound tense. **Haber** is the most commonly used auxiliary verb in Spanish.

Los chicos **han** visto los elefantes.
*The children **have** seen the elephants.*

Espero que **hayas** comido.
*I hope you **have** eaten.*

Reflexive verb A verb that describes an action performed by the subject on itself and is always used with a reflexive pronoun.

Me compré un carro nuevo.
*I bought **myself** a new car.*

Pedro y Adela **se levantan** muy temprano.
*Pedro and Adela **get (themselves) up** very early.*

Spelling-change verb A verb that undergoes a predictable change in spelling, in order to reflect its actual pronunciation in the various conjugations.

practicar	c→qu	practico	practiqué
dirigir	g→j	dirigí	dirijo
almorzar	z→c	almorzó	almorcé

Stem-changing verb A verb whose stem vowel undergoes one or more predictable changes in the various conjugations.

entender (e:ie)	entiendo
pedir (e:i)	piden
dormir (o:ue, u)	duermo, durmieron

Verb Conjugation Tables

The verb lists

The list of verbs below and the model verb tables that start on page 158 show you how to conjugate every verb taught in DESCUBRE. Each verb in the list is followed by a model verb conjugated according to the same pattern. The number in parentheses indicates where in the verb tables you can find the conjugated forms of the model verb. If you want to find out how to conjugate **divertirse**, for example, look up number 33, **sentir**, the model for verbs that follow the e:ie stem-change pattern.

How to use the verb tables

In the tables you will find the infinitive, present and past participles, and all the simple forms of each model verb. The formation of the compound tenses of any verb can be inferred from the table of compound tenses, pages 158–159, either by combining the past participle of the verb with a conjugated form of **haber** or by combining the present participle with a conjugated form of **estar**.

abrazar (z:c) like cruzar (37)
abrir like vivir (3) *except* past participle is abierto
aburrir(se) like vivir (3)
acabar de like hablar (1)
acampar like hablar (1)
acompañar like hablar (1)
aconsejar like hablar (1)
acordarse (o:ue) like contar (24)
acostarse (o:ue) like contar (24)
adelgazar (z:c) like cruzar (37)
afeitarse like hablar (1)
ahorrar like hablar (1)
alegrarse like hablar (1)
aliviar like hablar (1)
almorzar (o:ue) like contar (24) *except* (z:c)
alquilar like hablar (1)
andar like hablar (1) *except* preterite stem is anduv-
anunciar like hablar (1)
apagar (g:gu) like llegar (41)
aplaudir like vivir (3)
apreciar like hablar (1)
aprender like comer (2)
apurarse like hablar (1)
arrancar (c:qu) like tocar (43)
arreglar like hablar (1)
asistir like vivir (3)
aumentar like hablar (1)

ayudar(se) like hablar (1)
bailar like hablar (1)
bajar(se) like hablar (1)
bañarse like hablar (1)
barrer like comer (2)
beber like comer (2)
besar(se) like hablar (1)
borrar like hablar (1)
brindar like hablar (1)
bucear like hablar (1)
buscar (c:qu) like tocar (43)
caber (4)
caer(se) (5)
calentarse (e:ie) like pensar (30)
calzar (z:c) like cruzar (37)
cambiar like hablar (1)
caminar like hablar (1)
cantar like hablar (1)
casarse like hablar (1)
cazar (z:c) like cruzar (37)
celebrar like hablar (1)
cenar like hablar (1)
cepillarse like hablar (1)
cerrar (e:ie) like pensar (30)
cobrar like hablar (1)
cocinar like hablar (1)
comenzar (e:ie) (z:c) like empezar (26)
comer (2)
compartir like vivir (3)
comprar like hablar (1)
comprender like comer (2)

comprometerse like comer (2)
comunicarse (c:qu) like tocar (43)
conducir (c:zc) (6)
confirmar like hablar (1)
conocer (c:zc) (35)
conseguir (e:i) (gu:g) like seguir (32)
conservar like hablar (1)
consumir like vivir (3)
contaminar like hablar (1)
contar (o:ue) (24)
contestar like hablar (1))
contratar like hablar (1)
controlar like hablar (1)
conversar like hablar (1)
correr like comer (2)
costar (o:ue) like contar (24)
creer (y) (36)
cruzar (z:c) (37)
cuidar like hablar (1)
cumplir like vivir (3)
dañar like hablar (1)
dar (7)
deber like comer (2)
decidir like vivir (3)
decir (e:i) (8)
declarar like hablar (1)
dejar like hablar (1)
depositar like hablar (1)
desarrollar like hablar (1)
desayunar like hablar (1)

descansar like hablar (1)
descargar (g:gu) like llegar (41)
describir like vivir (3) *except* past participle is descrito
descubrir like vivir (3) *except* past participle is descubierto
desear like hablar (1)
despedirse (e:i) like pedir (29)
despertarse (e:ie) like pensar (30)
destruir (y) (38)
dibujar like hablar (1)
dirigir like vivir (3) *except* (g:j)
disfrutar like hablar (1)
divertirse (e:ie) like sentir (33)
divorciarse like hablar (1)
doblar like hablar (1)
doler (o:ue) like volver (34) *except* past participle is regular
dormir(se) (o:ue) (25)
ducharse like hablar (1)
dudar like hablar (1)
durar like hablar (1)
echar like hablar (1)
elegir (e:i) like pedir (29) *except* (g:j)
emitir like vivir (3)
empezar (e:ie) (z:c) (26)

Verb Conjugation Tables

enamorarse like hablar (1)
encantar like hablar (1)
encontrar(se) (o:ue) like contar (24)
enfermarse like hablar (1)
engordar like hablar (1)
enojarse like hablar (1)
enseñar like hablar (1)
ensuciar like hablar (1)
entender (e:ie) (27)
entrenarse like hablar (1)
entrevistar like hablar (1)
enviar (envío) (39)
escalar like hablar (1)
escanear like hablar (1)
escoger (g:j) like proteger (42)
escribir like vivir (3) *except* past participle is escrito
escuchar like hablar (1)
esculpir like vivir (3)
esperar like hablar (1)
esquiar (esquío) like enviar (39)
establecer (c:zc) like conocer (35)
estacionar like hablar (1)
estar (9)
estornudar like hablar (1)
estudiar like hablar (1)
evitar like hablar (1)
explicar (c:qu) like tocar (43)
faltar like hablar (1)
fascinar like hablar (1)
firmar like hablar (1)
fumar like hablar (1)
funcionar like hablar (1)
ganar like hablar (1)
gastar like hablar (1)
grabar like hablar (1)
graduarse (gradúo) (40)
guardar like hablar (1)
gustar like hablar (1)
haber (hay) (10)
hablar (1)
hacer (11)
importar like hablar (1)
imprimir like vivir (3)
indicar (c:qu) like tocar (43)
informar like hablar (1)
insistir like vivir (3)
interesar like hablar (1)
invertir (e:ie) like sentir (33)
invitar like hablar (1)
ir(se) (12)

jubilarse like hablar (1)
jugar (u:ue) (g:gu) (28)
lastimarse like hablar (1)
lavar(se) like hablar (1)
leer (y) like creer (36)
levantar(se) like hablar (1)
limpiar like hablar (1)
llamar(se) like hablar (1)
llegar (g:gu) (41)
llenar like hablar (1)
llevar(se) like hablar (1)
llover (o:ue) like volver (34) *except* past participle is regular
luchar like hablar (1)
mandar like hablar (1)
manejar like hablar (1)
mantener(se) like tener (20)
maquillarse like hablar (1)
mejorar like hablar (1)
merendar (e:ie) like pensar (30)
mirar like hablar (1)
molestar like hablar (1)
montar like hablar (1)
morir (o:ue) like dormir (25) *except* past participle is muerto
mostrar (o:ue) like contar (24)
mudarse like hablar (1)
nacer (c:zc) like conocer (35)
nadar like hablar (1)
navegar (g:gu) like llegar (41)
necesitar like hablar (1)
negar (e:ie) like pensar (30) *except* (g:gu)
nevar (e:ie) like pensar (30)
obedecer (c:zc) like conocer (35)
obtener like tener (20)
ocurrir like vivir (3)
odiar like hablar (1)
ofrecer (c:zc) like conocer (35)
oír (y) (13)
olvidar like hablar (1)
pagar (g:gu) like llegar (41)
parar like hablar (1)
parecer (c:zc) like conocer (35)
pasar like hablar (1)
pasear like hablar (1)
patinar like hablar (1)

pedir (e:i) (29)
peinarse like hablar (1)
pensar (e:ie) (30)
perder (e:ie) like entender (27)
pescar (c:qu) like tocar (43)
pintar like hablar (1)
planchar like hablar (1)
poder (o:ue) (14)
poner(se) (15)
practicar (c:qu) like tocar (43)
preferir (e:ie) like sentir (33)
preguntar like hablar (1)
prender like comer (2)
preocuparse like hablar (1)
preparar like hablar (1)
presentar like hablar (1)
prestar like hablar (1)
probar(se) (o:ue) like contar (24)
prohibir like vivir (3)
proteger (g:j) (42)
publicar (c:qu) like tocar (43)
quedar(se) like hablar (1)
querer (e:ie) (16)
quitar(se) like hablar (1)
recetar like hablar (1)
recibir like vivir (3)
reciclar like hablar (1)
recoger (g:j) like proteger (42)
recomendar (e:ie) like pensar (30)
recordar (o:ue) like contar (24)
reducir (c:zc) like conducir (6)
regalar like hablar (1)
regatear like hablar (1)
regresar like hablar (1)
reír(se) (e:i) (31)
relajarse like hablar (1)
renunciar like hablar (1)
repetir (e:i) like pedir (29)
resolver (o:ue) like volver (34)
respirar like hablar (1)
revisar like hablar (1)
rogar (o:ue) like contar (24) *except* (g:gu)
romper(se) like comer (2) *except* past participle is roto
saber (17)
sacar (c:qu) like tocar (43)
sacudir like vivir (3)

salir (18)
saludar(se) like hablar (1)
secar(se) (c:q) like tocar (43)
seguir (e:i) (32)
sentarse (e:ie) like pensar (30)
sentir(se) (e:ie) (33)
separarse like hablar (1)
ser (19)
servir (e:i) like pedir (29)
solicitar like hablar (1)
sonar (o:ue) like contar (24)
sonreír (e:i) like reír(se) (31)
sorprender like comer (2)
subir like vivir (3)
sudar like hablar (1)
sufrir like vivir (3)
sugerir (e:ie) like sentir (33)
suponer like poner (15)
temer like comer (2)
tener (20)
terminar like hablar (1)
tocar (c:qu) (43)
tomar like hablar (1)
torcerse (o:ue) like volver (34) *except* (c:z) and past participle is regular; e.g. yo tuerzo
toser like comer (2)
trabajar like hablar (1)
traducir (c:zc) like conducir (6)
traer (21)
transmitir like vivir (3)
tratar like hablar (1)
usar like hablar (1)
vencer (c:z) (44)
vender like comer (2)
venir (22)
ver (23)
vestirse (e:i) like pedir (29)
viajar like hablar (1)
visitar like hablar (1)
vivir (3)
volver (o:ue) (34)
votar like hablar (1)

Regular verbs: simple tenses

Infinitive	INDICATIVE					SUBJUNCTIVE		IMPERATIVE
	Present	Imperfect	Preterite	Future	Conditional	Present	Past	
1 hablar	hablo	hablaba	hablé	hablaré	hablaría	hable	hablara	
	hablas	hablabas	hablaste	hablarás	hablarías	hables	hablaras	habla tú (no hables)
Participles:	habla	hablaba	habló	hablará	hablaría	hable	hablara	hable Ud.
hablando	hablamos	hablábamos	hablamos	hablaremos	hablaríamos	hablemos	habláramos	hablemos
hablado	habláis	hablabais	hablasteis	hablaréis	hablaríais	habléis	hablarais	hablad (no habléis)
	hablan	hablaban	hablaron	hablarán	hablarían	hablen	hablaran	hablen Uds.
2 comer	como	comía	comí	comeré	comería	coma	comiera	
	comes	comías	comiste	comerás	comerías	comas	comieras	come tú (no comas)
Participles:	come	comía	comió	comerá	comería	coma	comiera	coma Ud.
comiendo	comemos	comíamos	comimos	comeremos	comeríamos	comamos	comiéramos	comamos
comido	coméis	comíais	comisteis	comeréis	comeríais	comáis	comierais	comed (no comáis)
	comen	comían	comieron	comerán	comerían	coman	comieran	coman Uds.
3 vivir	vivo	vivía	viví	viviré	viviría	viva	viviera	
	vives	vivías	viviste	vivirás	vivirías	vivas	vivieran	vive tú (no vivas)
Participles:	vive	vivía	vivió	vivirá	viviría	viva	viviera	viva Ud.
viviendo	vivimos	vivíamos	vivimos	viviremos	viviríamos	vivamos	viviéramos	vivamos
vivido	vivís	vivíais	vivisteis	viviréis	viviríais	viváis	vivierais	vivid (no viváis)
	viven	vivían	vivieron	vivirán	vivirían	vivan	vivieran	vivan Uds.

All verbs: compound tenses

PERFECT TENSES						
INDICATIVE					SUBJUNCTIVE	
Present Perfect	Past Perfect	Future Perfect	Conditional Perfect	Present Perfect	Past Perfect	
he	había	habré	habría	haya	hubiera	
has	habías	habrás	habrías	hayas	hubieras	
ha } hablado	habías } hablado	habrá } hablado	habría } hablado	haya } hablado	hubiera } hablado	
hemos comido	habíamos comido	habremos comido	habríamos comido	hayamos comido	hubiéramos comido	
habéis vivido	habíais vivido	habréis vivido	habríais vivido	hayáis vivido	hubierais vivido	
han	habían	habrán	habrían	hayan	hubieran	

Verb Conjugation Tables

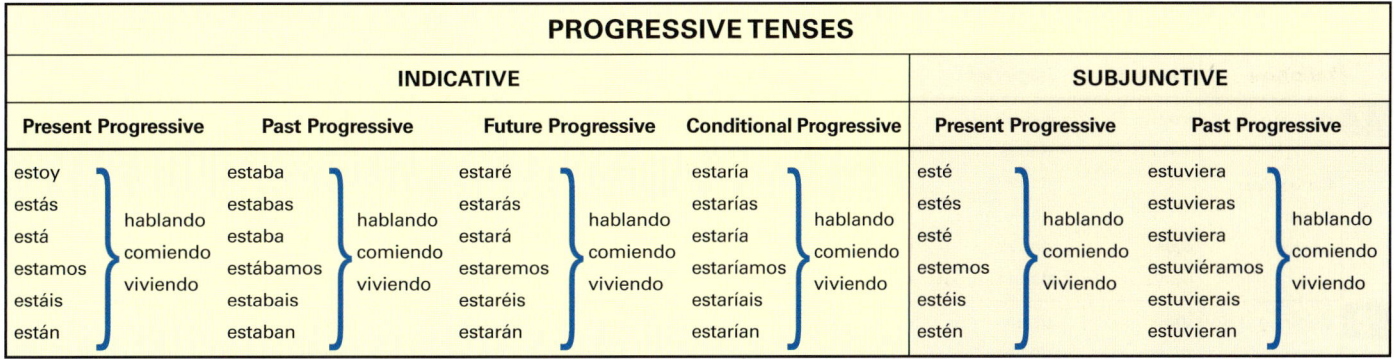

		PROGRESSIVE TENSES					
		INDICATIVE				SUBJUNCTIVE	
	Present Progressive	Past Progressive	Future Progressive	Conditional Progressive		Present Progressive	Past Progressive
	estoy	estaba	estaré	estaría		esté	estuviera
	estás	estabas	estarás	estarías		estés	estuvieras
	está hablando	estaba hablando	estará hablando	estaría hablando		esté hablando	estuviera hablando
	estamos comiendo	estábamos comiendo	estaremos comiendo	estaríamos comiendo		estemos comiendo	estuviéramos comiendo
	estáis viviendo	estabais viviendo	estaréis viviendo	estaríais viviendo		estéis viviendo	estuvierais viviendo
	están	estaban	estarán	estarían		estén	estuvieran

Irregular verbs

	Infinitive	INDICATIVE					SUBJUNCTIVE		IMPERATIVE
		Present	Imperfect	Preterite	Future	Conditional	Present	Past	
4	caber	quepo	cabía	cupe	cabré	cabría	quepa	cupiera	
		cabes	cabías	cupiste	cabrás	cabrías	quepas	cupieras	cabe tú (no quepas)
	Participles:	cabe	cabía	cupo	cabrá	cabría	quepa	cupiera	quepa Ud.
	cabiendo	cabemos	cabíamos	cupimos	cabremos	cabríamos	quepamos	cupiéramos	quepamos
	cabido	cabéis	cabíais	cupisteis	cabréis	cabríais	quepáis	cupierais	cabed (no quepáis)
		caben	cabían	cupieron	cabrán	cabrían	quepan	cupieran	quepan Uds.
5	caer(se)	caigo	caía	caí	caeré	caería	caiga	cayera	
		caes	caías	caíste	caerás	caerías	caigas	cayeras	cae tú (no caigas)
	Participles:	cae	caía	cayó	caerá	caería	caiga	cayera	caiga Ud.
	cayendo	caemos	caíamos	caímos	caeremos	caeríamos	caigamos	cayéramos	caigamos
	caído	caéis	caíais	caísteis	caeréis	caeríais	caigáis	cayerais	caed (no caigáis)
		caen	caían	cayeron	caerán	caerían	caigan	cayeran	caigan Uds.
6	conducir (c:zc)	conduzco	conducía	conduje	conduciré	conduciría	conduzca	condujera	
		conduces	conducías	condujiste	conducirás	conducirías	conduzcas	condujeras	conduce tú (no conduzcas)
		conduce	conducía	condujo	conducirá	conduciría	conduzca	condujera	conduzca Ud.
	Participles:	conducimos	conducíamos	condujimos	conduciremos	conduciríamos	conduzcamos	condujéramos	conduzcamos
	conduciendo	conducís	conducíais	condujisteis	conduciréis	conduciríais	conduzcáis	condujerais	conducid (no conduzcáis)
	conducido	conducen	conducían	condujeron	conducirán	conducirían	conduzcan	condujeran	conduzcan Uds.

Infinitive	INDICATIVE					SUBJUNCTIVE		IMPERATIVE
	Present	Imperfect	Preterite	Future	Conditional	Present	Past	
7 dar	doy	daba	di	daré	daría	dé	diera	
	das	dabas	diste	darás	darías	des	dieras	da tú (no des)
Participles:	da	daba	dio	dará	daría	dé	diera	dé Ud.
dando	damos	dábamos	dimos	daremos	daríamos	demos	diéramos	demos
dado	dais	dabais	disteis	daréis	daríais	deis	dierais	dad (no deis)
	dan	daban	dieron	darán	darían	den	dieran	den Uds.
8 decir (e:i)	digo	decía	dije	diré	diría	diga	dijera	
	dices	decías	dijiste	dirás	dirías	digas	dijeras	di tú (no digas)
Participles:	dice	decía	dijo	dirá	diría	diga	dijera	diga Ud.
diciendo	decimos	decíamos	dijimos	diremos	diríamos	digamos	dijéramos	digamos
dicho	decís	decíais	dijisteis	diréis	diríais	digáis	dijerais	decid (no digáis)
	dicen	decían	dijeron	dirán	dirían	digan	dijeran	digan Uds.
9 estar	estoy	estaba	estuve	estaré	estaría	esté	estuviera	
	estás	estabas	estuviste	estarás	estarías	estés	estuvieras	está tú (no estés)
Participles:	está	estaba	estuvo	estará	estaría	esté	estuviera	esté Ud.
estando	estamos	estábamos	estuvimos	estaremos	estaríamos	estemos	estuviéramos	estemos
estado	estáis	estabais	estuvisteis	estaréis	estaríais	estéis	estuvierais	estad (no estéis)
	están	estaban	estuvieron	estarán	estarían	estén	estuvieran	estén Uds.
10 haber	he	había	hube	habré	habría	haya	hubiera	
	has	habías	hubiste	habrás	habrías	hayas	hubieras	
Participles:	ha	había	hubo	habrá	habría	haya	hubiera	
habiendo	hemos	habíamos	hubimos	habremos	habríamos	hayamos	hubiéramos	
habido	habéis	habíais	hubisteis	habréis	habríais	hayáis	hubierais	
	han	habían	hubieron	habrán	habrían	hayan	hubieran	
11 hacer	hago	hacía	hice	haré	haría	haga	hiciera	
	haces	hacías	hiciste	harás	harías	hagas	hicieras	haz tú (no hagas)
Participles:	hace	hacía	hizo	hará	haría	haga	hiciera	haga Ud.
haciendo	hacemos	hacíamos	hicimos	haremos	haríamos	hagamos	hiciéramos	hagamos
hecho	hacéis	hacíais	hicisteis	haréis	haríais	hagáis	hicierais	haced (no hagáis)
	hacen	hacían	hicieron	harán	harían	hagan	hicieran	hagan Uds.
12 ir	voy	iba	fui	iré	iría	vaya	fuera	
	vas	ibas	fuiste	irás	irías	vayas	fueras	ve tú (no vayas)
Participles:	va	iba	fue	irá	iría	vaya	fuera	vaya Ud.
yendo	vamos	íbamos	fuimos	iremos	iríamos	vayamos	fuéramos	vamos (no vayamos)
ido	vais	ibais	fuisteis	iréis	iríais	vayáis	fuerais	id (no vayáis)
	van	iban	fueron	irán	irían	vayan	fueran	vayan Uds.
13 oír (y)	oigo	oía	oí	oiré	oiría	oiga	oyera	
	oyes	oías	oíste	oirás	oirías	oigas	oyeras	oye tú (no oigas)
Participles:	oye	oía	oyó	oirá	oiría	oiga	oyera	oiga Ud.
oyendo	oímos	oíamos	oímos	oiremos	oiríamos	oigamos	oyéramos	oigamos
oído	oís	oíais	oísteis	oiréis	oiríais	oigáis	oyerais	oíd (no oigáis)
	oyen	oían	oyeron	oirán	oirían	oigan	oyeran	oigan Uds.

Verb Conjugation Tables

		INDICATIVE					SUBJUNCTIVE		IMPERATIVE
	Infinitive	Present	Imperfect	Preterite	Future	Conditional	Present	Past	
14	poder (o:ue)	puedo	podía	pude	podré	podría	pueda	pudiera	
		puedes	podías	pudiste	podrás	podrías	puedas	pudieras	puede tú (no puedas)
	Participles:	puede	podía	pudo	podrá	podría	pueda	pudiera	pueda Ud.
	pudiendo	podemos	podíamos	pudimos	podremos	podríamos	podamos	pudiéramos	podamos
	podido	podéis	podíais	pudisteis	podréis	podríais	podáis	pudierais	poded (no podáis)
		pueden	podían	pudieron	podrán	podrían	puedan	pudieran	puedan Uds.
15	poner	pongo	ponía	puse	pondré	pondría	ponga	pusiera	
		pones	ponías	pusiste	pondrás	pondrías	pongas	pusieras	pon tú (no pongas)
	Participles:	pone	ponía	puso	pondrá	pondría	ponga	pusiera	ponga Ud.
	poniendo	ponemos	poníamos	pusimos	pondremos	pondríamos	pongamos	pusiéramos	pongamos
	puesto	ponéis	poníais	pusisteis	pondréis	pondríais	pongáis	pusierais	poned (no pongáis)
		ponen	ponían	pusieron	pondrán	pondrían	pongan	pusieran	pongan Uds.
16	querer (e:ie)	quiero	quería	quise	querré	querría	quiera	quisiera	
		quieres	querías	quisiste	querrás	querrías	quieras	quisieras	quiere tú (no quieras)
	Participles:	quiere	quería	quiso	querrá	querría	quiera	quisiera	quiera Ud.
	queriendo	queremos	queríamos	quisimos	querremos	querríamos	queramos	quisiéramos	queramos
	querido	queréis	queríais	quisisteis	querréis	querríais	queráis	quisierais	quered (no queráis)
		quieren	querían	quisieron	querrán	querrían	quieran	quisieran	quieran Uds.
17	saber	sé	sabía	supe	sabré	sabría	sepa	supiera	
		sabes	sabías	supiste	sabrás	sabrías	sepas	supieras	sabe tú (no sepas)
	Participles:	sabe	sabía	supo	sabrá	sabría	sepa	supiera	sepa Ud.
	sabiendo	sabemos	sabíamos	supimos	sabremos	sabríamos	sepamos	supiéramos	sepamos
	sabido	sabéis	sabíais	supisteis	sabréis	sabríais	sepáis	supierais	sabed (no sepáis)
		saben	sabían	supieron	sabrán	sabrían	sepan	supieran	sepan Uds.
18	salir	salgo	salía	salí	saldré	saldría	salga	saliera	
		sales	salías	saliste	saldrás	saldrías	salgas	salieras	sal tú (no salgas)
	Participles:	sale	salía	salió	saldrá	saldría	salga	saliera	salga Ud.
	saliendo	salimos	salíamos	salimos	saldremos	saldríamos	salgamos	saliéramos	salgamos
	salido	salís	salíais	salisteis	saldréis	saldríais	salgáis	salierais	salid (no salgáis)
		salen	salían	salieron	saldrán	saldrían	salgan	salieran	salgan Uds.
19	ser	soy	era	fui	seré	sería	sea	fuera	
		eres	eras	fuiste	serás	serías	seas	fueras	sé tú (no seas)
	Participles:	es	era	fue	será	sería	sea	fuera	sea Ud.
	siendo	somos	éramos	fuimos	seremos	seríamos	seamos	fuéramos	seamos
	sido	sois	erais	fuisteis	seréis	seríais	seáis	fuerais	sed (no seáis)
		son	eran	fueron	serán	serían	sean	fueran	sean Uds.
20	tener	tengo	tenía	tuve	tendré	tendría	tenga	tuviera	
		tienes	tenías	tuviste	tendrás	tendrías	tengas	tuvieras	ten tú (no tengas)
	Participles:	tiene	tenía	tuvo	tendrá	tendría	tenga	tuviera	tenga Ud.
	teniendo	tenemos	teníamos	tuvimos	tendremos	tendríamos	tengamos	tuviéramos	tengamos
	tenido	tenéis	teníais	tuvisteis	tendréis	tendríais	tengáis	tuvierais	tened (no tengáis)
		tienen	tenían	tuvieron	tendrán	tendrían	tengan	tuvieran	tengan Uds.

		INDICATIVE					SUBJUNCTIVE		IMPERATIVE
	Infinitive	Present	Imperfect	Preterite	Future	Conditional	Present	Past	
21	traer	**traigo**	traía	**traje**	traeré	traería	**traiga**	**trajera**	
		traes	traías	**trajiste**	traerás	traerías	**traigas**	**trajeras**	trae tú (no **traigas**)
	Participles:	trae	traía	**trajo**	traerá	traería	**traiga**	**trajera**	**traiga** Ud.
	trayendo	traemos	traíamos	**trajimos**	traeremos	traeríamos	**traigamos**	**trajéramos**	**traigamos**
	traído	traéis	traíais	**trajisteis**	traeréis	traeríais	**traigáis**	**trajerais**	traed (no **traigáis**)
		traen	traían	**trajeron**	traerán	traerían	**traigan**	**trajeran**	**traigan** Uds.
22	venir	**vengo**	venía	**vine**	vendré	vendría	**venga**	**viniera**	
		vienes	venías	**viniste**	vendrás	vendrías	**vengas**	**vinieras**	**ven** tú (no **vengas**)
	Participles:	**viene**	venía	**vino**	vendrá	vendría	**venga**	**viniera**	**venga** Ud.
	viniendo	venimos	veníamos	**vinimos**	vendremos	vendríamos	**vengamos**	**viniéramos**	**vengamos**
	venido	venís	veníais	**vinisteis**	vendréis	vendríais	**vengáis**	**vinierais**	venid (no **vengáis**)
		vienen	venían	**vinieron**	vendrán	vendrían	**vengan**	**vinieran**	**vengan** Uds.
23	ver	**veo**	veía	**vi**	veré	vería	**vea**	viera	
		ves	veías	viste	verás	verías	veas	vieras	ve tú (no **veas**)
	Participles:	ve	veía	**vio**	verá	vería	**vea**	viera	**vea** Ud.
	viendo	vemos	veíamos	vimos	veremos	veríamos	**veamos**	viéramos	**veamos**
	visto	**veis**	**veíais**	visteis	veréis	veríais	**veáis**	vierais	ved (no **veáis**)
		ven	veían	vieron	verán	verían	**vean**	vieran	**vean** Uds.

Stem-changing verbs

		INDICATIVE					SUBJUNCTIVE		IMPERATIVE
	Infinitive	Present	Imperfect	Preterite	Future	Conditional	Present	Past	
24	contar	**cuento**	contaba	conté	contaré	contaría	**cuente**	contara	
	(o:ue)	**cuentas**	contabas	contaste	contarás	contarías	**cuentes**	contaras	**cuenta** tú (no **cuentes**)
		cuenta	contaba	contó	contará	contaría	**cuente**	contara	**cuente** Ud.
	Participles:	contamos	contábamos	contamos	contaremos	contaríamos	contemos	contáramos	contemos
	contando	contáis	contabais	contasteis	contaréis	contaríais	contéis	contarais	contad (no contéis)
	contado	**cuentan**	contaban	contaron	contarán	contarían	**cuenten**	contaran	**cuenten** Uds.
25	dormir	**duermo**	dormía	dormí	dormiré	dormiría	**duerma**	**durmiera**	
	(o:ue)	**duermes**	dormías	dormiste	dormirás	dormirías	**duermas**	**durmieras**	**duerme** tú (no **duermas**)
		duerme	dormía	**durmió**	dormirá	dormiría	**duerma**	**durmiera**	**duerma** Ud.
	Participles:	dormimos	dormíamos	dormimos	dormiremos	dormiríamos	**durmamos**	**durmiéramos**	**durmamos**
	durmiendo	dormís	dormíais	dormisteis	dormiréis	dormiríais	**durmáis**	**durmierais**	dormid (no **durmáis**)
	dormido	**duermen**	dormían	**durmieron**	dormirán	dormirían	**duerman**	**durmieran**	**duerman** Uds.
26	empezar	**empiezo**	empezaba	**empecé**	empezaré	empezaría	**empiece**	empezara	
	(e:ie) (z:c)	**empiezas**	empezabas	empezaste	empezarás	empezarías	**empieces**	empezaras	**empieza** tú (no **empieces**)
		empieza	empezaba	empezó	empezará	empezaría	**empiece**	empezara	**empiece** Ud.
	Participles:	empezamos	empezábamos	empezamos	empezaremos	empezaríamos	**empecemos**	empezáramos	**empecemos**
	empezando	empezáis	empezabais	empezasteis	empezaréis	empezaríais	**empecéis**	empezarais	empezad (no **empecéis**)
	empezado	**empiezan**	empezaban	empezarán	empezarán	empezarían	**empiecen**	empezaran	**empiecen** Uds.

Verb Conjugation Tables

		INDICATIVE				SUBJUNCTIVE		IMPERATIVE
Infinitive	Present	Imperfect	Preterite	Future	Conditional	Present	Past	
27 entender (e:ie)	**entiendo**	entendía	entendí	entenderé	entendería	**entienda**	entendiera	
	entiendes	entendías	entendiste	entenderás	entenderías	**entiendas**	entendieras	**entiende** tú (no **entiendas**)
	entiende	entendía	entendió	entenderá	entendería	**entienda**	entendiera	**entienda** Ud.
Participles:	entendemos	entendíamos	entendimos	entenderemos	entenderíamos	entendamos	entendiéramos	entendamos
entendiendo	entendéis	entendíais	entendisteis	entenderéis	entenderíais	entendáis	entendierais	entended (no entendáis)
entendido	**entienden**	entendían	entendieron	entenderán	entenderían	**entiendan**	entendieran	**entiendan** Uds.
28 jugar (u:ue) (g:gu)	**juego**	jugaba	**jugué**	jugaré	jugaría	**juegue**	jugara	
	juegas	jugabas	jugaste	jugarás	jugarías	**juegues**	jugaras	**juega** tú (no **juegues**)
	juega	jugaba	jugó	jugará	jugaría	**juegue**	jugara	**juegue** Ud
Participles:	jugamos	jugábamos	jugamos	jugaremos	jugaríamos	**juguemos**	jugáramos	**juguemos**
jugando	jugáis	jugabais	jugasteis	jugaréis	jugaríais	**juguéis**	jugarais	jugad (no **juguéis**)
jugado	**juegan**	jugaban	jugaron	jugarán	jugarían	**jueguen**	jugaran	**jueguen** Uds.
29 pedir (e:i)	**pido**	pedía	pedí	pediré	pediría	**pida**	**pidiera**	
	pides	pedías	pediste	pedirás	pedirías	**pidas**	**pidieras**	**pide** tú (no **pidas**)
	pide	pedía	**pidió**	pedirá	pediría	**pida**	**pidiera**	**pida** Ud.
Participles:	pedimos	pedíamos	pedimos	pediremos	pediríamos	**pidamos**	**pidiéramos**	**pidamos**
pidiendo	pedís	pedíais	pedisteis	pediréis	pediríais	**pidáis**	**pidierais**	pedid (no **pidáis**)
pedido	**piden**	pedían	**pidieron**	pedirán	pedirían	**pidan**	**pidieran**	**pidan** Uds.
30 pensar (e:ie)	**pienso**	pensaba	pensé	pensaré	pensaría	**piense**	pensara	
	piensas	pensabas	pensaste	pensarás	pensarías	**pienses**	pensaras	**piensa** tú (no **pienses**)
	piensa	pensaba	pensó	pensará	pensaría	**piense**	pensara	**piense** Ud.
Participles:	pensamos	pensábamos	pensamos	pensaremos	pensaríamos	pensemos	pensáramos	pensemos
pensando	pensáis	pensabais	pensasteis	pensaréis	pensaríais	penséis	pensarais	pensad (no penséis)
pensado	**piensan**	pensaban	pensaron	pensarán	pensarían	**piensen**	pensaran	**piensen** Uds.
31 reír (e:i)	**río**	reía	reí	reiré	reiría	**ría**	riera	
	ríes	reías	**reíste**	reirás	reirías	**rías**	rieras	**ríe** tú (no **rías**)
Participles:	**ríe**	reía	**rió**	reirá	reiría	**ría**	riera	**ría** Ud.
riendo	**reímos**	reíamos	**reímos**	reiremos	reiríamos	**riamos**	**riéramos**	**riamos**
reído	reís	reíais	**reísteis**	reiréis	reiríais	**riáis**	rierais	reíd (no **riáis**)
	ríen	reían	**rieron**	reirán	reirían	**rían**	rieran	**rían** Uds.
32 seguir (e:i) (gu:g)	**sigo**	seguía	seguí	seguiré	seguiría	**siga**	**siguiera**	
	sigues	seguías	seguiste	seguirás	seguirías	**sigas**	**siguieras**	**sigue** tú (no **sigas**)
	sigue	seguía	**siguió**	seguirá	seguiría	**siga**	**siguiera**	**siga** Ud.
Participles:	seguimos	seguíamos	seguimos	seguiremos	seguiríamos	**sigamos**	**siguiéramos**	**sigamos**
siguiendo	seguís	seguíais	seguisteis	seguiréis	seguiríais	**sigáis**	**siguierais**	seguid (no **sigáis**)
seguido	**siguen**	seguían	**siguieron**	seguirán	seguirían	**sigan**	**siguieran**	**sigan** Uds.
33 sentir (e:ie)	**siento**	sentía	sentí	sentiré	sentiría	**sienta**	**sintiera**	
	sientes	sentías	sentiste	sentirás	sentirías	**sientas**	**sintieras**	**siente** tú (no **sientas**)
	siente	sentía	**sintió**	sentirá	sentiría	**sienta**	**sintiera**	**sienta** Ud.
Participles:	sentimos	sentíamos	sentimos	sentiremos	sentiríamos	**sintamos**	**sintiéramos**	**sintamos**
sintiendo	sentís	sentíais	sentisteis	sentiréis	sentiríais	**sintáis**	**sintierais**	sentid (no **sintáis**)
sentido	**sienten**	sentían	**sintieron**	sentirán	sentirían	**sientan**	**sintieran**	**sientan** Uds.

Infinitive	INDICATIVE					SUBJUNCTIVE		IMPERATIVE
	Present	Imperfect	Preterite	Future	Conditional	Present	Past	
34 volver (o:ue)	**vuelvo**	volvía	volví	volveré	volvería	**vuelva**	volviera	
	vuelves	volvías	volviste	volverás	volverías	**vuelvas**	volvieras	**vuelve** tú (no **vuelvas**)
	vuelve	volvía	volvió	volverá	volvería	**vuelva**	volviera	**vuelva** Ud.
Participles:	volvemos	volvíamos	volvimos	volveremos	volveríamos	volvamos	volviéramos	volvamos
volviendo	volvéis	volvíais	volvisteis	volveréis	volveríais	volváis	volvierais	volved (no volváis)
vuelto	**vuelven**	volvían	volvieron	volverán	volverían	**vuelvan**	volvieran	**vuelvan** Uds.

Verbs with spelling changes only

Infinitive	INDICATIVE					SUBJUNCTIVE		IMPERATIVE
	Present	Imperfect	Preterite	Future	Conditional	Present	Past	
35 conocer (c:zc)	**conozco**	conocía	conocí	conoceré	conocería	**conozca**	conociera	
	conoces	conocías	conociste	conocerás	conocerías	**conozcas**	conocieras	conoce tú (no **conozcas**)
	conoce	conocía	conoció	conocerá	conocería	**conozca**	conociera	**conozca** Ud.
Participles:	conocemos	conocíamos	conocimos	conoceremos	conoceríamos	**conozcamos**	conociéramos	**conozcamos**
conociendo	conocéis	conocíais	conocisteis	conoceréis	conoceríais	**conozcáis**	conocierais	conoced (no **conozcáis**)
conocido	conocen	conocían	conocieron	conocerán	conocerían	**conozcan**	conocieran	**conozcan** Uds.
36 creer (y)	creo	creía	creí	creeré	creería	crea	**creyera**	
	crees	creías	**creíste**	creerás	creerías	creas	**creyeras**	cree tú (no creas)
Participles:	cree	creía	**creyó**	creerá	creería	crea	**creyera**	crea Ud.
creyendo	creemos	creíamos	**creímos**	creeremos	creeríamos	creamos	**creyéramos**	creamos
creído	creéis	creíais	**creísteis**	creeréis	creeríais	creáis	**creyerais**	creed (no creáis)
	creen	creían	**creyeron**	creerán	creerían	crean	**creyeran**	crean Uds.
37 cruzar (z:c)	cruzo	cruzaba	**crucé**	cruzaré	cruzaría	**cruce**	cruzara	
	cruzas	cruzabas	cruzaste	cruzarás	cruzarías	**cruces**	cruzaras	cruza tú (no **cruces**)
Participles:	cruza	cruzaba	cruzó	cruzará	cruzaría	**cruce**	cruzara	**cruce** Ud.
cruzando	cruzamos	cruzábamos	cruzamos	cruzaremos	cruzaríamos	**crucemos**	cruzáramos	**crucemos**
cruzado	cruzáis	cruzabais	cruzasteis	cruzaréis	cruzaríais	**crucéis**	cruzarais	cruzad (no **crucéis**)
	cruzan	cruzaban	cruzaron	cruzarán	cruzarían	**crucen**	cruzaran	**crucen** Uds.
38 destruir (y)	**destruyo**	destruía	destruí	destruiré	destruiría	**destruya**	**destruyera**	
	destruyes	destruías	destruiste	destruirás	destruirías	**destruyas**	**destruyeras**	**destruye** tú (no **destruyas**)
Participles:	**destruye**	destruía	**destruyó**	destruirá	destruiría	**destruya**	**destruyera**	**destruya** Ud.
destruyendo	destruimos	destruíamos	destruimos	destruiremos	destruiríamos	**destruyamos**	**destruyéramos**	**destruyamos**
destruido	destruís	destruíais	destruisteis	destruiréis	destruiríais	**destruyáis**	**destruyerais**	destruid (no **destruyáis**)
	destruyen	destruían	**destruyeron**	destruirán	destruirían	**destruyan**	**destruyeran**	**destruyan** Uds.
39 enviar (envío)	**envío**	enviaba	envié	enviaré	enviaría	**envíe**	enviara	
	envías	enviabas	enviaste	enviarás	enviarías	**envíes**	enviaras	**envía** tú (no **envíes**)
	envía	enviaba	envió	enviará	enviaría	**envíe**	enviara	**envíe** Ud.
Participles:	enviamos	enviábamos	enviamos	enviaremos	enviaríamos	enviemos	enviáramos	enviemos
enviando	enviáis	enviabais	enviasteis	enviaréis	enviaríais	enviéis	enviarais	enviad (no enviéis)
enviado	**envían**	enviaban	enviaron	enviarán	enviarían	**envíen**	enviaran	**envíen** Uds.

Verb Conjugation Tables

		INDICATIVE					SUBJUNCTIVE		IMPERATIVE
	Infinitive	Present	Imperfect	Preterite	Future	Conditional	Present	Past	
40	graduarse (gradúo)	**gradúo**	graduaba	gradué	graduaré	graduaría	**gradúe**	graduara	
		gradúas	graduabas	graduaste	graduarás	graduarías	**gradúes**	graduaras	**gradúa** tú (no **gradúes**)
		gradúa	graduaba	graduó	graduará	graduaría	**gradúe**	graduara	**gradúe** Ud.
	Participles:	graduamos	graduábamos	graduamos	graduaremos	graduaríamos	graduemos	graduáramos	graduemos
	graduando	graduáis	graduabais	graduasteis	graduaréis	graduaríais	graduéis	graduarais	graduad (no graduéis)
	graduado	**gradúan**	graduaban	graduaron	graduarán	graduarían	**gradúen**	graduaran	**gradúen** Uds.
41	llegar (g:gu)	llego	llegaba	**llegué**	llegaré	llegaría	**llegue**	llegara	
		llegas	llegabas	llegaste	llegarás	llegarías	**llegues**	llegaras	llega tú (no **llegues**)
	Participles:	llega	llegaba	llegó	llegará	llegaría	**llegue**	llegara	**llegue** Ud.
	llegando	llegamos	llegábamos	llegamos	llegaremos	llegaríamos	**lleguemos**	llegáramos	**lleguemos**
	llegado	llegáis	llegabais	llegasteis	llegaréis	llegaríais	**lleguéis**	llegarais	llegad (no **lleguéis**)
		llegan	llegaban	llegaron	llegarán	llegarían	**lleguen**	llegaran	**lleguen** Uds.
42	proteger (g:j)	**protejo**	protegía	protegí	protegeré	protegería	**proteja**	protegiera	
		proteges	protegías	protegiste	protegerás	protegerías	**protejas**	protegieras	protege tú (no **protejas**)
		protege	protegía	protegió	protegerá	protegería	**proteja**	protegiera	**proteja** Ud.
	Participles:	protegemos	protegíamos	protegimos	protegeremos	protegeríamos	**protejamos**	protegiéramos	**protejamos**
	protegiendo	protegéis	protegíais	protegisteis	protegeréis	protegeríais	**protejáis**	protegierais	proteged (no **protejáis**)
	protegido	protegen	protegían	protegieron	protegerán	protegerían	**protejan**	protegieran	**protejan** Uds.
43	tocar (c:qu)	toco	tocaba	**toqué**	tocaré	tocaría	**toque**	tocara	
		tocas	tocabas	tocaste	tocarás	tocarías	**toques**	tocaras	toca tú (no **toques**)
	Participles:	toca	tocaba	tocó	tocará	tocaría	**toque**	tocara	**toque** Ud.
	tocando	tocamos	tocábamos	tocamos	tocaremos	tocaríamos	**toquemos**	tocáramos	**toquemos**
	tocado	tocáis	tocabais	tocasteis	tocaréis	tocaríais	**toquéis**	tocarais	tocad (no **toquéis**)
		tocan	tocaban	tocaron	tocarán	tocarían	**toquen**	tocaran	**toquen** Uds.
44	vencer (c:z)	**venzo**	vencía	vencí	venceré	vencería	**venza**	venciera	
		vences	vencías	venciste	vencerás	vencerías	**venzas**	vencieras	vence tú (no **venzas**)
	Participles:	vence	vencía	venció	vencerá	vencería	**venza**	venciera	**venza** Ud.
	venciendo	vencemos	vencíamos	vencimos	venceremos	venceríamos	**venzamos**	venciéramos	**venzamos**
	vencido	vencéis	vencíais	vencisteis	venceréis	venceríais	**venzáis**	vencierais	venced (no **venzáis**)
		vencen	vencían	vencieron	vencerán	vencerían	**venzan**	vencieran	**venzan** Uds.

Vocabulario

Guide to Vocabulary

Contents of the glossary
This glossary contains the words and expressions listed on the **Vocabulario** page found at the end of each lesson in **DESCUBRE** as well as other useful vocabulary. The number following an entry indicates the **DESCUBRE** level and lesson where the word or expression was introduced. Check the **Estructura** sections of each lesson for words and expressions related to those grammar topics.

Abbreviations used in this glossary

adj.	adjective	*f.*	feminine	*m.*	masculine	*prep.*	preposition
adv.	adverb	*fam.*	familiar	*n.*	noun	*pron.*	pronoun
art.	article	*form.*	formal	*obj.*	object	*ref.*	reflexive
conj.	conjunction	*indef.*	indefinite	*p.p.*	past participle	*sing.*	singular
def.	definite	*interj.*	interjection	*pl.*	plural	*sub.*	subject
d.o.	direct object	*i.o.*	indirect object	*poss.*	possessive	*v.*	verb

Note on alphabetization
In current practice, for purposes of alphabetization, **ch** and **ll** are not treated as separate letters, but **ñ** still follows **n**. Therefore, in this glossary you will find that **año**, for example, appears after **anuncio**.

Spanish-English

A

a *prep.* at; to 1.1
　a bordo aboard 1.1
　a la derecha to the right 1.2
　a la izquierda to the left 1.2
　a la(s) + *time* at + *time* 1.1
　a nombre de in the name of 1.5
　¿A qué hora...? At what time...? 1.1
　a ver let's see 1.2
abeja *f.* bee
abierto/a *adj.* open 1.5
abrazo *m.* hug
abrigo *m.* coat 1.6
abril *m.* April 1.5
abrir *v.* to open 1.3
abuelo/a *m., f.* grandfather; grandmother 1.3
abuelos *pl.* grandparents 1.3
aburrido/a *adj.* bored; boring 1.5
aburrir *v.* to bore 1.7
acabar de (+ *inf.***)** *v.* to have just (done something) 1.6
acampar *v.* to camp 1.5
aceite *m.* oil 1.8
acordarse (de) (o:ue) *v.* to remember 1.7
acostarse (o:ue) *v.* to go to bed 1.7
acuático/a *adj.* aquatic 1.4
adicional *adj.* additional
adiós *m.* good-bye 1.1
adjetivo *m.* adjective
administración de empresas *f.* business administration 1.2

adolescencia *f.* adolescence 1.9
¿adónde? *adv.* where (to)? (*destination*) 1.2
aduana *f.* customs 1.5
aeropuerto *m.* airport 1.5
afeitarse *v.* to shave 1.7
aficionado/a *adj.* fan 1.4
afirmativo/a *adj.* affirmative
agencia de viajes *f.* travel agency 1.5
agente de viajes *m., f.* travel agent 1.5
agosto *m.* August 1.5
agradable *adj.* pleasant
agua *f.* water 1.8
　agua mineral mineral water 1.8
ahora *adv.* now 1.2
　ahora mismo right now 1.5
aire *m.* air 1.5
ajo *m.* garlic 1.8
al (*contraction of* **a + el**) 1.2
　al aire libre open-air 1.6
　al lado de beside 1.2
alegre *adj.* happy; joyful 1.5
alegría *f.* happiness 1.9
alemán, alemana *adj.* German 1.3
algo *pron.* something; anything 1.7
algodón *m.* cotton 1.6
alguien *pron.* someone; somebody; anyone 1.7
algún, alguno/a(s) *adj.* any; some 1.7
alimento *m.* food
alimentación *f.* diet
allá *adv.* over there 1.2
allí *adv.* there 1.2
almacén *m.* department store 1.6

almorzar (o:ue) *v.* to have lunch 1.4
almuerzo *m.* lunch 1.8
alto/a *adj.* tall 1.3
amable *adj.* nice; friendly 1.5
amarillo/a *adj.* yellow 1.3
amigo/a *m., f.* friend 1.3
amistad *f.* friendship 1.9
amor *m.* love 1.9
anaranjado/a *adj.* orange 1.6
andar *v.* **en patineta** to skateboard 1.4
aniversario (de bodas) *m.* (wedding) anniversary 1.9
anoche *adv.* last night 1.6
anteayer *adv.* the day before yesterday 1.6
antes *adv.* before 1.7
　antes de *prep.* before 1.7
antipático/a *adj.* unpleasant 1.3
año *m.* year 1.5
　año pasado last year 1.6
aparato *m.* appliance
apellido *m.* last name 1.3
aprender (a + *inf.***)** *v.* to learn 1.3
aquel, aquella *adj.* that 1.6
aquél, aquélla *pron.* that 1.6
aquello *neuter pron.* that; that thing; that fact 1.6
aquellos/as *pl. adj.* those (over there) 1.6
aquéllos/as *pl. pron.* those (ones) (over there) 1.6
aquí *adv.* here 1.1
　Aquí está... Here it is... 1.5
　Aquí estamos en... Here we are at/in...
Argentina *f.* Argentina 1.1
argentino/a *adj.* Argentine 1.3

Vocabulario

Spanish-English

arqueología *f.* archaeology 1.2
arriba *adv.* up
arroz *m.* rice 1.8
arte *m.* art 1.2
artista *m., f.* artist 1.3
arveja *m.* pea 1.8
asado/a *adj.* roast 1.8
ascensor *m.* elevator 1.5
asistir (a) *v.* to attend 1.3
atún *m.* tuna 1.8
aunque *conj.* although
autobús *m.* bus 1.1
automático/a *adj.* automatic
auto(móvil) *m.* auto(mobile) 1.5
avenida *f.* avenue
avergonzado/a *adj.* embarrassed 1.5
avión *m.* airplane 1.5
¡Ay! *interj.* Oh!
  ¡Ay, qué dolor! Oh, what pain!
ayer *adv.* yesterday 1.6
azúcar *m.* sugar 1.8
azul *adj.* blue 1.3

B

bailar *v.* to dance 1.2
bajo/a *adj.* short (*in height*) 1.3
bajo control under control 1.7
baloncesto *m.* basketball 1.4
banana *f.* banana 1.8
bandera *f.* flag
bañarse *v.* to bathe; to take a bath 1.7
baño *m.* bathroom 1.7
barato/a *adj.* cheap 1.6
barco *m.* boat 1.5
beber *v.* to drink 1.3
bebida *f.* drink 1.8
béisbol *m.* baseball 1.4
beso *m.* kiss 1.9
biblioteca *f.* library 1.2
bicicleta *f.* bicycle 1.4
bien *adj., adv.* well 1.1
billete *m.* paper money; ticket
billón *m.* trillion
biología *f.* biology 1.2
bisabuelo/a *m.* great-grandfather; great-grandmother 1.3
bistec *m.* steak 1.8
bizcocho *m.* biscuit
blanco/a *adj.* white 1.3
(blue)jeans *m., pl.* jeans 1.6
blusa *f.* blouse 1.6
boda *f.* wedding 1.9
bolsa *f.* purse, bag 1.6
bonito/a *adj.* pretty 1.3
borrador *m.* eraser 1.2
bota *f.* boot 1.6
botella *f.* bottle 1.9
  botella de vino bottle of wine 1.9
botones *m., f. sing* bellhop 1.5
brindar *v.* to toast (*drink*) 1.9
bucear *v.* to scuba dive 1.4
bueno *adv.* well 1.2

buen, bueno/a *adj.* good 1.3, 1.6
  ¡Buen viaje! Have a good trip! 1.1
  Buena idea. Good idea. 1.4
  Buenas noches. Good evening.; Good night. 1.1
  Buenas tardes. Good afternoon. 1.1
  buenísimo extremely good
  ¿Bueno? Hello. (*on telephone*)
  Buenos días. Good morning. 1.1
bulevar *m.* boulevard
buscar *v.* to look for 1.2

C

caballo *m.* horse 1.5
cada *adj.* each 1.6
café *m.* café 1.4; *adj.* brown 1.6; *m.* coffee 1.8
cafetería *f.* cafeteria 1.2
caja *f.* cash register 1.6
calcetín (calcetines) *m.* sock(s) 1.6
calculadora *f.* calculator 1.2
caldo *m.* soup
calidad *f.* quality 1.6
calor *m.* heat 1.4
calzar *v.* to take size... shoes 1.6
cama *f.* bed 1.5
camarero/a *m., f.* waiter/waitress 1.8
camarón *m.* shrimp 1.8
cambiar (de) *v.* to change 1.9
cambio *m.* **de moneda** currency exchange
caminar *v.* to walk 1.2
camino *m.* road
camión *m* truck; bus
camisa *f.* shirt 1.6
camiseta *f.* t-shirt 1.6
campo *m.* countryside 1.5
canadiense *adj.* Canadian 1.3
cansado/a *adj.* tired 1.5
cantar *v.* to sing 1.2
capital *f.* capital city 1.1
cara *f.* face 1.7
caramelo *m.* caramel 1.9
carne *f.* meat 1.8
  carne de res *f.* beef 1.8
caro/a *adj.* expensive 1.6
carta *f.* letter 1.4; (*playing*) card 1.5
cartera *f.* wallet 1.6
casa *f.* house; home 1.2
casado/a *adj.* married 1.9
casarse (con) *v.* to get married (to) 1.9
catorce *n., adj.* fourteen 1.1
cebolla *f.* onion 1.8
celebrar *v.* to celebrate 1.9
cena *f.* dinner 1.8
cenar *v.* to have dinner 1.2
centro *m.* downtown 1.4

centro comercial shopping mall 1.6
cepillarse los dientes/el pelo *v.* to brush one's teeth/one's hair 1.7
cerca de *prep.* near 1.2
cerdo *m.* pork 1.8
cereales *m., pl.* cereal; grains 1.8
cero *m.* zero 1.1
cerrado/a *adj.* closed 1.5
cerrar (e:ie) *v.* to close 1.4
cerveza *f.* beer 1.8
ceviche *m.* marinated fish dish 1.8
  ceviche de camarón *m.* lemon-marinated shrimp 1.8
chaleco *m.* vest
champán *m.* champagne 1.9
champiñón *m.* mushroom 1.8
champú *m.* shampoo 1.7
chaqueta *f.* jacket 1.6
chau *fam. interj.* bye 1.1
chévere *adj., fam.* terrific
chico/a *m., f.* boy; girl 1.1
chino/a *adj.* Chinese 1.3
chocar (con) *v.* to run into
chocolate *m.* chocolate 1.9
chuleta *f.* chop (*food*) 1.8
  chuleta de cerdo *f.* pork chop 1.8
cibercafé *m.* cybercafé
ciclismo *m.* cycling 1.4
cien(to) *n., adj.* one hundred 1.2
ciencia *f.* science 1.2
cinco *n., adj.* five 1.1
cincuenta *n., adj.* fifty 1.2
cine *m.* movie theater 1.4
cinta *f.* (audio)tape
cinturón *m.* belt 1.6
cita *f.* date; appointment 1.9
ciudad *f.* city 1.4
clase *f.* class 1.2
cliente/a *m., f.* customer 1.6
color *m.* color 1.3, 1.6
comenzar (e:ie) *v.* to begin 1.4
comer *v.* to eat 1.3
comida *f.* food; meal 1.8
como *prep., conj.* like; as 1.8
¿cómo? *adv.* what?; how? 1.1
  ¿Cómo es...? What's... like? 1.3
  ¿Cómo está usted? *form.* How are you? 1.1
  ¿Cómo estás? *fam.* How are you? 1.1
  ¿Cómo se llama (usted)? *form.* What's your name? 1.1
  ¿Cómo te llamas (tú)? *fam.* What's your name? 1.1
cómodo/a *adj.* comfortable 1.5
compañero/a de clase *m., f.* classmate 1.2
compañero/a de cuarto *m., f.* roommate 1.2

compartir *v.* to share 1.3
completamente *adv.* completely 1.5
comprar *v.* to buy 1.2
compras *f., pl.* purchases 1.5
   ir de compras to go shopping 1.5
comprender *v.* to understand 1.3
comprobar (o:ue) *v.* to check
comprometerse (con) *v.* to get engaged (to) 1.9
computación *f.* computer science 1.2
computadora *f.* computer 1.1
comunidad *f.* community 1.1
con *prep.* with 1.2
   Con permiso. Pardon me.; Excuse me. 1.1
concordar (o:ue) *v.* to agree
conducir *v.* to drive 1.6
conductor(a) *m., f.* driver 1.1
confirmar *v.* to confirm 1.5
   confirmar *v.* **una reservación** *f.* to confirm a reservation 1.5
confundido/a *adj.* confused 1.5
conmigo *pron.* with me 1.4, 1.9
conocer *v.* to know; to be acquainted with 1.6
conocido/a *adj.; p.p.* known
conseguir (e:i) *v.* to get; to obtain 1.4
consejo *m.* advice
construir *v.* to build
contabilidad *f.* accounting 1.2
contar (o:ue) *v.* to count; to tell 1.4
contento/a *adj.* happy; content 1.5
contestar *v.* to answer 1.2
contigo *fam. pron.* with you 1.9
control *m.* control 1.7
conversación *f.* conversation 1.1
conversar *v.* to converse, to chat 1.2
corbata *f.* tie 1.6
correo electrónico *m.* e-mail 1.4
correr *v.* to run 1.3
cortesía *f.* courtesy
corto/a *adj.* short (in length) 1.6
cosa *f.* thing 1.1
Costa Rica *f.* Costa Rica 1.1
costar (o:ue) *f.* to cost 1.6
costarricense *adj.* Costa Rican 1.3
creer (en) *v.* to believe (in) 1.3
crema de afeitar *f.* shaving cream 1.7
cuaderno *m.* notebook 1.1

¿cuál(es)? *pron.* which?; which one(s)? 1.2
   ¿Cuál es la fecha de hoy? What is today's date? 1.5
cuando *conj.* when 1.7
¿cuándo? *adv.* when? 1.2
¿cuánto(s)/a(s)? *adj.* how much/how many? 1.1
   ¿Cuánto cuesta...? How much does... cost? 1.6
   ¿Cuántos años tienes? How old are you? 1.3
cuarenta *n., adj.* forty 1.2
cuarto *m.* room 1.2; 1.7
   cuarto de baño *m.* bathroom 1.7
cuarto/a *n., adj.* fourth 1.5
   menos cuarto quarter to (*time*)
   y cuarto quarter after (*time*) 1.1
cuatro *n., adj.* four 1.1
cuatrocientos/as *n., adj.* four hundred 1.2
Cuba *f.* Cuba 1.1
cubano/a *adj.* Cuban 1.3
cubiertos *m., pl.* silverware
cubierto/a *p.p.* covered
cubrir *v.* to cover
cultura *f.* culture 1.2
cuenta *f.* bill 1.8
cuidado *m.* care 1.3
cumpleaños *m., sing.* birthday 1.9
cumplir años *v.* to have a birthday 1.9
cuñado/a *m., f.* brother-in-law; sister-in-law 1.3
curso *m.* course 1.2

D

dar *v.* to give 1.6, 1.9
   dar un consejo *v.* to give advice
de *prep.* of; from 1.1
   ¿De dónde eres? *fam.* Where are you from? 1.1
   ¿De dónde es usted? *form.* Where are you from? 1.1
   ¿de quién...? whose...? *sing.* 1.1
   ¿de quiénes...? whose...? *pl.* 1.1
   de algodón (made) of cotton 1.6
   de buen humor in a good mood 1.5
   de compras shopping 1.5
   de cuadros plaid 1.6
   de excursión hiking 1.4
   de hecho in fact
   de ida y vuelta roundtrip 1.5
   de la mañana in the morning; A.M. 1.1

de la noche in the evening; at night; P.M. 1.1
de la tarde in the afternoon; in the early evening; P.M. 1.1
de lana (made) of wool 1.6
de lunares polka-dotted 1.6
de mal humor in a bad mood 1.5
de moda in fashion 1.6
De nada. You're welcome. 1.1
de rayas striped 1.6
de repente *adv.* suddenly 1.6
de seda (made) of silk 1.6
debajo de *prep.* below; under 1.2
deber (+ *inf.***)** *v.* should; must; ought to 1.3
   Debe ser... It must be... 1.6
decidir (+ *inf.***)** *v.* to decide 1.3
décimo/a *adj.* tenth 1.5
decir (e:i) *v.* to say; to tell 1.4, 1.9
   decir la respuesta to say the answer 1.4
   decir la verdad to tell the truth 1.4
   decir mentiras to tell lies 1.4
dejar una propina *v.* to leave a tip 1.9
del (contraction of **de + el**) of the; from the
delante de *prep.* in front of 1.2
delgado/a *adj.* thin; slender 1.3
delicioso/a *adj.* delicious 1.8
demás *adj.* the rest
demasiado *adj., adv.* too much 1.6
dependiente/a *m., f.* clerk 1.6
deporte *m.* sport 1.4
deportista *m.* sports person
deportivo/a *adj.* sports-related 1.4
derecha *f.* right 1.2
   a la derecha de to the right of 1.2
derecho *adj.* straight (ahead)
desayunar *v.* to have breakfast 1.2
desayuno *m.* breakfast 1.8
descansar *v.* to rest 1.2
describir *v.* to describe 1.3
desde *prep.* from 1.6
desear *v.* to wish; to desire 1.2
desordenado/a *adj.* disorderly 1.5
despedida *f.* farewell; good-bye
despedirse (e:i) (de) *v.* to say good-bye (to)
despejado/a *adj.* clear (*weather*)
despertador *m.* alarm clock 1.7
despertarse (e:ie) *v.* to wake up 1.7
después *adv.* afterwards; then 1.7

Vocabulario — Spanish-English

después de *prep.* after 1.7
detrás de *prep.* behind 1.2
día *m.* day 1.1
   día de fiesta holiday 1.9
diario/a *adj.* daily 1.7
diccionario *m.* dictionary 1.1
diciembre *m.* December 1.5
diecinueve *n., adj.* nineteen 1.1
dieciocho *n., adj.* eighteen 1.1
dieciséis *n., adj.* sixteen 1.1
diecisiete *n., adj.* seventeen 1.1
diente *m.* tooth 1.7
diez *n., adj.* ten 1.1
difícil *adj.* difficult; hard 1.3
dinero *m.* money 1.6
diseño *m.* design
diversión *f.* fun activity; entertainment; recreation 1.4
divertido/a *adj.* fun 1.7
divertirse (e:ie) *v.* to have fun 1.9
divorciado/a *adj.* divorced 1.9
divorciarse (de) *v.* to get divorced (from) 1.9
divorcio *m.* divorce 1.9
doble *adj.* double
doce *n., adj.* twelve 1.1
doctor(a) *m., f.* doctor 1.3
documentos de viaje *m., pl.* travel documents
domingo *m.* Sunday 1.2
don *m.* Mr.; sir 1.1
doña *m.* Mrs.; ma'am 1.1
donde *prep.* where
   ¿dónde? *adv.* where? 1.1
   ¿Dónde está...? Where is...? 1.2
dormir (o:ue) *v.* to sleep 1.4
dormirse (o:ue) *v.* to go to sleep; to fall asleep 1.7
dos *n., adj.* two 1.1
   dos veces *f.* twice; two times 1.6
doscientos/as *n., adj.* two hundred 1.2
ducha *f.* shower 1.7
ducharse *v.* to shower; to take a shower 1.7
dueño/a *m., f.* owner; landlord 1.8
dulces *m., pl.* sweets; candy 1.9
durante *prep.* during 1.7

E

e *conj.* (used instead of *y* before words beginning with *i* and *hi*) and 1.4
economía *f.* economics 1.2
Ecuador *m.* Ecuador 1.1
ecuatoriano/a *adj.* Ecuadorian 1.3
edad *f.* age 1.9
(en) efectivo *m.* cash 1.6
el *m., sing., def. art.* the 1.1
él *sub. pron.* he 1.1; *pron., obj. of prep.* him 1.9
elegante *adj.* elegant 1.6
ella *sub. pron.* she 1.1; *pron., obj. of prep.* her 1.9
ellos/as *sub. pron.* they 1.1; *pron., obj. of prep.* them 1.9
emocionante *adj.* exciting
empezar (e:ie) *v.* to begin 1.4
empleado/a *m., f.* employee 1.5
en *prep.* in; on; at 1.2
   en casa at home 1.7
   en línea inline 1.4
   en mi nombre in my name
   en punto on the dot; exactly; sharp (*time*) 1.1
   en qué in what; how 1.2
   ¿En qué puedo servirles? How can I help you? 1.5
enamorado/a (de) *adj.* in love (with) 1.5
enamorarse (de) *v.* to fall in love (with) 1.9
encantado/a *adj.* delighted; pleased to meet you 1.1
encantar *v.* to like very much; to love (*inanimate objects*) 1.7
encima de *prep.* on top of 1.2
encontrar (o:ue) *v.* to find 1.4
enero *m.* January 1.5
enojado/a *adj.* mad; angry 1.5
enojarse (con) *v.* to get angry (with) 1.7
ensalada *f.* salad 1.8
enseguida *adv.* right away 1.8
enseñar *v.* to teach 1.2
entender (e:ie) *v.* to understand 1.4
entonces *adv.* then 1.7
entre *prep.* between; among 1.2
entremeses *m., pl.* hors d'oeuvres; appetizers 1.8
equipaje *m.* luggage 1.5
equipo *m.* team 1.4
equivocado/a *adj.* wrong 1.5
eres *fam.* you are 1.1
es he/she/it is 1.1
   Es de... He/She is from... 1.1
   Es la una. It's one o'clock. 1.1
esa(s) *f., adj.* that; those 1.6
ésa(s) *f., pron.* those (ones) 1.6
escalar *v.* to climb 1.4
   escalar montañas *v.* to climb mountains 1.4
escoger *v.* to choose 1.8
escribir *v.* to write 1.3
   escribir un mensaje electrónico to write an e-mail message 1.4
   escribir una carta to write a letter 1.4
   escribir una postal to write a postcard
escritorio *m.* desk 1.2
escuchar *v.* to listen (to) 1.2
escuchar la radio to listen to the radio 1.2
escuchar música to listen to music 1.2
escuela *f.* school 1.1
ese *m., sing., adj.* that 1.6
ése *m., sing., pron.* that (one) 1.6
eso *neuter pron.* that; that thing 1.6
esos *m., pl., adj.* those 1.6
ésos *m., pl., pron.* those (ones) 1.6
España *f.* Spain 1.1
español *m.* Spanish (language) 1.2
español(a) *adj.* Spanish 1.3
espárragos *m., pl.* asparagus 1.8
especialización *f.* major 1.2
espejo *m.* mirror 1.7
esperar (+ *inf.*) *v.* to wait (for); to hope 1.2
esposo/a *m., f.* husband; wife; spouse 1.3
esquí (acuático) *m.* (water) skiing 1.4
esquiar *v.* to ski 1.4
está he/she/it is, you are 1.2
   Está (muy) despejado. It's (very) clear. (*weather*)
   Está lloviendo. It's raining. 1.5
   Está nevando. It's snowing. 1.5
   Está (muy) nublado. It's (very) cloudy. (*weather*) 1.5
esta(s) *f., adj.* this; these 1.6
esta noche tonight 1.4
ésta(s) *f., pron.* this (one); these (ones) 1.6
Ésta es... *f.* This is... (*introducing someone*) 1.1
estación *f.* station; season 1.5
   estación de autobuses bus station 1.5
   estación del metro subway station 1.5
   estación de tren train station 1.5
estadio *m.* stadium 1.2
estado civil *m.* marital status 1.9
Estados Unidos *m.* (EE.UU.; E.U.) United States 1.1
estadounidense *adj.* from the United States 1.3
estampado/a *adj.* print
estar *v.* to be 1.2
   estar aburrido/a to be bored 1.5
   estar bajo control to be under control 1.7
   estar de moda to be in fashion 1.6

Vocabulario

estar de vacaciones to be on vacation 1.5
estar seguro/a to be sure 1.5
No está nada mal. It's not bad at all. 1.5
este *m., sing., adj.* this 1.6
éste *m., sing., pron.* this (one) 1.6
  Éste es... *m.* This is... (*introducing someone*) 1.1
estilo *m.* style
esto *neuter pron.* this; this thing 1.6
estos *m., pl., adj.* these 1.6
éstos *m., pl., pron.* these (ones) 1.6
estudiante *m., f.* student 1.1, 1.2
estudiantil *adj.* student 1.2
estudiar *v.* to study 1.2
estupendo/a *adj.* stupendous 1.5
etapa *f.* stage 1.9
examen *m.* test; exam 1.2
excelente *adj.* excellent 1.5
excursión *f.* hike; tour; excursion 1.4
excursionista *m., f.* hiker
explicar *v.* to explain 1.2
explorar *v.* to explore
expresión *f.* expression

F

fabuloso/a *adj.* fabulous 1.5
fácil *adj.* easy 1.3
falda *f.* skirt 1.6
faltar *v.* to lack; to need 1.7
familia *f.* family 1.3
fascinar *v.* to fascinate 1.7
favorito/a *adj.* favorite 1.4
febrero *m.* February 1.5
fecha *f.* date 1.5
feliz *adj.* happy 1.5
  ¡Feliz cumpleaños! Happy birthday! 1.9
  ¡Felicidades! Congratulations! 1.9
  ¡Felicitaciones! Congratulations! 1.9
fenomenal *adj.* great, phenomenal 1.5
feo/a *adj.* ugly 1.3
fiesta *f.* party 1.9
fijo/a *adj.* fixed, set 1.6
fin *m.* end 1.4
  fin de semana weekend 1.4
física *f.* physics 1.2
flan (de caramelo) *m.* baked (caramel) custard 1.9
folleto *m.* brochure
foto(grafía) *f.* photograph 1.1
francés, francesa *adj.* French 1.3

frenos *m., pl.* brakes
fresco/a *adj.* cool 1.5
frijoles *m., pl.* beans 1.8
frío/a *adj.* cold 1.5
frito/a *adj.* fried 1.8
fruta *f.* fruit 1.8
frutilla *f.* strawberry
fuera *adv.* outside
fútbol *m.* soccer 1.4
fútbol americano *m.* football 1.4

G

gafas (de sol) *f., pl.* (sun)glasses 1.6
gafas (oscuras) *f., pl.* (sun)glasses
galleta *f.* cookie 1.9
ganar *v.* to win 1.4
ganga *f.* bargain 1.6
gastar *v.* to spend (*money*) 1.6
gemelo/a *m., f.* twin 1.3
gente *f.* people 1.3
geografía *f.* geography 1.2
gimnasio *m.* gymnasium 1.4
golf *m.* golf 1.4
gordo/a *adj.* fat 1.3
gracias *f., pl.* thank you; thanks 1.1
  Gracias por todo. Thanks for everything. 1.9
  Gracias una vez más. Thanks again. 1.9
graduarse (de/en) *v.* to graduate (from/in) 1.9
gran, grande *adj.* big; large 1.3
grillo *m.* cricket
gris *adj.* gray 1.6
gritar *v.* to scream 1.7
guantes *m., pl.* gloves 1.6
guapo/a *adj.* handsome; good-looking 1.3
guía *m., f.* guide
gustar *v.* to be pleasing to; to like 1.2
  Me gustaría... I would like...
gusto *m.* pleasure 1.1
  El gusto es mío. The pleasure is mine. 1.1
  Mucho gusto. Pleased to meet you. 1.1

H

habitación *f.* room 1.5
  habitación doble double room 1.5
  habitación individual single room 1.5
hablar *v.* to talk; to speak 1.2
hacer *v.* to do; to make 1.4
  Hace buen tiempo. The weather is good. 1.5

  Hace (mucho) calor. It's (very) hot. (*weather*) 1.5
  Hace fresco. It's cool. (*weather*) 1.5
  Hace (mucho) frío. It's very cold. (*weather*) 1.5
  Hace mal tiempo. The weather is bad. 1.5
  Hace (mucho) sol. It's (very) sunny. (*weather*) 1.5
  Hace (mucho) viento. It's (very) windy. (*weather*) 1.5
  hacer juego (con) to match (with) 1.6
  hacer las maletas to pack (one's) suitcases 1.5
  hacer (wind)surf to (wind)surf 1.5
  hacer turismo to go sightseeing
  hacer un viaje to take a trip 1.5
  hacer una excursión to go on a hike; to go on a tour
hambre *f.* hunger 1.3
hamburguesa *f.* hamburger 1.8
hasta *prep.* until 1.6; toward
  Hasta la vista. See you later. 1.1
  Hasta luego. See you later. 1.1
  Hasta mañana. See you tomorrow. 1.1
  Hasta pronto. See you soon. 1.1
hay *v.* there is; there are 1.1
  Hay (mucha) contaminación. It's (very) smoggy.
  Hay (mucha) niebla. It's (very) foggy.
  No hay de qué. You're welcome. 1.1
helado/a *adj.* iced 1.8
helado *m.* ice cream 1.9
hermanastro/a *m., f.* stepbrother; stepsister 1.3
hermano/a *m., f.* brother; sister 1.3
hermano/a mayor/menor *m., f.* older/younger brother/sister 1.3
hermanos *m., pl.* siblings (brothers and sisters) 1.3
hermoso/a *adj.* beautiful 1.6
hijastro/a *m., f.* stepson; stepdaughter 1.3
hijo/a *m., f.* son; daughter 1.3
  hijo/a único/a *m., f.* only child 1.3
hijos *m., pl.* children 1.3
historia *f.* history 1.2
hockey *m.* hockey 1.4
hola *interj.* hello; hi 1.1
hombre *m.* man 1.1

Vocabulario — Spanish-English

hora *f.* hour 1.1; the time
horario *m.* schedule 1.2
hotel *m.* hotel 1.5
hoy *adv.* today 1.2
   hoy día *adv.* nowadays
   Hoy es... Today is... 1.2
huésped *m., f.* guest 1.5
huevo *m.* egg 1.8
humanidades *f., pl.* humanities 1.2

I

ida *f.* one way (*travel*)
idea *f.* idea 1.4
iglesia *f.* church 1.4
igualmente *adv.* likewise 1.1
impermeable *m.* raincoat 1.6
importante *adj.* important 1.3
importar *v.* to be important to; to matter 1.7
increíble *adj.* incredible 1.5
individual *adj.* private (*room*) 1.5
ingeniero/a *m., f.* engineer 1.3
inglés *m.* English (*language*) 1.2
inglés, inglesa *adj.* English 1.3
inodoro *m.* toilet 1.7
inspector(a) de aduanas *m., f.* customs inspector 1.5
inteligente *adj.* intelligent 1.3
intercambiar *v.* to exchange
interesante *adj.* interesting 1.3
interesar *v.* to be interesting to; to interest 1.7
invierno *m.* winter 1.5
invitado/a *m., f.* guest 1.9
invitar *v.* to invite 1.9
ir *v.* to go 1.4
   ir a (+ *inf.*) to be going to *do something* 1.4
   ir de compras to go shopping 1.5
   ir de excursión (a las montañas) to go on a hike (in the mountains) 1.4
   ir de pesca to go fishing
   ir de vacaciones to go on vacation 1.5
   ir en autobús to go by bus 1.5
   ir en auto(móvil) to go by car 1.5
   ir en avión to go by plane 1.5
   ir en barco to go by boat 1.5
   ir en metro to go by subway
   ir en motocicleta to go by motorcycle 1.5
   ir en taxi to go by taxi 1.5
   ir en tren to go by train
irse *v.* to go away; to leave 1.7
italiano/a *adj.* Italian 1.3
izquierdo/a *adj.* left 1.2
   a la izquierda de to the left of 1.2

J

jabón *m.* soap 1.7
jamás *adv.* never; not ever 1.7
jamón *m.* ham 1.8
japonés, japonesa *adj.* Japanese 1.3
joven *adj. m., f., sing.* (**jóvenes** *pl.*) young 1.3
joven *m., f., sing.* (**jóvenes** *pl.*) youth; young person 1.1
jubilarse *v.* to retire (*from work*) 1.9
juego *m.* game
jueves *m., sing.* Thursday 1.2
jugador(a) *m., f.* player 1.4
jugar (u:ue) *v.* to play 1.4
   jugar a las cartas to play cards 1.5
jugo *m.* juice 1.8
   jugo de fruta *m.* fruit juice 1.8
julio *m.* July 1.5
junio *m.* June 1.5
juntos/as *adj.* together 1.9
juventud *f.* youth 1.9

L

la *f., sing., def. art.* the 1.1
la *f., sing., d.o. pron.* her, it; *form.* you 1.5
laboratorio *m.* laboratory 1.2
lana *f.* wool 1.6
langosta *f.* lobster 1.8
lápiz *m.* pencil 1.1
largo/a *adj.* long 1.6
las *f., pl., def. art.* the 1.1
las *f., pl., d.o. pron.* them; *form.* you 1.5
lavabo *m.* sink 1.7
lavarse *v.* to wash oneself 1.7
   lavarse la cara to wash one's face 1.7
   lavarse las manos to wash one's hands 1.7
le *sing., i.o. pron.* to/for him, her; *form.* you 1.6
   Le presento a... *form.* I would like to introduce you to (name). 1.1
lección *f.* lesson 1.1
leche *f.* milk 1.8
lechuga *f.* lettuce 1.8
leer *v.* to read 1.3
   leer correo electrónico to read e-mail 1.4
   leer un periódico to read a newspaper 1.4
   leer una revista to read a magazine 1.4
lejos de *prep.* far from 1.2
lengua *f.* language 1.2
   lenguas extranjeras *f., pl.* foreign languages 1.2
lentes (de sol) (sun)glasses
lentes de contacto *m., pl.* contact lenses
les *pl., i.o. pron.* to/for them; *form.* you 1.6
levantarse *v.* to get up 1.7
libre *adj.* free 1.4
librería *f.* bookstore 1.2
libro *m.* book 1.2
limón *m.* lemon 1.8
limpio/a *adj.* clean 1.5
línea *f.* line
listo/a *adj.* ready; smart 1.5
literatura *f.* literature 1.2
llamarse *v.* to be called; to be named 1.7
llave *f.* key 1.5
llegada *f.* arrival 1.5
llegar *v.* to arrive 1.2
llevar *v.* to carry 1.2; to wear; to take 1.6
   llevarse bien/mal (con) to get along well/badly (with) 1.9
llover (o:ue) *v.* to rain 1.5
   Llueve. It's raining. 1.5
lo *m., sing., d.o. pron.* him, it; *form.* you 1.5
   Lo siento. I'm sorry. 1.1
   Lo siento muchísimo. I'm so sorry. 1.4
loco/a *adj.* crazy 1.6
los *m., pl., def. art.* the 1.1
los *m., pl., d.o. pron.* them; *form.* you 1.5
luego *adv.* then 1.7; *adv.* later 1.1
lugar *m.* place 1.4
lunares *m.* polka dots 1.6
lunes *m., sing.* Monday 1.2

M

madrastra *f.* stepmother 1.3
madre *f.* mother 1.3
madurez *f.* maturity; middle age 1.9
magnífico/a *adj.* magnificent 1.5
maíz *m.* corn 1.8
mal, malo/a *adj.* bad 1.3
maleta *f.* suitcase 1.1
mamá *f.* mom 1.3
mano *f.* hand 1.1
   ¡Manos arriba! Hands up!
mantequilla *f.* butter 1.8
manzana *f.* apple 1.8
mañana *f.* morning, A.M. 1.1; tomorrow 1.1

Vocabulario — Spanish-English

mapa *m.* map 1.2
maquillaje *m.* makeup 1.7
maquillarse *v.* to put on makeup 1.7
mar *m.* sea 1.5
maravilloso/a *adj.* marvelous 1.5
margarina *f.* margarine 1.8
mariscos *m., pl.* shellfish 1.8
marrón *adj.* brown 1.6
martes *m., sing.* Tuesday 1.2
marzo *m.* March 1.5
más *pron.* more 1.2
   más de (+ *number***)** more than 1.8
   más tarde later (on) 1.7
   más... que more... than 1.8
matemáticas *f., pl.* mathematics 1.2
materia *f.* course 1.2
matrimonio *m.* marriage 1.9
mayo *m.* May 1.5
mayonesa *f.* mayonnaise 1.8
mayor *adj.* older 1.3
   el/la mayor *adj.* the eldest 1.8; the oldest
me *sing., d.o. pron.* me 1.5; *sing. i.o. pron.* to/for me 1.6
   Me gusta... I like... 1.2
   No me gustan nada. I don't like them at all. 1.2
   Me llamo... My name is... 1.1
   Me muero por... I'm dying to (for)...
mediano/a *adj.* medium
medianoche *f.* midnight 1.1
medias *f., pl.* pantyhose, stockings 1.6
médico/a *m., f.* doctor 1.3
medio/a *adj.* half 1.3
   medio/a hermano/a *m., f.* half-brother; half-sister 1.3
   mediodía *m.* noon 1.1
   y media thirty minutes past the hour (*time*) 1.1
mejor *adj.* better 1.8
   el/la mejor *adj.* the best 1.8
melocotón *m.* peach 1.8
menor *adj.* younger 1.3
   el/la menor *adj.* the youngest 1.8
menos *adv.* less
   menos cuarto..., menos quince... quarter to... (*time*) 1.1
   menos de (+ *number***)** fewer than 1.8
   menos... que less... than 1.8
mensaje electrónico *m.* e-mail message 1.4
mentira *f.* lie 1.4
menú *m.* menu 1.8
mercado *m.* market 1.6

mercado al aire libre *m.* open-air market 1.6
merendar (e:ie) *v.* to snack 1.8; to have an afternoon snack
mes *m.* month 1.5
mesa *f.* table 1.2
metro *m.* subway 1.5
mexicano/a *adj.* Mexican 1.3
México *m.* Mexico 1.1
mí *pron., obj. of prep.* me 1.9
mi(s) *poss. adj.* my 1.3
miedo *m.* fear 1.3
miércoles *m., sing.* Wednesday 1.2
mil *m.* one thousand 1.2
   Mil perdones. I'm so sorry. (*lit.* A thousand pardons.) 1.4
mil millones *m.* billion
millón *m.* million 1.2
millones (de) *m.* millions (of)
minuto *m.* minute 1.1
mirar *v.* to look (at); to watch 1.2
   mirar (la) televisión to watch television 1.2
mismo/a *adj.* same 1.3
mochila *f.* backpack 1.2
moda *f.* fashion 1.6
módem *m.* modem
molestar *v.* to bother; to annoy 1.7
montaña *f.* mountain 1.4
montar a caballo *v.* to ride a horse 1.5
monumento *m.* monument 1.4
mora *f.* blackberry 1.8
morado/a *adj.* purple 1.6
moreno/a *adj.* brunet(te) 1.3
morir (o:ue) *v.* to die 1.8
mostrar (o:ue) *v.* to show 1.4
motocicleta *f.* motorcycle 1.5
motor *m.* motor
muchacho/a *m., f.* boy; girl 1.3
mucho/a *adj., adv.* a lot of; much 1.2; many 1.3
   (Muchas) gracias. Thank you (very much).; Thanks (a lot). 1.1
   Muchísimas gracias. Thank you very, very much. 1.9
   Mucho gusto. Pleased to meet you. 1.1
muchísimo very much 1.2
muela *f.* tooth; molar
muerte *f.* death 1.9
mujer *f.* woman 1.1
   mujer policía *f.* female police officer
multa *f.* fine
mundial *adj.* worldwide
municipal *adj.* municipal
museo *m.* museum 1.4
música *f.* music 1.2

muy *adv.* very 1.1
   Muy amable. That's very kind of you. 1.5
   (Muy) bien, gracias. (Very) well, thanks. 1.1

N

nacer *v.* to be born 1.9
nacimiento *m.* birth 1.9
nacionalidad *f.* nationality 1.1
nada *pron., adv.* nothing 1.1; not anything 1.7
   nada mal not bad at all 1.5
nadar *v.* to swim 1.4
nadie *pron.* no one, nobody, not anyone 1.7
naranja *f.* orange 1.8
natación *f.* swimming 1.4
Navidad *f.* Christmas 1.9
necesitar (+ *inf.***)** *v.* to need 1.2
negativo/a *adj.* negative
negro/a *adj.* black 1.3
nervioso/a *adj.* nervous 1.5
nevar (e:ie) *v.* to snow 1.5
   Nieva. It's snowing. 1.5
ni... ni neither... nor 1.7
niebla *f.* fog
nieto/a *m., f.* grandson; granddaughter 1.3
nieve *f.* snow
ningún, ninguno/a(s) *adj., pron.* no; none; not any 1.7
   ningún problema no problem
niñez *f.* childhood 1.9
niño/a *m., f.* child 1.3
no *adv.* no; not 1.1
   ¿no? right? 1.1
   No está nada mal. It's not bad at all. 1.5
   no estar de acuerdo to disagree
   No estoy seguro. I'm not sure.
   no hay there is not; there are not 1.1
   No hay de qué. You're welcome. 1.1
   No hay problema. No problem. 1.7
   No me gustan nada. I don't like them at all. 1.2
   no muy bien not very well 1.1
   No quiero. I don't want to. 1.4
   No sé. I don't know.
   No se preocupe. (*form.*) Don't worry. 1.7
   No te preocupes. (*fam.*) Don't worry. 1.7
   no tener razón to be wrong 1.3

Vocabulario — Spanish-English

noche *f.* night 1.1
nombre *m.* name 1.1
norteamericano/a *adj.* (North) American 1.3
nos *pl., d.o. pron.* us 1.5; *pl., i.o. pron.* to/for us 1.6
  Nos vemos. See you. 1.1
nosotros/as *sub. pron.* we 1.1; *pron., obj. of prep.* us 1.9
novecientos/as *n., adj.* nine hundred 1.2
noveno/a *n., adj.* ninth 1.5
noventa *n., adj.* ninety 1.2
noviembre *m.* November 1.5
novio/a *m., f.* boyfriend/girlfriend 1.3
nublado/a *adj.* cloudy 1.5
  Está (muy) nublado. It's very cloudy. 1.5
nuera *f.* daughter-in-law 1.3
nuestro(s)/a(s) *poss. adj.* our 1.3
nueve *n., adj.* nine 1.1
nuevo/a *adj.* new 1.6
número *m.* number 1.1; (shoe) size 1.6
nunca *adv.* never; not ever 1.7

O

o *conj.* or 1.7
  o... o; either... or 1.7
océano *m.* ocean
ochenta *n., adj.* eighty 1.2
ocho *n., adj.* eight 1.1
ochocientos/as *n., adj.* eight hundred 1.2
octavo/a *n., adj.* eighth 1.5
octubre *m.* October 1.5
ocupado/a *adj.* busy 1.5
odiar *v.* to hate 1.9
ofrecer *v.* to offer 1.6
oír *v.* to hear 1.4
  Oiga./Oigan. *form., sing./pl.* Listen. (*in conversation*) 1.1
  Oye. *fam., sing.* Listen. (*in conversation*) 1.1
once *n., adj.* eleven 1.1
ordenado/a *adj.* orderly 1.5
ordinal *adj.* ordinal (number)
ortografía *f.* spelling
ortográfico/a *adj.* spelling
os *fam., pl., d.o. pron.* you 1.5; *fam., pl., i.o. pron.* to/for you 1.6
otoño *m.* autumn 1.5
otro/a *adj.* other; another 1.6
  otra vez *adv.* again

P

padrastro *m.* stepfather 1.3
padre *m.* father 1.3
  padres *m., pl.* parents 1.3
pagar *v.* to pay 1.6, 1.9
  pagar la cuenta to pay the bill 1.9
país *m.* country 1.1
paisaje *m.* landscape 1.5
palabra *f.* word 1.1
pan *m.* bread 1.8
  pan tostado *m.* toasted bread 1.8
pantalones *m., pl.* pants 1.6
  pantalones cortos *m., pl.* shorts 1.6
pantuflas *f., pl.* slippers 1.7
papa *f.* potato 1.8
  papas fritas *f., pl.* fried potatoes; French fries 1.8
papá *m.* dad 1.3
  papás *m., pl.* parents 1.3
papel *m.* paper 1.2
papelera *f.* wastebasket 1.2
par *m.* pair 1.6
  par de zapatos *m.* pair of shoes 1.6
parecer *v.* to seem 1.6
pareja *f.* (married) couple; partner 1.9
parientes *m., pl.* relatives 1.3
parque *m.* park 1.4
párrafo *m.* paragraph
partido *m.* game; match (*sports*) 1.4
pasado/a *adj.* last; past 1.6
  pasado *p.p.* passed
pasaje *m.* ticket 1.5
  pasaje de ida y vuelta *m.* roundtrip ticket 1.5
pasajero/a *m., f.* passenger 1.1
pasaporte *m.* passport 1.5
pasar *v.* to go through 1.5
  pasar por la aduana to go through customs
  pasar tiempo to spend time
  pasarlo bien/mal to have a good/bad time 1.9
pasatiempo *m.* pastime; hobby 1.4
pasear *v.* to take a walk; to stroll 1.4
  pasear en bicicleta to ride a bicycle 1.4
  pasear por to walk around 1.4
pasta *f.* **de dientes** toothpaste 1.7
pastel *m.* cake; pie 1.9
  pastel de chocolate *m.* chocolate cake 1.9
  pastel de cumpleaños *m.* birthday cake
patata *f.* potato 1.8
  patatas fritas *f., pl.* fried potatoes; French fries 1.8
patinar (en línea) *v.* to (inline) skate 1.4
patineta *f.* skateboard 1.4
pavo *m.* turkey 1.8
pedir (e:i) *v.* to ask for; to request 1.4; to order (*food*) 1.8
peinarse *v.* to comb one's hair 1.7
película *f.* movie 1.4
pelirrojo/a *adj.* red-haired 1.3
pelo *m.* hair 1.7
pelota *f.* ball 1.4
pensar (e:ie) *v.* to think 1.4
  pensar (+ inf.) *v.* to intend to; to plan to (*do something*) 1.4
  pensar en *v.* to think about 1.4
pensión *f.* boardinghouse
peor *adj.* worse 1.8
  el/la peor *adj.* the worst 1.8
pequeño/a *adj.* small 1.3
pera *f.* pear 1.8
perder (e:ie) *v.* to lose; to miss 1.4
Perdón. Pardon me.; Excuse me. 1.1
perezoso/a *adj.* lazy
perfecto/a *adj.* perfect 1.5
periódico *m.* newspaper 1.4
periodismo *m.* journalism 1.2
periodista *m., f.* journalist 1.3
permiso *m.* permission
pero *conj.* but 1.2
persona *f.* person 1.3
pesca *f.* fishing
pescado *m.* fish (*cooked*) 1.8
pescador(a) *m., f.* fisherman/fisherwoman
pescar *v.* to fish 1.5
pimienta *f.* black pepper 1.8
piña *f.* pineapple 1.8
piscina *f.* swimming pool 1.4
piso *m.* floor (*of a building*) 1.5
pizarra *f.* blackboard 1.2
planes *m., pl.* plans
planta baja *f.* ground floor 1.5
plato *m.* dish (*in a meal*) 1.8
  plato principal *m.* main dish 1.8
playa *f.* beach 1.5
plaza *f.* city or town square 1.4
pluma *f.* pen 1.2
pobre *adj.* poor 1.6
pobreza *f.* poverty
poco/a *adj.* little; few 1.5
poder (o:ue) *v.* to be able to; can 1.4
pollo *m.* chicken 1.8
  pollo asado *m.* roast chicken 1.8
ponchar *v.* to go flat
poner *v.* to put; to place 1.4
ponerse (+ adj.) *v.* to become (+ *adj.*) 1.7; to put on 1.7

Vocabulario

por *prep.* in exchange for; for; by; in; through; around; along; during; because of; on account of; on behalf of; in search of; by way of
   por avión by plane
   por favor please 1.1
   por la mañana in the morning 1.7
   por la noche at night 1.7
   por la tarde in the afternoon 1.7
   ¿por qué? why? 1.2
   por teléfono by phone; on the phone
   por último finally 1.7
porque *conj.* because 1.2
posesivo/a *adj.* possessive 1.3
postal *f.* postcard
postre *m.* dessert 1.9
practicar *v.* to practice 1.2
   practicar deportes *m., pl.* to play sports 1.4
precio (fijo) *m.* (fixed; set) price 1.6
preferir (e:ie) *v.* to prefer 1.4
pregunta *f.* question
preguntar *v.* to ask (a question) 1.2
preocupado/a (por) *adj.* worried (about) 1.5
preocuparse (por) *v.* to worry (about) 1.7
preparar *v.* to prepare 1.2
preposición *f.* preposition
presentación *f.* introduction
presentar *v.* to introduce
   Le presento a… I would like to introduce you to (name). 1.1
   Te presento a… I would like to introduce you to (name). *(fam.)* 1.1
prestado/a *adj.* borrowed
prestar *v.* to lend; to loan 1.6
primavera *f.* spring 1.5
primer, primero/a *n., adj.* first 1.5
primo/a *m., f.* cousin 1.3
principal *adj.* main 1.8
prisa *f.* haste 1.3
probar (o:ue) *v.* to taste; to try 1.8
probarse (o:ue) *v.* to try on 1.7
problema *m.* problem 1.1
profesión *f.* profession 1.3
profesor(a) *m., f.* teacher 1.1, 1.2
programa *m.* 1.1
programador(a) *m., f.* computer programmer 1.3
pronombre *m.* pronoun
propina *f.* tip 1.8
prueba *f.* test; quiz 1.2

psicología *f.* psychology 1.2
pueblo *m.* town 1.4
puerta *f.* door 1.2
Puerto Rico *m.* Puerto Rico 1.1
puertorriqueño/a *adj.* Puerto Rican 1.3
pues *conj.* well 1.2

Q

que *conj.* that; which
   ¡Qué…! How…! 1.3
   ¡Qué dolor! What pain!
   ¡Qué ropa más bonita! What pretty clothes! 1.6
   ¡Qué sorpresa! What a surprise!
   ¿qué? *pron.* what? 1.1
   ¿Qué día es hoy? What day is it? 1.2
   ¿Qué hay de nuevo? What's new? 1.1
   ¿Qué hora es? What time is it? 1.1
   ¿Qué les parece? What do you (pl.) think?
   ¿Qué pasa? What's happening?; What's going on? 1.1
   ¿Qué precio tiene? What is the price?
   ¿Qué tal…? How are you?; How is it going? 1.1; How is/are…? 1.2
   ¿Qué talla lleva/usa? What size do you wear? *(form.)* 1.6
   ¿Qué tiempo hace? How's the weather? 1.5
   ¿En qué…? In which…? 1.2
quedar *v.* to be left over; to fit (clothing) 1.7
quedarse *v.* to stay; to remain 1.7
querer (e:ie) *v.* to want; to love 1.4
queso *m.* cheese 1.8
quien(es) *pron.* who; whom
   ¿Quién es…? Who is…? 1.1
   ¿quién(es)? *pron.* who?; whom? 1.1
química *f.* chemistry 1.2
quince *n., adj.* fifteen 1.1
   menos quince quarter to *(time)* 1.1
   y quince quarter after *(time)* 1.1
quinceañera *f.* young woman celebrating her fifteenth birthday 1.9
quinientos/as *n., adj.* five hundred 1.2
quinto/a *n., adj.* fifth 1.5
quitarse *v.* to take off 1.7
quizás *adv.* maybe 1.5

R

radio *f.* radio (*medium*) 1.2
radio *m.* radio (*set*) 1.2
ratos libres *m., pl.* spare (*free*) time 1.4
raya *f.* stripe 1.6
razón *f.* reason 1.3
rebaja *f.* sale 1.6
recibir *v.* to receive 1.3
recién casado/a *m., f.* newlywed 1.9
recomendar (e:ie) *v.* to recommend 1.8
recordar (o:ue) *v.* to remember 1.4
recorrer *v.* to tour an area
refresco *m.* soft drink 1.8
regalar *v.* to give (a gift) 1.9
regalo *m.* gift 1.6
regatear *v.* to bargain 1.6
regresar *v.* to return 1.2
regular *adj.* so-so; OK 1.1
reírse (e:i) *v.* to laugh 1.9
relaciones *f., pl.* relationships
relajarse *v.* to relax 1.9
reloj *m.* clock; watch 1.2
repetir (e:i) *v.* to repeat 1.4
residencia estudiantil *f.* dormitory 1.2
respuesta *f.* answer
restaurante *m.* restaurant 1.4
revista *f.* magazine 1.4
rico/a *adj.* rich 1.6; tasty; delicious 1.8
riquísimo/a *adj.* extremely delicious 1.8
rojo/a *adj.* red 1.3
romper (con) *v.* to break up (with) 1.9
ropa *f.* clothing; clothes 1.6
   ropa interior *f.* underwear 1.6
rosado/a *adj.* pink 1.6
rubio/a *adj.* blond(e) 1.3
ruso/a *adj.* Russian 1.3
rutina *f.* routine 1.7
   rutina diaria *f.* daily routine 1.7

S

sábado *m.* Saturday 1.2
saber *v.* to know; to know how 1.6; to taste 1.8
   saber (a) to taste (like) 1.8
sabrosísimo/a *adj.* extremely delicious 1.8
sabroso/a *adj.* tasty; delicious 1.8
sacar *v.* to take out
   sacar fotos to take photos 1.5
sal *f.* salt 1.8
salchicha *f.* sausage 1.8

Vocabulario

salida *f.* departure; exit 1.5
salir *v.* to leave 1.4; to go out
  salir (con) to go out (with); to date 1.9
  salir de to leave from
  salir para to leave for (*a place*)
salmón *m.* salmon 1.8
saludo *m.* greeting 1.1
  saludos a... greetings to... 1.1
sandalia *f.* sandal 1.6
sandía *f.* watermelon
sándwich *m.* sandwich 1.8
se *ref. pron.* himself, herself, itself; *form.* yourself, themselves, yourselves 1.7
secarse *v.* to dry oneself 1.7
sección de (no) fumar *f.* (non) smoking section 1.8
secuencia *f.* sequence
sed *f.* thirst 1.3
seda *f.* silk 1.6
seguir (e:i) *v.* to follow; to continue 1.4
según *prep.* according to
segundo/a *n., adj.* second 1.5
seguro/a *adj.* sure; safe 1.5
seis *n., adj.* six 1.1
seiscientos/as *n., adj.* six hundred 1.2
semana *f.* week 1.2
  fin *m.* **de semana** weekend 1.4
  semana *f.* **pasada** last week 1.6
semestre *m.* semester 1.2
sentarse (e:ie) *v.* to sit down 1.7
sentir(se) (e:ie) *v.* to feel 1.7
señor (Sr.) *m.* Mr.; sir 1.1
señora (Sra.) *f.* Mrs.; ma'am 1.1
señorita (Srta.) *f.* Miss 1.1
separado/a *adj.* separated 1.9
separarse (de) *v.* to separate (from) 1.9
septiembre *m.* September 1.5
séptimo/a *adj.* seventh 1.5
ser *v.* to be 1.1
  ser aficionado/a (a) to be a fan (of) 1.4
serio/a *adj.* serious
servir (e:i) *v.* to serve 1.8; to help 1.5
sesenta *n., adj.* sixty 1.2
setecientos/as *n., adj.* seven hundred 1.2
setenta *n., adj.* seventy 1.2
sexto/a *n., adj.* sixth 1.5
sí *adv.* yes 1.1
si *conj.* if 1.4
siempre *adv.* always 1.7
siete *n., adj.* seven 1.1
silla *f.* seat 1.2
similar *adj.* similar

simpático/a *adj.* nice; likeable 1.3
sin *prep.* without 1.2
  sin duda without a doubt
  sin embargo however
sino *conj.* but (rather) 1.7
situado/a *adj., p.p.* located
sobre *prep.* on; over 1.2
sobrino/a *m., f.* nephew; niece 1.3
sociología *f.* sociology 1.2
sol *m.* sun 1.4; 1.5
soleado/a *adj.* sunny
sólo *adv.* only 1.3
solo *adj.* alone
soltero/a *adj.* single 1.9
sombrero *m.* hat 1.6
Son las dos. It's two o'clock. 1.1
sonreír (e:i) *v.* to smile 1.9
sopa *f.* soup 1.8
sorprender *v.* to surprise 1.9
sorpresa *f.* surprise 1.9
soy I am 1.1
  Soy yo. That's me. 1.1
  Soy de... I'm from... 1.1
su(s) *poss. adj.* his, her, its; *form.* your, their 1.3
sucio/a *adj.* dirty 1.5
suegro/a *m., f.* father-in-law; mother-in-law 1.3
sueño *m.* sleep 1.3
suerte *f.* luck 1.3
suéter *m.* sweater 1.6
suponer *v.* to suppose 1.4
sustantivo *m.* noun

T

tabla de (wind)surf *f.* surf board/sailboard 1.5
tal vez *adv.* maybe 1.5
talla *f.* size 1.6
  talla grande *f.* large
también *adv.* also; too 1.2; 1.7
tampoco *adv.* neither; not either 1.7
tan *adv.* so 1.5
  tan... como as... as 1.8
tanto *adv.* so much
  tanto... como as much... as 1.8
  tantos/as... como as many... as 1.8
tarde *adv.* late 1.7
tarde *f.* afternoon; evening; P.M. 1.1
tarea *f.* homework 1.2
tarjeta *f.* card
  tarjeta de crédito *f.* credit card 1.6
  tarjeta postal *f.* postcard
taxi *m.* taxi 1.5
te *sing., fam., d.o. pron.* you 1.5; *sing., fam., i.o. pron.* to/for you 1.6

Te presento a... *fam.* I would like to introduce you to (name). 1.1
¿Te gusta(n)...? Do you like...? 1.2
té *m.* tea 1.8
  té helado *m.* iced tea 1.8
televisión *f.* television 1.2
temprano *adv.* early 1.7
tener *v.* to have 1.3
  tener... años to be... years old 1.3
  Tengo... años. I'm... years old. 1.3
  tener (mucho) calor to be (very) hot 1.3
  tener (mucho) cuidado to be (very) careful 1.3
  tener (mucho) frío to be (very) cold 1.3
  tener ganas de (+ *inf.*) to feel like (*doing something*) 1.3
  tener (mucha) hambre to be (very) hungry 1.3
  tener (mucho) miedo (de) to be (very) afraid (of); to be (very) scared (of) 1.3
  tener miedo (de) que to be afraid that
  tener planes to have plans
  tener (mucha) prisa to be in a (big) hurry 1.3
  tener que (+ *inf.*) *v.* to have to (*do something*) 1.3
  tener razón to be right 1.3
  tener (mucha) sed to be (very) thirsty 1.3
  tener (mucho) sueño to be (very) sleepy 1.3
  tener (mucha) suerte *f.* to be (very) lucky 1.3
  tener tiempo to have time 1.4
  tener una cita to have a date; to have an appointment 1.9
tenis *m.* tennis 1.4
tercer, tercero/a *n., adj.* third 1.5
terminar *v.* to end; to finish 1.2
  terminar de (+ *inf.*) *v.* to finish (*doing something*) 1.4
ti *pron., obj. of prep., fam.* you 1.9
tiempo *m.* time 1.4; weather 1.5
  tiempo libre free time
tienda *f.* shop; store 1.6
  tienda de campaña tent
tinto/a *adj.* red (wine) 1.8
tío/a *m., f.* uncle; aunt 1.3
tíos *m.* aunts and uncles 1.3
título *m.* title
tiza *f.* chalk 1.2
toalla *f.* towel 1.7
todavía *adv.* yet; still 1.5

todo *m.* everything 1.5
  Todo está bajo control. Everything is under control. 1.7
todo(s)/a(s) *adj.* all; whole 1.4
todos *m., pl.* all of us; everybody; everyone
tomar *v.* to take; to drink 1.2
  tomar clases to take classes 1.2
  tomar el sol to sunbathe 1.4
  tomar en cuenta to take into account
  tomar fotos to take photos 1.5
tomate *m.* tomato 1.8
tonto/a *adj.* silly; foolish 1.3
tortilla *f.* tortilla 1.8
  tortilla de maíz corn tortilla 1.8
tostado/a *adj.* toasted 1.8
trabajador(a) *adj.* hard-working 1.3
trabajar *v.* to work 1.2
traducir *v.* to translate 1.6
traer *v.* to bring 1.4
traje *m.* suit 1.6
  traje de baño *m.* bathing suit 1.6
tranquilo/a *adj.* calm
  Tranquilo. Relax. 1.7
trece *n., adj.* thirteen 1.1
treinta *n., adj.* thirty 1.1, 1.2
  y treinta thirty minutes past the hour (*time*) 1.1
tren *m.* train 1.5
tres *n., adj.* three 1.1
trescientos/as *n., adj.* three hundred 1.2
trimestre *m.* trimester; quarter 1.2
triste *adj.* sad 1.5
tú *fam. sub. pron.* you 1.1
  Tú eres... You are... 1.1
tu(s) *fam. poss. adj.* your 1.3
turismo *m.* tourism 1.5
turista *m., f.* tourist 1.1
turístico/a *adj.* touristic

U

Ud. *form. sing.* you 1.1
Uds. *form., pl.* you 1.1
último/a *adj.* last
un, uno/a *indef. art.* a, an; one 1.1
  uno/a *m., f., sing. pron.* one 1.1
  a la una at one o'clock 1.1
  una vez *adv.* once; one time 1.6
  una vez más one more time 1.9
unos/as *m., f., pl. indef. art.* some; *pron.* some 1.1

único/a *adj.* only 1.3
universidad *f.* university; college 1.2
usar *v.* to wear; to use 1.6
usted (Ud.) *form. sing.* you 1.1
  ustedes (Uds.) *form., pl.* you 1.1
útil *adj.* useful
uva *f.* grape 1.8

V

vacaciones *f. pl.* vacation 1.5
vamos let's go 1.4
varios/as *adj., pl.* various; several 1.8
veces *f., pl.* times 1.6
veinte *n., adj.* twenty 1.1
veinticinco *n., adj.* twenty-five 1.1
veinticuatro *n., adj.* twenty-four 1.1
veintidós *n., adj.* twenty-two 1.1
veintinueve *n., adj.* twenty-nine 1.1
veintiocho *n., adj.* twenty-eight 1.1
veintiséis *n., adj.* twenty-six 1.1
veintisiete *n., adj.* twenty-seven 1.1
veintitrés *n., adj.* twenty-three 1.1
veintiún, veintiuno/a *n., adj.* twenty-one 1.1
vejez *f.* old age 1.9
vendedor(a) *m., f.* salesperson 1.6
vender *v.* to sell 1.6
venir *v.* to come 1.3
ventana *f.* window 1.2
ver *v.* to see 1.4
  a ver let's see 1.2
  ver películas to see movies 1.4
verano *m.* summer 1.5
verbo *m.* verb
verdad *f.* truth
  ¿verdad? right? 1.1
verde *adj.* green 1.3
verduras *f., pl.* vegetables 1.8
vestido *m.* dress 1.6
vestirse (e:i) *v.* to get dressed 1.7
vez *f.* time 1.6
viajar *v.* to travel 1.2
viaje *m.* trip 1.5
viajero/a *m., f.* traveler 1.5
vida *f.* life 1.9
video *m.* video 1.1
videojuego *m.* video game 1.4
viejo/a *adj.* old 1.3
viento *m.* wind 1.5
viernes *m., sing.* Friday 1.2

vinagre *m.* vinegar 1.8
vino *m.* wine 1.8
  vino blanco *m.* white wine 1.8
  vino tinto *m.* red wine 1.8
visitar *v.* to visit 1.4
  visitar monumentos to visit monuments 1.4
viudo/a *adj.* widower; widow 1.9
vivir *v.* to live 1.3
vivo/a *adj.* bright; lively; living
vóleibol *m.* volleyball 1.4
volver (o:ue) *v.* to return 1.4
vos *pron.* you
vosotros/as *pron., form., pl.* you 1.1
vuelta *f.* return trip
vuestro(s)/a(s) *form., poss. adj.* your 1.3

W

walkman *m.* walkman

Y

y *conj.* and 1.1
  y cuarto quarter after (*time*) 1.1
  y media half-past (*time*) 1.1
  y quince quarter after (*time*) 1.1
  y treinta thirty (minutes past the hour) 1.1
  ¿Y tú? *fam.* And you? 1.1
  ¿Y usted? *form.* And you? 1.1
ya *adv.* already 1.6
yerno *m.* son-in-law 1.3
yo *sub. pron.* I 1.1
  Yo soy... I'm... 1.1
yogur *m.* yogurt 1.8

Z

zanahoria *f.* carrot 1.8
zapatos *m., pl.* shoes
  zapatos de tenis tennis shoes, sneakers 1.6

English-Spanish

A

a un, uno/a *m., f., sing.; indef. art.* 1.1
A.M. mañana *f.* 1.1
able: be able to poder (o:ue) *v.* 1.4
aboard a bordo 1.1
accounting contabilidad *f.* 1.2
acquainted: be acquainted with conocer *v.* 1.6
additional adicional *adj.*
adjective adjetivo *m.*
adolescence adolescencia *f.* 1.9
advice consejo *m.* 1.6
 give advice dar consejos 1.6
affirmative afirmativo/a *adj.*
afraid: be (very) afraid (of) tener (mucho) miedo (de) 1.3
 be afraid that tener miedo (de) que
after después de *prep.* 1.7
afternoon tarde *f.* 1.1
afterward después *adv.* 1.7
again *adv.* otra vez
age edad *f.* 1.9
agree concordar (o:ue) *v.*
airplane avión *m.* 1.5
airport aeropuerto *m.* 1.5
alarm clock despertador *m.* 1.7
all todo(s)/a(s) *adj.* 1.4
 all of us todos 1.1
 all over the world en todo el mundo
alleviate aliviar *v.*
alone solo/a *adj.*
already ya *adv.* 1.6
also también *adv.* 1.2; 1.7
although *conj.* aunque
always siempre *adv.* 1.7
American (North) norteamericano/a *adj.* 1.3
among entre *prep.* 1.2
amusement diversión *f.*
and y 1.1, e (before words beginning with *i* or *hi*) 1.4
 And you? ¿Y tú? *fam.* 1.1; ¿Y usted? *form.* 1.1
angry enojado/a *adj.* 1.5
 get angry (with) enojarse *v.* (con) 1.7
anniversary aniversario *m.* 1.9
 (wedding) anniversary aniversario *m.* (de bodas) 1.9
annoy molestar *v.* 1.7
another otro/a *adj.* 1.6
answer contestar *v.* 1.2; respuesta *f.*
any algún, alguno/a(s) *adj.* 1.7
anyone alguien *pron.* 1.7
anything algo *pron.* 1.7
appear parecer *v.*
appetizers entremeses *m., pl.* 1.8
apple manzana *f.* 1.8
appointment cita *f.* 1.9
 have an appointment tener *v.* una cita 1.9
April abril *m.* 1.5
aquatic acuático/a *adj.* 1.4
archaeology arqueología *f.* 1.2
Argentina Argentina *f.* 1.1
Argentine argentino/a *adj.* 1.3
arrival llegada *f.* 1.5
arrive llegar *v.* 1.2
art arte *m.* 1.2
artist artista *m., f.* 1.3
as como 1.8
 as... as tan... como 1.8
 as many... as tantos/as... como 1.8
 as much... as tanto... como 1.8
ask (a question) preguntar *v.* 1.2
ask for pedir (e:i) *v.* 1.4
asparagus espárragos *m., pl.* 1.8
at a *prep.* 1.1; en *prep.* 1.2
 at + *time* a la(s) + *time* 1.1
 at home en casa 1.7
 at night por la noche 1.7
 At what time...? ¿A qué hora...? 1.1
attend asistir (a) *v.* 1.3
attract atraer *v.* 1.4
August agosto *m.* 1.5
aunt tía *f.* 1.3
 aunts and uncles tíos *m., pl.* 1.3
automatic automático/a *adj.*
automobile automóvil *m.* 1.5
autumn otoño *m.* 1.5
avenue avenida *f.*

B

backpack mochila *f.* 1.2
bad mal, malo/a *adj.* 1.3
 It's not at all bad. No está nada mal. 1.5
bag bolsa *f.* 1.6
ball pelota *f.* 1.4
banana banana *f.* 1.8
bargain ganga *f.* 1.6; regatear *v.* 1.6
baseball (*game*) béisbol *m.* 1.4
basketball (*game*) baloncesto *m.* 1.4
bathe bañarse *v.* 1.7
bathing suit traje *m.* de baño 1.6
bathroom baño *m.* 1.7; cuarto de baño 1.7
be ser *v.* 1.1; estar *v.* 1.2
 be... years old tener... años 1.3
beach playa *f.* 1.5
beans frijoles *m., pl.* 1.8
beautiful hermoso/a *adj.* 1.6
because porque *conj.* 1.2
become (+ *adj.*) ponerse (+ *adj.*) 1.7; convertirse (e:ie) *v.*
bed cama *f.* 1.5
 go to bed acostarse (o:ue) *v.* 1.7
beef carne de res *f.* 1.8
before antes *adv.* 1.7; antes de *prep.* 1.7
begin comenzar (e:ie) *v.* 1.4; empezar (e:ie) *v.* 1.4
behind detrás de *prep.* 1.2
believe (in) creer *v.* (en) 1.3
bellhop botones *m., f. sing.* 1.5
below debajo de *prep.* 1.2
belt cinturón *m.* 1.6
beside al lado de *prep.* 1.2
best mejor *adj.*
 the best el/la mejor *adj.* 1.8
better mejor *adj.* 1.8
between entre *prep.* 1.2
bicycle bicicleta *f.* 1.4
big gran, grande *adj.* 1.3
bill cuenta *f.* 1.9
billion *m.* mil millones
biology biología *f.* 1.2
birth nacimiento *m.* 1.9
birthday cumpleaños *m., sing.* 1.9
 have a birthday cumplir *v.* años 1.9
biscuit bizcocho *m.*
black negro/a *adj.* 1.3
blackberry mora *f.* 1.8
blackboard pizarra *f.* 1.2
blond(e) rubio/a *adj.* 1.3
blouse blusa *f.* 1.6
blue azul *adj.* 1.3
boardinghouse pensión *f.*
boat barco *m.* 1.5
book libro *m.* 1.2
bookstore librería *f.* 1.2
boot bota *f.* 1.6
bore aburrir *v.* 1.7
bored aburrido/a *adj.* 1.5
 be bored estar *v.* aburrido/a 1.5
boring aburrido/a *adj.* 1.5
born: be born nacer *v.* 1.9
borrowed prestado/a *adj.*
bother molestar *v.* 1.7
bottle botella *f.* 1.9
bottom fondo *m.*
boulevard bulevar *m.*
boy chico *m.* 1.1; muchacho *m.* 1.3
boyfriend novio *m.* 1.3
brakes frenos *m., pl.*
bread pan *m.* 1.8
break up (with) romper *v.* (con) 1.9
breakfast desayuno *m.* 1.2, 1.8
 have breakfast desayunar *v.* 1.2
bring traer *v.* 1.4

Vocabulario

English-Spanish

brochure **folleto** m.
brother **hermano** m. 1.3
  brothers and sisters **hermanos** m., pl. 1.3
brother-in-law **cuñado** m. 1.3
brown **café** adj. 1.6; **marrón** adj. 1.6
brunet(te) **moreno/a** adj. 1.3
brush **cepillar** v. 1.7
  brush one's hair **cepillarse el pelo** 1.7
  brush one's teeth **cepillarse los dientes** 1.7
build **construir** v. 1.4
bus **autobús** m. 1.1
  bus station **estación** f. **de autobuses** 1.5
business administration **administración** f. **de empresas** 1.2
busy **ocupado/a** adj. 1.5
but **pero** conj. 1.2; (rather) **sino** conj. (in negative sentences) 1.7
butter **mantequilla** f. 1.8
buy **comprar** v. 1.2
by plane **en avión** 1.5
bye **chau** interj. fam. 1.1

C

café **café** m. 1.4
cafeteria **cafetería** f. 1.2
cake **pastel** m. 1.9
  chocolate cake **pastel de chocolate** m. 1.9
calculator **calculadora** f. 1.2
call **llamar** v.
  call on the phone **llamar por teléfono**
  be called **llamarse** v. 1.7
camp **acampar** v. 1.5
can **poder (o:ue)** v. 1.4
Canadian **canadiense** adj. 1.3
candy **dulces** m., pl. 1.9
capital city **capital** f. 1.1
car **auto(móvil)** m. 1.5
caramel **caramelo** m. 1.9
card **tarjeta** f.;
  (playing) **carta** f. 1.5
care **cuidado** m. 1.3
careful: be (very) careful **tener** v. **(mucho) cuidado** 1.3
carrot **zanahoria** f. 1.8
carry **llevar** v. 1.2
cash **(en) efectivo** 1.6
cash register **caja** f. 1.6
cashier **cajero/a** m., f.
celebrate **celebrar** v. 1.9
celebration **celebración** f.
  young woman's fifteenth birthday celebration **quinceañera** f. 1.9
cereal **cereales** m., pl. 1.8
chalk **tiza** f. 1.2
champagne **champán** m. 1.9

change **cambiar** v. **(de)** 1.9
chat **conversar** v. 1.2
chauffeur **conductor(a)** m., f. 1.1
cheap **barato/a** adj. 1.6
cheese **queso** m. 1.8
chemistry **química** f. 1.2
chicken **pollo** m. 1.8
child **niño/a** m., f. 1.3
childhood **niñez** f. 1.9
children **hijos** m., pl. 1.3
Chinese **chino/a** adj. 1.3
chocolate **chocolate** m. 1.9
  chocolate cake **pastel** m. **de chocolate** 1.9
choose **escoger** v. 1.8
chop (food) **chuleta** f. 1.8
Christmas **Navidad** f. 1.9
church **iglesia** f. 1.4
city **ciudad** f. 1.4
class **clase** f. 1.2
  take classes **tomar clases** 1.2
classmate **compañero/a** m., f. **de clase** 1.2
clean **limpio/a** adj. 1.5
clear (weather) **despejado/a** adj.
  It's (very) clear. (weather) **Está (muy) despejado.**
clerk **dependiente/a** m., f. 1.6
climb **escalar** v. 1.4
  climb mountains **escalar montañas** 1.4
clock **reloj** m. 1.2
close **cerrar (e:ie)** v. 1.4
closed **cerrado/a** adj. 1.5
clothes **ropa** f. 1.6
clothing **ropa** f. 1.6
cloudy **nublado/a** adj. 1.5
  It's (very) cloudy. **Está (muy) nublado.** 1.5
coat **abrigo** m. 1.6
coffee **café** m. 1.8
cold **frío** m. 1.5;
  be (feel) (very) cold **tener (mucho) frío** 1.3
  It's (very) cold. (weather) **Hace (mucho) frío.** 1.5
college **universidad** f. 1.2
color **color** m. 1.3, 1.6
comb one's hair **peinarse** v. 1.7
come **venir** v. 1.3
comfortable **cómodo/a** adj. 1.5
community **comunidad** f. 1.1
comparison **comparación** f.
computer **computadora** f. 1.1
  computer disc **disco** m.
  computer programmer **programador(a)** m., f. 1.3
  computer science **computación** f. 1.2
confirm **confirmar** v. 1.5
  confirm a reservation **confirmar una reservación** 1.5
confused **confundido/a** adj. 1.5
Congratulations! **¡Felicidades!; ¡Felicitaciones!** f. pl. 1.9
contamination **contaminación** f.

content **contento/a** adj. 1.5
continue **seguir (e:i)** v. 1.4
control **control** m.
  be under control **estar bajo control** 1.7
conversation **conversación** f. 1.1
converse **conversar** v. 1.2
cookie **galleta** f. 1.9
cool **fresco/a** adj. 1.5
  Be cool. **Tranquilo/a.**
  It's cool. (weather) **Hace fresco.** 1.5
corn **maíz** m. 1.8
cost **costar (o:ue)** v. 1.6
Costa Rica **Costa Rica** f. 1.1
Costa Rican **costarricense** adj. 1.3
cotton **algodón** f. 1.6
  (made of) cotton **de algodón** 1.6
count (on) **contar (o:ue)** v. **(con)** 1.4
country (nation) **país** m. 1.1
countryside **campo** m. 1.5
couple (married) **pareja** f. 1.9
course **curso** m. 1.2; **materia** f. 1.2
courtesy **cortesía** f.
cousin **primo/a** m., f. 1.3
cover **cubrir** v.
covered **cubierto** p.p.
crazy **loco/a** adj. 1.6
create **crear** v.
credit **crédito** m. 1.6
  credit card **tarjeta** f. **de crédito** 1.6
Cuba **Cuba** f. 1.1
Cuban **cubano/a** adj. 1.3
culture **cultura** f. 1.2
currency exchange **cambio** m. **de moneda**
custard (baked) **flan** m. 1.9
custom **costumbre** f. 1.1
customer **cliente/a** m., f. 1.6
customs **aduana** f. 1.5
  customs inspector **inspector(a)** m., f. **de aduanas** 1.5
cycling **ciclismo** m. 1.4

D

dad **papá** m. 1.3
daily **diario/a** adj. 1.7
  daily routine **rutina** f. **diaria** 1.7
dance **bailar** v. 1.2
date (appointment) **cita** f. 1.9;
  (calendar) **fecha** f. 1.5;
  (someone) **salir** v. **con (alguien)** 1.9
  have a date **tener una cita** 1.9
daughter **hija** f. 1.3
daughter-in-law **nuera** f. 1.3
day **día** m. 1.1

Vocabulario — English-Spanish

day before yesterday **anteayer** *adv.* 1.6
death **muerte** *f.* 1.9
December **diciembre** *m.* 1.5
decide **decidir** *v.* (+ *inf.*) 1.3
delicious **delicioso/a** *adj.* 1.8; **rico/a** *adj.* 1.8; **sabroso/a** *adj.* 1.8
delighted **encantado/a** *adj.* 1.1
department store **almacén** *m.* 1.6
departure **salida** *f.* 1.5
describe **describir** *v.* 1.3
design **diseño** *m.*
desire **desear** *v.* 1.2
desk **escritorio** *m.* 1.2
dessert **postre** *m.* 1.9
diary **diario** *m.* 1.1
dictionary **diccionario** *m.* 1.1
die **morir (o:ue)** *v.* 1.8
difficult **difícil** *adj.* 1.3
dinner **cena** *f.* 1.2, 1.8
  have dinner **cenar** *v.* 1.2
dirty **ensuciar** *v.*; **sucio/a** *adj.* 1.5
disagree **no estar de acuerdo**
dish **plato** *m.* 1.8
  main dish *m.* **plato principal** 1.8
disk **disco** *m.*
disorderly **desordenado/a** *adj.* 1.5
dive **bucear** *v.* 1.4
divorce **divorcio** *m.* 1.9
divorced **divorciado/a** *adj.* 1.9
  get divorced (from) **divorciarse** *v.* (**de**) 1.9
do **hacer** *v.* 1.4
  (I) don't want to. **No quiero.** 1.4
doctor **doctor(a)** *m., f.* 1.3; **médico/a** *m., f.* 1.3
domestic **doméstico/a** *adj.*
  domestic appliance **electrodoméstico** *m.*
door **puerta** *f.* 1.2
dormitory **residencia** *f.* **estudiantil** 1.2
double **doble** *adj.* 1.5
  double room **habitación** *f.* **doble** 1.5
downtown **centro** *m.* 1.4
draw **dibujar** *v.* 1.2
dress **vestido** *m.* 1.6
  get dressed **vestirse (e:i)** *v.* 1.7
drink **beber** *v.* 1.3; **tomar** *v.* 1.2
  bebida *f.* 1.8
drive **conducir** *v.* 1.6
driver **conductor(a)** *m., f.* 1.1
dry oneself **secarse** *v.* 1.7
during **durante** *prep.* 1.7

E

each **cada** *adj.* 1.6
eagle **águila** *f.*
early **temprano** *adv.* 1.7
ease **aliviar** *v.*
easy **fácil** *adj.* 1.3
eat **comer** *v.* 1.3
economics **economía** *f.* 1.2
Ecuador **Ecuador** *m.* 1.1
Ecuadorian **ecuatoriano/a** *adj.* 1.3
effective **eficaz** *adj.*
egg **huevo** *m.* 1.8
eight **ocho** *n., adj.* 1.1
eight hundred **ochocientos/as** *n., adj.* 1.2
eighteen **dieciocho** *n., adj.* 1.1
eighth **octavo/a** *adj.* 1.5
eighty **ochenta** *n., adj.* 1.2
either... or **o... o** *conj.* 1.7
eldest **el/la mayor** *adj.* 1.8
elegant **elegante** *adj.* 1.6
elevator **ascensor** *m.* 1.5
eleven **once** *n., adj.* 1.1
e-mail **correo** *m.* **electrónico** 1.4
  e-mail message **mensaje** *m.* **electrónico** 1.4
  read e-mail **leer** *v.* **el correo electrónico** 1.4
embarrassed **avergonzado/a** *adj.* 1.5
employee **empleado/a** *m., f.* 1.5
end **fin** *m.* 1.4; **terminar** *v.* 1.2
engaged: get engaged (to) **comprometerse** *v.* (**con**) 1.9
engineer **ingeniero/a** *m., f.* 1.3
English (*language*) **inglés** *m.* 1.2; **inglés, inglesa** *adj.* 1.3
entertainment **diversión** *f.* 1.4
eraser **borrador** *m.* 1.2
establish **establecer** *v.*
evening **tarde** *f.* 1.1
everybody **todos** *m., pl.*
everything **todo** *m.* 1.5
  Everything is under control. **Todo está bajo control.** 1.7
exactly **en punto** 1.1
exam **examen** *m.* 1.2
excellent **excelente** *adj.* 1.5
exciting **emocionante** *adj.*
excursion **excursión** *f.*
excuse **disculpar** *v.*
  Excuse me. (*May I?*) **Con permiso.** 1.1; (*I beg your pardon.*) **Perdón.** 1.1
exit **salida** *f.* 1.5
expensive **caro/a** *adj.* 1.6
explain **explicar** *v.* 1.2
explore **explorar** *v.*
expression **expresión** *f.*
extremely delicious **riquísimo/a** *adj.* 1.8

F

fabulous **fabuloso/a** *adj.* 1.5
face **cara** *f.* 1.7
fact: in fact **de hecho**
fall (*season*) **otoño** *m.* 1.5
fall: fall asleep **dormirse (o:ue)** *v.* 1.7
  fall in love (with) **enamorarse** *v.* (**de**) 1.9
family **familia** *f.* 1.3
fan **aficionado/a** *adj.* 1.4
  be a fan (of) **ser aficionado/a (a)** 1.4
far from **lejos de** *prep.* 1.2
farewell **despedida** *f.* 1.1
fascinate **fascinar** *v.* 1.7
fashion **moda** *f.* 1.6
  be in fashion **estar de moda** 1.6
fast **rápido/a** *adj.*
fat **gordo/a** *adj.* 1.3
father **padre** *m.* 1.3
father-in-law **suegro** *m.* 1.3
favorite **favorito/a** *adj.* 1.4
fear **miedo** *m.* 1.3
February **febrero** *m.* 1.5
feel **sentir(se) (e:ie)** *v.* 1.7
  feel like (*doing something*) **tener ganas de** (+ *inf.*) 1.3
few **pocos/as** *adj., pl.*
fewer than **menos de** (+ *number*) 1.8
field: major field of study **especialización** *f.*
fifteen *n., adj.* **quince** 1.1
  fifteen-year-old girl **quinceañera** *f.* 1.9
  young woman celebrating her fifteenth birthday **quinceañera** *f.* 1.9
fifth **quinto/a** *n., adj.* 1.5
fifty **cincuenta** *n., adj.* 1.2
figure (*number*) **cifra** *f.*
finally **por último** 1.7
find **encontrar (o:ue)** *v.* 1.4
  find (each other) **encontrar(se)** *v.*
fine **multa** *f.*
finish **terminar** *v.* 1.2
  finish (*doing something*) **terminar** *v.* **de** (+ *inf.*) 1.4
first **primer, primero/a** *n., adj.* 1.5
fish (*food*) **pescado** *m.* 1.8
fisherman **pescador** *m.*
fisherwoman **pescadora** *f.*
fishing **pesca** *f.* 1.5
fit (*clothing*) **quedar** *v.* 1.7
five **cinco** *n., adj.* 1.1
five hundred **quinientos/as** *n., adj.* 1.2
fixed **fijo/a** *adj.* 1.6
flag **bandera** *f.*
flank steak **lomo** *m.* 1.8

Vocabulario

English-Spanish

floor (*of a building*) **piso** *m.* 1.5
  ground floor **planta** *f.* **baja** 1.5
  top floor **planta** *f.* **alta**
fog **niebla** *f.*
follow **seguir (e:i)** *v.* 1.4
food **comida** *f.* 1.8; **alimento** *m.*
foolish **tonto/a** *adj.* 1.3
football **fútbol** *m.* **americano** 1.4
for me **para mí** 1.8
forbid **prohibir** *v.*
foreign languages **lenguas** *f. pl.* **extranjeras** 1.2
forty **cuarenta** *n., adj.* 1.2
four **cuatro** *n., adj.* 1.1
four hundred **cuatrocientos/as** *n., adj.*
fourteen **catorce** *n., adj.* 1.1
fourth **cuarto/a** *n., adj.* 1.5
free **libre** *adj.* 1.4
  free time **tiempo libre**; **ratos libres** 1.4
French **francés, francesa** *adj.* 1.3
French fries **papas** *f., pl.* **fritas** 1.8; **patatas** *f., pl.* **fritas** 1.8
Friday **viernes** *m., sing.* 1.2
fried **frito/a** *adj.* 1.8
  fried potatoes **papas** *f., pl.* **fritas** 1.8; **patatas** *f., pl.* **fritas** 1.8
friend **amigo/a** *m., f.* 1.3
friendly **amable** *adj.* 1.5
friendship **amistad** *f.* 1.9
from **de** *prep.* 1.1; **desde** *prep.* 1.6
  from the United States **estadounidense** *adj.* 1.3
  He/She/It is from... **Es de....** 1.1
  I'm from... **Soy de...** 1.1
fruit **fruta** *f.* 1.8
  fruit juice **jugo** *m.* **de fruta** 1.8
fun **divertido/a** *adj.* 1.7
  fun activity **diversión** *f.* 1.4
  have fun **divertirse (e:ie)** *v.* 1.9
function **funcionar** *v.*

G

game **juego** *m.*; (*match*) **partido** *m.* 1.4
garlic **ajo** *m.* 1.8
geography **geografía** *f.* 1.2
German **alemán, alemana** *adj.* 1.3
get **conseguir (e:i)** *v.* 1.4
  get along well/badly (with) **llevarse bien/mal (con)** 1.9
  get up **levantarse** *v.* 1.7
gift **regalo** *m.* 1.6
girl **chica** *f.* 1.1; **muchacha** *f.* 1.3
girlfriend **novia** *f.* 1.3
give **dar** *v.* 1.6, 1.9; (*as a gift*) **regalar** 1.9
glasses **gafas** *f., pl.* 1.6
  sunglasses **gafas** *f., pl.* **de sol** 1.6
gloves **guantes** *m., pl.* 1.6
go **ir** *v.* 1.4
  go away **irse** 1.7
  go by boat **ir en barco** 1.5
  go by bus **ir en autobús** 1.5
  go by car **ir en auto(móvil)** 1.5
  go by motorcycle **ir en motocicleta** 1.5
  go by taxi **ir en taxi** 1.5
  go down **bajar(se)** *v.*
  go on a hike (in the mountains) **ir de excursión (a las montañas)** 1.4
  go out **salir** *v.* 1.9
  go out (with) **salir** *v.* (**con**) 1.9
  go up **subir** *v.*
  Let's go. **Vamos.** 1.4
  be going to (*do something*) **ir a** (+ *inf.*) 1.4
golf **golf** *m.* 1.4
good **buen, bueno/a** *adj.* 1.3, 1.6
  Good afternoon. **Buenas tardes.** 1.1
  Good evening. **Buenas noches.** 1.1
  Good idea. **Buena idea.** 1.4
  Good morning. **Buenos días.** 1.1
  Good night. **Buenas noches.** 1.1
good-bye **adiós** *m.* 1.1
  say good-bye (to) **despedirse (e:i) (de)** *v.*
good-looking **guapo/a** *adj.* 1.3
graduate (from/in) **graduarse** *v.* **(de/en)** 1.9
grains **cereales** *m., pl.* 1.8
granddaughter **nieta** *f.* 1.3
grandfather **abuelo** *m.* 1.3
grandmother **abuela** *f.* 1.3
grandparents **abuelos** *m. pl.* 1.3
grandson **nieto** *m.* 1.3
grape **uva** *f.* 1.8
gray **gris** *adj.* 1.6
great **fenomenal** *adj.* 1.5
great-grandfather **bisabuelo** *m.* 1.3
great-grandmother **bisabuela** *f.* 1.3
green **verde** *adj.* 1.3
greeting **saludo** *m.* 1.1
  Greetings to... **Saludos a...** 1.1
grilled flank steak **lomo** *m.* **a la plancha** 1.8
ground floor **planta baja** *f.* 1.5
guest (at a house/hotel) **huésped** *m., f.* 1.5; (*invited to a function*) **invitado/a** *m., f.* 1.9
gymnasium **gimnasio** *m.* 1.4

H

hair **pelo** *m.* 1.7
half **medio/a** *adj.* 1.3
  half-past... (*time*) ...**y media** 1.1
half-brother **medio hermano** 1.3
half-sister **media hermana** 1.3
ham **jamón** *m.* 1.8
hamburger **hamburguesa** *f.* 1.8
hand **mano** *f.* 1.1
  Hands up! **¡Manos arriba!**
handsome **guapo/a** *adj.* 1.3
happiness **alegría** *v.* 1.9
happy **alegre** *adj.* 1.5; **contento/a** *adj.* 1.5; **feliz** *adj.* 1.5
  Happy birthday! **¡Feliz cumpleaños!** 1.9
hard **difícil** *adj.* 1.3
hard-working **trabajador(a)** *adj.* 1.3
haste **prisa** *f.* 1.3
hat **sombrero** *m.* 1.6
hate **odiar** *v.* 1.9
have **tener** *v.* 1.3
  Have a good trip! **¡Buen viaje!** 1.1
  have time **tener tiempo** 1.4
  have to (*do something*) **tener que** (+ *inf.*) 1.3; **deber** (+ *inf.*)
he **él** *sub. pron.* 1.1
hear **oír** *v.* 1.4
heat **calor** *m.* 1.5
Hello. **Hola.** 1.1
help **servir (e:i)** *v.* 1.5
her **su(s)** *poss. adj.* 1.3; **la** *f., sing., d.o. pron.* 1.5
  to/for her **le** *f., sing., i.o. pron.* 1.6
here **aquí** *adv.* 1.1
  Here it is. **Aquí está.** 1.5
  Here we are at/in... **Aquí estamos en...**
Hi. **Hola.** 1.1
hike **excursión** *f.* 1.4
  go on a hike **hacer una excursión**; **ir de excursión** 1.4
hiker **excursionista** *m., f.*
hiking **de excursión** 1.4
him **lo** *m., sing., d.o. pron.* 1.5
  to/for him **le** *m., sing., i.o. pron.* 1.6
his **su(s)** *poss. adj.* 1.3
history **historia** *f.* 1.2
hobby **pasatiempo** *m.* 1.4

Vocabulario

English-Spanish

hockey **hockey** m. 1.4
holiday **día** m. **de fiesta** 1.9
home **casa** f. 1.2
homework **tarea** f. 1.2
hope **esperar** v. (+ inf.) 1.2
hors d'oeuvres **entremeses** m., pl. 1.8
horse **caballo** m. 1.5
hot: be (feel) (very) hot **tener (mucho) calor** 1.3
  It's (very) hot **Hace (mucho) calor** 1.5
hotel **hotel** m. 1.5
hour **hora** f. 1.1
house **casa** f. 1.2
How…! **¡Qué…!** 1.3
  how? **¿cómo?** adv. 1.1
  How are you? **¿Qué tal?** 1.1
  How are you? **¿Cómo estás?** fam. 1.1
  How are you? **¿Cómo está usted?** form. 1.1
  How can I help you? **¿En qué puedo servirles?** 1.5
  How is it going? **¿Qué tal?** 1.1
  How is/are…? **¿Qué tal…?** 1.2
  How much/many? **¿Cuánto(s)/a(s)?** 1.1
  How much does… cost? **¿Cuánto cuesta…?** 1.6
  How old are you? **¿Cuántos años tienes?** fam. 1.3
however **sin embargo**
humanities **humanidades** f., pl. 1.2
hundred **cien, ciento** n., adj. 1.2
hunger **hambre** f. 1.3
hungry: be (very) hungry **tener** v. **(mucha) hambre** 1.3
hurry
  be in a (big) hurry **tener** v. **(mucha) prisa** 1.3
husband **esposo** m. 1.3

I

I **Yo** sub. pron. 1.1
  I am… **Yo soy…** 1.1
ice cream **helado** m. 1.9
iced **helado/a** adj. 1.8
  iced tea **té** m. **helado** 1.8
idea **idea** f. 1.4
if **si** conj. 1.4
important **importante** adj. 1.3
  be important to **importar** v. 1.7
in **en** prep. 1.2
  in a bad mood **de mal humor** 1.5
  in a good mood **de buen humor** 1.5
in front of **delante de** prep. 1.2
  in love (with) **enamorado/a (de)** 1.5

in the afternoon **de la tarde** 1.1; **por la tarde** 1.7
in the direction of **para** prep. 1.1
in the early evening **de la tarde** 1.1
in the evening **de la noche** 1.1; **por la tarde** 1.7
in the morning **de la mañana** 1.1; **por la mañana** 1.7
incredible **increíble** adj. 1.5
inside **dentro** adv.
intelligent **inteligente** adj. 1.3
intend to **pensar** v. (+ inf.) 1.4
interest **interesar** v. 1.7
interesting **interesante** adj. 1.3
  be interesting to **interesar** v. 1.7
introduction **presentación** f.
  I would like to introduce you to (name). **Le presento a…** form. 1.1; **Te presento a…** fam. 1.1
invite **invitar** v. 1.9
it **lo/la** sing., d.o., pron. 1.5
  It's me. **Soy yo.** 1.1
Italian **italiano/a** adj. 1.3
its **su(s)** poss. adj. 1.3

J

jacket **chaqueta** f. 1.6
January **enero** m. 1.5
Japanese **japonés, japonesa** adj. 1.3
jeans **(blue)jeans** m., pl. 1.6
jog **correr** v.
journalism **periodismo** m. 1.2
journalist **periodista** m., f. 1.3
joy **alegría** f. 1.9
  give joy **dar** v. **alegría** 1.9
joyful **alegre** adj. 1.5
juice **jugo** m. 1.8
July **julio** m. 1.5
June **junio** m. 1.5
just **apenas** adv.
  have just (done something) **acabar de** (+ inf.) 1.6

K

key **llave** f. 1.5
kind: That's very kind of you. **Muy amable.** 1.5
kiss **beso** m. 1.9
know **saber** v. 1.6; **conocer** v. 1.6
  know how **saber** v. 1.6

L

laboratory **laboratorio** m. 1.2
lack **faltar** v. 1.7
landlord **dueño/a** m., f. 1.8
landscape **paisaje** m. 1.5

language **lengua** f. 1.2
large **grande** adj. 1.3; (clothing size) **talla grande**
last **pasado/a** adj. 1.6; **último/a** adj.
  last name **apellido** m. 1.3
  last night **anoche** adv. 1.6
  last week **semana** f. **pasada** 1.6
  last year **año** m. **pasado** 1.6
late **tarde** adv. 1.7
later (on) **más tarde** 1.7
  See you later. **Hasta la vista.** 1.1; **Hasta luego.** 1.1
laugh **reírse (e:i)** v. 1.9
lazy **perezoso/a** adj.
learn **aprender** v. (a + inf.) 1.3
leave **salir** v. 1.4; **irse** v. 1.7
  leave a tip **dejar una propina** 1.9
  leave for (a place) **salir para**
  leave from **salir de**
left **izquierdo/a** adj. 1.2
  be left over **quedar** v. 1.7
  to the left of **a la izquierda de** 1.2
lemon **limón** m. 1.8
lend **prestar** v. 1.6
less **menos** adv.
  less… than **menos… que** 1.8
  less than **menos de** (+ number) 1.8
lesson **lección** f. 1.1
let's see **a ver** 1.2
letter **carta** f. 1.4
lettuce **lechuga** f. 1.8
library **biblioteca** f. 1.2
lie **mentira** f. 1.4
life **vida** f. 1.9
like **como** prep. 1.8; **gustar** v. 1.2
  Do you like…? **¿Te gusta(n)…?** 1.2
  I don't like them at all. **No me gustan nada.** 1.2
  I like… **Me gusta(n)…** 1.2
  like very much **encantar** v.; **fascinar** v. 1.7
likeable **simpático/a** adj. 1.3
likewise **igualmente** adv. 1.1
line **línea** f.
listen (to) **escuchar** v. 1.2
  Listen! (command) **¡Oye!** fam., sing. 1.1; **¡Oiga/Oigan!** form., sing./pl. 1.1
  listen to music **escuchar música** 1.2
  listen (to) the radio **escuchar la radio** 1.2
literature **literatura** f. 1.2
little (quantity) **poco/a** adj. 1.5
live **vivir** v. 1.3
loan **prestar** v. 1.6
lobster **langosta** f. 1.8

181

Vocabulario — English-Spanish

long **largo/a** *adj.* 1.6
look (at) **mirar** *v.* 1.2
 look for **buscar** *v.* 1.2
lose **perder (e:ie)** *v.* 1.4
lot of, a **mucho/a** *adj.* 1.2, 1.3
love (*another person*) **querer (e:ie)** *v.* 1.4; (*inanimate objects*) **encantar** *v.* 1.7; **amor** *m.* 1.9
 in love **enamorado/a** *adj.* 1.5
luck **suerte** *f.* 1.3
lucky: be (very) lucky **tener (mucha) suerte** 1.3
luggage **equipaje** *m.* 1.5
lunch **almuerzo** *m.* 1.8
 have lunch **almorzar (o:ue)** *v.* 1.4

M

ma'am **señora (Sra.)** *f.* 1.1
mad **enojado/a** *adj.* 1.5
magazine **revista** *f.* 1.4
magnificent **magnífico/a** *adj.* 1.5
main **principal** *adj.* 1.8
major **especialización** *f.* 1.2
make **hacer** *v.* 1.4
makeup **maquillaje** *m.* 1.7
 put on makeup **maquillarse** *v.* 1.7
man **hombre** *m.* 1.1
many **mucho/a** *adj.* 1.3
map **mapa** *m.* 1.2
March **marzo** *m.* 1.5
margarine **margarina** *f.* 1.8
marinated fish **ceviche** *m.* 1.8
 lemon-marinated shrimp **ceviche** *m.* **de camarón** 1.8
marital status **estado** *m.* **civil** 1.9
market **mercado** *m.* 1.6
 open-air market **mercado al aire libre** 1.6
marriage **matrimonio** *m.* 1.9
married **casado/a** *adj.* 1.9
 get married (to) **casarse** *v.* **(con)** 1.9
marvelous **maravilloso/a** *adj.* 1.5
match (*sports*) **partido** *m.* 1.4
 match (with) **hacer** *v.* **juego (con)** 1.6
mathematics **matemáticas** *f., pl.* 1.2
matter **importar** *v.* 1.7
maturity **madurez** *f.* 1.9
May **mayo** *m.* 1.5
maybe **tal vez** *adv.* 1.5; **quizás** *adv.* 1.5
mayonnaise **mayonesa** *f.* 1.8
me **me** *sing., d.o. pron.* 1.5; **mí** *pron., obj. of prep.* 1.9
 to/for me **me** *sing., i.o. pron.* 1.6

meal **comida** *f.* 1.8
meat **carne** *f.* 1.8
medium **mediano/a** *adj.*
meet (*each other*) **conocer(se)** *v.* 1.8
menu **menú** *m.* 1.8
message **mensaje** *m.*
Mexican **mexicano/a** *adj.* 1.3
Mexico **México** *m.* 1.1
middle age **madurez** *f.* 1.9
midnight **medianoche** *f.* 1.1
milk **leche** *f.* 1.8
million **millón** *m.* 1.2
 million of **millón de** *m.* 1.2
mineral water **agua** *f.* **mineral** 1.8
minute **minuto** *m.* 1.1
mirror **espejo** *m.* 1.7
Miss **señorita (Srta.)** *f.* 1.1
miss **perder (e:ie)** *v.* 1.4
mistaken **equivocado/a** *adj.*
modem **módem** *m.*
mom **mamá** *f.* 1.3
Monday **lunes** *m., sing.* 1.2
money **dinero** *m.* 1.6
month **mes** *m.* 1.5
monument **monumento** *m.* 1.4
more **más** 1.2
 more… than **más… que** 1.8
 more than **más de (+** *number***)** 1.8
morning **mañana** *f.* 1.1
mother **madre** *f.* 1.3
mother-in-law **suegra** *f.* 1.3
motor **motor** *m.*
motorcycle **motocicleta** *f.* 1.5
mountain **montaña** *f.* 1.4
movie **película** *f.* 1.4
movie theater **cine** *m.* 1.4
Mr. **señor (Sr.); don** *m.* 1.1
Mrs. **señora (Sra.); doña** *f.* 1.1
much **mucho/a** *adj.* 1.2, 1.3
 very much **muchísimo/a** *adj.* 1.2
municipal **municipal** *adj. m., f.*
museum **museo** *m.* 1.4
mushroom **champiñón** *m.* 1.8
music **música** *f.* 1.2
must **deber** *v.* **(+** *inf.***)** 1.3
 It must be… **Debe ser…** 1.6
my **mi(s)** *poss. adj.* 1.3

N

name **nombre** *m.* 1.1
 be named **llamarse** *v.* 1.7
 in the name of **a nombre de** 1.5
 last name *m.* **apellido**
 My name is… **Me llamo…** 1.1
nationality **nacionalidad** *f.* 1.1
near **cerca de** *prep.* 1.2
need **faltar** *v.* 1.7; **necesitar** *v.* **(+** *inf.***)** 1.2

negative **negativo/a** *adj.*
neither **tampoco** *adv.* 1.7
neither… nor **ni… ni** *conj.* 1.7
nephew **sobrino** *m.* 1.3
nervous **nervioso/a** *adj.* 1.5
never **nunca** *adv.* 1.7; **jamás** *adv.* 1.7
new **nuevo/a** *adj.* 1.6
newlywed **recién casado/a** *m., f.* 1.9
newspaper **periódico** *m.* 1.4
next to **al lado de** *prep.* 1.2
nice **simpático/a** *adj.* 1.3; **amable** *adj.* 1.5
niece **sobrina** *f.* 1.3
night **noche** *f.* 1.1
nine **nueve** *n., adj.* 1.1
nine hundred **novecientos/as** *n., adj.* 1.2
nineteen **diecinueve** *n., adj.* 1.1
ninety **noventa** *n., adj.* 1.2
ninth **noveno/a** *n., adj.* 1.5
no **no** *adv.* 1.1; **ningún, ninguno/a(s)** *adj.* 1.7
 no one **nadie** *pron.* 1.7
 No problem. **No hay problema.** 1.7
nobody **nadie** *pron.* 1.7
none **ningún, ninguno/a(s)** *pron.* 1.7
noon **mediodía** *m.* 1.1
nor **ni** *conj.* 1.7
not **no** 1.1
 not any **ningún, ninguno/a(s)** *adj.* 1.7
 not anyone **nadie** *pron.* 1.7
 not anything **nada** *pron.* 1.7
 not bad at all **nada mal** 1.5
 not either **tampoco** *adv.* 1.7
 not ever **nunca** *adv.* 1.7; **jamás** *adv.* 1.7
 Not very well. **No muy bien.** 1.1
notebook **cuaderno** *m.* 1.1
nothing **nada** *pron.* 1.1; 1.7
noun **sustantivo** *m.*
November **noviembre** *m.* 1.5
now **ahora** *adv.* 1.2
nowadays **hoy día** *adv.*
number **número** *m.* 1.1

O

obtain **conseguir (e:i)** *v.* 1.4
o'clock: It's… o'clock. **Son las…** 1.1
 It's one o'clock. **Es la una.** 1.1
October **octubre** *m.* 1.5
of **de** *prep.* 1.1
offer **ofrecer** *v.* 1.6
Oh! **¡Ay!**
oil **aceite** *m.* 1.8
OK **regular** *adj.* 1.1
 It's okay. **Está bien.**
old **viejo/a** *adj.* 1.3

Vocabulario

English-Spanish

old age **vejez** *f.* 1.9
older **mayor** *adj.* 1.3
   older brother/sister **hermano/a mayor** *m., f.* 1.3
oldest **el/la mayor** *adj.* 1.8
on **en** *prep.* 1.2; **sobre** *prep.* 1.2
   on the dot **en punto** 1.1
   on top of **encima de** 1.2
once **una vez** 1.6
one **un, uno/a** *m., f., sing. pron.* 1.1
   one hundred **cien(to)** *n., adj.* 1.2
   one million **un millón** *m.* 1.2
   one more time **una vez más** 1.9
   one thousand **mil** *n., adj.* 1.2
   one time **una vez** 1.6
onion **cebolla** *f.* 1.8
only **sólo** *adv.* 1.3; **único/a** *adj.* 1.3
   only child **hijo/a único/a** *m., f.* 1.3
open **abierto/a** *adj.* 1.5; **abrir** *v.* 1.3
open-air **al aire libre** 1.6
or **o** *conj.* 1.7
orange **anaranjado/a** *adj.* 1.6; **naranja** *f.* 1.8
order *(food)* **pedir (e:i)** *v.* 1.8
orderly **ordenado/a** *adj.* 1.5
ordinal *(numbers)* **ordinal** *adj.*
other **otro/a** *adj.* 1.6
ought to **deber** *v.* (*+ inf.*) 1.3
our **nuestro(s)/a(s)** *poss. adj.* 1.3
over **sobre** *prep.* 1.2
over there **allá** *adv.* 1.2
owner **dueño/a** *m., f.* 1.8

P

P.M. **tarde** *f.* 1.1
pack (one's suitcases) **hacer** *v.* **las maletas** 1.5
pair **par** *m.* 1.6
   pair of shoes **par de zapatos** *m.* 1.6
pants **pantalones** *m., pl.* 1.6
pantyhose **medias** *f., pl.* 1.6
paper **papel** *m.* 1.2
Pardon me. *(May I?)* **Con permiso.** 1.1; *(Excuse me.)* Pardon me. **Perdón.** 1.1
parents **padres** *m., pl.* 1.3; **papás** *m., pl.* 1.3
park **parque** *m.* 1.4
partner *(one of a married couple)* **pareja** *f.* 1.9
party **fiesta** *f.* 1.9
passed **pasado/a** *adj., p.p.*
passenger **pasajero/a** *m., f.* 1.1
passport **pasaporte** *m.* 1.5
past **pasado/a** *adj.* 1.6
pastime **pasatiempo** *m.* 1.4

pay **pagar** *v.* 1.6
   pay the bill **pagar la cuenta** 1.9
pea **arveja** *m.* 1.8
peach **melocotón** *m.* 1.8
pear **pera** *f.* 1.8
pen **pluma** *f.* 1.2
pencil **lápiz** *m.* 1.1
people **gente** *f.* 1.3
pepper *(black)* **pimienta** *f.* 1.8
perfect **perfecto/a** *adj.* 1.5
perhaps **quizás** *adv.;* **tal vez** *adv.*
permission **permiso** *m.*
person **persona** *f.* 1.3
phenomenal **fenomenal** *adj.* 1.5
photograph **foto(grafía)** *f.* 1.1
physician **doctor(a)** *m., f.,* **médico/a** *m., f.* 1.3
physics **física** *f. sing.* 1.2
pie **pastel** *m.* 1.9
pineapple **piña** *f.* 1.8
pink **rosado/a** *adj.* 1.6
place **lugar** *m.* 1.4; **poner** *v.* 1.4
plaid **de cuadros** 1.6
plans **planes** *m., pl.*
   have plans **tener planes**
play **jugar (u:ue)** *v.* 1.4; *(cards)* **jugar a (las cartas)** 1.5
   play sports **practicar deportes** 1.4
player **jugador(a)** *m., f.* 1.4
pleasant **agradable** *adj.*
please **por favor** 1.1
   Pleased to meet you. **Mucho gusto.** 1.1; **Encantado/a.** *adj.* 1.1
pleasing: be pleasing to **gustar** *v.* 1.2, 1.7
pleasure **gusto** *m.* 1.1
   The pleasure is mine. **El gusto es mío.** 1.1
polka-dotted **de lunares** 1.6
pool **piscina** *f.* 1.4
poor **pobre** *adj.* 1.6
pork **cerdo** *m.* 1.8
   pork chop **chuleta** *f.* **de cerdo** 1.8
possessive **posesivo/a** *adj.* 1.3
postcard **postal** *f.*
potato **papa** *f.* 1.8; **patata** *f.* 1.8
practice **practicar** *v.* 1.2
prefer **preferir (e:ie)** *v.* 1.4
prepare **preparar** *v.* 1.2
preposition **preposición** *f.*
pretty **bonito/a** *adj.* 1.3
price **precio** *m.* 1.6
   (fixed, set) price **precio** *m.* **fijo** 1.6
print **estampado/a** *adj*
private *(room)* **individual** *adj.*
problem **problema** *m.* 1.1
profession **profesión** *f.* 1.3
professor **profesor(a)** *m., f.*
program **programa** *m.* 1.1

programmer **programador(a)** *m., f.* 1.3
pronoun **pronombre** *m.*
psychology **psicología** *f.* 1.2
Puerto Rican **puertorriqueño/a** *adj.* 1.3
Puerto Rico **Puerto Rico** *m.* 1.1
pull a tooth **sacar una muela**
purchases **compras** *f., pl.* 1.5
purple **morado/a** *adj.* 1.6
purse **bolsa** *f.* 1.6
put **poner** *v.* 1.4
   put on *(clothing)* **ponerse** *v.* 1.7
   put on makeup **maquillarse** *v.* 1.7

Q

quality **calidad** *f.* 1.6
quarter **trimestre** *m.* 1.2
   quarter after *(time)* **y cuarto** 1.1; **y quince** 1.1
   quarter to *(time)* **menos cuarto** 1.1; **menos quince** 1.1
question **pregunta** *f.* 1.2
quiz **prueba** *f.* 1.2

R

radio *(medium)* **radio** *f.* 1.2
rain **llover (o:ue)** *v.* 1.5
   It's raining. **Llueve.** 1.5; **Está lloviendo.** 1.5
raincoat **impermeable** *m.* 1.6
read **leer** *v.* 1.3.
   read e-mail **leer correo electrónico** 1.4
   read a magazine **leer una revista** 1.4
   read a newspaper **leer un periódico** 1.4
ready **listo/a** *adj.* 1.5
receive **recibir** *v.* 1.3
recommend **recomendar (e:ie)** *v.* 1.8
recreation **diversión** *f.* 1.4
red **rojo/a** *adj.* 1.3
red-haired **pelirrojo/a** *adj.* 1.3
relatives **parientes** *m., pl.* 1.3
relax **relajarse** *v.* 1.9; **Tranquilo/a.** 1.7
remain **quedarse** *v.* 1.7
remember **acordarse (o:ue)** *v.* **(de)** 1.7; **recordar (o:ue)** *v.* 1.4
repeat **repetir (e:i)** *v.* 1.4
request **pedir (e:i)** *v.* 1.4
reservation **reservación** *f.* 1.5
rest **descansar** *v.* 1.2
restaurant **restaurante** *m.* 1.4
retire *(from work)* **jubilarse** *v.* 1.9
return **regresar** *v.* 1.2; **volver (o:ue)** *v.* 1.4

Vocabulario — English-Spanish

return trip **vuelta** *f.*
rice **arroz** *m.* 1.8
rich **rico/a** *adj.* 1.6
ride: ride a bicycle **pasear** *v.* **en bicicleta** 1.4
  ride a horse **montar** *v.* **a caballo** 1.5
right **derecha** *f.* 1.2
  be right **tener razón** 1.3
  right away **enseguida** *adv.* 1.9
  right now **ahora mismo** 1.5
  to the right of **a la derecha de** 1.2
  right? (*question tag*) **¿no?** 1.1; **¿verdad?** 1.1
road **camino** *m.*
roast **asado/a** *adj.* 1.8
roast chicken **pollo** *m.* **asado** 1.8
rollerblade **patinar en línea** *v.*
room **habitación** *f.* 1.5; **cuarto** *m.* 1.2; 1.7
roommate **compañero/a** *m., f.* **de cuarto** 1.2
roundtrip **de ida y vuelta** 1.5
  roundtrip ticket **pasaje** *m.* **de ida y vuelta** 1.5
routine **rutina** *f.* 1.7
run **correr** *v.* 1.3
Russian **ruso/a** *adj.* 1.3

S

sad **triste** *adj.* 1.5
safe **seguro/a** *adj.* 1.5
sailboard **tabla de windsurf** *f.* 1.5
salad **ensalada** *f.* 1.8
sale **rebaja** *f.* 1.6
salesperson **vendedor(a)** *m., f.* 1.6
salmon **salmón** *m.* 1.8
salt **sal** *f.* 1.8
same **mismo/a** *adj.* 1.3
sandal **sandalia** *f.* 1.6
sandwich **sándwich** *m.* 1.8
Saturday **sábado** *m.* 1.2
sausage **salchicha** *f.* 1.8
say **decir** *v.* 1.4
  say (that) **decir (que)** *v.* 1.4, 1.9
  say the answer **decir la respuesta** 1.4
scared: be (very) scared (of) **tener (mucho) miedo (de)** 1.3
schedule **horario** *m.* 1.2
school **escuela** *f.* 1.1
science *f.* **ciencia** 1.2
scuba dive **bucear** *v.* 1.4
sea **mar** *m.* 1.5
season **estación** *f.* 1.5
seat **silla** *f.* 1.2
second **segundo/a** *n., adj.* 1.5
see **ver** *v.* 1.4
  see movies **ver películas** 1.4
  See you. **Nos vemos.** 1.1
  See you later. **Hasta la vista.** 1.1; **Hasta luego.** 1.1
  See you soon. **Hasta pronto.** 1.1
  See you tomorrow. **Hasta mañana.** 1.1
seem **parecer** *v.* 1.6
sell **vender** *v.* 1.6
semester **semestre** *m.* 1.2
separate (from) **separarse** *v.* **(de)** 1.9
separated **separado/a** *adj.* 1.9
September **septiembre** *m.* 1.5
sequence **secuencia** *f.*
serve **servir (e:i)** *v.* 1.8
set (*fixed*) **fijo/a** *adj.* 1.6
seven **siete** *n., adj.* 1.1
seven hundred **setecientos/as** *n., adj.* 1.2
seventeen **diecisiete** *n., adj.* 1.1
seventh **séptimo/a** *n., adj.* 1.5
seventy **setenta** *n., adj.* 1.2
several **varios/as** *adj. pl.* 1.8
shampoo **champú** *m.* 1.7
share **compartir** *v.* 1.3
sharp (*time*) **en punto** 1.1
shave **afeitarse** *v.* 1.7
shaving cream **crema** *f.* **de afeitar** 1.7
she **ella** *sub. pron.* 1.1
shellfish **mariscos** *m., pl.* 1.8
ship **barco** *m.*
shirt **camisa** *f.* 1.6
shoe **zapato** *m.* 1.6
  shoe size **número** *m.* 1.6
  tennis shoes **zapatos** *m., pl.* **de tenis** 1.6
shop **tienda** *f.* 1.6
shopping: to go shopping **ir de compras** 1.5
shopping mall **centro comercial** *m.* 1.6
short (*in height*) **bajo/a** *adj.* 1.3; (*in length*) **corto/a** *adj.* 1.6
shorts **pantalones cortos** *m., pl.* 1.6
should (*do something*) **deber** *v.* **(+ *inf.*)** 1.3
show **mostrar (o:ue)** *v.* 1.4
shower **ducha** *f.* 1.7; **ducharse** *v.* 1.7
shrimp **camarón** *m.* 1.8
siblings **hermanos/as** *m., f. pl.* 1.3
silk **seda** *f.* 1.6
  (made of) silk **de seda** 1.6
silly **tonto/a** *adj.* 1.3
since **desde** *prep.*
sing **cantar** *v.* 1.2
single **soltero/a** *adj.* 1.9
  single room **habitación** *f.* **individual** 1.5
sink **lavabo** *m.* 1.7
sir **señor (Sr.)** *m.* 1.1
sister **hermana** *f.* 1.3
sister-in-law **cuñada** *f.* 1.3
sit down **sentarse (e:ie)** *v.* 1.7
six **seis** *n., adj.* 1.1
six hundred **seiscientos/as** *n., adj.* 1.2
sixteen **dieciséis** *n., adj.* 1.1
sixth **sexto/a** *n., adj.* 1.5
sixty **sesenta** *n., adj.* 1.2
size **talla** *f.* 1.6
  shoe size **número** *m.* 1.6
skate (in-line) **patinar** *v.* **(en línea)** 1.4
skateboard **andar en patineta** *v.* 1.4
ski **esquiar** *v.* 1.4
skiing **esquí** *m.* 1.4
  waterskiing **esquí** *m.* **acuático** 1.4
skirt **falda** *f.* 1.6
sleep **dormir (o:ue)** *v.* 1.4; **sueño** *m.* 1.3
  go to sleep **dormirse (o:ue)** *v.* 1.7
sleepy: be (very) sleepy **tener (mucho) sueño** 1.3
slender **delgado/a** *adj.* 1.3
slippers **pantuflas** *f.* 1.7
small **pequeño/a** *adj.* 1.3
smart **listo/a** *adj.* 1.5
smile **sonreír (e:i)** *v.* 1.9
smoggy: It's (very) smoggy. **Hay (mucha) contaminación.**
smoke **fumar** *v.* 1.8
smoking section **sección** *f.* **de fumar** 1.8
  nonsmoking section *f.* **sección de no fumar** 1.8
snack **merendar** *v.* 1.8
sneakers **los zapatos de tenis** 1.6
snow **nevar (e:ie)** *v.* 1.5; **nieve** *f.*
snowing: It's snowing. **Nieva.** 1.5; **Está nevando.** 1.5
so **tan** *adv.* 1.5
  so much **tanto** *adv.*
  so-so **regular** 1.1
soap **jabón** *m.* 1.7
soccer **fútbol** *m.* 1.4
sociology **sociología** *f.* 1.2
sock(s) **calcetín (calcetines)** *m.* 1.6
soft drink **refresco** *m.* 1.8
some **algún, alguno/a(s)** *adj.* 1.7; **unos/as** *pron. m., f. pl.; indef. art.* 1.1
somebody **alguien** *pron.* 1.7
someone **alguien** *pron.* 1.7
something **algo** *pron.* 1.7
son **hijo** *m.* 1.3
son-in-law **yerno** *m.* 1.3
soon **pronto** *adv.*
  See you soon. **Hasta pronto.** 1.1

Vocabulario — English-Spanish

sorry
   I'm sorry. **Lo siento.** 1.4
   I'm so sorry. **Mil perdones.** 1.4; **Lo siento muchísimo.** 1.4
soup **sopa** *f.* 1.8
Spain **España** *f.* 1.1
Spanish (*language*) **español** *m.* 1.2; **español(a)** *adj.* 1.3
spare time **ratos libres** 1.4
speak **hablar** *v.* 1.2
spelling **ortografía** *f.*; **ortográfico/a** *adj.*
spend (*money*) **gastar** *v.* 1.6
sport **deporte** *m.* 1.4
sports-related **deportivo/a** *adj.* 1.4
spouse **esposo/a** *m., f.* 1.3
spring **primavera** *f.* 1.5
square (city or town) **plaza** *f.* 1.4
stadium **estadio** *m.* 1.2
stage **etapa** *f.* 1.9
station **estación** *f.* 1.5
status: marital status **estado civil** 1.9
stay **quedarse** *v.* 1.7
steak **bistec** *m.* 1.8
step **etapa** *f.*
stepbrother **hermanastro** *m.* 1.3
stepdaughter **hijastra** *f.* 1.3
stepfather **padrastro** *m.* 1.3
stepmother **madrastra** *f.* 1.3
stepsister **hermanastra** *f.* 1.3
stepson **hijastro** *m.* 1.3
still **todavía** *adv.* 1.5
stockings **medias** *f., pl.* 1.6
store **tienda** *f.* 1.6
strawberry **frutilla** *f.*; **fresa** *f.*
stripe **raya** *f.* 1.6
   striped **de rayas** 1.6
stroll **pasear** *v.* 1.4
student **estudiante** *m., f.* 1.1, 1.2; **estudiantil** *adj.* 1.2
study **estudiar** *v.* 1.2
stupendous **estupendo/a** *adj.* 1.5
style **estilo** *m.*
subway **metro** *m.* 1.5
   subway station **estación** *f.* **del metro** 1.5
such as **tales como**
suddenly **de repente** *adv.* 1.6
sugar **azúcar** *m.* 1.8
suit **traje** *m.* 1.6
suitcase **maleta** *f.* 1.1
summer **verano** *m.* 1.5
sun **sol** *m.* 1.5
sunbathe **tomar** *v.* **el sol** 1.4
Sunday **domingo** *m.* 1.2
sunglasses **gafas** *f., pl.* **de sol** 1.6
sunny: It's (very) sunny. **Hace (mucho) sol.** 1.5
suppose **suponer** *v.* 1.4
sure **seguro/a** *adj.* 1.5
   be sure **estar seguro/a** 1.5
surfboard **tabla de surf** *f.* 1.5
surprise **sorprender** *v.* 1.9; **sorpresa** *f.* 1.9
sweater **suéter** *m.* 1.6
sweets **dulces** *m., pl.* 1.9
swim **nadar** *v.* 1.4
swimming **natación** *f.* 1.4
swimming pool **piscina** *f.* 1.4

T

table **mesa** *f.* 1.2
take **tomar** *v.* 1.2; **llevar** *v.* 1.6
   take a bath **bañarse** *v.* 1.7
   take (*wear*) a shoe size *v.* **calzar** 1.6
   take a shower **ducharse** *v.* 1.7
   take off **quitarse** *v.* 1.7
   take photos **tomar fotos** 1.5; **sacar fotos** 1.5
talk *v.* **hablar** 1.2
tall **alto/a** *adj.* 1.3
tape (*audio*) **cinta** *f.*
taste **probar (o:ue)** *v.* 1.8; **saber** *v.* 1.8
   taste (like) **saber (a)** 1.8
tasty **rico/a** *adj.* 1.8; **sabroso/a** *adj.* 1.8
taxi **taxi** *m.* 1.5
tea **té** *m.* 1.8
teach **enseñar** *v.* 1.2
teacher **profesor(a)** *m., f.* 1.1, 1.2
team **equipo** *m.* 1.4
television **televisión** *f.* 1.2
tell **contar (o:ue)** *v.* 1.4; **decir** *v.* 1.4
tell (that) **decir** *v.* **(que)** 1.4, 1.9
   tell lies **decir mentiras** 1.4
   tell the truth **decir la verdad** 1.4
ten **diez** *n., adj.* 1.1
tennis **tenis** *m.* 1.4
tennis shoes **zapatos** *m., pl.* **de tenis** 1.6
tent **tienda** *f.* **de campaña**
tenth **décimo/a** *n., adj.* 1.5
terrific **chévere** *adj.*
test **prueba** *f.* 1.2; **examen** *m.* 1.2
Thank you. **Gracias.** 1.1
   Thank you (very much). **(Muchas) gracias.** 1.1
   Thank you very, very much. **Muchísimas gracias.** 1.9
   Thanks (a lot). **(Muchas) gracias.** 1.1
   Thanks again. (*lit. Thanks one more time.*) **Gracias una vez más.** 1.9
   Thanks for everything. **Gracias por todo.** 1.9
that (one) **ése, ésa, eso** *pron.* 1.6; **ese, esa** *adj.* 1.6
that (*over there*) **aquél, aquélla, aquello** *pron.* 1.6; **aquel, aquella** *adj.* 1.6
that's me **soy yo** 1.1
the **el** *m., sing.* **la** *f. sing.* **los** *m., pl.* **las** *f., pl.*
their **su(s)** *poss. adj.* 1.3
them **los/las** *pl., d.o. pron.* 1.5; **ellos/as** *pron., obj. of prep.* 1.9
   to/for them **les** *pl., i.o. pron.* 1.6
then **después** (*afterward*) *adv.* 1.7; **entonces** (*as a result*) *adv.* 1.7; **luego** (*next*) *adv.* 1.7
there **allí** *adv.* 1.2
   There is/are... **Hay...** 1.1
   There is/are not... **No hay...** 1.1
these **éstos, éstas** *pron.* 1.6; **estos, estas** *adj.* 1.6
they **ellos** *m., pron.* **ellas** *f., pron.*
thin **delgado/a** *adj.* 1.3
thing **cosa** *f.* 1.1
think **pensar (e:ie)** *v.* 1.4; (*believe*) **creer** *v.*
   think about **pensar en** *v.* 1.4
third **tercero/a** *n., adj.* 1.5
thirst **sed** *f.* 1.3
thirsty: be (very) thirsty **tener (mucha) sed** 1.3
thirteen **trece** *n., adj.* 1.1
thirty **treinta** *n., adj.* 1.1; 1.2
   thirty minutes past the hour **y treinta; y media** 1.1
this **este, esta** *adj.*; **éste, ésta, esto** *pron.* 1.6
   This is... (*introduction*) **Éste/a es...** 1.1
those **ésos, ésas** *pron.* 1.6; **esos, esas** *adj.* 1.6
those (*over there*) **aquéllos, aquéllas** *pron.* 1.6; **aquellos, aquellas** *adj.* 1.6
thousand **mil** *n., adj.* 1.6
three **tres** *n., adj.* 1.1
three hundred **trescientos/as** *n., adj.* 1.2
Thursday **jueves** *m., sing.* 1.2
thus (*in such a way*) **así** *adj.*
ticket **pasaje** *m.* 1.5
tie **corbata** *f.* 1.6
time **vez** *f.* 1.6; **tiempo** *m.* 1.4
   have a good/bad time **pasarlo bien/mal** 1.9
   What time is it? **¿Qué hora es?** 1.1
   (At) What time...? **¿A qué hora...?** 1.1
times **veces** *f., pl.* 1.6
   two times **dos veces** 1.6
tip **propina** *f.* 1.9
tired **cansado/a** *adj.* 1.5
   be tired **estar cansado/a** 1.5

Vocabulario — English-Spanish

to **a** *prep.* 1.1
toast (*drink*) **brindar** *v.* 1.9
toasted **tostado/a** *adj.* 1.8
   toasted bread **pan tostado** *m.* 1.8
today **hoy** *adv.* 1.2
   Today is… **Hoy es…** 1.2
together **juntos/as** *adj.* 1.9
toilet **inodoro** *m.* 1.7
tomato **tomate** *m.* 1.8
tomorrow **mañana** *f.* 1.1
   See you tomorrow. **Hasta mañana.** 1.1
tonight **esta noche** *adv.* 1.4
too **también** *adv.* 1.2; 1.7
   too much **demasiado** *adv.* 1.6
tooth **diente** *m.* 1.7
toothpaste **pasta** *f.* **de dientes** 1.7
tortilla **tortilla** *f.* 1.8
tour **excursión** *f.* 1.4
   tour an area **recorrer** *v.*
tourism **turismo** *m.* 1.5
tourist **turista** *m., f.* 1.1; **turístico/a** *adj.*
towel **toalla** *f.* 1.7
town **pueblo** *m.* 1.4
train **tren** *m.* 1.5
   train station **estación** *f.* **(de) tren** *m.* 1.5
translate **traducir** *v.* 1.6
travel **viajar** *v.* 1.2
travel agent **agente** *m., f.* **de viajes** 1.5
traveler **viajero/a** *m., f.* 1.5
trillion **billón** *m.*
trimester **trimestre** *m.* 1.2
trip **viaje** *m.* 1.5
   take a trip **hacer un viaje** 1.5
truth **verdad** *f.*
try **intentar** *v.*; **probar (o:ue)** *v.* 1.8
   try on **probarse (o:ue)** *v.* 1.7
t-shirt **camiseta** *f.* 1.6
Tuesday **martes** *m., sing.* 1.2
tuna **atún** *m.* 1.8
turkey **pavo** *m.* 1.8
twelve **doce** *n., adj.* 1.1
twenty **veinte** *n., adj.* 1.1
twenty-eight **veintiocho** *n., adj.* 1.1
twenty-five **veinticinco** *n., adj.* 1.1
twenty-four **veinticuatro** *n., adj.* 1.1
twenty-nine **veintinueve** *n., adj.* 1.1
twenty-one **veintiún, veintiuno/a** *n., adj.* 1.1
twenty-seven **veintisiete** *n., adj.* 1.1
twenty-six **veintiséis** *n., adj.* 1.1
twenty-three **veintitrés** *n., adj.* 1.1
twenty-two **veintidós** *n., adj.* 1.1
twice **dos veces** *adv.* 1.6
twin **gemelo/a** *m., f.* 1.3
two **dos** *n., adj.* 1.1
   two hundred **doscientos/as** *n., adj.* 1.2
   two times **dos veces** *adv.* 1.6

U

ugly **feo/a** *adj.* 1.3
uncle **tío** *m.* 1.3
under **bajo** *adv.* 1.7; **debajo de** *prep.* 1.2
understand **comprender** *v.* 1.3; **entender (e:ie)** *v.* 1.4
underwear **ropa interior** *f.* 1.6
United States **Estados Unidos (EE.UU.)** *m. pl.* 1.1
university **universidad** *f.* 1.2
unmarried **soltero/a** *adj.*
unpleasant **antipático/a** *adj.* 1.3
until **hasta** *prep.* 1.6
us **nos** *pl., d.o. pron.* 1.5
   to/for us **nos** *pl., i.o. pron.* 1.6
use **usar** *v.* 1.6
useful **útil** *adj.*

V

vacation **vacaciones** *f. pl.* 1.5
   be on vacation **estar de vacaciones** 1.5
   go on vacation **ir de vacaciones** 1.5
various **varios/as** *adj., pl.* 1.8
vegetables **verduras** *pl., f.* 1.8
verb **verbo** *m.*
very **muy** *adv.* 1.1
   very much **muchísimo** *adv.* 1.2
   (Very) well, thank you. **(Muy) bien gracias.** 1.1
video **video** *m.* 1.1
video game **videojuego** *m.* 1.4
vinegar **vinagre** *m.* 1.8
visit **visitar** *v.* 1.4
   visit monuments **visitar monumentos** 1.4
volleyball **vóleibol** *m.* 1.4

W

wait (for) **esperar** *v.* (+ *inf.*) 1.2
waiter/waitress **camarero/a** *m., f.* 1.8
wake up **despertarse (e:ie)** *v.* 1.7
walk **caminar** *v.* 1.2
   take a walk **pasear** *v.* 1.4
   walk around **pasear por** 1.4
walkman **walkman** *m.*
wallet **cartera** *f.* 1.6
want **querer (e:ie)** *v.* 1.4
wash **lavar** *v.*
   wash one's face/hands **lavarse la cara/las manos** 1.7
   wash oneself **lavarse** *v.* 1.7
wastebasket **papelera** *f.* 1.2
watch **mirar** *v.* 1.2; **reloj** *m.* 1.2
   watch television **mirar (la) televisión** 1.2
water **agua** *f.* 1.8
waterskiing *m.* **esquí acuático** 1.4
we **nosotros(as)** *m., f. sub. pron.* 1.1
wear **llevar** *v.* 1.6; **usar** *v.* 1.6
weather **tiempo** *m.*
   The weather is bad. **Hace mal tiempo.** 1.5
   The weather is good. **Hace buen tiempo.** 1.5
wedding **boda** *f.* 1.9
Wednesday **miércoles** *m., sing.* 1.2
week **semana** *f.* 1.2
weekend **fin** *m.* **de semana** 1.4
well **pues** *adv.* 1.2; **bueno** *adv.* 1.2
   (Very) well, thanks. **(Muy) bien, gracias.** 1.1
well organized **ordenado/a** *adj.*
what? **¿qué?** *pron.* 1.1
   At what time…? **¿A qué hora…?** 1.1
   What day is it? **¿Qué día es hoy?** 1.2
   What do you guys think? **¿Qué les parece?** 1.9
   What is today's date? **¿Cuál es la fecha de hoy?** 1.5
   What nice clothes! **¡Qué ropa más bonita!** 1.6
   What size do you take? **¿Qué talla lleva (usa)?** 1.6
   What time is it? **¿Qué hora es?** 1.1
   What's going on? **¿Qué pasa?** 1.1
   What's happening? **¿Qué pasa?** 1.1
   What's… like? **¿Cómo es…?** 1.3
   What's new? **¿Qué hay de nuevo?** 1.1
   What's the weather like? **¿Qué tiempo hace?** 1.5
   What's your name? **¿Cómo se llama usted?** *form.* 1.1
   What's your name? **¿Cómo te llamas (tú)?** *fam.* 1.1
when **cuando** *conj.* 1.7
   When? **¿Cuándo?** *adv.* 1.2
where **donde** *prep.*
   where (to)? (*destination*)

Vocabulario

English-Spanish

¿adónde? *adv.* 1.2;
  (*location*)
¿dónde? *adv.* 1.1
Where are you from? **¿De
  dónde eres (tú)?** *fam.* 1.1;
  ¿De dónde es (usted)?
  form. 1.1
Where is…? **¿Dónde
  está…?** 1.2
which? **¿cuál?** *pron.* 1.2; **¿qué?**
  adj. 1.2
  In which…? **¿En qué…?** 1.2
  which one(s)? **¿cuál(es)?** *pron.*
  1.2
white **blanco/a** *adj.* 1.3
  white wine **vino blanco** 1.8
who? **¿quién(es)?** *pron.* 1.1
  Who is…? **¿Quién es…?** 1.1
whole **todo/a** *adj.*
whose **¿de quién(es)?** *pron., adj.*
  1.1
why? **¿por qué?** *adv.* 1.2
widower/widow **viudo/a**
  adj. 1.9
wife **esposa** *f.* 1.3
win **ganar** *v.* 1.4
wind **viento** *m.* 1.5
window **ventana** *f.* 1.2
windy: It's (very) windy. **Hace
  (mucho) viento.** 1.5
wine **vino** *m.* 1.8
  red wine **vino tinto** 1.8
  white wine **vino blanco** 1.8
winter **invierno** *m.* 1.5
wish **desear** *v.* 1.2
with **con** *prep.* 1.2
  with me **conmigo** 1.4; 1.9
  with you **contigo** *fam.* 1.9
without **sin** *prep.* 1.2
woman **mujer** *f.* 1.1
wool **lana** *f.* 1.6
  (made of) wool **de lana** 1.6
word **palabra** *f.* 1.1
work **trabajar** *v.* 1.2
worldwide **mundial** *adj.*
worried (about) **preocupado/a
  (por)** *adj.* 1.5
worry (about) **preocuparse** *v.*
  (por) 1.7
  Don't worry. **No se preocupe.**
    form. 1.7; **No te preocupes.**
    fam. 1.7; **Tranquilo.** *adj.*
worse **peor** *adj.* 1.8
worst **el/la peor** *adj.* **lo peor** *n.*
  1.8
Would you like to…? **¿Te
  gustaría…?** *fam.* 1.4
write **escribir** *v.* 1.3
  write a letter/e-mail message
  **escribir una carta/un
  mensaje electrónico** 1.4
wrong **equivocado/a** *adj.* 1.5
  be wrong **no tener razón** 1.3

X

x-ray **radiografía** *f.*

Y

year **año** *m.* 1.5
  be… years old **tener…
    años** 1.3
yellow **amarillo/a** *adj.* 1.3
yes **sí** *interj.* 1.1
yesterday **ayer** *adv.* 1.6
yet **todavía** *adv.* 1.5
yogurt **yogur** *m.* 1.8
you *sub pron.* **tú** *fam. sing.*,
  usted (Ud.) *form. sing.*,
  vosotros/as *fam. pl.*, **ustedes
  (Uds.)** *form. pl.* 1.1; *d. o.
  pron.* **te** *fam. sing.*, **lo/la** *form.
  sing.*, **os** *fam. pl.*, **los/las** *form.
  pl.* 1.5; *obj. of prep.* **ti** *fam.
  sing.*, **usted (Ud.)** *form. sing.*,
  vosotros/as *fam. pl.*, **ustedes
  (Uds.)** *form. pl.* 1.9
  (to, for) you *i.o. pron.* **te**
    fam. sing., **le** *form. sing.*, **os**
    fam. pl., **les** *form. pl.* 1.6
  You are… **Tú eres…** 1.1
  You're welcome. **De nada.**
    1.1; **No hay de qué.** 1.1
young **joven** *adj., sing.* (**jóvenes**
  pl.) 1.3
  young person **joven** *m., f., sing.*
    (**jóvenes** *pl.*) 1.1
  young woman **señorita
    (Srta.)** *f.*
younger **menor** *adj.* 1.3
  younger brother/sister *m.,
    f.* **hermano/a menor** 1.3
youngest **el/la menor** *m., f.* 1.8
your **su(s)** *poss. adj. form.* 1.3;
  tu(s) *poss. adj. fam. sing.* 1.3;
  vuestro/a(s) *poss. adj. form.
  pl.* 1.3
youth *f.* **juventud** 1.9

Z

zero **cero** *m.* 1.1

MATERIAS	ACADEMIC SUBJECTS
la administración de empresas	business administration
la agronomía	agriculture
el alemán	German
el álgebra	algebra
la antropología	anthropology
la arqueología	archaeology
la arquitectura	architecture
el arte	art
la astronomía	astronomy
la biología	biology
la bioquímica	biochemistry
la botánica	botany
el cálculo	calculus
el chino	Chinese
las ciencias políticas	political science
la computación	computer science
las comunicaciones	communications
la contabilidad	accounting
la danza	dance
el derecho	law
la economía	economics
la educación	education
la educación física	physical education
la enfermería	nursing
el español	Spanish
la filosofía	philosophy
la física	physics
el francés	French
la geografía	geography
la geología	geology
el griego	Greek
el hebreo	Hebrew
la historia	history
la informática	computer science
la ingeniería	engineering
el inglés	English
el italiano	Italian
el japonés	Japanese
el latín	Latin
las lenguas clásicas	classical languages
las lenguas romances	Romance languages
la lingüística	linguistics
la literatura	literature
las matemáticas	mathematics
la medicina	medicine
el mercadeo/ la mercadotecnia	marketing
la música	music
los negocios	business
el periodismo	journalism
el portugués	Portuguese
la psicología	psychology
la química	chemistry
el ruso	Russian
los servicios sociales	social services
la sociología	sociology
el teatro	theater
la trigonometría	trigonometry

LOS ANIMALES	ANIMALS
la abeja	bee
la araña	spider
la ardilla	squirrel
el ave (f.), el pájaro	bird
la ballena	whale
el burro	donkey
la cabra	goat
el caimán	alligator
el camello	camel
la cebra	zebra
el ciervo, el venado	deer
el cochino, el cerdo, el puerco	pig
el cocodrilo	crocodile
el conejo	rabbit
el coyote	coyote
la culebra, la serpiente, la víbora	snake
el elefante	elephant
la foca	seal
la gallina	hen
el gallo	rooster
el gato	cat
el gorila	gorilla
el hipopótamo	hippopotamus
la hormiga	ant
el insecto	insect
la jirafa	giraffe
el lagarto	lizard
el león	lion
el lobo	wolf
el loro, la cotorra, el papagayo, el perico	parrot
la mariposa	butterfly
el mono	monkey
la mosca	fly
el mosquito	mosquito
el oso	bear
la oveja	sheep
el pato	duck
el perro	dog
el pez	fish
la rana	frog
el ratón	mouse
el rinoceronte	rhinoceros
el saltamontes, el chapulín	grasshopper
el tiburón	shark
el tigre	tiger
el toro	bull
la tortuga	turtle
la vaca	cow
el zorro	fox

EL CUERPO HUMANO Y LA SALUD

THE HUMAN BODY AND HEALTH

El cuerpo humano / The human body

la barba	beard
el bigote	mustache
la boca	mouth
el brazo	arm
la cabeza	head
la cadera	hip
la ceja	eyebrow
el cerebro	brain
la cintura	waist
el codo	elbow
el corazón	heart
la costilla	rib
el cráneo	skull
el cuello	neck
el dedo	finger
el dedo del pie	toe
la espalda	back
el estómago	stomach
la frente	forehead
la garganta	throat
el hombro	shoulder
el hueso	bone
el labio	lip
la lengua	tongue
la mandíbula	jaw
la mejilla	cheek
el mentón, la barba, la barbilla	chin
la muñeca	wrist
el músculo	muscle
el muslo	thigh
las nalgas, el trasero, las asentaderas	buttocks
la nariz	nose
el nervio	nerve
el oído	(inner) ear
el ojo	eye
el ombligo	navel, belly button
la oreja	(outer) ear
la pantorrilla	calf
el párpado	eyelid
el pecho	chest
la pestaña	eyelash
el pie	foot
la piel	skin
la pierna	leg
el pulgar	thumb
el pulmón	lung
la rodilla	knee
la sangre	blood
el talón	heel
el tobillo	ankle
el tronco	torso, trunk
la uña	fingernail
la uña del dedo del pie	toenail
la vena	vein

Los cinco sentidos / The five senses

el gusto	taste
el oído	hearing
el olfato	smell
el tacto	touch
la vista	sight

La salud / Health

el accidente	accident
alérgico/a	allergic
el antibiótico	antibiotic
la aspirina	aspirin
el ataque cardiaco, el ataque al corazón	heart attack
el cáncer	cancer
la cápsula	capsule
la clínica	clinic
congestionado/a	congested
el consultorio	doctor's office
la curita	adhesive bandage
el/la dentista	dentist
el/la doctor(a), el/la médico/a	doctor
el dolor (de cabeza)	(head)ache, pain
embarazada	pregnant
la enfermedad	illness, disease
el/la enfermero/a	nurse
enfermo/a	ill, sick
la erupción	rash
el examen médico	physical exam
la farmacia	pharmacy
la fiebre	fever
la fractura	fracture
la gripe	flu
la herida	wound
el hospital	hospital
la infección	infection
el insomnio	insomnia
la inyección	injection
el jarabe	(cough) syrup
mareado/a	dizzy, nauseated
el medicamento	medication
la medicina	medicine
las muletas	crutches
la operación	operation
el/la paciente	patient
el/la paramédico/a	paramedic
la pastilla, la píldora	pill, tablet
los primeros auxilios	first aid
la pulmonía	pneumonia
los puntos	stitches
la quemadura	burn
el quirófano	operating room
la radiografía	x-ray
la receta	prescription
el resfriado	cold (illness)
la sala de emergencia(s)	emergency room
saludable	healthy, healthful
sano/a	healthy
el seguro médico	medical insurance
la silla de ruedas	wheelchair
el síntoma	symptom
el termómetro	thermometer
la tos	cough
la transfusión	transfusion

la vacuna	vaccination	la hoja de actividades	activity sheet
la venda	bandage	el horario de clases	class schedule
el virus	virus	la oración, las oraciones	sentence(s)
		el párrafo	paragraph
cortar(se)	to cut (oneself)	la persona	person
curar	to cure, to treat	presente	present
desmayar(se)	to faint	la prueba	test, quiz
enfermarse	to get sick	siguiente	following
enyesar	to put in a cast	la tarea	homework
estornudar	to sneeze		
guardar cama	to stay in bed	**Expresiones útiles**	**Useful expressions**
hinchar(se)	to swell	Abra(n) su(s) libro(s).	Open your book(s).
internar(se) en el hospital	to check into the hospital	Cambien de papel.	Change roles.
lastimarse (el pie)	to hurt (one's foot)	Cierre(n) su(s) libro(s).	Close your book(s).
mejorar(se)	to get better; to improve	¿Cómo se dice ___ en español?	How do you say ___ in Spanish?
operar	to operate	¿Cómo se escribe ___ en español?	How do you write ___ in Spanish?
quemar(se)	to burn	¿Comprende(n)?	Do you understand?
respirar (hondo)	to breathe (deeply)	(No) comprendo.	I (don't) understand.
romperse (la pierna)	to break (one's leg)	Conteste(n) las preguntas.	Answer the questions.
sangrar	to bleed	Continúe(n), por favor.	Continue, please.
sufrir	to suffer	Escriba(n) su nombre.	Write your name.
tomarle la presión a alguien	to take someone's blood pressure	Escuche(n) el audio.	Listen to the audio.
tomarle el pulso a alguien	to take someone's pulse	Estudie(n) la Lección tres.	Study Lesson three.
torcerse (el tobillo)	to sprain (one's ankle)	Haga(n) la actividad (el ejercicio) número cuatro.	Do activity (exercise) number four.
vendar	to bandage	Lea(n) la oración en voz alta.	Read the sentence aloud.

EXPRESIONES ÚTILES PARA LA CLASE / USEFUL CLASSROOM EXPRESSIONS

Palabras útiles	**Useful words**	Levante(n) la mano.	Raise your hand(s).
ausente	absent	Más despacio, por favor.	Slower, please.
el departamento	department	No sé.	I don't know.
el dictado	dictation	Páse(n)me los exámenes.	Pass me the tests.
la conversación, las conversaciones	conversation(s)	¿Qué significa ___?	What does ___ mean?
la expresión, las expresiones	expression(s)	Repita(n), por favor.	Repeat, please.
		Siénte(n)se, por favor.	Sit down, please.
el examen, los exámenes	test(s), exam(s)	Siga(n) las instrucciones.	Follow the instructions.
la frase	sentence	¿Tiene(n) alguna pregunta?	Do you have any questions?
		Vaya(n) a la página dos.	Go to page two.

COUNTRIES & NATIONALITIES / PAÍSES Y NACIONALIDADES

North America / Norteamérica

Canada	**Canadá**	*canadiense*
Mexico	**México**	*mexicano/a*
United States	**Estados Unidos**	*estadounidense*

Central America / Centroamérica

Belize	**Belice**	*beliceño/a*
Costa Rica	**Costa Rica**	*costarricense*
El Salvador	**El Salvador**	*salvadoreño/a*
Guatemala	**Guatemala**	*guatemalteco/a*
Honduras	**Honduras**	*hondureño/a*
Nicaragua	**Nicaragua**	*nicaragüense*
Panama	**Panamá**	*panameño/a*

The Caribbean / El Caribe

English	Español	Nacionalidad
Cuba	Cuba	*cubano/a*
Dominican Republic	República Dominicana	*dominicano/a*
Haiti	Haití	*haitiano/a*
Puerto Rico	Puerto Rico	*puertorriqueño/a*

South America / Suramérica

English	Español	Nacionalidad
Argentina	Argentina	*argentino/a*
Bolivia	Bolivia	*boliviano/a*
Brazil	Brasil	*brasileño/a*
Chile	Chile	*chileno/a*
Colombia	Colombia	*colombiano/a*
Ecuador	Ecuador	*ecuatoriano/a*
Paraguay	Paraguay	*paraguayo/a*
Peru	Perú	*peruano/a*
Uruguay	Uruguay	*uruguayo/a*
Venezuela	Venezuela	*venezolano/a*

Europe / Europa

English	Español	Nacionalidad
Armenia	Armenia	*armenio/a*
Austria	Austria	*austríaco/a*
Belgium	Bélgica	*belga*
Bosnia	Bosnia	*bosnio/a*
Bulgaria	Bulgaria	*búlgaro/a*
Croatia	Croacia	*croata*
Czech Republic	República Checa	*checo/a*
Denmark	Dinamarca	*danés, danesa*
England	Inglaterra	*inglés, inglesa*
Estonia	Estonia	*estonio/a*
Finland	Finlandia	*finlandés, finlandesa*
France	Francia	*francés, francesa*
Germany	Alemania	*alemán, alemana*
Great Britain (United Kingdom)	Gran Bretaña (Reino Unido)	*británico/a*
Greece	Grecia	*griego/a*
Hungary	Hungría	*húngaro/a*
Iceland	Islandia	*islandés, islandesa*
Ireland	Irlanda	*irlandés, irlandesa*
Italy	Italia	*italiano/a*
Latvia	Letonia	*letón, letona*
Lithuania	Lituania	*lituano/a*
Netherlands (Holland)	Países Bajos (Holanda)	*holandés, holandesa*
Norway	Noruega	*noruego/a*
Poland	Polonia	*polaco/a*
Portugal	Portugal	*portugués, portuguesa*
Romania	Rumania	*rumano/a*
Russia	Rusia	*ruso/a*
Scotland	Escocia	*escocés, escocesa*
Serbia	Serbia	*serbio/a*
Slovakia	Eslovaquia	*eslovaco/a*
Slovenia	Eslovenia	*esloveno/a*
Spain	España	*español(a)*
Sweden	Suecia	*sueco/a*
Switzerland	Suiza	*suizo/a*
Ukraine	Ucrania	*ucraniano/a*
Wales	Gales	*galés, galesa*

Asia / Asia

Bangladesh	Bangladés	*bangladesí*
Cambodia	Camboya	*camboyano/a*
China	China	*chino/a*
India	India	*indio/a*
Indonesia	Indonesia	*indonesio/a*
Iran	Irán	*iraní*
Iraq	Iraq, Irak	*iraquí*

Israel	Israel	*israelí*
Japan	Japón	*japonés, japonesa*
Jordan	Jordania	*jordano/a*
Korea	Corea	*coreano/a*
Kuwait	Kuwait	*kuwaití*
Lebanon	Líbano	*libanés, libanesa*
Malaysia	Malasia	*malasio/a*
Pakistan	Pakistán	*pakistaní*
Russia	Rusia	*ruso/a*
Saudi Arabia	Arabia Saudí	*saudí*
Singapore	Singapur	*singapurés, singapuresa*
Syria	Siria	*sirio/a*
Taiwan	Taiwán	*taiwanés, taiwanesa*
Thailand	Tailandia	*tailandés, tailandesa*
Turkey	Turquía	*turco/a*
Vietnam	Vietnam	*vietnamita*

Africa / África

Algeria	Argelia	*argelino/a*
Angola	Angola	*angoleño/a*
Cameroon	Camerún	*camerunés, camerunesa*
Congo	Congo	*congolés, congolesa*
Egypt	Egipto	*egipcio/a*
Equatorial Guinea	Guinea Ecuatorial	*ecuatoguineano/a*
Ethiopia	Etiopía	*etíope*
Ivory Coast	Costa de Marfil	*marfileño/a*
Kenya	Kenia, Kenya	*keniano/a, keniata*
Libya	Libia	*libio/a*
Mali	Malí	*maliense*
Morocco	Marruecos	*marroquí*
Mozambique	Mozambique	*mozambiqueño/a*
Nigeria	Nigeria	*nigeriano/a*
Rwanda	Ruanda	*ruandés, ruandesa*
Somalia	Somalia	*somalí*
South Africa	Sudáfrica	*sudafricano/a*
Sudan	Sudán	*sudanés, sudanesa*
Tunisia	Tunicia, Túnez	*tunecino/a*
Uganda	Uganda	*ugandés, ugandesa*
Zambia	Zambia	*zambiano/a*
Zimbabwe	Zimbabue	*zimbabuense*

Australia and the Pacific / Australia y el Pacífico

Australia	Australia	*australiano/a*
New Zealand	Nueva Zelanda	*neozelandés, neozelandesa*
Philippines	Filipinas	*filipino/a*

MONEDAS DE LOS PAÍSES HISPANOS / CURRENCIES OF HISPANIC COUNTRIES

País / Country	Moneda / Currency
Argentina	el peso
Bolivia	el boliviano
Chile	el peso
Colombia	el peso
Costa Rica	el colón
Cuba	el peso
Ecuador	el dólar estadounidense
El Salvador	el dólar estadounidense
España	el euro
Guatemala	el quetzal
Guinea Ecuatorial	el franco
Honduras	el lempira
México	el peso
Nicaragua	el córdoba
Panamá	el balboa, el dólar estadounidense
Paraguay	el guaraní
Perú	el nuevo sol
Puerto Rico	el dólar estadounidense
República Dominicana	el peso
Uruguay	el peso
Venezuela	el bolívar

EXPRESIONES Y REFRANES / EXPRESSIONS AND SAYINGS

Expresiones y refranes con partes del cuerpo / Expressions and sayings with parts of the body

A cara o cruz	Heads or tails
A corazón abierto	Open heart
A ojos vistas	Clearly, visibly
Al dedillo	Like the back of one's hand
¡Choca/Vengan esos cinco!	Put it there!/Give me five!
Codo con codo	Side by side
Con las manos en la masa	Red-handed
Costar un ojo de la cara	To cost an arm and a leg
Darle a la lengua	To chatter/To gab
De rodillas	On one's knees
Duro de oído	Hard of hearing
En cuerpo y alma	In body and soul
En la punta de la lengua	On the tip of one's tongue
En un abrir y cerrar de ojos	In a blink of the eye
Entrar por un oído y salir por otro	In one ear and out the other
Estar con el agua al cuello	To be up to one's neck with/in
Estar para chuparse los dedos	To be delicious/To be finger-licking good
Hablar entre dientes	To mutter/To speak under one's breath
Hablar por los codos	To talk a lot/To be a chatterbox
Hacer la vista gorda	To turn a blind eye on something
Hombro con hombro	Shoulder to shoulder
Llorar a lágrima viva	To sob/To cry one's eyes out
Metérsele (a alguien) algo entre ceja y ceja	To get an idea in your head
No pegar ojo	Not to sleep a wink
No tener corazón	Not to have a heart
No tener dos dedos de frente	Not to have an ounce of common sense
Ojos que no ven, corazón que no siente	Out of sight, out of mind
Perder la cabeza	To lose one's head
Quedarse con la boca abierta	To be thunderstruck
Romper el corazón	To break someone's heart
Tener buen/mal corazón	Have a good/bad heart
Tener un nudo en la garganta	Have a knot in your throat
Tomarse algo a pecho	To take something too seriously
Venir como anillo al dedo	To fit like a charm/To suit perfectly

Expresiones y refranes con animales / Expressions and sayings with animals

A caballo regalado no le mires el diente.	Don't look a gift horse in the mouth.
Comer como un cerdo	To eat like a pig
Cuando menos se piensa, salta la liebre.	Things happen when you least expect it.
Llevarse como el perro y el gato	To fight like cats and dogs
Perro ladrador, poco mordedor./Perro que ladra no muerde.	His/her bark is worse than his/her bite.
Por la boca muere el pez.	Talking too much can be dangerous.
Poner el cascabel al gato	To stick one's neck out
Ser una tortuga	To be a slowpoke

Expresiones y refranes con alimentos / Expressions and sayings with food

Agua que no has de beber, déjala correr.	If you're not interested, don't ruin it for everybody else.
Con pan y vino se anda el camino.	Things never seem as bad after a good meal.
Contigo pan y cebolla.	You are all I need.
Dame pan y dime tonto.	I don't care what you say, as long as I get what I want.
Descubrir el pastel	To let the cat out of the bag
Dulce como la miel	Sweet as honey
Estar como agua para chocolate	To furious/To be at the boiling point
Estar en el ajo	To be in the know
Estar en la higuera	To have one's head in the clouds
Estar más claro que el agua	To be clear as a bell
Ganarse el pan	To earn a living/To earn one's daily bread
Llamar al pan, pan y al vino, vino.	Not to mince words.
No hay miel sin hiel.	Every rose has its thorn./There's always a catch.
No sólo de pan vive el hombre.	Man doesn't live by bread alone.
Pan con pan, comida de tontos.	Variety is the spice of life.
Ser agua pasada	To be water under the bridge
Ser más bueno que el pan	To be kindness itself
Temblar como un flan	To shake/tremble like a leaf

Expresiones y refranes con colores / Expressions and sayings with colors

Estar verde	To be inexperienced/wet behind the ears
Poner los ojos en blanco	To roll one's eyes
Ponerle a alguien un ojo morado	To give someone a black eye
Ponerse rojo	To turn red/To blush
Ponerse rojo de ira	To turn red with anger
Ponerse verde de envidia	To be green with envy
Quedarse en blanco	To go blank
Verlo todo de color de rosa	To see the world through rose-colored glasses

Refranes / Sayings

- A buen entendedor, pocas palabras bastan. — A word to the wise is enough.
- Ande o no ande, caballo grande. — Bigger is always better.
- A quien madruga, Dios le ayuda. — The early bird catches the worm.
- Cuídate, que te cuidaré. — Take care of yourself, and then I'll take care of you.
- De tal palo tal astilla. — A chip off the old block.
- Del dicho al hecho hay mucho trecho. — Easier said than done.
- Dime con quién andas y te diré quién eres. — A man is known by the company he keeps.
- El saber no ocupa lugar. — One never knows too much.
- Lo que es moda no incomoda. — You have to suffer in the name of fashion.
- Más vale maña que fuerza. — Brains are better than brawn.
- Más vale prevenir que curar. — Prevention is better than cure.
- Más vale solo que mal acompañado. — Better alone than with people you don't like.
- Más vale tarde que nunca. — Better late than never.
- No es oro todo lo que reluce. — All that glitters is not gold.
- Poderoso caballero es don Dinero. — Money talks.

COMMON FALSE FRIENDS

False friends are Spanish words that look similar to English words but have very different meanings. While recognizing the English relatives of unfamiliar Spanish words you encounter is an important way of constructing meaning, there are some Spanish words whose similarity to English words is deceptive. Here is a list of some of the most common Spanish false friends.

actualmente ≠ actually
actualmente = nowadays, currently
actually = **de hecho, en realidad, en efecto**

argumento ≠ argument
argumento = plot
argument = **discusión, pelea**

armada ≠ army
armada = navy
army = **ejército**

balde ≠ bald
balde = pail, bucket
bald = **calvo/a**

batería ≠ battery
batería = drum set
battery = **pila**

bravo ≠ brave
bravo = wild; fierce
brave = **valiente**

cándido/a ≠ candid
cándido/a = innocent
candid = **sincero/a**

carbón ≠ carbon
carbón = coal
carbon = **carbono**

casual ≠ casual
casual = accidental, chance
casual = **informal, despreocupado/a**

casualidad ≠ casualty
casualidad = chance, coincidence
casualty = **víctima**

colegio ≠ college
colegio = school
college = **universidad**

collar ≠ collar (of a shirt)
collar = necklace
collar = **cuello (de camisa)**

comprensivo/a ≠ comprehensive
comprensivo/a = understanding
comprehensive = **completo, extensivo**

constipado ≠ constipated
estar constipado/a = to have a cold
to be constipated = **estar estreñido/a**

crudo/a ≠ crude
crudo/a = raw, undercooked
crude = **burdo/a, grosero/a**

divertir ≠ to divert
divertirse = to enjoy oneself
to divert = **desviar**

educado/a ≠ educated
educado/a = well-mannered
educated = **culto/a, instruido/a**

embarazada ≠ embarrassed
estar embarazada = to be pregnant
to be embarrassed = **estar avergonzado/a; dar/tener vergüenza**

eventualmente ≠ eventually
eventualmente = possibly
eventually = **finalmente, al final**

éxito ≠ exit
éxito = success
exit = **salida**

físico/a ≠ physician
físico/a = physicist
physician = **médico/a**

fútbol ≠ football
fútbol = soccer
football = **fútbol americano**

lectura ≠ lecture
lectura = reading
lecture = **conferencia**

librería ≠ library
librería = bookstore
library = **biblioteca**

máscara ≠ mascara
máscara = mask
mascara = **rímel**

molestar ≠ to molest
molestar = to bother, to annoy
to molest = **abusar**

oficio ≠ office
oficio = trade, occupation
office = **oficina**

rato ≠ rat
rato = while, time
rat = **rata**

realizar ≠ to realize
realizar = to carry out; to fulfill
to realize = **darse cuenta de**

red ≠ red
red = net
red = **rojo/a**

revolver ≠ revolver
revolver = to stir, to rummage through
revolver = **revólver**

sensible ≠ sensible
sensible = sensitive
sensible = **sensato/a, razonable**

suceso ≠ success
suceso = event
success = **éxito**

sujeto ≠ subject (topic)
sujeto = fellow; individual
subject = **tema, asunto**

LOS ALIMENTOS / FOODS

Frutas / Fruits

la aceituna	olive
el aguacate	avocado
el albaricoque, el damasco	apricot
la banana, el plátano	banana
la cereza	cherry
la ciruela	plum
el dátil	date
la frambuesa	raspberry
la fresa, la frutilla	strawberry
el higo	fig
el limón	lemon; lime
el melocotón, el durazno	peach
la mandarina	tangerine
el mango	mango
la manzana	apple
la naranja	orange
la papaya	papaya
la pera	pear
la piña	pineapple
el pomelo, la toronja	grapefruit
la sandía	watermelon
las uvas	grapes

Vegetales / Vegetables

la alcachofa	artichoke
el apio	celery
la arveja, el guisante	pea
la berenjena	eggplant
el brócoli	broccoli
la calabaza	squash; pumpkin
la cebolla	onion
el champiñón, la seta	mushroom
la col, el repollo	cabbage
la coliflor	cauliflower
los espárragos	asparagus
las espinacas	spinach
los frijoles, las habichuelas	beans
las habas	fava beans
las judías verdes, los ejotes	string beans, green beans
la lechuga	lettuce
el maíz, el choclo, el elote	corn
la papa, la patata	potato
el pepino	cucumber
el pimentón	bell pepper
el rábano	radish
la remolacha	beet
el tomate, el jitomate	tomato
la zanahoria	carrot

El pescado y los mariscos / Fish and shellfish

la almeja	clam
el atún	tuna
el bacalao	cod
el calamar	squid
el cangrejo	crab
el camarón, la gamba	shrimp
la langosta	lobster
el langostino	prawn
el lenguado	sole; flounder
el mejillón	mussel
la ostra	oyster
el pulpo	octopus
el salmón	salmon
la sardina	sardine
la vieira	scallop

La carne / Meat

la albóndiga	meatball
el bistec	steak
la carne de res	beef
el chorizo	hard pork sausage
la chuleta de cerdo	pork chop
el cordero	lamb
los fiambres	cold cuts, food served cold
el filete	fillet
la hamburguesa	hamburger
el hígado	liver
el jamón	ham
el lechón	suckling pig, roasted pig
el pavo	turkey
el pollo	chicken
el cerdo	pork
la salchicha	sausage
la ternera	veal
el tocino	bacon

Otras comidas / Other foods

el ajo	garlic
el arroz	rice
el azúcar	sugar
el batido	milkshake
el budín	pudding
el cacahuete, el maní	peanut
el café	coffee
los fideos	noodles, pasta
la harina	flour
el huevo	egg
el jugo, el zumo	juice
la leche	milk
la mermelada	marmalade, jam
la miel	honey
el pan	bread
el queso	cheese
la sal	salt
la sopa	soup
el té	tea
la tortilla	omelet (Spain), tortilla (Mexico)
el yogur	yogurt

Cómo describir la comida / Ways to describe food

Español	English
a la plancha, a la parrilla	grilled
ácido/a	sour
al horno	baked
amargo/a	bitter
caliente	hot
dulce	sweet
duro/a	tough
frío/a	cold
frito/a	fried
fuerte	strong, heavy
ligero/a	light
picante	spicy
sabroso/a	tasty
salado/a	salty

DÍAS FESTIVOS / HOLIDAYS

enero / January
- Año Nuevo (1) — New Year's Day
- Día de los Reyes Magos (6) — Three Kings Day (Epiphany)
- Día de Martin Luther King, Jr. — Martin Luther King, Jr. Day

febrero / February
- Día de San Blas (Paraguay) (3) — St. Blas Day (Paraguay)
- Día de San Valentín, Día de los Enamorados (14) — Valentine's Day
- Día de los Presidentes — Presidents' Day
- Carnaval — Carnival (Mardi Gras)

marzo / March
- Día de San Patricio (17) — St. Patrick's Day
- Nacimiento de Benito Juárez (México) (21) — Benito Juárez's Birthday (Mexico)

abril / April
- Semana Santa — Holy Week
- Pésaj — Passover
- Pascua — Easter
- Declaración de la Independencia de Venezuela (19) — Declaration of Independence of Venezuela
- Día de la Tierra (22) — Earth Day

mayo / May
- Día del Trabajo (1) — Labor Day
- Cinco de Mayo (5) (México) — Cinco de Mayo (May 5th) (Mexico)
- Día de las Madres — Mother's Day
- Independencia Patria (Paraguay) (15) — Independence Day (Paraguay)
- Día Conmemorativo — Memorial Day

junio / June
- Día de los Padres — Father's Day
- Día de la Bandera (14) — Flag Day
- Día del Indio (Perú) (24) — Native People's Day (Peru)

julio / July
- Día de la Independencia de los Estados Unidos (4) — Independence Day (United States)
- Día de la Independencia de Venezuela (5) — Independence Day (Venezuela)
- Día de la Independencia de la Argentina (9) — Independence Day (Argentina)
- Día de la Independencia de Colombia (20) — Independence Day (Colombia)
- Nacimiento de Simón Bolívar (24) — Simón Bolívar's Birthday
- Día de la Revolución (Cuba) (26) — Revolution Day (Cuba)
- Día de la Independencia del Perú (28) — Independence Day (Peru)

agosto / August
- Día de la Independencia de Bolivia (6) — Independence Day (Bolivia)
- Día de la Independencia del Ecuador (10) — Independence Day (Ecuador)
- Día de San Martín (Argentina) (17) — San Martín Day (anniversary of his death) (Argentina)
- Día de la Independencia del Uruguay (25) — Independence Day (Uruguay)

septiembre / September
- Día del Trabajo (EE. UU.) — Labor Day (U.S.)
- Día de la Independencia de Costa Rica, El Salvador, Guatemala, Honduras y Nicaragua (15) — Independence Day (Costa Rica, El Salvador, Guatemala, Honduras, Nicaragua)
- Día de la Independencia de México (16) — Independence Day (Mexico)
- Día de la Independencia de Chile (18) — Independence Day (Chile)
- Año Nuevo Judío — Jewish New Year
- Día de la Virgen de las Mercedes (Perú) (24) — Day of the Virgin of Mercedes (Peru)

octubre / October
- Día de la Raza (12) — Columbus Day
- Noche de Brujas (31) — Halloween

noviembre / November
- Día de los Muertos (2) — All Souls Day
- Día de los Veteranos (11) — Veterans' Day
- Día de la Revolución Mexicana (20) — Mexican Revolution Day
- Día de Acción de Gracias — Thanksgiving
- Día de la Independencia de Panamá (28) — Independence Day (Panama)

diciembre / December
- Día de la Virgen (8) — Day of the Virgin
- Día de la Virgen de Guadalupe (México) (12) — Day of the Virgin of Guadalupe (Mexico)
- Januká — Chanukah
- Nochebuena (24) — Christmas Eve
- Navidad (25) — Christmas
- Año Viejo (31) — New Year's Eve

NOTE: In Spanish, dates are written with the day first, then the month. Christmas Day is **el 25 de diciembre**. In Latin America and in Europe, abbreviated dates also follow this pattern. Halloween, for example, falls on 31/10. You may also see the numbers in dates separated by periods: 27.4.16. When referring to centuries, roman numerals are always used. The 16th century, therefore, is **el siglo XVI**.

PESOS Y MEDIDAS / WEIGHTS AND MEASURES

Longitud / Length

El sistema métrico / Metric system — **El equivalente estadounidense** / U.S. equivalent

- **milímetro = 0,001 metro** / millimeter = 0.001 meter = 0.039 inch
- **centímetro = 0,01 metro** / centimeter = 0.01 meter = 0.39 inch
- **decímetro = 0,1 metro** / decimeter = 0.1 meter = 3.94 inches
- **metro** / meter = 39.4 inches
- **decámetro = 10 metros** / dekameter = 10 meters = 32.8 feet
- **hectómetro = 100 metros** / hectometer = 100 meters = 328 feet
- **kilómetro = 1.000 metros** / kilometer = 1,000 meters = .62 mile

El sistema estadounidense / U.S. system — **El equivalente métrico** / Metric equivalent

- inch / **pulgada** = 2.54 centimeters / **= 2,54 centímetros**
- foot = 12 inches / **pie = 12 pulgadas** = 30.48 centimeters / **= 30,48 centímetros**
- yard = 3 feet / **yarda = 3 pies** = 0.914 meter / **= 0,914 metro**
- mile = 5,280 feet / **milla = 5.280 pies** = 1.609 kilometers / **= 1,609 kilómetros**

Superficie / Surface Area

El sistema métrico / Metric system — **El equivalente estadounidense** / U.S. equivalent

- **metro cuadrado** / square meter = 10.764 square feet
- **área = 100 metros cuadrados** / area = 100 square meters = 0.025 acre
- **hectárea = 100 áreas** / hectare = 100 ares = 2.471 acres

El sistema estadounidense / U.S. system — **El equivalente métrico** / Metric equivalent

- **yarda cuadrada = 9 pies cuadrados = 0,836 metros cuadrados** / square yard = 9 square feet = 0.836 square meters
- **acre = 4.840 yardas cuadradas = 0,405 hectáreas** / acre = 4,840 square yards = 0.405 hectares

Capacidad / Capacity

El sistema métrico / Metric system — **El equivalente estadounidense** / U.S. equivalent

- **mililitro = 0,001 litro** / milliliter = 0.001 liter = 0.034 ounces
- **centilitro = 0,01 litro** / centiliter = 0.01 liter = 0.34 ounces
- **decilitro = 0,1 litro** / deciliter = 0.1 liter = 3.4 ounces
- **litro** / liter = 1.06 quarts
- **decalitro = 10 litros** / dekaliter = 10 liters = 2.64 gallons
- **hectolitro = 100 litros** / hectoliter = 100 liters = 26.4 gallons
- **kilolitro = 1.000 litros** / kiloliter = 1,000 liters = 264 gallons

El sistema estadounidense / U.S. system — **El equivalente métrico** / Metric equivalent

- ounce / **onza** = 29.6 milliliters / **= 29,6 mililitros**
- cup = 8 ounces / **taza = 8 onzas** = 236 milliliters / **= 236 mililitros**
- pint = 2 cups / **pinta = 2 tazas** = 0.47 liters / **= 0,47 litros**
- quart = 2 pints / **cuarto = 2 pintas** = 0.95 liters / **= 0,95 litros**
- gallon = 4 quarts / **galón = 4 cuartos** = 3.79 liters / **= 3,79 litros**

Peso / Weight

El sistema métrico / Metric system — **El equivalente estadounidense** / U.S. equivalent

- **miligramo = 0,001 gramo** / milligram = 0.001 gram
- **gramo** / gram = 0.035 ounce
- **decagramo = 10 gramos** / dekagram = 10 grams = 0.35 ounces
- **hectogramo = 100 gramos** / hectogram = 100 grams = 3.5 ounces
- **kilogramo = 1.000 gramos** / kilogram = 1,000 grams = 2.2 pounds
- **tonelada (métrica) = 1.000 kilogramos** / metric ton = 1,000 kilograms = 1.1 tons

El sistema estadounidense / U.S. system — **El equivalente métrico** / Metric equivalent

- ounce / **onza** = 28.35 grams / **= 28,35 gramos**
- pound = 16 ounces / **libra = 16 onzas** = 0.45 kilograms / **= 0,45 kilogramos**
- ton = 2,000 pounds / **tonelada = 2.000 libras** = 0.9 metric tons / **= 0,9 toneladas métricas**

Temperatura / Temperature

Grados centígrados / Degrees Celsius
To convert from Celsius to Fahrenheit, multiply by $\frac{9}{5}$ and add 32.

Grados Fahrenheit / Degrees Fahrenheit
To convert from Fahrenheit to Celsius, subtract 32 and multiply by $\frac{5}{9}$.

NÚMEROS

Números ordinales

primer, primero/a	1º/1ª
segundo/a	2º/2ª
tercer, tercero/a	3º/3ª
cuarto/a	4º/4ª
quinto/a	5º/5ª
sexto/a	6º/6ª
séptimo/a	7º/7ª
octavo/a	8º/8ª
noveno/a	9º/9ª
décimo/a	10º/10ª

Fracciones

$\frac{1}{2}$	un medio, la mitad
$\frac{1}{3}$	un tercio
$\frac{1}{4}$	un cuarto
$\frac{1}{5}$	un quinto
$\frac{1}{6}$	un sexto
$\frac{1}{7}$	un séptimo
$\frac{1}{8}$	un octavo
$\frac{1}{9}$	un noveno
$\frac{1}{10}$	un décimo
$\frac{2}{3}$	dos tercios
$\frac{3}{4}$	tres cuartos
$\frac{5}{8}$	cinco octavos

Decimales

un décimo	0,1
un centésimo	0,01
un milésimo	0,001

NUMBERS

Ordinal numbers

first	1st
second	2nd
third	3rd
fourth	4th
fifth	5th
sixth	6th
seventh	7th
eighth	8th
ninth	9th
tenth	10th

Fractions

one half
one third
one fourth (quarter)
one fifth
one sixth
one seventh
one eighth
one ninth
one tenth
two thirds
three fourths (quarters)
five eighths

Decimals

one tenth	0.1
one hundredth	0.01
one thousandth	0.001

OCUPACIONES	OCCUPATIONS
el/la abogado/a	lawyer
el actor, la actriz	actor
el/la administrador(a) de empresas	business administrator
el/la agente de bienes raíces	real estate agent
el/la agente de seguros	insurance agent
el/la agricultor(a)	farmer
el/la arqueólogo/a	archaeologist
el/la arquitecto/a	architect
el/la artesano/a	artisan
el/la auxiliar de vuelo	flight attendant
el/la basurero/a	garbage collector
el/la bibliotecario/a	librarian
el/la bombero/a	firefighter
el/la cajero/a	bank teller, cashier
el/la camionero/a	truck driver
el/la cantinero/a	bartender
el/la carnicero/a	butcher
el/la carpintero/a	carpenter
el/la científico/a	scientist
el/la cirujano/a	surgeon
el/la cobrador(a)	bill collector
el/la cocinero/a	cook, chef
el/la comprador(a)	buyer
el/la consejero/a	counselor, advisor
el/la contador(a)	accountant
el/la corredor(a) de bolsa	stockbroker
el/la diplomático/a	diplomat
el/la diseñador(a) (gráfico/a)	(graphic) designer
el/la electricista	electrician
el/la empresario/a de pompas fúnebres	funeral director
el/la especialista en dietética	dietician
el/la fisioterapeuta	physical therapist
el/la fotógrafo/a	photographer
el/la higienista dental	dental hygienist
el hombre/la mujer de negocios	businessperson
el/la ingeniero/a en computación	computer engineer
el/la intérprete	interpreter
el/la juez(a)	judge
el/la maestro/a	elementary school teacher
el/la marinero/a	sailor
el/la obrero/a	manual laborer
el/la obrero/a de la construcción	construction worker
el/la oficial de prisión	prison guard
el/la optometrista	optometrist
el/la panadero/a	baker
el/la paramédico/a	paramedic
el/la peluquero/a	hairdresser
el/la piloto	pilot
el/la pintor(a)	painter
el/la plomero/a	plumber
el/la político/a	politician
el/la programador(a)	computer programer
el/la psicólogo/a	psychologist
el/la quiropráctico/a	chiropractor
el/la redactor(a)	editor
el/la reportero/a	reporter
el/la sastre	tailor
el/la secretario/a	secretary
el/la supervisor(a)	supervisor
el/la técnico/a (en computación)	(computer) technician
el/la vendedor(a)	sales representative
el/la veterinario/a	veterinarian

Índice

A

absolute superlatives (8) **286**
acabar de + *infinitive* (6) **207**
academic courses (2) **40, 41, 76**
accents (4) **123**
adjectives
    demonstrative (6) **210**
    descriptive (3), (6) **88, 114, 192, 224**
    nationality (3) **89, 114**
    position (3) **90**
    possessive (3) **93**
    ser with adjectives (3) **88**
age questions (3) **83, 101**
al (contraction) (4) **126**
alphabet, Spanish (1) **9**
articles, definite and indefinite (1) **14**

B

b (5) **161**
bathroom objects (7) **226, 260**
birthdays (9) **300, 330**
body parts (7) **226, 260**
buildings
    campus (2) **40, 76**
    general (4) **118, 150**

C

c (8) **271**
campus buildings (2) **40, 76**
celebrations (9) **300, 330**
classroom objects and people (2) **40, 76**
clothing (6) **190, 224**
colors (3), (6) **89, 114, 192, 224**
comparisons (8) **281**
conducir
    present tense (6) **200**
    preterite tense (9) **310**
conocer and **saber** (6) **200**
courses (academic) (2) **40, 76**
courtesy expressions (1) **2, 7, 38**
Cultura
    Carolina Herrera (6) **199**
    Las cataratas del Iguazú (5) **162**
    ¿Cómo te llamas? (3) **86**
    La escuela secundaria (2) **48**
    La familia real española (3) **87**
    Ferran Adrià: arte en la cocina (8) **273**
    Festival de Viña del Mar (9) **309**
    Frutas y verduras de América (8) **272**
    El INFRAMEN (2) **49**
    El mate (7) **235**
    Los mercados al aire libre (6) **198**
    Miguel Cabrera y Paola Espinosa (4) **125**
    La plaza principal (1) **11**
    Punta del Este (5) **163**
    Real Madrid y Barça: rivalidad total (4) **124**
    Saludos y besos en los países hispanos (1) **10**
    Semana Santa: vacaciones y tradición (9) **308**
    La siesta (7) **234**

D

d (6) **197**
daily schedules (7) **226, 260**
dar
    expressions (6) **203**
    present tense (6) **203**
    preterite tense (9) **311**
dates (months) (5) **154**
days of the week (2) **42, 76**
decir
    expressions (4) **136**
    present tense (4) **133**
    preterite tense (9) **310**
definite articles (1) **14**
del (contraction) (1) **20**
demonstrative adjectives and pronouns (6) **210**
describing clothes (6) **190, 195, 224**
describing routines (7) **226, 260**
descriptive adjectives (3), (6) **88, 114, 192, 224**
diphthongs and linking (3) **85**
direct objects: nouns and pronouns (5) **174**
diversions, related verbs (9) **300, 330**
double object pronouns (8) **277**

E

entertainment, related verbs (9) **300, 330**
estar
    comparing **ser** and **estar** (5) **170**
    present tense (2) **59**
    preterite tense (9) **310**
    with conditions (5) **164**
    with emotions (5) **164**
    with health conditions (2) **59**
    with location (2) **59**

F

family members and relatives (3) **78, 114**
farewells (1) **2, 38**
food and drink (8) **262, 264, 298**
    parties, related foods (9) **300, 330**
forming questions (2) **55**

G

g (9) **307**
greetings and introductions (1) **2, 38**
grooming, personal (7) **226, 260**
gusta(n), me/te (2) **45, 52**
gustar (2) **52**
    verbs like **gustar** (7) **246**

H

h (9) **307**
hacer
    present tense (4) **136**
    preterite tense (9) **310**
hay (1) **16**
health
    conditions with **estar** (5) **164**
    questions (1) **2, 38**
hotels (5) **152, 188**
hygiene, personal (7) **226, 260**

I

indefinite articles (1) **14**
indefinite words (7) **240**
indirect object pronouns (6) **202**
information questions (2) **55**
interrogative words (2) **56**
intonation, question (2) **55**
introductions (1) **2, 38**
ir
    present tense (4) **126**
    preterite tense (7) **244**
    ir a + *infinitive* (4) **126**
irregular verbs
    preterite tense (9) **310**

J

j (9) **307**

L

life's stages (9) **302, 330**
linking (3) **85**
ll (8) **271**
location with **estar** (2) **59**

M

meals (8) **264, 298**
months of the year (5) **154**

N

names of Spanish-speaking countries (1) **38**
negation with **no** (2) **51**
negative words (7) **240**
nouns (1) **12**
numbers
    0–30 (1) **16**

Índice

31 and higher (2) **63**
ordinal (5) **155, 188**

Ñ

ñ (8) **271**

O

object pronouns
   direct (5) **174**
   double (8) **277**
   indirect (6) **202**
   prepositional (9) **318**
   reflexive (7) **236**
occupations (3) **78, 114**
ofrecer, present tense (6) **200**
oír, present tense (4) **137**
ordinal numbers (5) **155, 188**

P

Panorama
   Canadá (1) **36**
   Chile (9) **328**
   Cuba (6) **222**
   Ecuador (3) **112**
   España (2) **74**
   Estados Unidos (1) **36**
   Guatemala (8) **296**
   México (4) **148**
   Perú (7) **258**
   Puerto Rico (5) **186**
participles
   present with progressive tenses (5) **166**
parties, related people, items, foods (9) **300, 330**
parts of the body (7) **226, 260**
pastimes (4) **116, 150**
pero vs. **sino** (7) **241**
personal **a** (5) **174**
pluralization of nouns (1) **13**
poder
   present tense (4) **130**
   preterite tense (9) **310**
poner
   present tense (4) **136**
   preterite tense (9) **310**
position of adjectives (3) **90**
possessive adjectives (3) **93**
prepositions often used with **estar** (2) **60**
prepositional object pronouns (9) **318**
preterite tense
   regular verbs (6) **206**
   irregular verbs (9) **310**
   verbs that change meaning (9) **314**
professions (3) **78, 114**
progressive tense
   present (5) **166**

pronouns
   demonstratives (6) **210**
   direct object (5) **174**
   double object (8) **277**
   indirect object (6) **202**
   prepositional object (9) **318**
   reflexive (7) **236**
   subject (1) **19**
   use and omission of subject pronouns (2) **52**

Q

querer, preterite tense (9) **310**
questions, forming (2) **55**
   age (3) **83**
   information questions (2) **55**
   intonation for questions (2) **55, 56**
   ¿qué? and ¿cuál? (9) **316**
   question words (2) **56**
   tag questions (2) **55**

R

r and **rr** (7) **233**
reflexive verbs (7) **236**
regular verbs
   present tense
      -ar verbs (2) **50**
      -er and -ir verbs (3) **96**
   preterite (6) **206**
restaurants (8) **269**
routines (7) **226, 260**

S

saber
   and **conocer** (6) **200**
   preterite tense (9) **310**
salir, present tense (4) **136**
school vocabulary (2) **40, 76**
se constructions
   reflexive verbs (7) **236**
seasons of the year (5) **154**
sequencing actions, words for (7) **226, 260**
ser
   comparing **ser** and **estar** (5) **170**
   present tense (1) **20**
   preterite tense (7) **244**
   to show identification (1) **20**
   to show origin (1) **21**
   to show possession (1) **20**
   with adjectives (3) **88**
   with nationalities (3) **89**
   with professions (1) **21**
shopping (6) **190, 224**
Spanish alphabet (1) **9**
Spanish-speaking countries, names of (1) **38**

sports and leisure activities (4) **116, 150**
stages of life (9) **302, 330**
stem-changing verbs
   present tense (4) **129, 133**
   preterite tense (8) **274**
stress and accent marks (4) **123**
subject pronouns (1) **19**
   use and omission (2) **52**
superlatives (8) **286**
   absolute superlatives (8) **286**

T

t (6) **197**
tag questions (2) **55**
tener
   expressions with (3) **101**
   present tense (3) **100**
   preterite tense (9) **310**
telling time (1) **24**
town places (4) **118, 150**
traducir
   present tense (6) **200**
   preterite tense (9) **310**
traer
   present tense (4) **136**
   preterite tense (9) **310**
travel terms (5) **152, 188**

V

v (5) **161**
vacation vocabulary (5) **152, 188**
venir
   present tense (3) **100**
   preterite tense (9) **310**
ver
   present tense (4) **137**
verbs describing routines and personal grooming (7) **226, 260**
verbs like **gustar** (7) **246**
verbs that change meaning in the preterite (9) **314**
verbs with irregular **yo** forms (**hacer, oír, poner, salir, traer,** and **ver**) (4) **136, 137**
vowels (2) **47**

W

weather expressions (5) **154**
work-related terms (3) **78, 114**

Y

years (e.g. 2007) (2) **64**

Z

z (8) **271**

Credits

Every effort has been made to trace the copyright holders of the works published herein. If proper copyright acknowledgment has not been made, please contact the publisher and we will correct the information in future printings.

Photography and Art Credits

All images © Vista Higher Learning unless otherwise noted.

Cover: Holly Wilmeth/Media Bakery.

Front Matter (SE): xviii: (l) Bettmann/Corbis; (r) Florian Biamm/123RF; **xix:** (l) Lawrence Manning/Corbis; (r) Design Pics Inc/Alamy; **xx:** José Blanco; **xxi:** (l) Digital Vision/Getty Images; (r) Andres/Big Stock Photo; **xxii:** Fotolia IV/Fotolia; **xxiii:** (l) Goodshoot/Corbis; (r) Tyler Olson/Shutterstock; **xxiv:** Shelly Wall/Shutterstock; **xxv:** (t) Colorblind/Corbis; (b) Moodboard/Fotolia; **xxvi:** (t) Digital Vision/Getty Images; (b) Purestock/Getty Images.

Front Matter (TE): T15: Mike Flippo/Shutterstock; **T16:** Jean Glueck/Media Bakery; **T35:** SimmiSimons/iStockphoto; **T39:** Monkeybusinessimages/Big Stock Photo.

Lesson 1: 1: Paula Díez; **2:** Oscar Artavia Solano; **3:** Martín Bernetti; **4:** Martín Bernetti; **10:** (l) Rachel Distler; (r) Stephen Coburn/Shutterstock; **11:** (r) Ken Welsh/Alamy; (l) Matt Sayles/AP/Corbis; (m) Paola Rios-Schaaf; **12:** (l) Janet Dracksdorf; (r) Tom Grill/Corbis; **16:** (l) José Girarte/iStockphoto; (r) Blend Images/Alamy; **19:** (l) Buzzshotz/Alamy; (m) Anne Loubet; (r) Elena Elisseeva/Shutterstock; **28:** (all) Martín Bernetti; **32:** Carolina Zapata; **33:** Paula Díez; **36:** (t) Jeremy Breningstall/ZUMA Press/Newscom; (m) Brandon Seidel/123RF; (b) Andresr/Shutterstock; **37:** (tl) PhotoDisc/Getty Images; (tr) Bill Bachmann/Alamy; (bl) Stocksnapper/Shutterstock; (br) Rmnoa357/Shutterstock.

Lesson 2: 39: Miodrag Gajic/Fotolia; **42:** Noam/Fotolia; **48:** (l) Hill Street Studios/AGE Fotostock; (r) David Ashley/Corbis; **49:** Guayo Fuentes/Shutterstock; **57:** Stephen Coburn/Shutterstock; **58:** Chris Schmidt/iStockphoto; **59:** (l) Paola Rios-Schaaf; (r) Image Source/Corbis; **64:** Martín Bernetti; **67:** (l) Rick Gomez/Corbis; (r) Aspen Stock/AGE Fotostock; **68:** José Blanco; **69:** (l) Gudrun Hommel; (r) Pascal Pernix; **70:** (t) Image Source/MaXx Images; (b) Martín Bernetti; **71:** Nora y Susana/Fotocolombia; **74:** (tl) Tupungato/123RF; (tr) José Blanco; (m) Darren Baker/Shutterstock; (b) Reuters/Corbis; **75:** (t) Sarah L. Voisin/The Washington Post/Getty Images; (ml) Erich Lessing/Art Resource, NY; (mr) José Blanco; (bl) Iconotec/Fotosearch; (br) Katie Wade.

Lesson 3: 77: Paul Bradbury/AGE Fotostock; **79:** Martín Bernetti; **80:** (tl) Anne Loubet; (tr) Blend Images/Alamy; (tml) Ana Cabezas Martín; (tmr) Blend Images/Shutterstock; (bml, bmr, br) Martín Bernetti; (bl) Kuzma/Big Stock Photo; **86:** (tl) David Cantor/AP Images; (tr) Rafael Perez/Reuters/Corbis; (b) Martial Trezzini/EPA/Corbis; **87:** (t) Dani Cardona/Reuters/Corbis; (b) LOTE/Splash News/Corbis; **90:** (all) Martín Bernetti; **92:** Andres Rodriguez/Alamy; **97:** (l) Tyler Olson/Fotolia; (r) Martín Bernetti; **98:** Martín Bernetti; **106:** (all) Martín Bernetti; **107:** (t) Yuri Arcurs/iStockphoto; (m) Image Source/MaXx Images; (b) Martín Bernetti; **108:** Monart Design/Fotolia; **109:** ImageShop/Corbis; **112:** (tr, tl, b) Martín Bernetti; (ml) Ivan Mejia; (mr) Lauren Krolick; **113:** (tl, ml, b) Martín Bernetti; (tr) *Madre y niño en azul* (1986), Oswaldo Guayasamín. Óleo sobre tela, 100 x 100 cm. Copyright © 2015 Herederos Guayasamín; (mr) Javarman/Shutterstock.

Lesson 4: 115: Franz Faltermaier/Westend61/AGE Fotostock; **117:** Blacqbook/Shutterstock; **119:** Nora y Susana/Fotocolombia; **124:** (l) Natursports/123RF; (r) Carl Juste/MCT/Newscom; **125:** (t) Photoworks/Shutterstock; (b) ZUMA Press/Alamy; **135:** Warner Bros/The Kobal Collection; **139:** Anne Loubet; **141:** Agan/Shutterstock; **142:** Martín Bernetti; **143:** Thais Llorca/EPA/Newscom; **144:** Martín Bernetti; **145:** Alexander Rochau/Fotolia; **148:** (tl) Randy Miramontez/Shutterstock; (tr) *Autorretrato con mono* (1938), Frida Kahlo. Albright-Knox Art Gallery/Corbis/© 2015 Banco de México Diego Rivera Frida Kahlo Museums Trust, Mexico, D.F./Artists Rights Society (ARS), New York; (ml) Ruben Varela; (mr) Carolina Zapata; (b) Brian Overcast/Alamy; **149:** (tl) Radius Images/Alamy; (tr) Bettmann/Corbis; (m) Corel/Corbis; (b) Ioan Florin Cnejevici/Shutterstock.

Television Credits

34 Courtesy of Mastercard.
72 Courtesy of Cencosud Supermercados.
110 Courtesy of Cinematheque Jean Marie Boursicot.
146 Courtesy of Diego Reves.